Rise of the Nones

The Importance of Freedom from Religion

Rise of the Nones

The Importance of Freedom from Religion

Adam Neiblum

HYPATIA
PRESS

Published by Hypatia Press in the United Kingdom in 2023

ISBN: 978-1-83919-557-0

www.hypatiapress.org

The hinting and intimating manner of writing that was formerly used on subjects of this kind [religion], produced skepticism, but not conviction. It is necessary to be bold. Some people can be reasoned into sense, and others must be shocked into it. Say a bold thing that will stagger them, and they will begin to think.

Thomas Paine
In a Letter to Elihu Palmer
February 21, 1802

This book is dedicated to god
Thanks for all your hard work
We've got it from here
Rest In Peace

And to
Mr. Tom Flynn
Long-time Editor of *Free Inquiry* magazine

Contents

Foreword to *Rise of the Nones*

By Dan Barker, co-president of the Freedom From Religion
Foundation

Not once during the nineteen years I was preaching the Gospel did
anyone come up after the service to ask, "Rev. Barker, what were your
sources for this morning's sermon?" Nobody ever inquired about the
definitions of words or how my remarks may have comported with
history, science, or logic. Or with other parts of the bible. I stood in
the pulpit with full confidence that what I was saying was unassailable.
Not that it *couldn't* be questioned—I knew it *wouldn't* be questioned.

People don't go to church primarily to think critically. They go to
worship.

I once spent more than a month preparing a carefully researched
sermon that I was certain the congregation would find enlightening.
My sermon was about what it meant for Jesus to be called the
"firstborn of all creation" in Colossians 1:15. (Bear with me here—
this won't take long.) Obviously, Jesus was not the first human born.
He had a mother. The genealogy of Matthew traces his ancestry back
to Abraham, and Luke takes it all the way back to Adam. The word
firstborn (*protótokos* in Greek) was not just a description of birth order.
It was a blessing. The Israelite blessing of the firstborn son was similar
to the right of primogeniture, but it was transferable. Abraham's
firstborn son was Ishmael, but Isaac (the second son) got the blessing.
(Muslims think it was the other way around.) Isaac's firstborn son was
Esau, but the younger brother Jacob tricked his father into bestowing
the blessing on himself. Jacob's firstborn son was Reuben, but the

blessing went to Joseph, the son of the "wife he loved." Joseph's firstborn son was Manassah, but his grandfather Jacob bestowed the blessing on the younger brother Ephraim. The final plague that convinced Pharaoh to free the Israelites was the killing of all the firstborn Egyptians, a massacre that the Jews escaped by sprinkling lamb's blood on their doorposts so the angel of death would pass over. Hence, Passover. Those spared Jewish children carried a "firstborn" blessing which was transferred to the tribe of Levi during an elaborate cow-counting ceremony in the wilderness. The Levites became the priests from that time on. The firstborn blessing was passed (over) to them. Since then, all clergy—priests and ministers, like I was—have become "Levites," ordained with the special "firstborn" status. When Jesus was called the "firstborn of all creation," this did not simply mean he was God's first son. It meant he carried the firstborn blessing *of all creation*. It also meant that God's other children—all of us Christians who were "born again"—were subject to the "high-priest" authority (Hebrews 4:14) of our older brother Jesus. Most Protestant denominations, unlike Catholics, preach the "priesthood of all believers," where Jesus is the priest of priests, king of kings, and lord of lords.

Did you follow that? Your eyes may have glazed over by this point, but that morning I was pleased with that profound sermon. I believed God had led me to a deep biblical truth and was certain that the congregation would feel enriched. But when the service was over...nothing. Nobody said a word, not that morning, not ever. I was surprised. I may have committed the sin of disappointment. (Is disappointment a sin?) I had never asked for praise, but I would have thought someone might have said *something*. Like maybe, "Thank you. That was interesting." I would have taken *any* reaction, even, "That was boring." Which it may have been, to them as much as it was to you.

I now understand two things about what happened that morning. First, that sermon was too much. What were the listeners supposed to do with those great thoughts? They didn't need to be convinced of anything. They had come to worship God and to fellowship with the community of believers, not to grapple with history or biblical interpretation. "That's fine," they might have said. "I just want to spend time with Jesus." (And they needed to get home from church in time to take the roast out of the oven.)

I often heard "Amens." I never heard any "Boos." But even if there *had* been criticism, I would not have heard it as criticism. It would not have crossed my mind that someone would dare to question the truth of God's word. I would have understood a "criticism" simply as a question that God would easily answer. In my mind, it was all top-down. God dispensed and we received. God directed and we followed. If you are a committed follower of Jesus, it doesn't really matter what the pastor might say in any particular sermon. You are on board for life. Of course, most Christians want to learn and grow in their faith, but primarily they want to be *saved*. They want heaven. They want to feel loved by their Lord.

The second thing I now understand is that people have to *want* to learn. A Sunday worship service is not a college lecture. Not everybody has a scholarly thirst for history, linguistics, theology, or apologetics. It takes time and energy to gather, read, compare and analyze resources. It also takes a certain posture of mind: "I am confident enough of my intelligence and judgment that I can independently understand the issues and the facts with the ability to arrive at justifiable conclusions." If you don't have that bottom-up attitude, you are a follower, not a thinker. You don't own your faith: your faith owns you.

That may be good enough for many people. But it is *not* good enough for me, or for Adam Neiblum, the author of this book.

I know I am over-simplifying. (Is that also a sin?) Believers come in many forms. Most are simply happy with faith, but some do want to dig deep. There are indeed theologians, scholars, and apologists who grapple with the literature. I was like that. A few of them, like Adam Neiblum, don't just *want* to think: they *have* to think.

If you are not that type of person, then I might dust off and hand you some of my old simple sermons about Jesus, God, heaven, love, and hope (that I didn't spend a month researching) that will make you feel good in your faith. But if you *are* that type of person—if you are honestly curious and thirsty for objective knowledge, willing to wrestle with serious issues—then this book is for you.

The title of this book—*The Rise of the Nones*—is not merely optimistic. It refers to an observable growth in the percentage of adults who do think for themselves and identify with "no religion" in the United States. Fifty years ago, in 1972, about five percent of Americans were nonreligious.[1] In 1991, the American Religious Identification Survey reported that that group had grown to about 14%.[2] Today that percentage has more than doubled to almost 30%, including more than a third under thirty who are nonreligious.[3] That is an astonishing rise. Religion is shrinking while nonreligion is growing phenomenally. These nonreligious people are commonly referred to as the Nones. As in none of the above. This group is currently the largest "denomination" in the United States. The Nones are not all nonbelievers. About half of the Nones seem to be atheists, agnostics, or secular humanists, while the rest can be described as some form of "spiritual but not religious." Either way, these are people who think for themselves, bottom-up, not top-down from religious authority. They are a non-priesthood.

---

[1] https://www.pewresearch.org/religion/2022/09/13/how-u-s-religious-composition-has-changed-in-recent-decades/

[2] https://digitalrepository.trincoll.edu/isssc/6/

[3] https://www.pewresearch.org/religion/2021/12/14/about-three-in-ten-u-s-adults-are-now-religiously-unaffiliated/

We can debate what non-affiliated or nonreligious means in those studies, but the interesting fact is the increase in that number. Something important is happening. "We are currently enjoying nothing less than a wholesale awakening," Adam Neiblum writes, "based upon a foundation of knowledge as good, and of reason as essential." Something is happening in America that appears to parallel what happened in Europe, where after centuries of fierce faith and sectarian strife, most people today are thoroughly secular. In Europe, there are hundreds of beautiful but largely empty churches that are visited by more tourists than worshippers, as Annie Laurie and I did recently at the *La Sagrada Familia* cathedral in Barcelona designed by Antonio Gaudí. It was like visiting a beautiful museum. We went to admire the architecture and the art, not to pray to Mary or her firstborn son.

But I do know what it means to worship. As a teenager, I confessed my sins and accepted Jesus as my savior. I felt the presence of God when I prayed. I got goosebumps as I experienced the joy, love, and meaning that came from adoring the Creator. I accepted what I was convinced was a call to the ministry, became ordained, and served as an associate pastor in three California churches, then spent years as a missionary, cross-country evangelist and Christian songwriter. But after almost two decades of preaching, I abandoned belief in the supernatural and left the pulpit. I didn't lose my faith: I threw it away. If you want to know the specific reasons, see my book *Godless: How an Evangelical Preacher Became One of America's Leading Atheists.*

Why would I do that? Why did Adam Neiblum do the same thing after years of believing in God?

In short, I learned that what I was preaching is not true. My heart could no longer embrace what my mind rejected. The participants in The Clergy Project—which at the time of writing has more than 1,200 ordained ministers, priests, rabbis, nuns and other professional clergy who have left the ministry, or are in the process of leaving—

report various reasons for abandoning belief in the supernatural. But for most of us, it was intellectual. We used to preach "the truth shall set you free," and that is what happened.[4]

And that is exactly what can happen to *you* as you read Adam Neiblum's thoughtful book. You'll have to decide for yourself, of course, but whatever your decision, you won't be able to say we nonbelievers don't have reasons.

The Apostle Paul got a few things right. "Test everything; hold fast to what is good," I used to preach. (I Thessalonians 5:21) That is excellent advice. That is precisely what I did when I was evolving out of the faith, and that is what Adam is doing in the pages of this book. Paul also confessed that Christians—at least the Christians of his day—were ignorant of many things. "We see through a glass darkly," he wrote in I Corinthians 13:12. There is nothing wrong with acknowledging ignorance. Indeed, it is praiseworthy. Ignorance can drive us to learn. Paul was certainly confident in his faith, but unlike many modern preachers, he was honest enough to declare that he didn't know everything. "But," he continued, hoping for a future encounter with his Lord, "then we shall know, face to face." I think we freethinkers can say something similar, not about an encounter with a Lord, but an encounter with truth. When we come face to face with facts—such as Adam Neiblum presents in this book—we can grow up a little. We can rise. Now let's circle back to the fact that, in *Rise of the Nones*, Adam concludes that, "We are currently enjoying nothing less than a wholesale awakening based upon a foundation of knowledge as good, and of reason as essential."

If it is not a sin for an atheist to borrow religious terminology, I can say "Amen" to that.

---

[4] https://clergyproject.org

Chapter 1
Introduction—Fiat Lux

First Cause

The human mind is not very rational. Much of what members of the *Homo sapiens* species think about, believe, and do, is determined by some very non-rational cognitive predispositions, traits which we have acquired in conjunction with the overall evolution of our uniquely complex brains. Huge steps forward can be made by simply embracing this reality. The evolutionary sciences have improved our understanding of the human brain as an evolved organ, within a biological organism. It is this biological organ which gives shape to all human belief and knowledge.

Religious belief is no exception. It is rooted in, caused, shaped, and perpetuated by a suite of largely non-rational propensities of the human brain.[5] Significant light can be shed upon the human inclination toward religion and belief in gods by understanding how instinct shapes both the form and content of our beliefs, rather than reason, and by understanding more about our cognitive biases and similarly irrational mental predispositions.

---

[5] Kahneman, Daniel, Shane Frederick, Dale Griffin, and Thomas Gilovich. "Representativeness Revisited: Attribution Substantiation in Intuitive Judgment." Essay. In *Heuristics and Biases: The Psychology of Intuitive Judgment*, 103–19. Cambridge: Cambridge University Press, 2013.

In 1972, scientific researchers Kahneman & Tversky officially recognized what we now call cognitive biases.[6] They described how these quirks of the human mind significantly affect our thinking, judgment, decision making, beliefs, and behaviors. According to the *Handbook of Evolutionary Psychology*, cognitive bias is "a systematic pattern of deviation from norm or rationality in judgment. Cognitive biases may sometimes lead to perceptual distortion, inaccurate judgment, illogical interpretation, or what is broadly called irrationality."[7] So, it's basically a universal, hardwired predisposition to get things wrong, to interpret phenomena in an inaccurate or faulty way, to allow specific instinctive predilections to shape our thoughts and beliefs regardless of what data, evidence, and reason tell us.

Among the most common of all the cognitive biases is *confirmation bias*. This refers to the well-documented propensity of human beings to retain their beliefs by interpreting all incoming information as confirming or affirming their previously held beliefs. Say some evidence comes to Ralph's attention which, objectively or rationally viewed, would challenge his treasured belief 'A.' But Ralph manages somehow to interpret that evidence as *confirming* belief 'A,' despite all reason. Confirmation bias in fact predisposes many to double down on their beliefs, to become even more adamant and self-assured in the face of conflicting evidence or data. So, Ralph not only irrationally thinks that the data affirms belief 'A,' he thinks it improves or strengthens the case for 'A.' Atheists immediately recognize this confirmation bias as an extremely familiar, common, and prominent feature of religious faith.

---

[6] Ibid.
[7] Buss, David M., Martie. G. Haselton, Daniel Nettle, & Paul W. Andrews, "The evolution of cognitive bias." In *The Handbook of Evolutionary Psychology*, 724-746. Hoboken, NJ, US: John Wiley & Sons Inc., 2005.

Another common example of a cognitive bias is the human propensity to trust authority figures. One phenomenon which is well documented is that people are more inherently inclined to believe the words of authority figures or persons in positions of power. This is commonly referred to as an *authority bias.*

When our ancestral forebears were but members of small family tribes on the African savannah four million, two million, one million, all the way up until only twenty to thirty thousand years ago, individuals survived best when they stayed tight together, worked as a unit, survived, and thrived as a tribe. Team human. Members of team human generally did better when they stayed glued to the group and were necessarily respectful of the authority which was such an essential characteristic of those family tribes. Team loyalty behind a strong leader, sometimes an individual, sometimes a council of elders for example, was a major part of how groups worked, and thereby how individuals thrived or not. Y'know, that whole survival of the fittest thing.

Natural selection favored this propensity to play follow the leader, resulting in the passing on from one generation to the next of any genetic predisposition to respect authority and defer to team unity. This propensity aided in increased likelihood of survival and successful reproduction for the individual: i.e., the passing on of such tendencies to subsequent generations. That's evolution by natural selection.

So today, rational or not, our brains are still inclined toward an instinctual tendency to defer to that which a trusted authority, such as an Imam, a priest, or the Pope, says. If you really want the people to stop eating pork, or stop enjoying homosexual pleasures, or masturbation, or at the very least to feel shame, guilt, and self-loathing over doing so, just tell them God, or one of his emissaries, said "cut it out"!

At this point, I am fairly certain that your agile brain is positively bursting with examples of how this could all go wrong, how this irrational instinctive propensity which we call the authority bias might lead us horribly astray. Adolph Hitler and his goose-stepping Nazis come to mind perhaps? Precisely! Stanley Milgram's infamous experiments on obedience to authority were essentially an effort to comprehend and explain the Nazi atrocities of World War II.[8] His work served to demonstrate that human beings defer to authority, and remain obedient, often to a shocking degree (warning: more tasteless 'dad' puns spotted on road ahead).

In a similar vein, let's consider "the banality of evil," from the subtitle of Hannah Arendt's book, *Eichmann in Jerusalem: A Report on the Banality of Evil.*[9] This refers to that disturbingly common rationale for so many of humanity's most heinous atrocities—*'I was just following orders'*—which attests to the ultimately irrational, and highly problematic, nature of many of the evolved traits and cognitive predispositions of human beings. These are cognitive biases. This was but one example of our cognitive instincts, of how our brain has evolved to work. Such instinctual yet irrational responses are an essential ingredient in religion, faith, and belief in gods.

Though not necessarily as irrational as these cognitive biases, there are a host of other similarly instinctual predispositions—our innate hunger for justice and morality, our curiosity and desire for knowledge and understanding, and of course, our apparent fear of death. These instincts also have a causal, explanatory role in answering questions as to why people invented religion and the thousands of gods which we have historically believed in for as long as history records.

---

[8] Milgram, Stanley. *Obedience to Authority: An Experimental View.* New York, NY: Harper Perennial Modern Thought, 2009.
[9] Arendt, Hannah. *Eichmann in Jerusalem: A Report on the Banality of Evil.* New York, NY: Viking Press, 1964.

Taken together, these instinctive impulses have given rise to millennia-old traditions and institutions like the Abrahamic religions of Islam and Christianity (AIC), the world's two most populace and powerful religions, to which well more than half of the planet's 8 billion+ human beings currently claim some degree of allegiance. These religious traditions represent extraordinarily powerful forces in human society. They shape our beliefs and behavior through narratives regarding our true nature, our self-conception, and how we fit into the wider cosmic scheme of things. Through contemporary religious interpretation of 2000-year-old mythology and scripture, these traditions can also serve as a catalyst for specific legislation and theocratic policies, and even violent conflict.

Humanity reached a distinct turning point in autumn of 1859, when Charles Darwin published his revolutionary *On the Origin of Species*, which is essentially a replacement for, and improvement upon, antiquated origin myths such as the AIC.[10] These older works are pseudoscientific and instinct-riddled efforts at defining and circumscribing human nature, whereas Darwin's *Origin* functions as a far more accurate origin story, less mythological and pseudoscientific than rational, factual, and scientific.

To our detriment, much of humanity is either completely ignorant of Darwin's work, or understands it inaccurately, and fails to grasp its significant and wide-ranging implications. Once the truth of evolution is well understood and its ramifications for our self-conception fully absorbed, Darwin's new and improved origin story will serve as a springboard for a revolutionary change in our fundamental understanding of who and what we are and how we fit into the larger cosmic

---

[10] Darwin, Charles. *On The Origin of Species by Means of Natural Selection or, the Preservation of Favored Races in the Struggle for Life*, (*1859*), and *The Descent of Man*. New York, NY: The Modern Library, 1977.

picture. This is not merely a good thing; it is quite possibly a matter of life or death.

Our antiquated self-conception is complicit in a number of the problems which human beings, and through us the rest of life on planet Earth, currently face. We are slowly shifting toward a more accurate conception of who we are and where we came from. A good, step-back look at our history, and we can see human progress and our slow but steady movement from the supernatural toward the natural, from the instinctual to the rational, from the religious to the secular.

Unfortunately, this more overarching, comprehensive progress seems very slow. Darwin's work was published well over a century and a half ago. 'Evolution' is a standard element in school curriculum, widely acknowledged to be an indispensable component in a good education. We have global communications to spread the word, to dispense and disperse the rapidly growing body of data which affirms and supports the theory. And yet, a Gallup poll taken in the United States tells a less satisfying story:

> Forty-six percent of Americans believe in the creationist view that God created humans in their present form at one time within the last 10,000 years. The prevalence of this creationist view of the origin of humans is essentially unchanged from 30 years ago, when Gallup first asked the question.[11]

However, this 2021 poll is a little bit dated, as Pew Research demonstrated a few years later, when they famously described the more recent rise of the '*nones*.'[12] This increase in rational thought is a

---

[11] Newport, Frank. "In U.S. 46% Hold Creationist View of Human Origins." Gallup. June 1, 2012.

[12] "Nones" on the Rise." Pew Research Center. Washington, D.C. October 9, 2012, https://www.pewresearch.org/religion/2012/10/09/nones-on-the-rise/ – Rise of the 'Nones': Many are by now no doubt familiar with the term. Rooted originally in the works of the Pew Research organization, the 'nones' in this context refers to the

sign of real progress. But overall progress is being significantly hampered by out clinging to the past, but our conservative death grip on the AIC's outmoded origin story, and our ignorance and misunderstanding of not just Darwin's work per se, but the 'new and improved' origin story which it represents.

Our limited grasp of Darwin's dangerous idea, as Professor Daniel Dennett referred to it,[13] has allowed our species to cling to an outdated and moribund self-conception, one which hinders our much-needed progress morally, ethically, socially, materially, technologically, and scientifically. The largest single force propping up this antiquated, irrational, and highly problematic mindset, and hindering our forward movement, is religion, and in particular, the Abrahamic religions of Islam and Christianity.

In a more general, philosophical sense, the problem facing us can be understood as a systematic tendency toward *epistemological inversion*. We humans are disinclined, largely just through innocent, systematic ignorance, to take into account the primacy of the human brain in knowing the world. We do not know the world directly, as if peering through a clear, clean window, in spite of our tendency to assume as much. Rather, knowing the world is more of an interpretive experience than an unfettered or unmitigated apprehension.

Thanks entirely to the work done over the last few hundred years in such sciences as evolution, biology, genetics, and psychology, we increasingly understand that everything we believe, think, and know is done through the evolved organ known as the human brain. The

---

rapidly growing number of people in the United States who are moving in significant numbers away from religion. This trend earned its name from the wording of Pew Research questionnaires, in which the participant was asked to note which religion they were a member of, or had affiliation with. The increasingly check-marked response was that which simply said 'none': ergo the 'rise of the nones.'

[13] Dennett, Daniel. *Darwin's Dangerous Idea.* New York, NY: Simon & Schuster, 1995.

ultimate cause of religion and belief in god are pre-wired cognitive instincts. The more we acknowledge and understand the intercessory and interpretive processes built into believing and knowing, such as our cognitive instincts, be they rational or irrational, the better equipped we will be to mediate our subsequent understanding, and to adjust our belief and knowledge accordingly.

Human Progress

Progress is the victory of a new thought over old superstitions.
– Elizabeth Cady Stanton[14]

My years as a student of philosophy drove home several important lessons. One of them: always define your terms. A point which Socrates was famous, and ultimately died, for. The unclear meaning of key terms can have a highly pernicious and undermining impact upon human thought and discourse. The import of this seemingly subtle concern is widely underappreciated. Words like *god, love, morality, and justice* have a dizzying array of applications and meanings, and in contemporary American culture, buzzwords such as *socialism, freedom, capitalism,* and *democracy* can also suffer a surfeit of interpretations and applications. *Progress* is another such word.

An important distinction must be made between the biological process known as *evolution* and the cultural process of human *progress*. The two words are misconstrued as synonyms in a systematic and persistent manner, which represents a significant and problematic misconception.

For many, progress refers merely to 'technological improvement' and either scientific or material development. We can make a more effective weapon – a gun, a nuclear missile, an aircraft carrier. But

---

[14] Elizabeth Cady Stanton, found in miscellaneous documents. Miller NAWSA Suffrage Scrapbooks, 1897-1911.

should we? Is that truly what we mean by progress? Is doing so in the best long-term interest of human beings, of all life in an interdependent biosphere, living beings interconnected with the wide variety of other living beings? If not, then it is not what I mean by progress. Progress, in this book, describes a more all-inclusive process of overall advancement and improvement. Progress, as I will use the term, must include an *ethical* or *moral* component.

Any kind of mere cumulative advance, or 'improvement' for its own sake, or with serious detrimental consequences down the road, would be a limited, even vacuous conception of progress. Progress without a moral component, progress that does not make the world more just, or comes at the expense of humans, other life forms, or the environment on which we depend, is not really progress for these purposes.

Accordingly, advancement which benefits some at the expense of others would also be off the table. It isn't progress when only the lighter-skinned people reap the benefits, for example. Enslaving Africans to do the hard labor greatly increased American productivity, and made white Americans and Europeans significantly wealthier. But I would not use the term 'progress' to describe the institution of American slavery. Modern America is a significantly more just society today than it was back then. And yet the progress we have made in terms of living by the rule of law is tainted by the fact that people of color in the United States are still subject to a differing set of standards. When the standards of the American justice system are applied equally to all, regardless of the amount of black in the skin or green in the wallet, that will be a distinct and important example of progress. Zero technology required.

A significant component in human improvement would be our movement toward an increasingly democratic, egalitarian, just, and sustainable society. It is not really an advancement to have the Dow

Jones Average go up, where the corporations and the wealthy get wealthier, while the lives of average people remain unaffected, or possibly become even more difficult. Similarly, in regard to our physical, shared, global environment, upon which we all depend for our very survival in the long term, it is not progress if it makes our world more toxic or damaged, poisons the oceans, or destabilizes our planetary climate.

The most fundamental definition of progress concerns 'movement toward an ideal.' Progress is an all-inclusive movement forward in a manner which distinctly incorporates valuative elements such as morality, ethics, and justice. Sustainability and justice are important ideals toward which we must move, if we are to be described as genuinely progressing. Sustainability requires lifestyles, attitudes, behaviors, and technology which are designed for the absolute long haul. They are those which can run indefinitely, without exhausting resources or creating toxicity with others or within an environment, and without destroying important ecological balancing acts. This does not mean merely less polluting. It certainly does not mean a little recycling in order to justify the perpetuation or increase in habits of intolerable mass consumption.

Progress means real steps toward genuinely sustainable practices or technology, meaning that we could continue to do X literally forever, and would not run out of materials, would not poison the air, soil, or water. It means practices and technologies that are either environmentally neutral, like solar-powered mass transit, or work harmoniously with the wider biosphere of which we are integral components, as in high-tech bicycles, which are exceptionally practical and comfortable, and keep us healthy and in touch with our natural environments, as well as with one another.

I am not one of those old-school futurists or idealists with a luddite, anti-tech mindset. Yet neither do I think we can rely upon technology to solve all of our problems. The truth lies somewhere in between these two extremes. Interestingly, with material advancement, there often appears to be an element of moral improvement as well. The most obvious example of this would be the manner in which human society has moved away from scarcity into a post-scarcity world in which, technically, there is no good reason that any given human should go without the basic necessities of life such as food, clothing, shelter, or fundamental medical care. We are fortunate to live in a time in which there is no longer any justification for anyone to go without the truly important things which constitute a good life.

Technological progress must be sublimated to the long-term, all-inclusive needs of *Homo sapiens*, and should not be based upon indifferent market forces, special interests, or impersonal technological advancement. It must work in service to humankind, viewed as a species living in an interdependent manner within a biosphere. That being said, technology can and will solve a goodly number of our problems going forward. Clean energy, environmental clean-up, sustainable agriculture, sustainable and human-healthy global transportation systems, clean cities, and cruelty-free, sustainable food production for our species are all areas of advance which will significantly improve the lives of human beings and the many other beings with whom we share our planetary environment.

An unjust state of economic affairs is ultimately unsustainable. It causes disharmony in human society, which leads inevitably to conflict. The master/slave dynamic is ultimately untenable and unsustainable. Equitable distribution of goods, resources, rights, and responsibilities is inevitable for a truly sustainable human civilization. Only movement in that direction can be considered genuine progress. Significant disparity in wealth must be eradicated. This is a goal which all should equally embrace, as it genuinely leads to the ultimate fulfillment of humankind, the fulfillment of humanity's highest potential. As such, it must ultimately come from within (education, knowledge, belief) and not from without (laws, mandate, violence).

Progress means movement toward a future civilization characterized by increasingly equitable and fair distribution of economic resources, specifically food, clothing, shelter, and health care, as a baseline for all; justice, mutual respect, and nonviolence dominating human discourse; the full and unencumbered embrace of sustainable technology; and education, enlightenment, and freedom from indoctrination as universalist ideals shared by all.

The Irrational Animal

Human beings are deeply resistant to new ideas. This is the case regardless of how true an idea may be, how much sense it might make when contrasted with the answers of old. The German philosopher Arthur Schopenhauer is credited with making the following pithy observation:[15]

> All truth passes through three stages on the way to acceptance:
> First, it appears laughable;
> second, it is fought against;
> third, it is considered self-evident.

Scientist Louis Agassiz is quoted as saying something somewhat similar, and equally insightful:[16]

> ...whenever a new and startling fact is brought to light in science, people first say, 'it is not true,' then that 'it is contrary to religion,' and lastly, 'that everybody knew it before.'

---

[15] Though attributed to, and consistent with, Schopenhauer, the true provenance of this quote is actually unknown.

[16] Sir Charles Lyell published *The Geologic Evidences of the Antiquity of Man* in 1863 and, within its pages, he quoted Agassiz as saying this, but he did not cite the quote. As such, this quote is also a case of provenance unknown.

Most people on our planet will laugh at or claim false what I describe and prescribe in this book. In time, eventually, the things I am talking about will be accepted as the self-evident and obvious truth. The gospel, if you will. I hope I'm still around when that day comes.

If indeed it were true that the animal *Homo sapiens* was intelligently designed, we would readily accept the truth as soon as it came rolling down the pike. After all, the truth usually tends to come in the form of better explanations for 'what is' than that which we previously believed. The truth presents itself in the form of more probable explanations. With the improved knowledge and explanatory value which the truth entails, a rational creature would surely embrace with immediacy any truth or improvement in overall understanding.

Unfortunately, *Homo sapiens* is not exactly such an intelligently designed animal, nor for that matter a very rational one. Thinking rationally does not come easily to we human beings. It requires effort, practice, some cognitive exertion. It does not come to our brains as readily as do more irrational cognitive states. Human beliefs and thoughts are dictated as much, perhaps more so, by instinct, emotion, cognitive biases, and all manner of other, less-than-rational propensities. Thinking scientifically and rationally requires more effort of will, and is less instinctual, less 'natural,' than thinking religiously, for example. This is why the latter is far more prevalent in human history, and still is to this day.

The Omen

I was struggling, vainly struggling against waves of cold, swirling, brown, viscous muck, threatening to drown me, sweep me away. Its power was overwhelming, tugging at my arms, legs, torso. I grasped and clawed for purchase, my vision filled with the detritus of hearth and home, the effluvia of civilization, bobbing like ice cubes in a gigantic, violently roiling vat of iced coffee. Chairs, tables, heavy beams of wood, smacked against my ribs, banged, unforgiving and solid, sharp and painful against my bony shins.

Plastic bags of garbage, televisions, even whole, intact cars floated by, headlights beaming in futility, bobbing up and under, up and under the swirling, chocolate-colored watery sludge. And people. Floating human bodies. Appearing already bloated, taut skin straining against tattered clothing. Face down in the water. I struggled against the overpowering tide, grasping at anything seemingly anchored.

I clutched, lost hold. Grasped, then bumped loose again. That was when it dawned on me that I was not alone. We were shouting back and forth, me... and someone. Someone else was with me. Some family member. Lives in peril, not just my own. The mortification and dread doubled down. Shot through me, supercharged by orders of magnitude. It's really happening, I thought. More of a feeling than a thought – a chest-gripping tightness. It's really fuckin' happening!

Ripping the sleep apnea mask off my face, I woke and sat up quickly. I took a deep breath, leaned back against the cool veneer of my wooden bed frame. A thin sheen of perspiration glistened across my arms and chest. Consciousness quickly came online, erasing the complex illustrated narrative of my dreamworld. I swam against the tide to recall the details, to get them down before they sublimed away.

That was the sense I had when I woke up: it was happening. Or...was going to happen. Damnit. My worst fears were coming true. I knew it, I knew it all along. We had to move out of this fucking floodplain. Right away. Immediately. I was filled with a sense of immediate foreboding. Terrified. It was an omen. I had special knowledge of impending doom. This was a warning! This was going to happen, an omen of things to come!

Wait a minute. What the fuck? I knew better than that. An omen? Don't be ridiculous. All of this lasted but an instant. Six, or maybe ten seconds had passed in all. As the light of conscious wakefulness began to illuminate the darkened recesses of my mind, to send the demons scurrying back into their shadows, I realized that interpreting this as an omen was some seriously primitive shit. My subconscious sleeping mind had merely woven together several disparate threads: my ongoing anxiety over having everything wrapped up in a family homestead: my life-long mate, our three young children, my beloved little dog friends, and every single thing we owned; every useful thing, every meaningful thing, situated just below sea level, in a floodplain, a river delta, merely a quarter mile at best from the immense, half-planet-sized Pacific Ocean, all during a rainy, El Niño winter. All of this stress was merged with imagery culled from the media, too much obsessive video watching of tsunamis devastating Banda Aceh and Fukushima, with stranded polar bears, mile-long splashes from calving glaciers, island nations disappearing under rising tides, and global temperatures steadily rising, rising, sea levels rising, rising...

This was my brain's instinctive response to feelings of anxiety regarding this combination of global warming, living below sea level, behind an embankment meant to hold back both a raging river and half a planet's worth of water, this synthesis of all my working anxieties as a husband and a dad too. I've experienced this kind of thing before. Awakening in the middle of the night, frightened by nightmares. Scary monsters. Super creeps. You turn on the lights. Wake your partner.

Ever check on the kids? Make sure the newborn is breathing? The doors and windows all locked and secure? Check the closet? Under the bed? Chase away the prehistoric, the instinctive, the detritus and effluvia of our lizard brain. Maybe afterwards process the real causes, pursue the naturalistic, rational explanation. It was not a monster in the closet. It was just a monster in your head.

Supernatural and superstitious interpretations of experience happen instinctively. They seem to be a part of our basic default setting, our initial wiring. The empirical, our experiences, something that happened during the day, images from books or our many viewscreens - these give form to the ghosts and demons, angels and monsters. Whether you knock on wood, cross your fingers, or throw salt over your shoulder: that all depends largely upon where and when you were born, upon culture and context.

But the origin of superstitious and supernatural beliefs? That runs deeper. It is more than pure nurture and has deep roots in our nature. Instinctive, prehistoric interpretations of experience, with which many of us are familiar, well up from the deeper recesses of the brain. Omens. Premonitions. Signs. Ghosts. Spirits. Jinxes. Coincidences that don't feel like coincidences. Communications from what feels like somewhere else, someone else.

As wakefulness increases, as the sun rises, as consciousness crests, the supernatural and the mythical fade into the shadows, and many of us choose the far more probable, rational interpretation. At least, this is the case for those of us who have had the good fortune to learn that supernatural explanations do not represent the best possible explanations. Unfortunately, those who have never been taught this rational option B, who have been raised to think and believe only option A, the supernatural option, do not have our freedom of choice. They are more or less permanently stuck with option A. Forever and ever. Amen.

My nightmare omen tale is an example of this. But my coming to consciousness and reason that morning is also a microscopic illustration of a macroscopic process happening to all humans today, mirroring the more general maturing of humanity as we progress from the supernatural to the natural. We are, as a species, all in the midst of this shift, this coming to consciousness, this movement upwards: away from the supernatural, toward the natural; away from the instinctive, toward the rational; away from religion, toward science, fact, and reason.

Conclusion to the Introductory Part of the Introduction...

These examples of supernatural and superstitious thinking and cognitive biases are intended to illustrate some of the ways in which our minds can, and frequently do, lead us astray, lead us away from the more rational, reasonable choice, and incline us to instead interpret phenomenon in instinctive, supernatural, and religious ways. The AIC are highly problematic, widespread, historically and socially acceptable manifestations of instinctual and stubborn beliefs, and serve to thwart human progress. Darwin's brilliant new origin story remains misunderstood and underappreciated because we struggle with new ideas, especially those which challenge such strongly held, even if highly irrational or problematic, entrenched and highly pervasive beliefs.

In summary, the human mind is largely irrational, interpreting reality through instinct, emotion, imagination, supernaturalist, and superstitious filters. Religion comes naturally, whereas science and reason require more effort on the part of the human brain. This is why we are just starting to get there, historically speaking. The gods have been with us from the very beginning. But science has only recently joined the party. We are only just beginning to wake up. We need more. More reason, less religion. Traditions like the AIC impede the best form of human progress. Darwin represented a huge leap forward. But his work and its ramifications need be better understood and embraced in order for this process of progress toward a better, more rational, just, sustainable, knowledgeable, and beautiful civilization to improve.

Revolutionary Change

...if I have seen further, it is by standing on the shoulders of giants.
– Isaac Newton, 1675[17]

Copernicus is credited with placing the heliocentric model of the universe front and center in the mind of humanity with the 1543 publication of his *De revolutionibus orbium coelestium (On the Revolutions of the Heavenly Spheres).*[18] Of course, as can be said of so many of humanity's great ideas, the ancient Greeks had long before beaten him to it. Thinkers such as Aristarchus of Samos had proposed a heliocentric model well before even the beginning of the Christian era. In the Islamic caliphates, from what is commonly referred to as the Golden Age of Islam over a millennium later, Muslim scholars also displaced the earth from the center of things, well before baby Copernicus was born into 15th century Poland. But it was Nicolaus Copernicus' heliocentric model which was ultimately widely accepted as the best explanation for the location of the earth within our planetary system. His revolutionary new model replaced the long-held geocentric model, preferred by the church, which had for centuries asserted that the earth, and 'man,' stood at the center of the universe.

In like manner, Charles Darwin's ideas also had deep roots, reaching back at least to the pre-Socratics again, most notably Anaximander of Miletus. Darwin stood on a number of shoulders, including his very own grandfather Erasmus Darwin, who's work presaged that of his

---

[17] Newton, Isaac. "Letter from Sir Isaac Newton to Robert Hook." *Historical Society of Pennsylvania.* 1675.

[18] Copernicus, Nicolaus. *De Revolutionibus Orbium Coelestium. (On The Revolutions of the Heavenly Spheres).* 1543.

grandson. In a medical work titled, *Zoonomia; or the Laws of Organic Life*, he authored this description of shared evolutionary ancestry:[19]

> ...in the great length of time, since the earth began to exist, perhaps millions of ages before the commencement of the history of mankind, would it be too bold to imagine, that all warm-blooded animals have arisen from one living filament...with the power of acquiring new parts attended with new propensities, directed by irritations, sensations, volitions, and associations; and thus possessing the faculty of continuing to improve by its own inherent activity, and of delivering down those improvements by generation to its posterity, world without end?

While a vague and somewhat Lamarckian take on the process, Grandfather Erasmus Darwin was definitely in the ballpark. And yet Charles Darwin stands alone: for grasping with such a high level of precision the simple-yet-elegant nature of evolution by natural selection; for understanding the process even though he was missing several important pieces of the puzzle (genetics, for example); for the sheer diligence with which he refined his work over decades of admirably studious research and disciplined investigation; and for having the temerity and resolve to publish his *Origin* in the face of what he most certainly realized was guaranteed to be, in the parlance of 19th century Victorian England, a veritable shit storm.

Along with a like-minded paper by a younger naturalist of the time, Alfred Russel Wallace, Darwin's work was publicly presented in 1859. His *On the Origin of Species by Means of Natural Selection, or the Preservation of Favoured Races in the Struggle for Life*, met with mixed reviews from the scientists of the age and, unsurprisingly, a great deal of religiously generated animosity on the part of both fellow scientists

---

[19] Darwin, Erasmus. *Zoonomia, or, the Laws of Organic Life*. Cambridge: Cambridge University Press, 1794.

and the general public. The major religious institutions of the time, Catholic and Protestant alike, also looked upon Darwin's work with considerable disdain, interpreting *Origin* as a direct affront to the Biblical account of creation and human nature. While official views softened over the years, in light of the veritable avalanche of incoming data confirming the theory of evolution, the Catholic church has yet to offer one of those too-little-too-late apologies for which it has become infamous in our own time.

A great deal of the difficulty, from 1859 to the present day, stems from a lack of comprehension. Not that the concepts are that difficult. At base, they are not. Evolution is simple, but elegant. A great deal of the trouble arises from reticence, conscious or otherwise, and even willful misconception, misunderstanding, and misrepresentation on the part of many, largely, though not entirely, as the result of Abrahamic indoctrination. A huge number of people do not actually understand Darwin's theory of evolution by natural selection, nor how it has developed over the years with our ever-increasing body of scientific knowledge. Not grasping the fundamentals, it is understandable that a huge number of people, all around the world, also fail to grasp its wider ramifications.

Copernicus's work was truly revolutionary. In less literal, more everyday vernacular, Darwin's work was even more revolutionary, because it speaks directly to our understanding of life itself, including us, we human beings and our nature as the animal *Homo sapiens*. Like the heliocentric model, evolution removes us from the center of the universe. If we understand Darwin and evolutionary science properly, it can help shed light upon the all-important gap between our *mis*conceptions and the truth regarding human nature.

Abrahamic Intolerance

More than half of our world's 8 billion human beings are self-identified members of the two largest monotheistic, proselytizing religious traditions: Islam and Christianity. These two are, in many respects, more like differing sects of one common religious tradition than they are genuinely distinct religions. Numerous stories in the *Quran*, compiled in the 7th century AD, are identical to those in the Christian *Bible*. Allah differs little from Yahweh, the Christian god of the Old Testament. In fact, the word Allah is simply the Arabic word for god. The difference between them is insignificant when contrasted with the difference between Norse Loki and Itzamna of the Mayans, or between Hindu's Ganesha and Shinto's Hachiman.

Deep-rooted intolerance of religious diversity is a central and definitive characteristic shared by both Islam and Christianity. If you do not see things as they do, you are condemned eternally. Period. No ifs, ands, or butts. The essential message, dominating the pages of both the *Bible* and the *Quran*, goes something like this:

> We have the one and only true answer, the one and only true God. If you believe as we believe, do as we say, you will be saved. Those who do not believe and practice as our book commands will suffer eternal damnation. Any different belief, or nonbelief for that matter, is an affront to the one true God. And not one that he takes lightly, either. He takes this shit real serious. Any and all other infidels, atheists, or idolaters are just wrong, and must either be converted, eradicated, or else suffer eternal damnation.

Brings to mind the *War of the Worlds* and brain-eating aliens and zombies from the B-movies of the McCarthy era: leave nothing unique, different, or alive standing, nothing new or different in their murderous, conformist wake. It is also quite contrary to the claims of many contemporary American Christians, profoundly un-American, and directly in conflict with the best of the American experiment: we of the codified separation of church and state, the oft expressed respect for diversity, the great 'melting pot,' with our statue of Lady Liberty standing proudly at our front door, illuminating the path, welcoming all:[20]

Give me your tired, your poor,
Your huddled masses yearning to breathe free,
The wretched refuse of your teeming shore.
Send these, the homeless, tempest-tossed to me,
I lift my lamp beside the golden door!
— Emma Lazarus, 1883

Importantly, not all religions are necessarily so intolerant. But Islam and Christianity are. How this particular tenet is expressed differs widely, contingent upon time and place. On one end of this spectrum, you might have a believer benevolently, privately, and silently praying for your soul. Perhaps you never even noticed. At the other extreme end of this spectrum, you may find yourself being tortured or beheaded at the hands of a true believer, a zealot, perhaps an angry mob of these faithful, whipped into a blood-lusting frenzy by love for their god, merely for being an infidel, heretic, blasphemer, idolater, or nonbeliever. This you would most certainly have noticed.

While most believers fall somewhere in between these two extremes, this core self-righteousness has remained a consistent theme throughout the millennia. Every Christian or Muslim, if they are true to their scripture, is a proselytizer. There is little 'live and let live,' if there is indeed any, in their similar dominance-oriented mindsets.

Central to both of these Abrahamic sects is the assertion that they are the sole means to salvation, atonement, divinity, grace, to get to

---

[20] Lazarus, Emma. *The New Colossus.* 1883.

heaven, to avoid going to hell, to get tight with God, to worship Allah. There is considerable irony in the fact that the two are born of one and the same tradition, share a distinct cultural commonality, and share the same proselytizing, intolerant, self-righteous message, with many of the details very much alike. Despite, or perhaps because of this commonality, the two have historically warred, shedding rivers of blood over the millennia, killing one another over which is right, which is the one and only true faith.

In recent years, as human beings have increasingly come to recognize the dangers and shortcomings inherent to these antiquated dominance mindsets, there have been some efforts at more conciliatory approaches. One can find Muslim-Christian unity efforts that would not have existed in earlier times. This is one small indicator of human progress, a process impinging upon both ancient traditions from the more secular and diversity-accepting world. But such conciliatory efforts are truly the exception which prove the rule.

Throughout the course of history, millions have been ostracized, shunned, tortured, or otherwise come to unpleasant ends, simply for being suspected of infidelity to the jealous God of Abraham. Not just a thing of the past, as in the Spanish Inquisition, the Holy Crusades, or the famed burning of witches in Europe and America, people today are still being shunned, threatened, tortured, imprisoned, and murdered at the hands of those motivated by the 2000-year-old religious beliefs they find within the scripture of the AIC.

Americans are generally surprised to learn that fellow human beings are being ostracized, tortured, and murdered for witchcraft today, in the early years of the 21st century, all around the world.[21] When we Americans think of witches burning at the stake, we tend to imagine

---

[21] Schons, Mary. "Witch Trials in the 21st Century," National Geographic Magazine, Resource Library Article. May 2022. – "...the number of witch trials around the world is increasing. They are almost always violent, and sometimes they are deadly..."

23

Salem, Massachusetts around 1700, or something similarly anti-quated, deeply buried away in our past. Yet modern cases abound in nations where Abrahamic intolerance and fear of the 'other' is at a similar fever pitch to that of medieval Europe and the American colonies of yore.

Homosexuality, real or imagined, will also get you killed today, both on the streets and in the courtrooms of predominantly Christian Uganda. Atheists are being murdered in the streets of Islamic Bangladesh, too. This shared animosity is the result of deeply entrenched religious intolerance. I have had multiple contacts with long-distance friends, in Pakistan and Indonesia, who have personally attested to this extreme oppression, refusing to own any atheist printed reading materials, living in perpetual fear of being discovered, of merely being suspected or accused of heresy, of blasphemy, of being infidels, their very lives in jeopardy.

In contemporary Euro-American culture this intolerance remains significant. One of the most unpopular characteristics a person can have is to be an 'atheist,' according to all the relevant polls. We generally fall near or even below Muslims, who also fare very poorly in this largely Christian nation.[22] A recent one-term American president played upon Christian Americans' strong anti-Muslim sentiments, exacerbating tensions and enacting anti-Muslim policies. Without America's constitution and the rule of law, he would have been more successful, thereby raising levels of friction considerably on a global scale.

And it was but a few years back, in merry old England, that one of the world's genuinely brilliant scientific minds became yet another casualty of Abrahamic intolerance. Despite rhetoric to the contrary, it

---

[22] "Americans Express Increasingly Warm Feelings Towards Religious Groups. "Pew Research Center. Washington, D.C. February 15, 2017.
https://www.pewresearch.org/religion/2012/10/09/nones-on-the-rise/

was as a result of religiously enflamed homophobia that the great Alan Turing met his untimely end. Alan Turing was a brilliant Englishman who is widely recognized to be one of the foremost minds behind the creation of computers, computer science, and artificial intelligence. He was prosecuted and persecuted for 'homosexual acts.' The state required him to undergo chemical castration as an alternative to prison. At a mere 41 years of age, Turing died from cyanide poisoning in what is widely considered to be an act of suicide.

Despite rhetoric to the contrary, religious intolerance, and religious indoctrination in homophobic intolerance, were the cause of Turing's untimely death. Without this religious influence, there is no reason at all to surmise that the British people, or their various representative bodies, would have held such viciously intolerant views. The fact that he was punished by a secular system, or that he died by his own hand — these are of no consequence. He was as much a casualty of religious intolerance as was the brilliant Hypatia, attacked in the streets of Alexandria, torn limb-from-limb by a mob of angry, and very intolerant, Christians.

Global Dominance

Missionary proselytizing and millennia of coercion and conversion, however definitive, are not the sole explanation for the AIC's outsized influence upon human society as a whole. Their joint impact is even greater than these already significant factors would suggest. The AIC are influential in an *outsized* manner. This dominance is partly the result of some very worldly factors. Military, economic, social, and political factors all weigh in, as do such seemingly mundane concerns as geographic location, location, location.

The AIC are historically rooted in what is undeniably the most well-traversed and central nexus in all of human history. From the very beginning, with the first members of the genus *Homo*: the waves of wandering *habilis, erectus,* and *sapiens,* migrating, wave after wave, out of Africa, up and out into Europe and Asia, migration which took place primarily through the corridor which we now know as the middle east.

This geographic primacy continued on for centuries: through various iterations of the Silk Road; the numerous highly influential civilizations of the region, including the Sumerians, Babylonians, Akkadians, Assyrians, Egyptians, Hittites, the brief but influential Alexander the Great, the Greeks, Spartans, and Ptolemaics, and finally mighty Rome itself. This was followed by more expansion under the Christian missionaries, half a millennium of powerful Islamic Caliphates, and on into modern times, with the economic and political dominance associated with Middle East oil. This central region has always been of the most singular importance and influence. That which transpired within the region, including not merely the technological or pragmatic, but equally so the ideas, thoughts, beliefs, as well as the wealth and the wars, all tended to spread outwards into the wider world.

The most recent half millennia saw the expansion of the political, military, and economic interests of Christian-dominated imperialist European nations, such as Spain, Portugal, France and England, followed in the twentieth century by the dominance of the thoroughly Christian, post-WW2 United States of America. Significant political, military, economic, and cultural forces continued to merge with the missionary interests of the AIC, working in powerful union to spread the Abrahamic gospel like a veritable plague across the planetary landscape.

Today, many lament Pizarro's destruction of the Inca peoples, or the North American genocide of the indigenous natives, perpetrated by white men armed with guns, booze, disease-infested blankets and, of course, their *Bibles*. But the last half century of imperialism has been carried out with a far more benign face, through the auspices of Christianized Euro-America and its major technological, economic, military, and cultural hegemony over the rest of the planet.

Instead of the sword and the gun leading the charge, the coin of conversion is now Coca Cola, McDonalds, KFC, Visa & AmEx, Star Treks & Wars, the iPhone, iPad, League of Legends, and World of Warcraft. Instead of the face of Hernán Cortés or Cristoforo Columbo leading the charge, the faces of Dwayne 'The Rock' Johnson, LeBron James, Oprah, Taylor Swift, Barack Obama, or Donald Trump have led the way as middle east Abrahamic hegemony transmogrified over time into a new kind of non-violent, Euro-American cultural and economic hegemony.

The influence of the AIC over two millennia has been extremely thorough, impacting far more than merely the religion of its victims, but every other aspect of their lives as well. The AIC missionaries were not content to change merely the religious beliefs of those they encountered, but also necessarily their practices, rituals, attire, appearance, mating, marriage, sex lives, language, their entire education, and their traditions. In short, their entire culture. This impact was in some measure the result of traditions that were intolerant, proselytizing, imperialistic, and even genocidal – culturally, if not literally.

Christians forced their whole weltanschauung down the throats of each and every aboriginal, tribal, and pagan people they encountered, all the way up through early Europe, beyond the Sahara and the Congo, deep into the teeming jungles of Amazonia, across the wide plains of America, into the desert island of Australia, and to the beatific islands beyond. In this manner, the lives of millions of European, Asian, African, North and South American, Australian and Oceanic peoples were subject to what can only be described as a process of ongoing cultural genocide.

Normalizing Atheism

The devout and the faithful have long been taught that atheists are anything from lost souls to the embodiment of pure evil. For average folk, the word calls to mind images of fringe lunatics, raging against religion in a manner which all too ironically reminds them of the ravings of evangelical, fundamentalist, and ultra-pious religious fanatics. We are oft stereotyped as those who, naively tossing out the baby with the bathwater, fail to recognize all of the good which religion brings to the world, in spite of the occasional pederast priest or suicide bomber.

Polls consistently demonstrate this distaste for the label 'atheist,' above and beyond other familiar groupings by which people are identified. We are always somewhere near the bottom of the pile.

Americans' Views of U.S. Religious and Spiritual Groups[23]				
	Total Positive (%)	Neutral (%)	Total Negative (%)	Net Positive (% pts)
Methodists	49	47	4	45
Jews	46	48	4	42
Baptists	45	44	10	35
Catholics	45	41	13	32
Evangelical Christians*	39	36	23	16
Fundamentalist Christians*	35	36	25	10
Latter-Day Saints, or Mormons	24	48	26	-2
Muslims	17	48	34	-17
Atheists	13	41	45	-32
Scientologists	7	37	52	-45
*Asked of a half sample				

According to *Scientific American* Magazine:[24]

Atheists are one of the most disliked groups in America. Only 45 percent of Americans say they would vote for a qualified atheist presidential candidate, and atheists are rated as the least desirable group for a potential son-in-law or daughter-in-law to belong to.

But we impious infidels still fare better here and now than we would in most other times or climes. There are currently thirteen nations in which atheism is on the books as a crime punishable by death. Ordinary, decent folk, like you and I, live in fear for their very lives,

---

[23] Gallup Panel Survey, Gallup Poll, March 24-27, 2008.
[24] Grewel, Daisy. "In Atheists We Distrust." *Scientific American.* January 17, 2012.

keeping their beliefs well hidden, living a significant part of their lives 'in the closet.' Were they to suddenly appear in the town square in these countries, the likes of Charles Darwin, Albert Einstein, Carl Sagan, Richard Dawkins, Neil DeGrasse Tyson, Christopher Hitchens, or Stephen Hawking may well be set upon by a blade-wielding gang of the pious and faithful, beheaded to the cheers of an iPhone brandishing throng, while authorities stand idly by.

In many respects, atheism is analogous with homosexuality. The AIC has for millennia made them both out to be socially disgraceful, shameful, and a serious, punishable sin in the eyes of the lord. Both the homosexual and the atheist have been forced to live lives of secrecy and fear, have spent centuries keeping their true selves locked away in the proverbial closet, shared only very tentatively, and then only with those most highly trusted and like-minded. In the Christian and Islamic worlds, homosexuals have lived like this for centuries.

But progress has begun to take place. This has especially been the case since the Stonewall Riots in New York City, which marked a noteworthy turning point around 1969. Fifty years hence, there are many parts of the developed world in which people are less and less likely to be condemned, disrespected, oppressed, bullied, or ostracized for being LGBT or Q.

This is a result of a process of *normalization*. Normalization does *not* mean that such non-mainstream persons change their lifestyles, in order to become more 'normal.' Heaven forbid! It is about seeing diversity as a good, rather than the old melting-pot ideals of homogeneity or assimilation. It means that the broader culture has progressed to become more tolerant, accepting, even joyfully embracing and celebrating diversity.

In much of Euro-American society, and increasingly in developed, cosmopolitan areas around the world, homosexuality has progressed toward this more enlightened state, one in which the 'alternative lifestyles' are viewed as a normal characteristic of an ideally diverse, inclusive, and pluralistically rich society. Instead of conformity to rigid, limited Abrahamic codes of 'morality,' accepting diverse persons and lifestyles *as they are* is increasingly considered not just a moral good, but morally obligatory. Normalization means that people once considered repugnant are now considered equal in terms of justice, morality, and overall social status, regardless of their LGBT or Q status.

My hope is that the negative social stigma associated with atheism can be similarly mitigated. It should be entirely safe and free of repercussion for atheists to come out of the closet. Neither your chances of being elected president of the United States of America, nor the integrity of the connection between your head and torso, should be endangered in any way.

Hard v. Soft Atheism

There is a useful distinction to be noted between what I describe as the *soft* and *hard* atheist positions. Many nonbelievers go no further than the subjective claim of nonbelief, and are unwilling to assert that the believer is mistaken. Many assert that the burden of proof rests on those who *do* believe to demonstrate evidence in support of the assertion that god/s exist. In other words, the soft atheist position is: *I do not believe. If I am to believe, I'll need some convincing evidence.* Such nonbelievers hold the position that neither is better or worse, and that both the atheist and the theist have views of equivalent validity. This represents what I refer to as *soft atheism.*

Hard atheism is somewhat different. We share the soft atheist belief that the burden of proof should rest on the side of those who assert the existence of a deity, especially in light of the complete and total lack of worldly evidence to that effect. Yet we can *also* accept the 'burden of proof' without fear. Rather than remain on the defensive, the atheist position is strong enough that we can safely assert that god does not exist. Instead of simply stopping at *I do not believe*, the hard atheist is willing to assert something with more epistemological heft than mere doubt.

Hard atheism begins with the firm and positive recognition that all of the gods are but products of the imperfect human brain. They are all beliefs, not beings. This *soft v. hard* distinction is intended to describe an epistemological state: the soft state of a mere belief, versus the more robust, assertive claim characteristic of certitude or knowledge. Hard atheism asserts that those who believe god is a being of some type, and not merely a fictitious belief, are fundamentally mis-guided and mistaken.

It is important not merely to be atheist, but to be publicly atheist. We have a moral obligation to be 'out,' out of the closet into which Christianity has systematically forced us over the centuries. We have an obligation to represent our position intelligently and in an in-formed manner. Not flag waving, or obnoxious, nor shoving it down people's throats, or anything of that sort. That would not help things at all. But neither does keeping it to ourselves, our dirty little secret, out of our conscientious, or fearful, effort to avoid upsetting our co-workers, or grandma Anne, or devout Uncle Jim and Aunt Ellen.

It is important to distinguish between the person and their beliefs, to respect the one even when disagreeing with the other. It is the reli-gions and their attendant beliefs that are problematic, not the adher-ents per se. I do not wish to insult or offend anyone. However, I do not think we need to be tolerant and respectful of mistaken or prob-lematic views.

This is a very important point. The dynamic is analogous with that of ignorance. I am genuinely respectful and compassionate regarding those who are ignorant, meaning under informed, misinformed, poorly or undereducated. It is precisely because of this fundamental respect for the person that I necessarily disrespect that which shackles, binds, and blinds them. I do not respect ignorance itself. When someone is genuinely ignorant, you hate on the ignorance because you *do not* hate on the person.

Those still under the sway of religious traditions, of their faith in god, in Allah, in scripture, are victims, duped by a quite natural, very convincing, longstanding, popular, and self-perpetuating tradition of lies, fables, and falsehoods. They are under the sway of authority figures, social indoctrination, peer pressure, and comforting traditions, all rooted in naturally occurring, instinctive, causal predispositions and cognitive biases. Unfortunately, however, as Daniel Dennett put it:[25]

> There's simply no polite way to tell people they've dedicated their lives to an illusion.

Truth as Priority

Atheism is ultimately about the search for truth. It is an offshoot or extension of our wider search for knowledge. It sees that religion and the god hypothesis have failed to properly address fundamental questions about life, the cosmos, and human being. Atheists see gods and religion as faulty and problematic explanations. We reject claims about human nature and the cosmos which the preponderance of evidence tells us are false, in favor of those which the totality of evidence informs us are far more probable.

And atheism is a far more interesting subject than most people realize! It concerns our search for the truth regarding our existence, the seemingly inexplicable and sudden awakening of conscious self-

---

[25] Quote by D. Dennett found in: Schuessler, Jennifer. "Philosophy that Stirs the Water." *The New York Times*. April 29, 2013.

awareness within organically evolved organisms, here and now, on this planet, orbiting one fairly common type of yellow star, in this spiral arm of this one amongst millions of galaxies, in this inconceivably vast and wondrous expanding universe. How do we comprehend it all, how can we know it, how best should we make sense of all this, of our place within it?

The answers we have inherited from the distant past do not accomplish the heavy lifting we require of them in the here and now. And it makes sense, when you think about it, that 2,000-year-old origin stories would get stale. Once upon a time, accumulated knowledge forced us to recognize the shortcomings in the geocentric model of the cosmos, and so we progressed onwards to embrace the more accurate heliocentric model. In the same manner, there came a time when antiquated religious notions of disease as a spiritual issue concerning god, moral judgment, demons, curses, and witches, was discarded for the more rational and accurate germ theory of disease. In precisely the same manner, the ever-expanding body of human knowledge has begun to show increasingly glaring cracks in the theistic model, and atheist conceptions are rushing in to fill the growing gaps. But don't panic: this is a good thing. Human beings are progressing, growing up, maturing as a species. It is truly, as they say, 'all good.'

Humanity is progressing away from belief in the supernatural, and toward an understanding rooted in the natural; away from instinct, and toward a more reason-based mode of understanding. Your average Christian rightfully scoffs at Odin, Zarathustra, Viracocha, Osiris, Shiva, Ereshkigal, and the thousands of other deities from differing periods and places. We atheists simply take that one logical next step. No one said it better than Richard Dawkins:[26]

---

[26] Dawkins, Richard. *The God Delusion*. New York, NY: Houghton Mifflin Harcourt, 2008.

We are all atheists about most of the gods that humanity has ever believed in.

Some of us just go one god further.

Concluding Thoughts

People who believe in the god of the *Bible* or the *Quran* are fundamentally and factually mistaken, and yet Christianity and Islam are dominant in our world today. This has significant ramifications, and actually causes human beings and the world at large more harm than good. It anchors individuals in delusion and ignorance, nurtures conformity and obedience, sets sibling against sibling in violent conflict, and slows our overall progress in multiple areas, including justice, morality, and science. It impedes the cultivation of reason and rational discourse, grounding beliefs in mythology, self-conceptions in origin stories characterized by arrogance and supernaturalism, and ultimately squelches the greatest qualities in humanity, hindering our pursuit of eudaimonia for the individual and utopia for our communities.

New and important truths, including Darwin's theory of evolution, offer us a significant step forward in understanding the true nature of life, human beings, and our overall place within the cosmic schema. Yet the AIC continue to be significant impediments. Atheism is at base the search for knowledge. It should not merely be decriminalized, destigmatized, and normalized in human society, it should be raised to the status of an ideal, a goal we should pursue, toward the end of enabling humanity as a whole to more accurately comprehend the truth regarding our origins, our true nature, human progress, and our overall place within the wider cosmos.

Atheism is a positive thing, an essential step forward, away from falsehood, toward truth. Atheism says something factual about reality or, at the very least, rejects falsehoods about reality. Understanding how theistic belief is highly problematic is both informative and beneficial. We have a moral obligation to seek the truth, embrace the real world as it truly is, and to promote that which is good. We have a moral obligation to normalize atheism, to bring it out of the closet, and to help dispel the manifold falsehoods and antiquated presuppositions which put it there in the first place.

There is no god, as it is understood by the vast majority of Christians and Muslims. The god of Abraham, Isaac, and Jacob is a fiction, a belief, and not a real, actual being in any sense.

Religions such as Islam and Christianity are more burden than boon. A world without religion is both possible and preferable.

But it takes time for us to learn, absorb the truth, and accept change. Humanity's challenge to embrace revolutionary new truths of a rational or scientific nature is characterized by a two-part tango. One part is the ability of any given person or persons to present their new and novel idea. But the second dancer in the duo is the overall level of cultural development, the rationality, sophistication, education, and overall preparedness of those to whom she or he is presenting the message. It's a combination of how well the package is wrapped, with how ready the audience is to receive said package.

Darwin did an excellent job at preparing his message for delivery. *Origin* alone is a bold, solid, world changing document, as anyone who has read it will readily attest. It was, it is, the receiving audience that is still too deep under the sway of instinct, of antiquated, superstitious, religious dogma, and of Christianity's anti-knowledge mindset, to fully understand and appreciate Darwin's more accurate and humble origin story.

This is all changing now, slowly but surely, after 160+ years. In our time, thanks to the work of such rational, secular thinkers as Dawkins, Hitchens, Sam Harris, Michael Shermer, Bill Nye, Dan Barker, Steven Pinker, Jerry Coyne, Neil DeGrasse Tyson and, of course, Carl Sagan, more and more people are becoming informed about Darwin's work and the implications of evolutionary science. Yet there remains much work to be done.

Chapter 2
Born to Believe

This chapter is an extended version of an essay originally featured in Free Inquiry Magazine under the title, "Are We Born to Believe?" (February/March 2020; Volume 40, No. 2).

Many an atheist has taken afront when presented with the argument that religious faith and god beliefs are 'natural' for the animal *Homo sapiens*. They pepper social media with memes proclaiming that 'we are all born atheists,' with adorably innocent cherubic babies pulling at our heartstrings. Like the true believers themselves, atheists are sometimes susceptible to confirmation bias, clinging to treasured beliefs in the face of evidence to the contrary. Perhaps the fear is based upon the mistaken assumption that 'natural' and 'inevitable' necessarily go hand in hand. But the truth is that honestly understanding the root causes of religious faith and god beliefs is an important step towards realizing freedom from religion. After all, knowledge is power. But, fortunately for us, nature is not destiny.

> Man is born free, yet everywhere he is in chains.[27]
> – Jean-Jacque Rousseau, 1762

---

[27] Rousseau, Jean-Jacques, *The Social Contract*, 1762.

The thought is not new that, in the proverbial state of nature, we humans are pure and innocent—a squeaky-clean *tabula rasa*.[28] Then 'The Man' gets his hands on us, and we are indoctrinated with all of society's bullshit, including the religion of whatever culture we are born into. This line of thinking says that, if you stop the brainwashing, everything will be hunky dory. Left unfettered, people will naturally come to the same god-free, rational conclusions that we freethinkers, skeptics, and atheists embrace.

I genuinely respect the fundamental optimism at the basis of such thinking. I was raised in a family which held just such classic idealistic notions of original purity and perfection in the state of nature. This was a pretty popular 60's hippie mindset – a counter to misanthropic viewpoints such as Christianity's 'original sin' – with Jean-Jacque Rousseau, Margaret Mead, and the noble savage weltanschauung paving the road to Woodstock, Star Trek, and beyond.

Indoctrination is clearly a central component in the acquisition and maintenance of religious belief. Muslim parents largely produce Muslim offspring. Catholic parents, Catholic offspring. No doubt atheist households tend, by and large, to produce atheist offspring. But there is more to the story. While there is often a clear emphasis upon the *nurture* side of the debate, it is important to recognize the existence of a *nature* side of things. Many freethinkers view religious belief as 100% nurture, and see atheistic perspectives as the natural, default position of human beings. However, this perspective discounts an abundance of evidence and data to the contrary.

---

[28] Latin for "clean slate" – The literal translation from Latin is 'scraped tablet,' though it is more commonly read as "clean slate." Tabula rasa refers to the philosophical notion that the human mind at birth has no innate ideas or predispositions, but is instead a clean slate upon which experience is subsequently written, wholly determining the cognitive content of the human mind.

And it's important that we get this right. Religion, love it or hate it, is a big deal. Its impact upon humanity is so vast as to be immeasurable. If, as the late Christopher Hitchens claimed, "religion poisons everything,"[29] it most certainly behooves us to be as knowledgeable as possible regarding its causal conditions. The tabula rasa mindset merits resistance because it is an oversimplification of a more complex truth that we need to understand. The more we pin down the exact nature of these religious phenomena, the better we will be at dealing with them in the most constructive manner possible.

And so, what if our default mode is not atheism, but rather religious belief? What if religious belief is in fact the fundamental default mode for the brain of the animal *Homo sapiens*?

As it turns out, we are, in fact, naturally predisposed in some respects toward seeing and interpreting our experiences in superstitious, supernatural, and religious ways. Evidence shows that we humans suffer from a whole suite of cognitive biases and irrational propensities with which the jerry-rigging, not-so-intelligently designed process of evolution has endowed us. These propensities and biases quite 'naturally' point us toward supernatural, religious (mis-) interpretations of reality. If not checked or countered by cross-cultural or critical analysis, a comprehensive general education, exposure to the sciences, or to an environment in which reason and critical thought are practiced, these natural cognitive inclinations generally result in the kind of problematic beliefs which currently populate the minds of the world's copious devout.

The following are a few examples of the kind of common experiences which cast doubt upon our notion of atheism as the default setting for the *Homo sapiens* brain. You can most likely think of

---

[29] Hitchens, Christopher. *God is not Great: How Religion Poisons Everything.* New York: Twelve; Hachette Book Group, 2009.

additional examples that illustrate our propensity toward irrational, superstitious, supernaturalist belief.

- Belief in a soul or self: The mind-body dualism (or mind-brain dualism), which philosophers are still arguing over to this very day, has its roots in our experience of ensoulment, our sense of having a coherent self or soul which somehow 'transcends' the body, feels like more than just the sum of its working parts (i.e., dendrites, neurons, axons, etc.).

- The experience of signs, of portents, of dreams as harbingers or similarly supra-natural phenomenon, of omens and the like, in which the ordinary is infused with some kind of extraordinary meaning.

- Human beings from all cultures experience phenomena such as spirits, animating forces, ghosts, ancestors visiting in one form or another, monsters in the closet or in the dark or under the bed, witches casting spells or curses, phantasms and spooks, and thousands of variations on these widespread 'spiritual' themes.

- The prevalence of superstition. I have yet to meet a sports fan who is not at least a wee bit superstitious. My dearly beloved wife, who is simultaneously a serious and truly authentic atheist, as well as a serious and truly authentic Golden State Warriors fan, puts on a Warriors hat, scarf, t-shirt, or pair of socks before every game we watch.

- Belief in cosmic karma: I know many otherwise fully rational people who absolutely believe in some concept of divine or cosmic karma. They believe that 'what goes around comes around,' but not merely in the rational, secular sense of our evolved, scientifically verifiable social reciprocity.

- Last but certainly not least: the absolute ubiquity and universality of gods, in some form or another, in nearly every culture, time, or place in the history of the human race.

Know the Enemy and Prepare to Fight It

Religion-free households that create nonbelievers may not be simply free and open spaces, passively devoid of indoctrination. They may actively serve to inoculate us against religious thinking. In something resembling the proverbial state of nature, we might find humans naturally tending to interpret their experience in a manner very familiar to animist and pagan minds, with spirits and magical forces employed to explain what our pre-scientific minds found baffling, awesome, or inexplicable.

Charles Darwin's brilliant work makes it abundantly clear that we are animals, the direct products of nature, sharing common ancestry with all of the other animals. This must be the starting point for any informed understanding of human nature. For example, as much as we like to admire the brain of *Homo sapiens,* to think it spectacular and wondrous, which it truly is, this same brain is also a jerry-rigged, MacGyver-y, hot fucking mess. Far from being an objective, clear and clean window into the world, a perfect and unsullied slate upon which our experience is objectively recorded, it is, in fact, a jumble of opportunistically pre-wired belief instincts, predilections, cognitive biases, and cerebral quirks.

To illustrate, consider the human propensity to interpret the world, to see and think, in terms of *In Group versus Out Group (IG/OG).* Few would argue with the claim that IG/OG instincts are very strong in our species, a kind of natural cognitive prejudice. A recent finding, both humorous and telling, informs us that feelings of affiliation with a group actually reduce the disgust sensation caused by the bodily odors of that particular group.[30] That's right: we all know that there is no difference between the fetid quality of the air in your opponent's locker room, as compared with your own team's. Yet people find their teammate's smell acceptable, even pleasant, while finding their opponent's rank and malodorous.

Racism is similarly natural. This is supported by a variety of findings, including one which concluded that babies surrounded by only white faces will freak out when they encounter their first dark-skinned person, and equally so vice versa.[31] Such findings merely skim the surface of the mountainous and growing body of data which confirms that people have natural predispositions to interpret the world in terms of IG/OG, toward loving fellow In Group members, whilst holding less generous sentiments toward members of the Out Group.

In the same manner, we humans appear to be hell bent upon interpreting the world religiously. Superstitious and supernatural thinking appear to come quite naturally to our species. Supportive data for this claim begins with the important recognition of religion's ubiquity, its universality. People from all around the world have religious beliefs, and with similar essential components. This is most telling, in and of itself. What they are indoctrinated in is not theistic thinking per se, but in which form or manner to express these natural theistic instincts: which religion, which sect, the widely varying degrees of zealotry, etc. They learn their mode of religious belief from the family and culture in which they are immersed.

Another analogy to help illustrate this indwelling and underlying aspect of our nature would be human language. Few would suggest that we are indoctrinated into being a language-using animal. Instead,

---

[30] Cepelewicz, Jordana. "Body Odor Is Less Repulsive When It Comes From 'One Of Us.'" *Scientific American*. Feb 23, 2016.

[31] Bloom, Paul. *Just Babies: The Origins of Good & Evil*. New York: Crown Publishers, 2013.

we understand that the human brain is predisposed toward language, hardwired to do language. Which language we speak, which dialect and such, these are all entirely determined by context, by the teachings of family and culture, by indoctrination. Both language and religious belief come naturally to the human brain.

This analogy breaks down, however, when it comes to the relative strength of the two differing inclinations. For humans, the language instinct is considerably hardier than is our belief instinct. As I will argue in the pages to come, it is not particularly difficult to override our evolved proclivity to fill the world with mysterious forces, spirits, deities, and the like. The language instinct, however, is far more robust.

Cerebral Compost

Quirks of the evolved organ which is the human brain – our cognitive biases, belief instincts, the intrinsic, hardwired cerebral compost from which religious thinking and belief in god blossoms – these are universal human phenomena. The ubiquity of religious belief is an effect of its genesis within the very structure of the human body, primarily, if not solely, the biological organ we know of as our brain.[32] Religion is partly an evolutionary bequest, much as is the propensity to use language, our bipedalism, and our opposable thumb.

Many of our traits evolved to be as they are during the millions of years in which our ancestors were hunters and gatherers: members of small, familial tribes in prehistoric Africa. It is generally thought that it was a cooling, drying Africa, a place of climatic changes, possibly

---

[32] Often the human mind is considered to be something super- or supra-natural. Such latent dualism easily slides into human awareness, thought, and belief. My take on mind/body dualism is that of the philosophical materialist. Brain is the bodily organ; mind is simply the subjective experience of the brain's day-to-day bio/chemical/electric functioning.

brought about by the impact of the Indian tectonic plate as it moved rapidly northward, ramming into the Eurasian plate, piling up the Himalayas, and thereby altering atmospheric air currents. In the subsequently drier, cooler Africa, shrinking pockets of jungle and forest squeezed our short-legged, arboreal ancestors out of the trees and into new environs, encouraging the evolution of our beautiful, lengthy legs, our elegant, elongated strides[33] and, ultimately, Usain Bolt and Betty Grable.

With similar universality, people from all different cultures instinctively believe in ensoulment, or the 'ghost in the machine.' This is the belief that the soul or, secularly speaking, the self, has some kind of existence independent of the body. Today, rather than embrace the scientific probability that our sense of self is merely a ploy on the part of our selfish genes to get us to survive and successfully reproduce, we not only tend to believe in an existing, continuous self, but think of this self or soul as existing independently of the various axons, dendrites, and neurons which in actual fact constitute its true nature. We are highly prone to think of the self or soul as somehow existing independently of body/brain, or, in other words, of it having supernatural properties.

Yet some traits, having initially evolved to become a part of a species' repertoire because they were beneficial at one point in space and time, will often become less valuable at another. Some examples include the whale's hind legs, the eyes of cave-dwelling fish, the emu's wings, etc. With changes in environment and context, traits can cease to benefit, and even become a drain on an animal's resources. Consider the strongly inculcated hominid instinct for consuming massive amounts of sugar and fat whenever available, which has certainly

---

[33] Maslin, Mark. "How Climate Change and Plate Tectonics Shaped Human Evolution" from The Conversation, *Scientific American*. November 14, 2013.

backfired on us of late. For humans, this list also includes predispositions toward certain beliefs, thought patterns, mental traits, and behaviors which may no longer be as valuable as they were in different contexts or in different times.

In addition, traits always interact, blend, and combine with other traits, which can lead to complex, multi-trait characteristics. Physical, psychological, and social predispositions that were once of value to us may, either by themselves or in concert, become increasingly detrimental. Taking my cue from Richard Dawkins,[34] Jesse Bering,[35] and others, I understand religion in this way. Evolutionarily inculcated cognitive instincts combine, predisposing us to interpret phenomenon in terms of supernatural forces, inclining us toward an instinctively, and distinctively, religious interpretation of the cosmos. Add in the process of familial, tribal, and cultural indoctrination, and you have a one-two punch combo far more effective than anything little Sugar Ray Leonard or mighty Muhammad Ali ever dished out.

Evolutionary Explanations

Ever since Darwin, it has become increasingly common to think of the traits of any given living organism in terms of their biologically adaptive value, of how they may have rendered the creature more or less 'fit.' Why are we bipedal, for example? Why do we have IG/OG propensities? This can be an extremely valuable approach, greatly improving our understanding of living organisms in general, and of human nature in particular. But this approach can also quite easily descend into a problematic reductionism, offering oversimplifications rather than enlightening explanations.

---

[34] Dawkins, Richard. *The God Delusion*. New York: Houghton Mifflin Harcourt, 2008.
[35] Bering, Jesse. *The Belief Instinct: The Psychology of Souls, Destiny, and the Meaning of Life*. New York: W. W. Norton & Company, 2011.

Many have sought to understand religion as one coherent, discrete phenomenon which, in and of itself, had some adaptive value, and was thereby inculcated into our evolutionary repertoire. But religion is far too complex for such an understanding. We would be in error if we embraced this kind of oversimplification in talking about evolved traits as the primal source for religious belief, and assuming that religion is itself, as a package, somehow a survival-enhancing adaptation.

The best explanation of religion as a natural phenomenon is that it is a result of a complex of traits, or what Ludwig Wittgenstein would describe in terms of a 'family resemblance' model of identification.[36] This is the notion that, in identifying or explaining any given complex phenomenon, such as *game*, or *art*, or *religion*, it is best to think in terms of a suite or family grouping of traits, with no one trait being definitive.

To the extent that religious belief is a natural phenomenon, it is not a directly adaptive response per se, as with increased webbing between the toes of a duck, more resilient teeth for a lion or a shark, or lactose tolerance for humans practicing animal husbandry. The base origin of religion appears to be an amalgam of cognitive tendencies hardwired by evolution into the human brain, in response to a variety of environmental factors.

Some of these components are cognitive biases, the non-rational, hardwired cognitive instincts introduced in chapter 1, traits with which the brain of *Homo sapiens* has been burdened by the evolutionary process. Such often less-than-ideal, irrational propensities combine with other, more familiar human predilections, such as our fear of

---

[36] Wittgenstein, Ludwig. *Philosophical Investigations.* (1953). – "Consider for example the proceedings that we call 'games.' I mean board-games, card-games, ballgames, Olympic games, and so on. What is common to them all? Don't say: 'There must be something common, or they would not be called 'games''— but look at them you will not see something that is common to all, but similarities, relationships, and a whole series of them at that."

death, our natural curiosity and quest for understanding, and our strong innate hunger for morality, justice, and equity in the case of moralizing religions such as the AIC. This amalgam, or suite of 'family resemblance' traits, is the foundation of religious belief. It is the ultimate, root cause of the AIC.

There are two important provisos to keep in mind. First of all, few, if any, people exist in the state of nature anymore. For our purposes, the 'state of nature' refers to the environmental context within which our brain evolved to have its current unique make-up. This means a couple million years of pre-civilization, living in the wild, on the African savannah, migrating into Asia and Europe in small, family-sized nomadic bands of eusocial, bipedal, toolmaking, fire-handling, and food-cooking hunters and gatherers, with huge caloric intake fueling the explosive evolutionary growth of our unique brains. This was the environmental context in which our brains took their current and uniquely large form.

But our lifestyles have transformed radically over the last 15,000 years, shifting from hunting & gathering to the far more sedentary, urban, 'civilized' lives associated with the rise of agriculture and animal husbandry. Any trait or traits which evolved into existence during the millions of years of the former may well be rendered superfluous or moot in the latter. Our IG/OG brain, our sugar-crazed palate, these things helped us to survive and thrive in the state of nature. But living in our contemporary, globalized, overpopulated, post-scarcity context, such traits may be less boon than bane.

The second is that *Homo sapiens* is what I refer to as 'the learning animal.' Much of human nature is a result of nurture dominating nature. Human nature is characterized less by instinct, and more by learning, than probably any other living organism. This is why indoctrination plays the admittedly significant role that it does. Some instincts are very difficult, if not genuinely impossible, to override. As noted, language is an excellent example of such a robust cognitive predisposition.

Others succumb fairly easily to the right countering influences. Male aggression comes to mind as an example. The male of our species is by far the more aggressive and violently inclined of the two primary genders. By far and away, men are responsible for the vast majority of violent assaults, crimes, conflicts, and wars. Yet it is notably the case that families, cultures, or contexts which emphasize nonviolent problem-solving skills, compassion, and empathy, tend to produce distinctly more peaceful, less violent males. A modicum of *nurture* fairly easily overrides this disposition of *nature*. Religion is likewise the result of an amalgam of instinctive predispositions which are fairly non-robust. Nature is not destiny.

Our natural, instinctive propensity toward religious belief is non-robust. It is a little bit nature, a whole lotta nurture. It is but a thin veneer which can be easily overwritten by environmental factors such as immersion in a normative value of skepticism and critical thinking, education in the sciences and the liberal arts, or simply being raised in a nonreligious context that stresses the use of reason.

Cognitive Bias No. 1: Agency Attribution

So, it is time to get specific and describe a couple examples of the kinds of cognitive biases at the root of religious faith and the god belief. One such predisposition is our propensity to instinctively attribute *agency*. Our brains are hardwired to interpret the phenomenon of experience through an agency-detecting filter. That is, we think *in terms* of 'agents' and 'agency.' The human brain perceives, interprets, and thinks of the world we experience in terms of beings with intentions, interests, and wills.

We think of the self as a being. We think of others as beings. But we also think *in terms of* beings more generally, and our brains have evolved to interpret various phenomena using the same cognitive set of tools. This is the source of our all-pervasive animistic beliefs and practices, the peopling of our world with individuated, animated entities with wills and wants, spirits and minds. The goddess *Sequana* animated the waters of the river Seine, *Futen* the winds in Japan, but *Gaol* if you lived amongst the Iroquois, while the mountains, rocks, and caves were the dwelling place for the spirit of *Apu* according to the Inca. Similar interpretations sit at the foundation of the polytheistic and pagan traditions which dominated the human world before their subjugation by the AIC.

Humans instinctively fill the universe around us with beings with agency: self/soul, ghosts, witches, dragons, werewolves, unicorns, mermaids, fairies, Santa and the Easter Bunny, seraphim and cherubim, serpents, ghouls, spirits, vampires, zombies, leprechauns, giants, ogres, yetis, sasquatch, kachinas, Iwa, warlocks, demons, angels, demi-gods like Hercules or Romulus & Remus, the spirit of the Buddha Dharma, your guardian angel, the little devil and angel on each shoulder, the millions of differing gods themselves, Mother Mary and Baby Jesus and, of course, the Father, the Son, and the Holy Ghost.

Animist religions were ubiquitous among the tribal, indigenous, native peoples all around our world, prior to the rise of the monotheistic traditions. Our early ancestors attributed agency to every rock, tree, river, or volcano, to the sun, moon, wind, and rain. In spite of Christian and Islamic missionary efforts, tribal, native peoples generally seek to keep their old gods alive, even as *Things Fall Apart*[37] all around them. Animist, polytheist, and pantheist traditions can still be

---

[37] Achebe, Chinua. *Things Fall Apart*. Nigeria: William Heinemann, Ltd., 1958. – An excellent consideration of the phenomenon in question.

discerned today, though generally buried, broken, and misshapen beneath the oppressive overlying stratum of monotheism. This blending, or syncretism, is how we get to Vodou, Santeria, Rastafarianism, the Easter Bunny, and Santa Claus as well.

Our instinct to think in terms of agency is a result of our evolving to be the *eusocial* animals we are. Human beings are not nearly as individual as we often think. The soul is complete fiction. But the self, as a unified, contiguous, individuated entity, is also more fiction and cognitive construct than reality. Instead, humans are animals who, not unlike ants or honeybees, are members of intensely interdependent, interwoven communities. We have evolved to thrive in complex social interaction, requiring teamwork and cooperation, with fellow tribemates whose interests, intentions, and desires are to our benefit to be intensely aware of and sensitive to. The development of our large brain is intimately linked with the development of this collectivist, eusocial nature, as well as with our innate, instinctive propensity to interpret the world of experience in terms of beings with interests or, in other words, agents.

Tucker, Sammy, and Polly

I have two charming little furry friends sitting at my feet as I type these words. Tucker is my tiny rat terrier, and Sammy is my little chiweenie. Whenever there is an unusual sound, an unexpected knocking, the mailbox creaking, footsteps at the front door, or even the electronic beeping of my wife's car door locking halfway down the block, these two set about an unrivaled paroxysm of small dog symphonics which, left unperturbed, will run for a full minute or more. That may not sound like much, but, trust me, in the ears of any sufferer within auditory range, a full minute of small dog yapping is a truly heinous, torturous eternity. In the absence of information to the contrary, their little mammalian brains' default assumption is toward agency of some kind. They are quick tuned to assume, on the level of doggy consciousness, the threat of a being with intentions, a will, and interests all its own. In human beings, such instinctive predispositions will, when in a general state of ignorance, often generate theistic interpretations of the experienced phenomenon.

Consciousness is not an on/off affair, but a matter of degree, as Darwin fully recognized. While *Canis lupus* are undoubtedly not conscious in the same sense that our species is, their behavior suggests an evolutionary correlation with the cognitive processes I am describing. Such traits have obvious evolutionary advantages. They were therefore adapted into subsequent populations. They led to automatic responses, responses which did not require conscious deliberation per se. Picture an ancient shaman awakening from a sleep vision, thinking "*omen*," then awakening fellow tribemates and getting them the hell out of that damned flood plain!

The parallel is so striking it has occurred to many, including Charles Darwin himself, whose beloved fox terrier Polly inspired the following insightful passage:[38]

> ...my dog, a full-grown and very sensible animal, was lying on the lawn during a hot and still day; but at a little distance a slight breeze occasionally moved an open parasol, which would have been wholly disregarded by the dog, had any one stood near it. As it was, every time that the parasol slightly moved, the dog growled fiercely and barked. He must, I think, have reasoned to himself in a rapid and unconscious manner, that movement without any apparent cause indicated the presence of some strange living agent, and that no stranger had a right to be on his territory.

---

[38] Darwin, Charles. *The Descent of Man and Selection in Relation to Sex.* NY: D. Appleton & Co., 1889.

For we humans, that scratching sound at night is a potential burglar, that shadow a ghost or ghoul, a stalker, some form of agent, quite possibly with evil intentions. Even a philosophical materialist and skeptic such as myself struggles with my mind's native talent for populating the unknown. In the city, dastardly ne'er-do-wells lurk in the shadows. Camping in the woods, I'll peer nervously out from the light and warmth of the central hearth, filling the surrounding darkness with all manner of imaginary beings, ears pricked for the tell-tale snap of twigs beneath predatory footfall, just as were those of my evolutionary forebears.

Fast forward tens of thousands of years and you've got Zeus hurling thunderbolts, Neptune swelling tsunamis to swallow Atlantis whole, Jahweh commanding the genocidal elimination of another Out Group, Allah recommending smiting and dismemberment on a scale that would titillate any contemporary online gamer, and, ultimately, the Scots praying:

> From ghoulies and ghosties
> And long-leggedy beasties
> And things that go bump in the night,
> Good Lord, deliver us!

Little do they realize that the good lord whom they were beseeching for deliverance was himself created by the exact same mental machinery responsible for populating the unknown darkness with the ghoulies, ghosties, and long-leggedy beasties in the first place.

We fill in the darkness, the space between things known, with a vast coterie of intentional actors. Monotheistic and Abrahamic gods are the ultimate of these intentional actors, the largest instantiation of a being with an agenda; the primary explanatory agent, writ large and projected across our internal cosmoscape. All around the world, people believe that he watches over us, controls us, and that we are all pawns and puppets in his divine plan.

Cognitive Bias No. 2: Teleology

Another example of cognitive instincts with which evolution has endowed us combines the human mind with our bipedalism, which freed up our hands for toolmaking and tool using abilities. We are instinctively inclined to think and understand *in terms of* purpose and utility, to think *teleologically*, through a filter which perceives, interprets, and thinks *teleofunctionally:* that is, in terms of the use-value of things. We have evolved to interpret the cosmos in this way because it is adaptively advantageous for our species to do so. We bring this particular mental prejudice to bear upon all the phenomena in our lives. This is very often to highly beneficial effect, as one can readily imagine.

What purpose can we put this stick to? A spear is born.

How can we use these trees? We can build a protective structure, or maybe a craft that will float us across the surface of the water, to the greener grass on the other side, or to follow the migrating herd.

To what purpose can we put this fire? The possibilities are virtually limitless…

Now, take this teleological predisposition, and add the uniquely *cumulative, shared,* and *applicable* form of intelligence humans possess. Fast forward for, say, a million years. Whaddya got? Magnificence! Centrally heated homes, electricity, doubled life-expectancy rates, personal computers with instantaneous global communication, encyclopedic information and knowledge at our fingertips, refrigerators full of healthy food, bullet trains and bicycles, fewer bedbugs, fleas, and bubonic plague, more Bach, Beatles and Clash, all up in my amazing new-fangled earbuds. You get Pandora, Skype, Lamborghinis, satellites, 3D printers, Facebook, aquaculture, women's rights, the Bill of Rights, the United Nations and the Universal Declaration of Human Rights, soap in every bathroom, hot, cold, and clean running water, flush toilets, vaccines for polio, tetanus, and yellow fever, renewable energy, the emergence of conscious sustainability and global civilization, sustainable technology, less and less violence, more and more cooperation, marriage equality, wind-generated electricity, tofu, plus, even more importantly, over a thousand ways to make tofu palatable, and much, much more...

Yet, as is the case with so many of evolution's endowments, our teleological instinct can go too far. If you think of a rock, stick, or fire in terms of use or purpose, you may be a genius. If you think of your family or friends in terms of use or purpose, you're just an asshole. And if you think of the whole universe that way, as if it were a clock made by a giant clockmaker, as something that was planned, designed, or built by an uber-being who created humans with a cosmic purpose and built the world around us to be useful to us ... Well, then, you're probably religious. But you are also probably mistaken.

This kind of projection is a very common human error. It is a form of cart-before-the-horse thinking which I have referred to as *epistemological inversion*. We think we are comprehending things accurately. But the way we see the world sometimes says less about *the world*, and more about *the way we see*.

Consider this example: many people today adamantly believe that some form of intelligence predates existence, that an intelligent force or being caused the cosmos. Used to be spirits and gods, now it's just as often the work of 'advanced' alien races, complex holographic simulations, or some form or another of Artificial Intelligence. In either case, the known universe is in some sense an effect, a result, of that intelligent entity's plan or blueprint. Yet so far, all of the evidence we possess suggests that intelligence is a purely biological phenomenon:

it is itself entirely the effect or result of evolutionary processes. Yet people think that intelligence somehow caused the evolution of intelligence in animals. They think of it as a *cause*, even though all the facts we have tell us that it's entirely *effect*. Cart before the horse. Epistemological inversion.

Intelligence is nothing more than one on a long list of traits – along with feathers, photosynthesis, seeds, sex, echolocation, the elephant's sensitive and versatile snout, the octopus's skilled and thinking tentacles, our bipedal gait, our cognitive biases – which evolutionary processes have cobbled into being from whatever scraps were at hand. If the trait benefits an organism in its effort to survive and successfully reproduce within a given specific context or set of complex variables, then the trait sticks around. So, thinking of intelligence as a cause is erroneous, cart-before-the-horse thinking. It is an example of a fundamental epistemological inversion. Not to mention it is also more than a tad anthropocentric.

There is no evidence-based, rational reason to assert that natural phenomena have such instrumental or utilitarian reasons for their existence. Rather, all the evidence we have strongly suggests that the phenomena of the universe *are* simply because they *are*, not *for* any reason. Neither planets, stars, moons, mountains, rivers, creeks, animals nor persons exist *for a purpose*. Human beings have no cosmic purpose, there is no master plan, and it's not all *for* anything. We are the ones who overlay the whole shebang with cognitive projections of utility, destiny, purpose, value, blueprint, or plan. We observe the non-teleologic cosmos through a cognitive filter which imposes telos, like a tinted pair of glasses imposes a hue or tone upon that which we perceive.

Thinking and seeing *in terms of* purpose and utility is a biologically adaptive, evolved trait. It helped our ancestors to survive and thrive. That is why we all come equipped with a propensity to think in this manner. And so, while thoughts of divine purpose, utility, and a god with a plan are unsupported by evidence and reason, they nevertheless arise quite naturally and spontaneously within the mind of the animal *Homo sapiens*, predisposing us toward theistic conclusions.

Suffice it to say that we are the source of teleology. Value exists only within the mind of the valuer, the being which has evolved to experience value. Use and purpose are not in the nature of what is observed, but only in the mind of the observer. Our teleofunctional cerebral instinct leads us to believe that our very lives, even the existence of our species as a whole, possesses a cosmic purpose, are in some ways an expression of a divine destiny or importance.

Thus is born the notion of god's plan, the religious belief that an overlord has a blueprint, that we humans figure into it prominently, and that the entirety of the natural realm is here for our use. Wrapped up in this package of biases, we find the roots of our belief in a designer, a god with a plan, as well as humanity's errant view of itself as special, separate, and superior to all other life forms, and predestined for some grand cosmic purpose. In other words, *human exceptionalism.*

Religious and teleological thinking are nearly indistinguishable in some respects, and work together to bias our understanding accordingly. Consider our deepest ontological and metaphysical inquiries, the very shape and form of the questions we consider to be deep and profound. As Dawkins[39] and others have observed, they are in fact actually rather vacuous and meaningless:

The question 'Why are we here?' biases our inquiry toward the teleofunctional perspective. This is patently absurd when one instead considers our existence from a scientific, evolutionary perspective. The answer has been so elusive because the question is fundamentally absurd.

---

[39] Dawkins, *The God Delusion*, 2008.

'What is our purpose?' is merely a variant on the above, and so suffers the same critique. Despite its profound appearance, it does more to confuse than enlighten us.

'What is the meaning of life?' presupposes not merely that it is intelligible to describe the existence of the animal *Homo sapiens* in terms of meaning, but also that such meaning is in some sense pre-ordained. This again presupposes some conception of a plan or blueprint. Our inability to grasp this divine destiny is chalked up to god's ways being perpetually mysterious, god's oft played get out of jail free card. The truth of the matter is far more probably that no such grandiose destiny exists, and that 'meaning' in a human life is to be understood in a far more humble, localized, and far less pompous manner, determined by what we have evolved to value, not pre-determined by a creator, cosmic overlord, or divine blueprint.

The mode of thought under consideration comes naturally to human beings. Children will answer questions about worldly phenomenon by emphasizing their teleofunctional value. When asked 'why are there apples?' they will answer 'for the deer to eat.' Or 'for people to bake into yummy apple turnovers.' However, as Jesse Bering observed:[40]

> It's only around fourth or fifth grade that children begin abandoning these incorrect teleofunctional answers in favor of scientifically accurate accounts. And without a basic science education, promiscuous teleology remains a fixture of adult thought.
> – Jesse Bering

Unchecked, this natural, instinctive 'promiscuous teleology' shapes our understanding of human nature, our world, and the universe as a

---

[40] Bering, *The Belief Instinct*, 2011.

whole. We are hardwired to project this telos—belief that the cosmos is purposeful, or has a purpose, of humans as having purpose or destiny, and of the two as closely related facts—Imax-style across both the internal and external firmament.

Promoting, Protecting, & Perpetuating

We have considered two examples of the kinds of cognitive instincts which are hardwired into the evolved circuitry that is the human brain: *agency attribution* and *teleology*. They sit at the root of religious belief, while social and environmental factors subsequently determine how they are expressed, or if they are expressed at all. While such cognitive biases have a *causal* role in initiating religious thought and belief, there is a different suite of built-in instincts which serve to *promote, protect,* and *perpetuate* such beliefs once they are in place.

Many an atheist or rational thinker has been vexed by the seeming incapacity of the devout to entertain even the tiniest bit of doubt as to their deeply entrenched religious beliefs. The following evolutionarily hardwired instincts, or cognitive biases, while not insurmountable, shed light upon why reason, rational discourse, science, and plain old common sense often seem to roll off the pious like water off the proverbial duck's back.

Cognitive Bias No. 3 – The Repetition Bias
Cognitive Bias No. 3 – The Repetition Bias

Human beings are hardwired to believe that which is repeated over and over again. It is a characteristic which we share with other animals. Think Pavlov and his dogs. If one hears something repeatedly, the mind starts to believe it, regardless of how ludicrous it may be. This *repetition bias* is simple and fairly obvious. Politicians and the advertising industry have famously taken advantage of this trait, toward the end of amassing great power and wealth. It is a cognitive bias of the utmost importance, as it is a very potent characteristic, and can be a significant barrier to human progress.

Islam and Christianity place considerable emphasis upon this element of repetition. Religious services and the religious life both consist of a high degree of repetition. Interestingly, the word *repetitive* is in fact a synonym for the word *mantra*. Prayer is another obvious case in point. The devout pray regularly, many times throughout the day. The second pillar of Islam, known as Salah or Salat, obliges every Muslim to perform a minimum of five daily prayers. Both the act of praying, and the content of the prayers themselves, are intensely repetitive. Belief in the fundamentally dependent relationship of the weak, sinful, imperfect human to an all-powerful, all-good, perfect, supernatural, intervening deity is perpetually reaffirmed, renewed, and reinforced. The AIC derive a great deal of their immense sticking power directly from this one human weakness: the repetition bias.

Cognitive Bias No. 4 – The Confirmation Bias

Another particularly troublesome propensity which is central to the intransigence of theistic beliefs is the *confirmation bias*. As introduced in chapter one, when confronted with data which shines the light of reasonable doubt upon their convictions, people often undervalue the incoming data, and irrationally cling all the more stubbornly to their original beliefs. We are inclined to hold our cognitive ground all the more obstinately in the face of contradictory evidence. Rather than allow a shadow of a doubt, the confirmation bias ensures that religious human beings will cling to and defend their convictions, however errant they may be. As mentioned earlier, they may indeed 'double down,' becoming even more deeply entrenched in their preferred position. Not looking so intelligently designed now, are we? Undoubtedly, the confirmation bias is extraordinarily familiar to us all. It is most certainly a major player in the game.

Unfortunately, this is a quirk of all human minds, and not merely the devout. Atheists can at times be as entrenched as the most adamant evangelical. When presented with the evidence-based argument that natural predispositions toward irrational and supernatural interpretations of experience serve as a foundation for religious belief, many atheists will completely disregard what the facts or data suggest. Instead, they hold fast to their *a priori* conviction that we are by nature blank slates, predisposed to rational, atheistic interpretations of the cosmos. They cling adamantly to the position that all religious belief is 100% the result of familial and cultural indoctrination. This particular bit of atheist hypocrisy sets my irony meter ringing big time.

Cognitive Bias No. 5 – The Authority Bias

Also introduced earlier, the *authority bias* refers to the manner in which, without conscious thought or rational deliberation, we lend extra credence to that which is uttered by authority figures, including the very fallible priests and popes, imams, and ayatollahs.

A number of Nobel Prize winners, in addition to being mostly brilliant in their specific recognized areas of expertise, have held positively ludicrous beliefs in other areas.[41] Some of these recognized geniuses were outspoken quacks, misogynists, racists, astrologers, warmongers, and anti-Semites, to name a few specifics. All of which simply serves to support the idea that our propensity to blindly follow any authority on many issues may not necessarily be ideal. Not every idea our idealized leaders have is consistently...well...ideal.

---

[41] Strauss, Mark. "Nobel Laureates Who Were Not Always Noble." *National Geographic*. Oct 6, 2015.

Humans are inclined to give the same kind of extra, 'authoritative' weight to that which is read in the scriptures of their religion of origin. The *Bible* and the *Quran* act as surrogate authority figures in this psychological sense. This is hardly surprising seeing as how these works are touted to be the literal word of god.

This follow-the-leader bias is well illustrated in the famous 'smoky room' experiments taught to students of Psychology. Social psychologists Darley and Latane placed unknowing volunteer participants in a waiting room, telling them to fill out forms or simply wait.[42] Soon the room began to fill with smoke, slowly leaking from a vent. The average participant fairly quickly rose up and proceeded to do something about it. The experimenters next placed informed confederates in the room. These confederates sat quietly, filling out forms, showing no concern as the vent proceeded to exude smoke. In multiple experiments, replicated in numerous variations, the amount of time the test subject waited before acting increased dramatically with the presence of these experimental confederates. These experiments brought our attention to the *herd effect*, which refers to the fact that, like other animals, human beings tend to follow the herd. Other people impact us, reducing or dispersing our sense of personal responsibility. We are psychologically predisposed to go with the crowd, to think and do as others think and do, regardless of how rational or irrational that may be.

If everyone in your tribe—your family, school, or circle of friends, your nation, your entire world—thinks, believes, and asserts that 'faith is a virtue,' only the very exceptional person is capable of questioning or resisting that belief. By far, the majority will, instead, think and believe more or less the same as their community members think and

---

[42] Darley John M., and Bibb Latane. "Bystander Intervention in Emergencies: Diffusion of Responsibility." *Journal of Personality and Social Psychology*, vol. 8, no. 4, Pt. 1. (1968): 377-83. https://doi.org/10.1037/h0025589.

believe. This herd effect, or group bias, is very powerful. We can all readily conceive a number of examples, whether from the front page or from our own lives, all attesting to the importance of this human weakness for the AIC's long reign of dominance.

These are some of the cognitive biases which safeguard our religious beliefs once they have been initially instilled. They work in concert with those more familiar, and somewhat more rational sources which have for so long been claimed to sit at the root of religious faith, such as our thirst for understanding, our preoccupation with death, or our hunger for the comfort which can accompany faith. All of the cognitive biases considered are but a sampling of the kind of instinctive predispositions which make religious faith and belief in god such a ubiquitous and intransigent phenomenon. Working together, they predispose us toward theism, both to cause it, as well as to protect and perpetuate it once it has taken root.

Born to Believe

The animal *Homo sapiens* has evolved a variety of characteristics which predispose us to theistic interpretations of existence, life, and the cosmos, as well as various instincts which incline us to hold onto those beliefs once formulated. Indoctrination determines much subsequently, including the form the subsequent belief takes, if any at all, while it can also play a significant role in nurturing, defending, and perpetuating religious faith. But religion is not 100% nurture, zero nature.

At the same time, our natural predisposition toward religious thinking is not robust, and is fairly easily steamrolled by a number of variants on the nurture side of the nature/nurture spectrum. Human neuroplasticity, our flexible, adaptable nature, and the fact that we are very much a learning animal, all allow us to enjoy great cognitive freedom. It is increasingly easy to be a rational, religion-free, secular infidel. Thank god!

Surroundings that are free of religious indoctrination, and/or characterized by well-rounded education, rational discourse, and scientific thinking, can, and do, readily override these religious inclinations. As author and professor Jesse Bering points out, without a basic science education, certain features of our 'belief instincts' can and often do remain a fixture of adult thought. While a proper education serves to counter theistic instincts and indoctrination, it is important to understand how populated the human mind is by the ghosts of old, and how closely they slumber just below the surface of human consciousness.

We should seek to normalize atheism. We should also not shy away from arguing the possibility that it is both a more accurate picture of reality, as well as better overall for humanity, as a foundation for rational, instinct-free human thought, belief, and behavior. But evolution is a slow, biological process, and our brains are more or less the same as they were 50,000 years ago. Our cognitive default mode may always be set to our ancestors' kind of supernatural and superstitious interpretations of the cosmos, those which are naturally inclined to generate religious belief. It is therefore very important that we know, understand, and guard against this tendency. We can choose to rise above these instinctive predilections. We can choose freedom from religion. Fortunately for us, nature is not destiny, and knowledge is power.

Chapter 3
Abrahamic Dualism

Truth v Comfort

[T]he bad thing about all religions is that, instead of being
able to confess their allegorical nature, they have to conceal it;
accordingly, they parade their doctrine in all seriousness as
true sensu proprio, and as absurdities form an essential part of
these doctrines, you have the great mischief of a continual
fraud.
– Arthur Schopenhauer[43]

There you have it. I am not really saying anything so radical or new.
One of history's great, renowned philosophers said something very
similar hundreds of years ago. So, if you like the argument from authority, that should do the job; you are now convinced. But, just in
case you're like me, and require more, I will offer rational argument
and worldly evidence to further state my case. After all, human
knowledge is cumulative and, without suggesting I know better than
Arthur Schopenhauer, much has changed since the early 1800s.
Thanks to our ability to stand on his shoulders, and those of numerous
others, we can see more, say more, know more.

The AIC emphasize comfort over truth. Religion is like that, offering pablum and placebo in place of accuracy and authenticity. Christianity and Islam are characterized by falsehoods. They lie. They lie

---

[43] Schopenhauer, Arthur. *The Christian System*, 1818.

big, and they lie often. Obviously, Jesus did not walk on water, nor did Moses part an actual sea. But these are not really the lies I am talking about. More to the point, I guess – the flagrantly fictional nature of holy scripture is but the very tip of the iceberg. It matters not a whit that 'everybody knows' they are but tales, allegory, origin myth, or allegedly moral fables. The impact is not diminished in the least.

The falsehoods and lies run far deeper than virgin birth, Noah's ark, or the ubiquitous medical miracles. The devout are discouraged from critically questioning their own religion's scriptures, its various rules, commandments, or even simple truisms and traditions. Self-criticism and brutal honesty are not religions' strong suits. And all of this falsehood and deception sets the stage for a stunning number of troubles in the real world, and concomitant denial as to the nature of those troubles.

It can be difficult to distinguish truth from falsehood, and the AIC do not make it any easier, to put it mildly. The demonization of the non-religious and the negative associations made with *atheists* or *atheism* are just one example of this. The devout portray us, at best, as lost souls. But even those with no strong religious convictions join in the culturally pervasive tendency to disregard and dismiss us as extremists, inclined to make a big deal over trivial matters. Idolators, infidels, and freethinkers all are maligned and ostracized. But this societal disapproval is all the more virulent for anyone associated with the specific label of 'atheist.' Thousands of years of indoctrination have convinced the people of our Christianity-infused social milieu that to be an atheist is particularly heinous, immoral, and even diabolically fiendish.

Historically, this can be understood as a part of the AIC's overall sales pitch. Many aspects of the AIC can be best understood in light of the central significance of proselytizing, the institutionalized and definitive focus on convincing people to join up. In spite of the fact that the religious portray us in a consistently negative light, it is simply false that we atheists are Satan-worshipping, pointy-tailed, baby-eating demons. But, by so demonizing us in everyone's hearts and minds, by making mere nonbelief itself into a sin, associated with the worst of evils, enrollment in the AIC increases. Atheism is not a bad thing. But telling people it is, gets them to line up and sign up.

Atheists and agnostics alike have been subjected to torture, burning at the stake, beheading, and similar atrocities. This very real, very life-and-limb threatening persecution has been perpetrated by the AIC for centuries. Hundreds of years ago, it was commonplace that merely accusing some neighbor, whom perhaps you simply disliked, or who owed you a chicken, or who had refused your sexual advances, of atheism, witchcraft, or being in league with the devil, would result in violent social censure, or angry mobs wielding pitchfork, machete, or sword. The merest whiff of suspicion could bring about extreme and odious consequences. Powerful, fear-based social and political pressures, rooted in Abrahamic ideology, ensured compliance and conformity.

We Americans think this entirely a thing of the past. But this is not true. In many parts of our world even today, nonbelievers live in a state of perpetual fear of being 'outed' or identified as nonbelievers due to extreme social pressure or state-sanctioned violence. Though most extreme today in theocratic Islamic nations, it is also true in other nations, of both Islamic and Christian majority, that being identified as an atheist can not only impact one's social status, but even be physically dangerous or injurious. While not often physical, other forms of extreme social pressures still exist in many parts of the United States of America. This is like a religious hangover, caused by the long-standing traditions and social habits of banning, shunning, and black listing, which have their own self-perpetuating, knock-on, ripple effects.

I am grateful for the fact that, where I currently live, I am not forced to use a pseudonym to protect my family, or to disguise my true feelings or thoughts. I can sport atheist bumper stickers without significant fear of being assaulted by some devout citizen experiencing a sudden and inexplicable case of road rage, so long as I don't drive too far into fundamentalist Christian sections of rural America where there is still extreme social pressure to conform. But even in the less flagrantly religious communities, contemporary misconceptions of atheists persist and thrive. Unfair stereotypes still represent us as shallow, live-for-the-moment hedonists. As reactionary, anti-social anarchists. As glass-half-empty nay-sayers. Or, as despairing, what's-the-fucking-point-anyway nihilists.

Another falsehood propagated by the AIC is that atheism renders us incapable of the deeper bearings which give human existence value and meaning. Yet research has shown that your average atheist or agnostic is better educated *on the very subject of religion itself* than is your average believer.[44] Contrary to popular misconceptions, we atheists are at least equally, if not more so, inclined to take it all quite seriously, to have a sense that it all matters, a sense that we human beings are a part of something bigger than ourselves, something which gives value, meaning, purpose, and context to our lives. The main difference between the two is that one belief is rooted in evidence and reason, while the other is based upon indoctrination, and rooted in faith and instinct.

> I am not an atheist by choice, I am a seeker of truth.
> Being an atheist is a side effect of that endeavor.
> – JD Stockman[45]

---

[44] Fahmy, Dalia. "Among Religious 'Nones,' Atheists and Agnostics Know the Most About Religion." Pew Research Center, Washington, D.C., Aug 21, 2019.
[45] JD Stockman is a contemporary blogger on the subject of atheism.

Of necessity, the search for truth entails the recognition and rejection of falsehood. The ability to recognize and reject poor, insufficient, or outdated answers to fundamental questions about human existence and our place within the cosmos is an essential part of winnowing down false claims to get to the reality.

> To kill an error is as good a service as, and sometimes even better than, the establishing of a new truth or fact.
> – Charles Darwin[46]

Religious falsehoods may offer people comfort and consolation in the short term, but they do so as they hinder our all-important search for knowledge, damaging the long-term process of maturation and, ultimately, humanity's overall progress. Unlearning religion and cultivating freedom from religion are part of an essential stage in the path of human progress and development. Far from being a vice, atheism is most definitely a virtue. It is a necessary step in the process of us discovering our true nature as a learning animal, capable of employing our reasoning capacities to create a socially, economically, and environmentally sustainable civilization characterized by peace, here and now, on planet Earth.

> Truth is the only safe ground to stand on.
> – Elizabeth Cady Stanton[47]

---

[46] Excerpt from *More Letter of Charles Darwin*, Vol. 2. eBook. Editors: F. Darwin and A.C. Seward. The Project Gutenberg. Release date: July 1, 2001. Available at: https://www.gutenberg.org/ebooks/2740
[47] This quote is widely attributed to Elizabeth Cady Stanton. However, the original source could not be verified.

The Learning Animal

A conception of human nature rooted in a solid understanding of the evolutionary sciences illuminates a great deal about who and what we are. It offers fresh, evidence-based, and rational answers to some of the age-old queries which have traditionally befuddled theologians and philosophers from time immemorial. We now know a significantly greater amount than ever before, sufficiently more to justify rewriting our fundamental origin story itself. We can—and indeed must—do this.

No longer are we the product of divine creation, nor are we made in god's image, nor are we the lone being straddling the line between the lowly natural and the divine supernatural realms. We are 100% animal now, the evolved species of the hominid known as *Homo sapiens*. We are, above all else, the learning animal. We have evolved to have a less instinctual way of life than any other organism in this planet's history.

Certainly, other animals do what we do. There are many other species who, in addition to instinct, can learn and share knowledge. Some groups of Orcas pass on unique familial hunting practices which demonstrates not only cumulative and shared knowledge, but considerable teamwork as well.[48] They will work together to maroon a Crabeater seal on a small float. They will then create waves sufficient to tip the float, and enjoy a yummy Crabeater seal treat. Other cetaceans have been discovered to have localized linguistic cultures, complete with dolphin and whale 'songs' unique to specific isolated groups, shared multi-generationally.

---

[48] Video: What Dramatic Orca Hunt Video Tells Us About Dolphin Intelligence. *National Geographic.* Found at:
https://www.nationalgeographic.com/science/article/orcas-hunt-seal-antarctica-ice-video-dolphin-intelligence-whale-culture-spd

Both apes and monkeys have demonstrated learned and shared food gathering techniques, particular to their groups, in the ways they use raw materials such as stems, sticks, and rocks to gather termites or crack open tasty hard-shelled nuts. One very clever macaque in Japan decided she preferred her sweet potato treats washed, and subsequent generations are still benefitting from this example of a learned and shared practice, passed from one generation to the next.[49] Cumulative and shared knowledge has also been demonstrated in elephant groups, a number of bird species, and various other creatures as well.

The difference between all of these and our own species is largely a matter of degree. We have evolved to have a less instinct-driven, more learning-based lifestyle than any other animal. This fact, that we are the learning animal, is both good and bad news.

The good news is all about our potential. Precisely because we are such a learning-focused animal, *Homo sapiens* has the potential for huge changes in lifestyle. There is only so much we can expect from a lion or an antelope, even a chimpanzee or bottlenose dolphin. But human beings have a far wider range of choices as to beliefs and behaviors than any other creature. We have a nonbiological adaptiveness which is unique. Unique in this context does not imply value judgment, as in 'superior to.' Merely unique,[50] as in one of a kind. Humans possess an exceptional malleability in our nature, and this bodes well for our future. Even when it comes to our prewired instincts and our

---

[49] Crair, Ben. "What Japan's Wild Snow Monkeys Can Teach Us About Animal Culture." *Smithsonian Magazine*. January 2021.

[50] My use of the term *unique*, unless otherwise made explicit, should be interpreted in an entirely value neutral manner. It absolutely does not mean superior, more advanced, better, or anything of the kind. Human intelligence is unique. But, so too is the intelligence of the octopus. It differs from our own in several respects. It is, by definition, equally unique. Our brain, that of the Neandertal, or that of the bottlenose dolphin – these are each unique as well. As is the 200 MPH dive speed of the peregrine falcon. Or the peacock's tail.

suite of genetic predispositions, there is very often a significant degree to which nurture can override nature.

As for the bad news, we can be trained to become the worst, most horrible creatures of all. As the direct result of religious indoctrination, much of humanity is essentially trained in a range of highly problematic beliefs and behaviors. Our fundamental malleability can go either way: toward that which is good, or toward that which is bad. We can, and often do, learn unhealthy, problematic, harmful things, which cause us to embrace the very worst beliefs and behaviors.

Indoctrination vs. Education

Education teaches one how to think, while indoctrination teaches one what to think.

The difference between education and indoctrination is that education opens the mind, while indoctrination closes it. Education is a process-driven approach to engaging in the knowledge and ideas of the world...Education opens doors of intellectual exploration and equips its students with the tools they will need to dissect, analyze, and interpret the information that they find.

Indoctrination, on the other hand, is a results-driven approach that aims to instill in people a set of habits and beliefs that align with an ideology or political agenda. Indoctrination narrows the lens through which we are able to see the world and [e]nsures that all of the information we receive is interpreted through the filter of the promoted ideology.[51]

In many respects, indoctrination is the biggest problem facing humanity today. The AIC of today are largely anti-education. They emphasize indoctrination, which, practiced over the course of many

---

[51] Canner, Jonah. The blog which I got this full quote from has been removed for an unstated reason. Half of the quote can be found at: https://medium.com/age-of-awareness/how-to-indoctrinate-your-students-7c9ebb9b3026

centuries, has had some extremely pernicious results. We are living with those results.

Because we are the learning animal, we have significant potential for change, and, furthermore, change which could happen in but a single generation! But we will have to overcome religious indoctrination. The best way for us to do that is not more indoctrination - counterindoctrination in a different mindset - but actual education as a distinctive approach and process. All of this helps explain why kids who spend four years getting a good secular university education on average tend to shift away from religion.[52] This is a very good thing, and something which it would behoove us to reproduce on a mass, global scale. Free university education for all *Homo sapiens*! Not the solution to all of our problems, necessarily, but a very good place to start.

There is a tendency, especially among the religiously devout, to conflate education and indoctrination. Admittedly, a fine line separates the two. But, at their more extreme ends, the differences are highly significant and readily apparent. Cognitive quirks, evolved predispositions, and instincts are the underlying source of religious belief. But it is social indoctrination, beginning at a very innocent and early age, which does the lion's share of the work keeping religion alive and thriving.

Religious indoctrination is why the overwhelming majority of human beings adhere to the religion of their upbringing. The more of this kind of training one has, the more one is inclined to be accordingly devout. The greater one's education, on the other hand, the less likely they are to have their beliefs determined in this way. The distinction between indoctrination and education may help explain an

[52] "In America, Does More Education Equal Less Religion?" Pew Research Center, Washington, D.C., April 26, 2017.

interesting phenomenon of which we atheists are particularly aware: why some people read the *Bible* and have their faith in god strengthened and renewed, while a good number of others read the very same book, and come to the conclusion that it's all bunk.

Christianity and Islam today do far more to hinder human progress than to help. They do so by a variety of means. One such mechanism is the promotion of falsehoods as truth. Believers by the billions are convinced not merely that Noah saved a bunch of animals from a flood, but that 'faith is a virtue,' that atheism and atheists are all inherently lost souls at best, or possibly evil and demonic at worst, and that we are all born sinners, but god or Jesus can save our otherwise doomed souls.

The Cosmic Logjam

Everyone has a god hypothesis. We atheists have a god hypothesis, too. We have thoughts, ideas, and beliefs about what god is and what it is not. Many, if not most, nones and atheists tend to believe that god is a belief, not a being. "He" exists only in the minds of the believers. However, such an extremely potent, mass-held belief has a tremendous impact upon the world of living beings. The Abrahamic god affects our lives immensely, and in a number of respects which most people are not entirely aware of, regardless of the fact that he is entirely fictional. Even though he is a 'mere' belief, it is a highly problematic belief which currently serves to hinder humanity from self-awareness and the kind of progress which is becoming more critical as the population of humans and our impact upon the planet increase.

If we atheists are right, then mere beliefs regarding what is functionally an entirely fictional entity, created in our image, are shaping a huge proportion of humanity's behaviors, as well as our origin stories, how we understand our existence, and indeed the entire cosmos within which we exist. This deity belief informs our ideals, our goals, our values, and what we think matters and what does not. This specific understanding is also what we pass on and teach to our children, one generation after the next. It dominates our learning process, shapes our laws, who we vote into power, and who we bomb into annihilation. It is a far more important topic than most people generally acknowledge.

In order to free ourselves from the significant, powerfully influential lies which religions tell, we must begin by acknowledging those ways of understanding which are faulty or misguided. In other words, in order to be freed from the lies, we need to recognize them as lies. In humanity's ongoing effort to do so, we have long suffered from one specific cosmic logjam, an epistemological impasse of the highest order. This is the time-honored belief that:

The existence of god can neither be proved nor disproved.

Epistemology is the branch of philosophy concerned with the nature of belief and knowledge. When it comes to knowledge itself, religion and the more naturalistic point of view differ considerably. What makes for valid knowledge in one sphere does not necessarily make for valid knowledge in the other. What is solid evidence to a believer differs considerably from solid evidence according to the secular, scientific, or humanist mind. This longstanding axiom points us toward a fundamental gap between religious and naturalistic ways of knowing the cosmos. This is the epistemological impasse.

There's a fundamental difference between scientific and religious epistemology. The difference has to do with what sort of things one accepts as validating any given claim, what constitutes good evidence. For *religious epistemology,* scripture, the written or spoken words of religious authorities, tradition, subjective or personal revelation, and faith are all paramount. *Scientific epistemology* discounts these in favor of worldly, naturalistic evidence, empirical data, the use of reason, and standards of objectivity.

The dualistic worldview still dominant today originates from pre-Abrahamic times, with roots no doubt extending well into the prehistoric. The 2,000-year-old ideas behind the AIC assert that the supernatural realm is the realm of the eternal. This 'spiritual' reality is that which truly matters, the qualitatively superior, and the divine. It holds that the natural realm is but a veil of illusion, the devil's playground, the lowly and inferior realm of the animal. The basic premise is that an ephemeral, unknowable 'beyond' is more real and is the superior, ideal realm.

This dualistic schism completely discredits that which we nonbelievers look to as the very font of viable information regarding our cosmos: empirical evidence of the natural universe, composed of matter and energy, with fixed laws governing their interplay. The adulation of the antiquated and the traditional is a familiar mindset associated with Christianity. But just because something is really old does not necessarily mean it is really good. Over the course of two millennia, supernatural explanations have become increasingly suspect and dubious. One important difference between religious and scientific ways of knowing is that the former is dualistic, with a supernatural realm separate from and superior to the natural one, whereas the other lacks this dualistic schism, and does not recognize the supernatural realm in any sense. And so, we find ourselves at an impasse. Holy scripture is valid 'evidence,' proof even, to one camp. The other side discounts such alleged evidence as entirely 'man-made' and mythical. The atheist's respect for naturalistic evidence falls upon deaf ears, while so too does the theist's faith in holy scripture. When we say to the devout 'show us the evidence,' they confound us by citing scripture as if it were evidence. They are equally confounded by the fact that we are confounded, presumably. The bottom line: differing epistemologies make for differing understandings of what constitutes viable evidence, of what it might mean to prove something, even as to what is a fact.

And thus, we arrive at our epistemological impasse. If we accept the fundamental duality, then neither side is clearly in favor. The theist and the atheist are placed upon equally solid or, for that matter, equally shaky ground. Since we can neither prove nor disprove god, atheism and religion become merely a matter of personal choice. Neither can be said to be right or wrong, neither can gain the clear upper hand. Choosing one over the other is essentially just a matter of personal, subjective preference.

Is v Ought: From Hume to Harris

Accepting this non-conclusive conclusion has led to our time-honored stalemate, bringing a diplomatic, if unsatisfying, end to any further debate, justifying a sort of 'live and let live' détente. Science and religion, battled to an insoluble deadlock, are each sent, bloodied and breathless, to their respective corners. Many today hold to some variant of this dualistic, separate-but-equal conception of science and religion.

One famous contemporary expression of this persistent dualism can be found in the works of Stephen Jay Gould, one of the most popular and influential scientists and science writers of the modern era. His conception of the 'Non-Overlapping Magisteria' was simultaneously persuasive and descriptive of this point of view.[53] His consideration of this topic exemplifies the widely held view that religion and science are best understood as separate-but-equal domains.

---

[53] Gould, Stephen J. "Non-Overlapping Magisteria." Originally published in *Natural History Magazine* in 1997, then subsequently in his book *Rocks of Ages* in 1999.

According to Gould, science should stay out of the values business, and keep its focus solely upon *description* and *matters of fact* (equivalent to the nature half of the duality). Religion, for its part, should stay out of the facts business altogether and concern itself primarily with *prescription* and *matters of value*. He apparently held considerable sympathy for the Christian view, common at the time, yet dwindling today in the United States, which affirmed the belief that religion is required for morality in society, and that religion thereby serves a valid and important service.

The provenance of this kind of dualistic thinking can be traced back a ways. Gould, too, stood upon the shoulders of those giants who had preceded him. One such luminary was 18th century Scottish philosopher David Hume. In *A Treatise of Human Nature* (1740), Hume presented what famously (well, ok - famous amongst philosophers, at least) came to be known as the *Naturalistic Fallacy*.[54] In rough form, this refers to our fundamental distinction between *facts* and *values*.

In somewhat less rough form, this refers to the contention that we cannot derive an *ought* (a prescriptive position, or a value claim) from an *is* (a descriptive position, or a factual claim). Both because I am a fan of this one particular old-dead-white guy, and because the subject is of some importance, I will present the relevant passage in its entirety. Be sure to read it in your very finest approximation of an antiquated Scottish brogue:[55]

> In every system of morality, which I have hitherto met with, I have always remarked, that the author proceeds for some time in the ordinary ways of reasoning, and establishes the being of

---

[54] Hume, David. *A Treatise of Human Nature: Being an Attempt to Introduce the Experimental Method of Reasoning into Moral Subjects.* Originally printed in 1739. Mineola, NY: Dover Publications, Reprint 2003. – The term 'Naturalistic Fallacy' was coined by G.E. Moore in his 1903 *Principia Ethica*.
[55] Ibid.

a God, or makes observations concerning human affairs; when all of a sudden I am surprised to find, that instead of the usual copulations of propositions, is, and is not, I meet with no proposition that is not connected with an ought, or an ought not. This change is imperceptible; but is however, of the last consequence. For as this ought, or ought not, expresses some new relation or affirmation, 'tis necessary that it should be observed and explained; and at the same time that a reason should be given; for what seems altogether inconceivable, how this new relation can be a deduction from others, which are entirely different from it. But as authors do not commonly use this precaution, I shall presume to recommend it to the readers; and am persuaded, that this small attention would subvert all the vulgar systems of morality, and let us see, that the distinction of vice and virtue is not founded merely on the relations of objects, nor is perceived by reason.

Hume is arguing that any move from an *is*, a fact-based claim or argument, to an *ought*, a value-laden, prescriptive claim such as is required for considerations in morality or justice, necessitates sufficient rational justification of some form, an argumentative consistency which thinkers heretofore had failed to properly appreciate the need for, and which will smooth the transition from the one to the other, from the *is* to the *ought*, from descriptions of matters of fact, to prescriptions regarding what we should or should not do, what is or is not good or right, how we should or should not live.

In order to serve as the foundation for a prescriptive, value-laden account, meaning something which helps us distinguish what is good from what is bad, naturalistic and entirely descriptive accounts must necessarily include some form of bridge, some validating criterion, some justifying explanation clearly articulating how the move from the one realm to the other is valid, or makes good sense. In 2010, Sam

Harris offered us just such a salient consistency in his work *The Moral Landscape: How Science Can Determine Human Values.*[56]

In *The Moral Landscape*, the commonly held belief that we cannot derive a prescriptive 'ought' from a descriptive 'is' is called into question. Harris' excellent argument is that we do, in fact, rightly base moral considerations upon matters of fact, specifically regarding those which nurture or impede the 'well-being of conscious creatures.' An illustrative example would be: slavery is morally wrong because, as a matter of fact, it is detrimental to the well-being of conscious creatures.

The longstanding impasse, in whichever form, is fallacious. Contrary to the beliefs of the late, great Gould, I contend that the general distinction between 'magisteria' is ill-conceived and erroneous. The impasse is an illusion, a falsehood, an epistemological error. The two realms can be considered in one consistent conversation, a conversation which does not benefit from Gould's, or scripture's, bifurcation. Science rules. Religion drools. Nature is real. The supernatural is not. That's it.

Morality and justice are not supernatural, divine phenomenon, but a natural expression of traits evolved by eusocial animals with highly complex brains. They can better be understood through entirely naturalistic, evidence-based, rational thought than through instinct or supposed divine fiat. Even when talking about spirituality in the sense of the human brain's more mysterious states or esoteric potential, we benefit not a whit, and find ourselves upon problematic tangents, when we employ supernatural explanations.

These extreme schisms, between the natural and the supernatural, between science and religion, between matters of fact and matters of

---

[56] Harris, Sam. *The Moral Landscape: How Science Can Determine Human Values.* New York: Free Press, 2010.

value, cause more problems than they assuage. To stick with the metaphor, religion and science may be apples and oranges. But, one of the fruits has rotted. We do not need it, and it should really just be tossed into the compost bin of history. We can get all that we want, and all that we need, and more, from the fresh, ripening fruit of a naturalistic, secular, humanist, and scientific perspective.

I'm not sure what's going on with all the fruit and food metaphors. It is about 5 a.m. and I haven't eaten yet. Probably it's getting near breakfast time. S'pose I need to listen to my body. Alright, alright...

Post-Breakfast Considerations

Ok, now...Where was I...

Oh, right. So, the aphorism which asserts that the existence of god can neither be proved nor disproved is fallacious and can be tossed completely. The alleged epistemological impasse is merely one of the many falsehoods which the AIC promotes and perpetuates. Teaching people to take explanations of a supernatural nature seriously is a highly problematic bit of indoctrination, and one which serves to hinder genuine education, knowledge, and human progress.

There are two important reasons why we can officially sweep such a dualism away, call it a done deal, and move on. One is that the fundamental premise of Abrahamic dualism is itself, in fact, a lie. The original distinction between the natural and supernatural realms is entirely fictitious. Abrahamic dualism is just another falsehood. There are no good reasons to surmise a supernatural realm. Ergo, those religious criteria in support of the claim are all necessarily rendered specious and spurious.

Ultimately, positing a deity to make sense of things may be comforting, but it amounts to nothing more than a god of the gaps move. Basically, the believer is injecting empty spiritual caulk into the gaps in their knowledge of the cosmos, because doing so eradicates or mitigates the 'feelings' associated with our very human needs: our curiosity, our need to understand, discover, and our need to have meaning and purpose within a wider context. It solves the problem, but only as a fix solves the junkie's problem; as scratching an infection of poison oak or ivy 'cures' an itch: it does not get at the real issue, and tends to do more harm than good. It feels like it's addressing the problem, but it's not.

The second reason why we can completely discount dualism is because we are more knowledgeable today than we were 500 or 1,000 years ago. That we could neither prove nor disprove the existence of god was a far more truthful epistemological claim 400 or 500 years ago, or in the time of Caesar, Cleopatra, and Christ, than it is in our own time. We know more. God, as characterized by the AIC, can be successfully argued to not exist. That's right. I said it. Gimme that *onus probandi*. That 'burden of proof.'[57] We can take it on now.

Human Progress: From the Supernatural to the Natural

Atheist concerns that religion is a negative phenomenon, that it 'poisons everything,'[58] that it is far more bane than boon in the world of today, are neither erroneous nor exaggerated. The lies and falsehoods promoted by the church are infinitely more heinous because the church advertises itself as a nexus of such goods as truth, morality, and justice. Just as with the extraordinary evil of entrusted religious

---

[57] *Onus Probandi* is Latin for the 'burden of proof.' Most atheists, technically meaning merely those who do not believe in god/s, contend that the burden of proof as to the existence of gods rests upon the person who claims god/s exist or are real in some sense. Ordinarily, atheists assert that the burden of proof is on the believer. I do not disagree. I am simply stating that we nonbelievers *could* take it on if we so chose, because the body of relevant data has changed so considerably, and shifted toward a more obviously secular, atheistic conclusion.

[58] Hitchens, *God is Not Great*, 2009.

authority figures sexually abusing young children, or 'merely' being complicit in any form of cover-up, the behavior is all the more horrific due to the presumed sanctity of its perpetrators. Such betrayal cuts all the deeper for the inherently unguarded state of the believer, their innocent trust placed unreservedly in the perpetrator's hands. The church is supposed to be a place of truth, of trustworthiness, and of moral goodness, literally the actual source of that which is good. When the church or the mosque tells lies, people are all the more willing to believe those lies wholeheartedly and without reserve. After all, it's the 'gospel' truth, right?

The Abrahamic god hypothesis itself is a falsehood. There is no god, and believing in him explains nothing. It does not help us, and if you have been told we need him for some reason, that, too, is a lie which keeps us from our full potential. There is no such thing as a soul, neither before, during, nor after our bodily existence. Our brains/minds have simply evolved to contrive a sense of continuity, a continuous self, because it is evolutionarily advantageous for us to believe that and think in that way. The religious simply extend this self into an imaginary eternity, and this is our alleged immortal soul.

But the truth is that, when you die, that's it. Just like you didn't exist for billions of years before you were born, now you won't exist again. That human beings exist after their body dies is another flagrant and disempowering lie. Comfort food for the mind, with zero nutritional content. There is no such thing as a soul. If it comforts you to believe that you are a part of something 'bigger' than yourself, recognize that this is obviously how a highly pro-social animal with a relatively large brain is going to think. But it's nothing more than instinct. It's not truth. The truth is that we are as much a 'part' as we are 'apart,' both being mere categories of the understanding within the human brain.

83

We are neither separate from nor superior to the rest of nature, not in any sense divine nor of a special quality. Neither we nor our planet are anywhere near as important as we tend to think. There is no divine plan. We do not have anything resembling a pre-written destiny. We merely enact a sadly irresponsible disempowerment when we think that we figure into a divine blueprint of some sort. He is not going to come down and rescue us. None of us.

That we are judged by god, that we are rewarded or punished, that there is any such thing as divine, cosmic karma (separate from the naturalistic realities of *social reciprocity* and our brain's capacity for *conscience*), all of these are falsehoods, promoted and perpetuated by religion and religious tradition. Not even good dogs go to heaven, because there's no such place.

We've been told some pretty significant lies. I, for one, am super glad to live in a time where we know better. The claim that *the existence of god can neither be proven nor disproven* is just another lie. Religious epistemology is not a separate-but-equal partner in the human pursuit of understanding and knowledge, nor merely a 'different perspective.' It is more accurately described as an instinct and bias-riddled mode of knowledge which is antiquated, and wholly inferior to our more contemporary scientific, naturalistic, atheistic, and humanistic ways of knowing. Knowledge of matters of fact about the natural realm, including human nature itself, is essential to help guide our understanding of who and what we are, as well as our values, our understanding of what we value, why, and even when and if we should. Science matters, and matters greatly, while religion, and the AIC in particular, has mostly just become a highly problematic albatross around the neck of our species. Removing this dead weight will ultimately result in a more accurate, all-around healthier human self-conception, a wiser understanding of who and what we are, of how we fit into the bigger picture, which will all dovetail with our progress toward an increasingly sustainable global civilization.

Scientific epistemology simply represents the finest means for acquiring reliable, accurate knowledge regarding the true nature of things which the species *Homo sapiens* has yet hit upon. That's the big claim. Scientific epistemology is not merely *different* from religious epistemology. It is *superior*. With the progressive development of naturalistic and scientific knowledge over the last few centuries in particular, our understanding is not merely different from that of the past, it is better, and improving still, day by day. Increasingly, we know more, and we know better.

Post-Theistic Progress

The naturalistic fallacy—the traditional belief that we cannot derive an 'ought,' a prescriptive claim, from an 'is,' a purely descriptive claim—stands in the way of us developing an entirely naturalistic picture of human nature. So, too, does the related dualism which holds science and religion to be separate but equal partners, such as Stephen Jay Gould's *Non-Overlapping Magisterium*. Such dualisms, as well as their ultimate source in the Abrahamic distinction between a lowly natural and a superior, divine, supernatural, are all faulty representations.

This recognition clears the way for a new, all-natural, science- and reason-based conception of *Homo sapiens,* as an interconnected, interdependent animal, contextually evolved to fit perfectly into our amazingly gorgeous, blue, green, and white marble, rolling through the proverbial heavens, right here, right now. If we all get this picture real soon, we might succeed in not fucking it up too much.

Ridding ourselves of dualistic misconceptions and embracing naturalistic, scientific thinking is allowing us to unclog the philosophical and theological logjam, the time-honored belief that the *existence of god could neither be proved nor disproved*. It can and is being disproved. The AIC are being exposed as guilty of falsehoods and fictions, slowly but surely. Without indoctrination, they might already be things of the past. Atheism is no longer for demons, sinners, and soulless hedonists, nor nay-sayers, narcissists, and nihilists, but is in fact a logical result of good education, and a necessary step on the path toward knowledge and a truth-based understanding of human nature and the cosmos.

With the slow but steady demise of Christianity's long reign comes clarification of the distinction between education and indoctrination. Long blurred, the fine line is being identified with greater and greater focus and precision. In so doing, we recognize one as a genuine good, the other as a recipe for blissful ignorance. Religion is largely a result of indoctrination, whereas atheism is the result of education, and specifically seeks to draw and clarify the line, rather than blur the line, between these distinctive modes of learning.

Homo sapiens is *THE* learning animal. This is why indoctrination is so effective and problematic. Equally so, why it is so important to challenge. We evolved to have this uniquely developed capacity for *accretive* and *mutualistic* intelligence. As our knowledge continually increases, we have moved from supernatural and pseudoscientific origin stories, explanations, and understandings, progressively toward more naturalistic, rational, and genuinely scientific ones.

As I will explore further in the pages to come, the extraordinary changes in human knowledge which have arisen during the last several hundred years, including our all-important transformation to global literacy and, ultimately, global communication and transportation, have all helped us transition away from the supernatural, increasingly toward the natural. The cumulative and shared nature of human intelligence results in a natural tendency toward ever-increasing human knowledge. As opposed to the bliss of ignorance, this leads in the opposite direction, toward the true fulfilment of our higher aspirations, our potential for good, through the rejection of past-oriented, conservative, theistic traditions, and the encouragement, cultivation, and embrace of future-oriented, rational, science-friendly, atheistic, humanistic progress.

Chapter 4

Knowing More & Knowing Better

No Knowledge, No Progress
Know Knowledge, Know Progress

Where ignorance is bliss, tis folly to be wise.
— Thomas Gray[59]

Religious authorities, and Americans by the millions, loudly decry the secularization of American society. Without any facts to support the claim, devout Americans consistently assert a causal connection between the fading relevance of religion in the average American's life, and every single one of society's perceived ills, from street violence, drug use, school shootings, and proliferating gangs, to the latest hurricane, tornado, or flood to befall our nation. There is a commonly held belief (more like a certainty) that more Bible reading and the restoration of religious faith would solve many, most, perhaps all of our various and sundry problems.

The reason this is not getting us anywhere is because it is just complete and total bullshit. In other words, it is yet another of the AIC's bold-faced lies. In the beginning, one of the first things god did was tell a big fat lie: he told Adam and Eve that knowledge was a bad thing. Right off the bat, falsehood extraordinaire. We've got Adam and Eve and a snake and an apple, and apparently the moral of the story is the

---

[59] Gray, Thomas. "Ode on a Distant Prospect at Eton College." *The Thomas Gray Archive*, 1742.

vague and counter-intuitive proposition that knowledge is somehow a bad thing, something to be eschewed, something for which one should and would be punished. Nothing could be further from the truth. Education and knowledge are in fact the very keys to the healthy, peaceful, beautiful, and sustainable civilization that represents our brightest possible future, the realization of our vast but slumbering human potential.

American Christianity emphasizes indoctrination in an anti-science, anti-education mindset. Here are just a few examples of real messages seen on American church billboards which demonstrate what Carl Sagan famously referred to as our "celebration of ignorance."[60]

The more "educated" we become,
the further we move away from God.

Darwin says to tell you he was wrong.
God

If your faith is big enough
facts don't matter.

American Christians are consistently indoctrinated not to trust education, science, higher education, academia, even just basic facts and evidence. The learned are dangerous, not to be trusted. The pious proclaim that discounting worldly evidence is evidence of the strength of their faith. Truly so. But faith, being the willingness to believe in something regardless of evidence to the contrary, is not necessarily a good thing. Faith is not a virtue.

The truth of the matter is the complete opposite. Precisely what the world needs now is to be freed from the limitations of religious

---

[60] Sagan, Carl. *The Demon Haunted World: Science as a Candle in the Dark*. Random House Publishing, 1996.

faith. To fulfill our greatest potential, to become knowledgeable and to make genuine progress, we need to unlearn the message of religious faith, the raising of ignorance to the status of an ideal. Instead of decrying worldly evidence and knowledge, we need to embrace human nature in its best form, including our wondrous gifts for intelligence, knowledge, curiosity, and real learning.

The very thing we need, the opposite of what the church proclaims, is the death of faith, and the embrace of our evolutionarily bestowed gift for *accretive* and *mutualistic* intelligence, for knowledge, the true source of genuine human progress. The bottom line is that, in order to make some real progress, Americans in particular are going to need to overcome their own indoctrination, to recognize that it stands in direct opposition to education, knowledge, human intelligence, and progress. This is the complete opposite of the beliefs stated at the outset, the commonly held idea that more *Bible* and *Quran*, more indoctrination, and less education, is what is needed.

The time period which we have had the good fortune to be born into is one characterized by continuing progress away from the supernatural and toward the natural. The AIC and their proponents think this is terribly bad news, when it is, as a matter of fact, truly the most excellent news we could possibly hope for.

Demonizing the Other

The AIC have always gone to considerable lengths to represent themselves as the proverbial, white-hatted good guys. Christ is the prince of peace, Islam the religion of peace. It is all about the sales pitch. The convincing lie. We outsiders, nonbelievers of any stripe, the educated and the atheists, are generally represented as lost souls, a danger to themselves and others, the ne'er-do-well bad guys, minions of the dark lord, hell-bent upon dragging the innocent, indeed dragging us all, down into nihilistic oblivion or eternal hellfire.

The history of Christianity and Islam are both replete with rampant insecurity and intolerance, characterized by consistent efforts to demonize the 'other,' such as the nonbeliever, to quell dissent, vanquish doubt, eradicate criticism. Importantly, this umbrella term 'other' refers to both the nonbeliever, as well as the person who believes, but does so in a different way. The latter famously includes each other, Christianity versus Islam, with millions of dead bodies attesting to the hatred so long fostered between these two most populous of the world's religions, all in spite of the significant common ground they share. The narrative of history is littered with the corpses of the devout, dead at one another's hands.

This millennium and a half of ongoing violence also includes internecine affairs, the result of the copious diffusion of splintering sects, both within Islam, and within Christianity. This common sectarian tension is familiar to us all, be it from the pages of history books, the daily news, from contemporary reports of hatred mutually expressed between Shi'ite and Sunni, between Catholic and Protestant, or from our own personal family histories. My own parents were ostracized from their respective clans for choosing to marry someone from a different religious background. Despite being in the alleged 'melting pot' of 1950s America, neither my mother's WASP (White Anglo-Saxon Protestant) family, nor my father's recently emigrated Jewish family, were very happy about their union.

Disputes are inevitably justified with reference to disagreements over the minutiae of scriptural interpretation, over who is or is not a genuine 'prophet,' or over whether it is morally egregious to draw a picture of god, and other similarly trivial details. Of course, religious differences are not always the primary driving factors behind these conflicts. People go to war over land, economic issues, and a variety of other, more secular reasons. Often religion is merely used as a smokescreen, a means of justifying the conflict on some allegedly higher, less 'worldly' plane.

That religion is not the real reason behind such conflicts does not in the least weaken my argument. In fact, it illustrates the very problem. The real reasons behind a conflict may well be partly or even entirely secular. But any savvy leadership knows it can count upon the religiously indoctrinated to rise to the bait, to be manipulated and coerced into a war-hungry frenzy, over differing interpretations of the same pages in a book, or similarly such indoctrinated, overblown concerns. These historically endless conflicts, wars, skirmishes, hatreds, and divisions are rooted not in knowledge of the 'other,' real-world knowledge of the true factors at play, but rather in indoctrinated beliefs regarding the 'other,' in entirely fabricated and exaggerated differences.

From an atheistic perspective, it becomes all the more ludicrous when one recognizes that all of these centuries of Abrahamic rivalry, hatred, warfare, oppression, and bloodshed, between religions, between sects, all take place regardless of one central, serious, deeply unsettling fact: the vast bulk of this dissention concerns matters of an *entirely fictional nature*. Imagine going to war over *Star Trek* versus *Star Wars*, fighting over whether it is Luke or Leah who is going to use the force and save the universe from the dark side, or splintering the congregation into separate factions, one devoted to the worship of Spock, the other Data.

You laugh now. Give it a few hundred years…

Commanded to Dominate

History strongly suggests that we humans are cognitively predetermined toward some measure of IG/OG conflict. But nature alone is not necessarily destiny. We also have a measure of control and choice regarding our actions, including our very beliefs to a certain extent. Even our more robust instincts and inclinations are only part of the picture. Nurture can, and frequently does, override or mediate nature. Humans have *free will*. If not actual free will, at least a super-close approximation, a fair stand-in for the real thing.

Our supposed bastions of morality, the AIC, in reality serve to exacerbate and enflame our IG/OG predispositions, our innate tendency to interpret the world through *us versus them* glasses, more so than to dampen or diminish them. This mindset predisposes us toward adversarialism, and a dominance-oriented paradigm of human interrelationship. This is the complete opposite of how they would like us to think of them. In a manner wholly consistent with such flagrant duplicity and misrepresentation, Christianity goes to great lengths to protect itself from even the slightest whiff of doubt or critical scrutiny. Much like an abusive relationship with a suspicious husband, possessive father, or hyper-jealous mate. If you think I may be overstating the case, take a moment to reflect upon the first four of the *Bible*'s ten commandments.

> I am the Lord your God.
> You shall have no other gods before me.
> You shall not make for yourself a graven image, you shall not bow down to them or serve them; for I the Lord your God am a jealous God, visiting the *iniquity* of the fathers upon the children to the third and the fourth generation of those who hate me...
> You shall not take the name of the Lord your God in vain; for the Lord will not hold him guiltless who takes his name in vain. Remember the sabbath day, to keep it holy... the seventh day is a sabbath to the Lord your God.

That's almost half of god's divinely proclaimed commandments, which many Christians devoutly believe serve as the very basis and foundational model for contemporary Euro-American morality, ethics, justice, and law. God is commanding us to be entirely devoted to him, to reassuring him that we love, and fear, and worship him, and him alone. Anyone who believes otherwise is wrong. Period. Wrong and headed for damnation. And these intolerant and divisive words represent a full 40% of god's holy commandments. In the Christian mind, to be morally good is equated with being exclusive, intolerant, and self-righteous about your faith in god.

Hallowed Ground

The simple pie chart below helps explain a great deal about our world. The primary point I wish to illustrate is the extent to which the AIC truly dominate. Nothing else even comes close. Though technically they, too, are members of the Abrahamic tradition, I have left the Jews out. The primary reason is because they do not have the imperialistic, intolerant, self-righteous emphasis upon proselytizing and conversion which so characterize Islam and Christianity, and their current world dominance. But it's also true that, historically, they've been through enough shit already.

Size of Major Religious Groups, 2010
Percentage of the global population

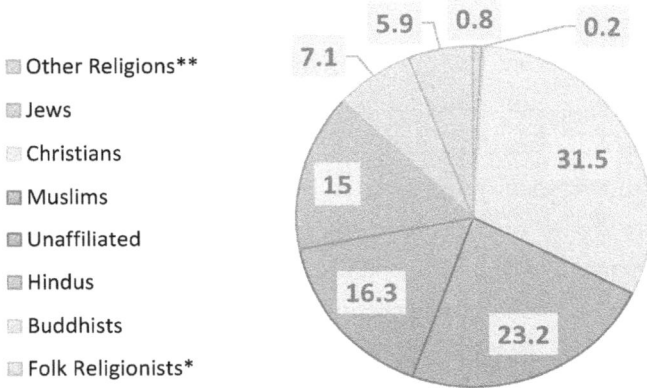

Other Religions**

Jews

Christians

Muslims

Unaffiliated

Hindus

Buddhists

Folk Religionists*

5.9   0.8   0.2

7.1

31.5

15

16.3

23.2

*Includes followers of African traditional religions, Chinese folk religions, Native American religions, and Australian aboriginal religions.
**Includes Bahai's, Jains, Sikhs, Shintoists, Taoists, followers of Tenrikyo, Wiccans, Zoroastrians, and many other faiths.[61]

The next largest group, after Christianity and Islam, has in fact grown somewhat larger in the decade since this chart was compiled. This consists of the many human beings with no stated religion or religious affiliation whatsoever, including many fellow atheists. After this, the fourth largest such grouping in the world is Hinduism, followed by Buddhism. And that's about it, in terms of major numbers. My goal here is simply to point out the significant dominance of the Abrahamic traditions of Islam and Christianity. They comprise more than half of the human race. They are more than ¾ of all religious persons. That's some serious domination.

---

[61] "The Global Religious Landscape." Pew Research Center, Washington, D.C., December 2012.

The AIC did not arrive at its current dominion by virtue of any moral righteousness on their behalf. Neither was it the result of a natural process of social development, a progression from animism to polytheism to monotheism. Nor is it the case that monotheism is inherently 'superior' to more 'primitive' polytheistic religions. In this work, you will encounter numerous descriptions, depictions, and arguments intended to illuminate the nature of human progress. But any movement toward Christianity and Islam is *not* a form of progress. Entirely the opposite. The truth is that any movement toward greater religiosity is a movement away from maximizing our potential, a movement toward a form of willing enslavement, a disempowerment, and an intentional dumbing down.

The truth is that the current dominance of the AIC is just another case of 'to the victor go the spoils.' We are taught about the innocent, godly Christians being fed to the lions in the Flavian amphitheater of Rome,[62] whilst the godless Roman pagans looked on and cheered. But it's always important to remember that history is written, pre-approved, edited, and redacted by the winners. The historical account, as it comes to us, would appear to be considerably skewed to represent the Christians as wholly innocent victims.

In its early years, Christianity was intensely focused upon demonizing any and all things non-Christian with a single-minded and unswerving devotion which today's Taliban would find wholly impressive. Considerable damage was done to pagan altars and places of worship, to pagan belief and believers, as well as all of that classical art and architecture, to important and irreplaceable libraries, to persons, their cultures, beliefs, and practices, from ancient Athens to Egyptian Alexandria, from Arabia to the Atlantic, as their missionary and

---

[62] The Flavian Amphitheater is the original name of that iconic structure in the center of Rome which we today think of simply as 'the coliseum.' It was built during the reign of Emperor Vespasian, around 70 AD.

proselytizing zeal gained traction. Christianity eventually won its undeclared war against paganism. Those first four commandments won the day in due course. And the stories were rewritten accordingly, painting the Christians out to be innocent victims and the white-hatted good guys.

Fast forward a millennium, into the time in Europe which, not coincidentally, is known as the Dark Ages. Christianity's ongoing efforts to eradicate doubt, dissent, and diversity included state and papally sanctioned violence of all sorts, including torture, inquisitions, various 'holy' wars, and, famously, the burning of witches. Such efforts at mass coercion, intended to permanently expunge even the tiniest iota of nonconformism or criticism, eventually resulted in the creation of a herd of fully obedient and pious sheep, largely untroubled by serious elements of free thought, from the time of Flavius Valerius Constantinus,[63] all the way up through the time of one Charles Robert Darwin, well over one thousand years of 'Dark Age' later.

If you really want to know how Christianity came to dominate the world, the bottom line is that it did so by a combination of dumbing us down and scaring the shit out of us. It all starts with the heavy-handed sales pitch on an imaginary afterlife in eternal hellfire and damnation, earned simply by virtue of being born as a human being, an inherently evil, immoral human baby. This is sold hand in hand, a 2-for-1 kind of deal, with the manufactured need for salvation, the need to be redeemed from this damned state. The sole source of redemption was their Abrahamic god, who was admittedly jealous,

---

[63] Also known as Constantine the Great, he was emperor of Rome from 306 AD to 337 AD. His personal transition, from being a traditional Roman 'pagan' to becoming a Christian, in the year 312, symbolically represents the wider historical transition of Mediterranean and European culture, away from the pagan and relatively diverse, to the far more restrictive, intolerant, uniform, and conformist Christian religion which dominated during the subsequent 1000-year period known as the Dark Ages.

angry, and vengeful if you did not buy his whole package deal. The original monopoly.

But 'original sin' is not the lone source of the terror. Burning at the stake, torture, and beheading infidels certainly had their quashing effects as well. They still do so in many parts of our world today, in both Muslim- and Christian-dominated countries. Many people are being accused of witchcraft, tortured, and killed even now, still, in the twenty-first century. Possibly even more so, in terms of sheer numbers, than in Euro-America's infamous witch-burning past.

The reason we do not hear about it is, to be perfectly honest, either because it happened outside of the borders of the U.S., or happened to people of color. America's nationalistic vanity is a privileged state of isolation and arrogance which causes most Americans to significantly devalue anything which does not have a noticeable impact upon our nation or its citizens, especially its white-skinned citizens. This ethnocentric self-obsession is common in powerful nations and empires. It is often expressed in varied forms of ethnocentrism, xenophobia, and racism. But America's unique history of race-based slavery has left us with a particularly racist version of this nationalistic myopia.

This history of American exceptionalism and particularly virulent racism means that many of America's atheists may be sadly unaware of the suffering of other peoples, the religious violence happening in our own time, or the fact that merely being accused of atheism or witchcraft can still result in censure, torture, even death. You will not hear about it on the evening news, unless it happens to some white Americans traveling or working abroad, perhaps. But it is happening as you read these pages. An atheist was beheaded recently in a Muslim nation in southern Asia.[64] A few years before that, a gay man was

---

[64] "American atheist blogger hacked to death in Bangladesh." *The Guardian*. February 27, 2015.

stoned to death in a Christian nation in sub-Saharan Africa.[65] The reign of Abrahamic terror is an ongoing tragedy, and one which, sadly, is not over yet.

Such heavy-handed and violent forms of coercion persist today, though not as frequently in Euro-America. Something closer to the rule of law has come to prevail over time in my neck of the woods. However, although this behavior may no longer be the norm here in the United States, we still feel the lingering effects of those prior stringent measures. The widespread contemporary disdain in which the terms *atheist* or *atheism* are held serves as testimony to this legacy. The unjust imbalance in dialogue is also a knock-on effect of centuries of this often-violent oppression: it's totally OK to talk shit about atheists, but it is considered in very bad taste to impugn the faithful among us. The reticence of millions, a huge percentage of the 'fence-sitting' type of agnostics, for example, undoubtedly owes something to this inheritance.

But, with the onset of eras such as the Renaissance and the Enlightenment, Christians have increasingly cultivated more clandestine approaches to coercing obedience, conformity, and compliance. Religious indoctrination and propaganda in Euro-America today serves some of the precise same goals as the torture, burnings, violence, and physical coercion of bygone eras. More subtle means of doing battle with criticism and doubt have taken the place of the Biblical tactics of other places and times. Religion today tells lies. It coerces hearts and minds. This physical nonviolence represents a form of progress. But it may also serve to make manipulative tactics more difficult to recognize, and thereby perhaps all that much harder to root out and eradicate.

---

[65] Gettleman, Jeffrey. "Ugandan Who Spoke Up for Gays is Beaten to Death." *The New York Times*. January 27, 2011.

For example, we are expected to venerate the sacred, to treat the religiously sanctified as 'hallowed ground.' But this linguistic turn of phrase, 'hallowed ground,' is itself a very revealing sort of double entendre. On the one hand, hallowed ground refers to that which is sacred and holy. However, it also has a potentially threatening connotation, as in 'hands off...or else!'

One of the more subtle ways that religion protects itself today is simply by emphasizing god's allegedly transcendent nature, by describing him always as omni-this or omni-that. By characterizing god as perpetually 'beyond,' despite the fact that the term 'beyond' is empty and devoid of meaning entirely, he is placed outside the realm of critical scrutiny. Christianity attempts to render itself bulletproof by characterizing god as ineffable and transcendent. Talking and thinking critically about the nature of god is off limits. Verboten. It is hallowed ground.

But now it's not that we will suffer at the hands of the inquisitor, or the angry, terrified mob. It's simply a matter of us reaching beyond our station, beyond our pay grade, so to speak. Those of us who care enough about the subject to try and seek genuine clarity and understanding are considered either hopelessly arrogant, naive, or even a touch mad.

God is the 'unmoved mover,' the 'uncaused cause,' to quote the venerated Saint Thomas Aquinas.[66] Are such utterances deep and profound? Or are they merely 'deepisms,' as in platitudes and bromides which feel full of insight, but are in fact devoid of content? Does 'beyond' actually describe something? Something meaningful? Something

---

[66] Saint Thomas Aquinas (1225–1274) is famous for his "Argument from Motion," in which he claimed that there must be an unmoved mover, or a first cause, which initiated all the motions of the world; also for his "Argument from Causation,' which asserted that something of necessity must have caused the world, and that uncaused-cause must be god.

real? Or does the language of transcendence merely serve the function of placing god outside the realm of meaningful discourse? Perhaps one gets a whole lot of wiggle room when one works in mysterious ways.

The Natural

> What worries me about religion is that it teaches people to be satisfied with not understanding the world they live in.
> – Richard Dawkins[67]

The bottom line is that humanity cannot make the progress which we need to make, the progress which we are ripe for, so long as the AIC continue to dominate as they have. Much as the age of enlightenment spelled the demise of the Dark Ages, we are again primed for a 100% positive shift, an all-good shift, away from the supernatural, toward the natural. The AIC place absolutely no emphasis upon human knowledge and progress. Rather, these ancient and venerable religious traditions today present indoctrination as if it were valuable in the way that genuine education actually is, while they present education itself as part of the problem, as a form of evil.

Intelligence is neither new, nor exclusive to humans. Evolution hit upon this particular trick many millions of years ago, and well before the first primate even came into existence. The octopus split evolutionary lineages from our own hundreds of millions of years ago, evolving what is clearly in some respects a similar kind of intelligence, yet in a radically different kind of brain.

The brain of the Octopus is not all bundled in one place, as are those of we primates. Instead, they have neurons spread throughout their body. In particular, they have neurons throughout the all-important 8 limb appendages which comprise so much of their body.

---

[67] Dawkins, Richard. "Heart Of The Matter: God Under The Microscope." BBC. 1996.

Octopus literally have brainy arms. In an excellent example of convergent evolution, we have separately evolved many surprisingly similar cognitive capacities. In spite of the enormous distances and differences between our two lineages, we can both figure out how to unscrew a jar if we want the yummy treat inside!

Octopus intelligence has been a real thing for nearly half a billion years. It would appear that having a good brain can be quite helpful for surviving and thriving within our world's oceanic environs. Over 400 million years later, a variety of cetacean species again evolved significant forms of intelligence. This was back when our primate ancestors most closely resembled something like a tarsier, squirrel, tree shrew, or rat. Comparable hominid intelligence is relatively new, only arriving on the scene within the last several million years.

These are only three examples. Countless others abound, countless organisms evolving differing forms and degrees of intelligence, employed to fulfill a wide range of adaptive functions. But, if an extraterrestrial came to visit Earth 200 million years ago, or even 20 million years ago, and, as we generally assume would be their top priority, sought out a kindred intelligence, their best bet would have been the ocean depths. I can hear many of my more misanthropic fellow atheists now, semi-sarcastically suggesting they'd be wise to do so still.

I have largely overcome the misanthropic tendencies of my cynical youth. This has been a direct result of reading and studying and learning about the world, becoming more learned and cultivating a very profound respect for the process of evolution, as well as for its numerous products: the animal *Homo sapiens*, for example, as well as the many other animals and organisms with whom we share this planet. I had never been a big animal guy. I was never even really huge on nature, per se. And I was not an environmentalist, nor an activist. Just so you get where this is all coming from.

I never approached this project with an environmentalist bias or agenda, an 'animals-are-people-too' mindset, or anything of the kind. No, it is entirely as a result of my research and studies that I have more recently awoken to this newfound respect and admiration. Simply put, at one point in my life, as a result of my education, I was genuinely thunderstruck by a recognition of the profoundly wondrous and enlightening nature of the process of evolution. I have been in love ever since, in awe of the process itself, its uncovering and discovering by Charles Darwin and others, and of what it tells us about human nature, and about life itself.

Recognition of the creative, dynamic, interconnected nature of the evolutionary process hit me like the proverbial ton of bricks. The more I continue to learn and understand, the greater becomes my appreciation for the dynamic process, for its numberless bounty of products, and for each organism evolved to thrive within each and every specific environmental niche and context. It's all seriously mind-boggling, the more you get to know it. This is far more mysterious, wondrous, profound, awesome, and mighty than any deity or theology which our minds can manufacture. I am in love with planet Earth, with life, with our species, and with the glowing future which recognizing our true, interdependent animal nature offers us.

The elephant and the octopus in particular astound me, and have helped me develop an increasingly passionate appreciation for the natural world. One thing of which these species are excellent examples is the notion that there are many different kinds of intelligence. Elephants, grazing leisurely over expansive habitats in family groups, interacting and communicating over miles with other family groups, have evolved significant social and emotional intelligence.

Not only is elephant social and emotional intelligence notable and underappreciated, so too is their memory. Memory is an important form of intelligence, and elephants have demonstrated significant capacity for this particular evolutionary trait. Elephants will regularly, as they meander through their wide-ranging homelands, visit the bones of their ancestors. Much as we do, they have been regularly documented to mourn. In fact, their capacity to remember and mourn their past ancestors and fallen family members can sometimes make the stereotypical human funeral, so often rife with insincerity, impatience, or indifference, pale by comparison.

The elephant's form of intelligence is particularly developed in the social and emotional direction. But such an emphasis would not have been as adaptively beneficial to the various species of octopus, most of whom live less social lifestyles. The octopus has evolved a cognitive skillset which differs in some relevant respects, including problem-solving skills, skills more apropos to its largely solitary lifestyle, pursuing a variety of different prey, and avoiding a variety of different predators by darting in and out and up and down the nooks and crannies of complex underwater reef and rock structures. This all requires a very distinct kind of intelligence from that which benefited the elephant.

All of this is to illustrate how it is not very accurate to speak in terms of one, singular, monolithic trait which we can call 'intelligence.' Ultimately, one day, this will be a far more developed and better understood scientific field. We are beginning to recognize how different humans have differing cognitive capacities and talents, even though our brains are all similar in structure. This cognitive diversity increases considerably when we are talking about intelligence in other species. Differing species of creatures evolve significantly divergent cognitive traits, capacities, and abilities as a direct result of a complex dynamic interplay between differing genetic factors, and widely divergent environmental and contextual variables.

Homo sapiens, as the learning animal we are, will come in time to identify these varied forms of intelligence, each of which evolved in response to the pressures of a specific given environment and overall context. In light of these facts, the antiquated notion of intelligence as a singular, quantifiable phenomenon, one which we can clearly measure with a single 'intelligence quotient,' one which humans have in abundance, and which the other species of animals have less or little of, will be recognized as problematic. It is largely pseudoscience, a result of human exceptionalist biases in our thought, a result of our penchant for idolizing all things human, and for using ourselves as the standard and metric by which all other life forms are to be measured, judged, and found wanting.

Such human exceptionalism represents an outdated interpretation of reality which will continue to thrive as long as we get our self-conception from books like the Bible or the Quran, but will fade into appropriate and harmless oblivion once we push such dusty old tomes to the side. Exceptionalist thought and belief will diminish as a greater percentage of us learn to practice science and think naturalistically with even greater diligence, as we better employ reason toward the end of cultivating a true and accurate understanding of the nature of things, one that isn't rooted in cognitive biases and instincts so much as our knowledge and awareness of the primacy of mind. Eventually we will cultivate an understanding which does not start with the assumption that we are 'made in god's image,' but with the recognition that we made him in our own, and which recognizes that we are not the alpha and the omega, the be-all-and-end-all, the sine qua non, the cat's meow or, generally speaking, the functional center of the universe.

Our self-conception, our fundamental understanding of what we are and how we fit into the bigger picture, suffers from an interpretive hangover, left over from our Abrahamic traditions, from religious thinking. Obviously, it behooves us to fully recover from this outdated and anthropomorphic bias ASAP. Not only does it hinder our capacity to formulate a healthy, sustainable civilization here and now on this amazingly beautiful planet, but it does not bode well for when the aliens, with their significantly different brains, show up, and we need to communicate with them respectfully and… er, um… intelligently.

The Learning Animal

Just as all of these other intelligent species have their own unique characteristics, so, too, does the animal Homo sapiens. Human intelligence has evolved to be uniquely accretive, mutualistic, and applicable. Our species has evolved a unique emphasis upon this one, specific type of intelligence. We rely upon it more than anyone else, do it more. This does not necessarily make us 'superior' or 'more advanced.' At this point, it is important to recognize that my analysis is distinctly and intentionally non-valuative. No value judgment is being made at this time. Our unique form of intelligence has simply evolved to emphasize knowledge accumulation and knowledge sharing more so, to greater degrees, than any other species. Different, but not necessarily better.

Human intelligence is accretive, meaning it builds and accumulates over time. This is true for the individual, the community, as well as the species as a whole. Our knowledge accumulates and transforms over the generations, centuries, and millennia. This is true through each success, but equally so through each failure. Each application, invention, ideation, experimentation, each gargantuan or minute success, and each tiny or spectacular failure equally so, all are a part of this definitive process.

Relatedly, human intelligence is uniquely mutualistic. It is shared between individuals within groups, and between groups, as well. It is shared from mother to child, and from culture to culture. It is shared in trade, within families, between friends. But this mutualistic intelligence is also happening in times of conflict, between adversaries. If your tribe is violently attacked, and you are kidnapped, brought back to be assaulted and raped, and become the victor's new 'wife,' you still bring along your bank of knowledge, your talent at finding different edible plants, your tribe's technology, toolmaking, or hunting skills. You were stolen and made a part of this new lineage. But so, too, was your storehouse of knowledge, ideas, skills and experiences.

Human knowledge is shared intentionally, and accidentally, for better or worse. And in all cases, this cumulative knowledge of ours not only builds mathematically, but it also builds exponentially. Our knowledge changes, and in turn, this changes us in a complex, interactive dynamic. Not merely in a quantitative manner, but qualitatively, as well. Through this cumulative and mutualistic intelligence, our species has been, is being, radically transformed. My dream car, the baby blue convertible '67 Ford Mustang, was not invented in the 1960s. Its roots trace back to the first wheel, the first glass, first metallurgy, electronics, the first engine... That classic car is really tens of thousands of years old and was made by literally millions of people.

There is a third characteristic that is worthy of mention, and that is applicability. The ability to apply our knowledge is an important element in the package deal which constitutes human intelligence. However, the capacity for application is hardly unique to human beings. While it can be reasonably asserted that we accumulate and share knowledge more so than do any other known species of animal, it is not equally viable to claim such uniqueness in regard to our capacity for application.

Human intelligence evolved step-by-step with the evolution of our specific kind of bipedalism, and our two ten-digited, opposable-thumbed, hands freed up by that aforementioned bipedalism. The recognition of this kind of co-evolution—that our brain evolved in lockstep with our bipedalism and specific manual dexterity—helps shed light upon the nature of our specific kind of intelligence. For example, our kind of toolmaking and tool use, and innate proclivity for teleological, teleofunctional thinking (thinking in terms of purpose, function, and applicability) make sense for a creature of our kind.

It is safe to assume that our particular form of intelligence would not be at all what it is today, if not for the reality of our primate evolution, including the subsequent shift to bipedalism a couple million years ago. All of this left us with these dangling hands. So, next time you're standing awkwardly at a party or some such social event, and you're standing there feeling awkward because you don't know what to do with your hands, remember that you wouldn't even be there, there probably would not even be this party, if not for these hands of ours. If not for them, there wouldn't be any such thing as a martini glass, or beer, keys to jangle nervously, a cigarette or joint to hold, or a cellphone to nervously pretend you're texting on.

Other organisms have evolved other forms of applicability, more relevant to their own individualized lives. The elephant's trunk can uproot a tree or gently pluck a piece of ripened fruit. And the octopus? Well, it's hard to imagine that any creature could possibly have more of an applicability skillset than these particular nine-brained, sucker-armed wonders. I envision a future dystopia in which, ethical considerations having succumbed to the hardcore demands of post-apocalyptic economics, everyone's favorite coffee shop will make a bundle on underpaid octopus baristas, capable of simultaneously making a blonde-triple-grande-pistachio-non-fat-latte, nuking and bagging a slice of banana bread, and accurately working the cash register – all at once.

While it cannot be said that our capacity for applying our intelligence is in any sense definitive or unique to our species in the manner that accretion and mutualism are, our particular form of applicability is still an important component in the overall picture of human intelligence.

Intelligence & Human Progress

It was big news when Jane Goodall first noted the Chimpanzees at Gombe learning how to use raw materials as tools, and again when she observed them sharing that knowledge with other members of their tribe. It was news when one particular Japanese Macaque figured out how to wash her food, and subsequently began to pass that knowledge throughout her tribe, as well. But what is big news for such animals is everyday stuff for us. We have evolved the capacity to do this to significantly greater orders of magnitude, and it is primarily this particular suite of adaptive traits, the capacity for accretive and mutualistic learning, which is our singular, most defining characteristic.

This is all stuff which we have learned about ourselves. When I write about the implications of Darwin's work, part of what I am referring to is the fact that we are animals, animals which have evolved these specific types of traits. This science- and reason-based conception is radically different from the pseudoscientific notion of us as created by an imaginary super-being, one who looks, thinks and acts much like a human adult male, yet is considered separate from and superior to the rest of the natural order, one who placed us here to dominate over all. There is a significant difference between the religious mindset, which holds indoctrination as a good, while it eyes curiosity, education, and knowledge with suspicion or even contempt, as distinct from an atheist, humanist perspective which holds the complete and total opposite. These conceptions could not be further apart. They cannot really coexist side by side, as the apologists would have it. It would appear to be an either/or proposition.

Our unique capacity for unparalleled degrees of accretive and mutualistic intelligence is the source of human culture, creativity, and progress. Completely foreign to the conservative traditions of the AIC, this progressive quality is essential to human well-being and fulfillment, as individuals, and as a species. These modes of intelligence are, slowly but surely, making us smarter and wiser than we were in past millennia. They will continue to do so increasingly to the extent that humanity can willingly embrace freedom from instinct, from indoctrination, from superstition, and from supernatural, religious beliefs.

Unfortunately, whether theistic or secular, popular conceptions of human progress tend to largely conceive of it in the narrower sense, such as the mere self-perpetuating, amoral trajectory of science and technology. Progress in the fullest sense of the word is not just about mastering fire or inventing engines, plate tectonics taking the place of Neptune or Noah, germ theory displacing karma and prayer, Darwin and evolution replacing creationism, Einstein amending Newton, or even our new-found ability to take the first tentative steps outside of our planetary womb.

Manifestations of the progress which results from our particular dynamic mode of intelligence, of our ever increasing human knowledge, and the resultant wisdom, also includes: significantly decreasing levels of worldwide warfare and overall violence, improvements in health care and the general standard of living, our ability to feed people better than ever in spite of our uncontrolled population growth, significant improvement in the rights of women, and increasing justice for other marginalized groups. Progress can also be measured by ever-increasing global concern for once abstruse priorities such as equal rights, social justice, global unity, environmentalism, and the cultivation of a sustainable human civilization. It is the case that when we know more, then we know better.

Last but most certainly not least, within the last several hundred years, during which a highly significant proportion of this purely secular, atheistic progress has been made, everything changed (once again), because humans went from 90% illiterate to 90% literate, with vast numbers of us suddenly capable of global intercommunication and knowledge acquisition more or less instantaneously.

Our knowledge and understanding do not merely change, nor do they noticeably 'evolve,' as some would inaccurately describe it. The progress I am describing is distinct from biological, evolutionary change. Our knowledge, our understanding: it improves, if allowed to. It progresses, if not thwarted. We become better, and continuously so. We can impede this process, or we can encourage it. But it is in our nature, within the structure of our particular form of intelligence, to learn, grow, and progress. So, we can confidently judge the knowledge of the past, and judge it as not merely different but, sometimes, as inferior.

Increasingly, and in particular within the last several centuries, humanity's knowledge has qualitatively transformed due to these accretive and mutualistic characteristics of our intelligence. Along with our knowledge, our god hypothesis is necessarily transforming, in spite of the conservative, intransigent nature of these dominant religious traditions, and the incessant, entrenched falsehoods which they perpetuate. One thing which we have learned is that Abrahamic, religious dualism is false. Understanding the fundamental construct of the cosmos as divided into a supernatural realm, with an intercessory creator deity that's separate from, and superior to, a created natural realm, with us straddling the divide, is simply inaccurate. At best it is baffling, self-contradictory, and antiquated allegory. More to the point, though, it is mythology, fantasy, fiction, and currently functions as harmful pseudoscience of the most problematic kind.

There are not two equal ways of looking at things. More accurately, there is an old, antiquated way, and there is a new, better way. We are simply in a period of transformation, growing from an old epistemology, one which continually, and problematically, reasserts itself, toward a new and better one. While it was once undoubtedly true that the existence of god could neither be proven nor disproven, today it is no longer the case, and this time-worn axiom is no longer accurate.

You know that timeless rhetorical query: "Who are we to judge?"[68] Well, today we are those who know better. Who are we to judge whether or not it is wrong for a fundamentalist Muslim or Christian to beat his child-bride and deny her an education? We are those who know better, largely because we have improving knowledge, shared and objectively validated, regarding what Sam Harris describes as the 'well-being of conscious creatures.'[69]

We are progressing from the supernatural to the natural. Our understanding of ourselves and of the cosmos, our beliefs, our knowledge, are increasingly determined by facts rather than faith, by data rather than by dogma, by reason rather than instinct, by education rather than indoctrination, by autonomy rather than obedience. And this is all good news.

Today's devout are inclined to conservatively romanticize the past as if the answers are back there, as if things were better in the old days

---

[68] I am well aware of the lengthy list of historical horrors perpetrated by a 'we' who 'know better.' The white, European male conquistadors and missionaries who genocidally spread the 'Good Word,' the *Bible*, along with class structure, smallpox, hard alcohol, and European culture, who sought to fully eradicate all vestiges of native culture, language, dress, art, or life-ways of the natives Americans, were confident that they knew better as well. What I am describing differs. The 'we' who knows better must be determined by standards which transcend culture, gender, ethnicity, politics, class, and other such divisive factors. It must be founded upon principles of objectivity, always upon facts and truth, and must be inclusive of universal rights and a fundamental respect for human autonomy, without fail and without bias.

[69] Harris, *The Moral Landscape*, 2010.

and we simply need to return to them. But life in biblical times was orders of magnitude worse than our lives today. Life throughout Christianity's long dominant reign of the Dark Ages was little better, except of course if you were fortunate enough to be one of the few members of your society's elite. The Bible and the Quran cannot possibly be the source for any enlightened solution to our world's problems, particularly because it is largely as a result of their long reign that we suffer so many of the problems we do.

Those living during the times described within the Bible and the Quran did not even know that a world without slavery was possible, much less that it was preferable. They would have laughed you out of the room if you had suggested that women should have an equal say in matters of any import. They would have considered you insane if you had talked about realistically decreasing worldly violence, or all of us living together, or the inhumane nature of the death penalty, or of equal rights for all peoples. The religious emphasis upon tradition and the conservative idealization of the past must give way to an increased enthusiasm for genuine positive change and real progress.

Chapter 5

From the Supernatural to the Natural

To the Victors Go the Spoils

History is always written by the winners. This has a deep impact upon the historical narrative, upon humanity's understanding of not merely our past, but of our own present, and our future as well. The received narrative is always significantly skewed toward the winners, be that win military, political, economic, or anything else. Some degree of digging or critical reflection is always warranted if what you are after is untainted truth.

Archeologists long ago recognized that those coming into power would re-carve stelae or hieroglyphics, touch up wall murals, or simply erase faces, eradicating previous regimes from the historical narrative with a few strokes of scouring stone, brush, or pen. Ancient sculptures and other forms of pre-literate, publicly visual art, even ancient literary works, from a variety of differing cultures, have been found to be re-purposed, given new features, wiped clean and started anew. Or they have not been found at all, despite our knowing through other means that they should be there.

Take for example the story of one of antiquity's truly startling works, *De Rerum Naturae - On the Nature of Things*, by Lucretius, Roman poet and philosopher, living and writing around 100 - 50 BCE. *De Rerum Naturae* was a decidedly unchristian work, one which undoubtedly rubbed early Christians the wrong way. We will never know how many copies of this precious historical document were destroyed by one means or another. If not for the eagle eye of one particularly astute scribe, working near the beginning of the Renaissance, this uniquely prescient and amazing work would have been entirely lost to us all. It has been theorized that the discovery of this lone surviving work was in some part responsible for the widespread, multicultural re-birth which followed.

The version of history we readily accept today is in fact highly redacted and edited, and does not accurately reflect the historical truth, so much as a narrative which significantly favors Christianity, the clear historical winner. Conflict began 2000 years ago, in the form of Christianity v. Paganism. All of the ancient Mediterranean world—thousands of years of Great Egypt, the Golden Age of Greece, Imperial Rome, and so much more—all were considered pagan, ergo subject to erasure and redaction by the growing numbers of Christians. Recalling the previous chapter, nearly half of god's divine commandments were specifically designed to address this one, singular scourge, intended to demonize, condemn, and eradicate the belief and practice of anyone deemed pagan.

The Christian Destruction of the Classical World[70] was essentially a *fait accompli* by the time the Roman Emperor Constantine publicly declared his conversion to Christianity in 312 CE (meaning Common Era, or AD as it was known in my youth: Anno Domini - "the year of our LORD"). Thus began approximately 1000 years of serious conformity, indoctrination, and control we know of as the Dark Ages in Europe, right up until around 1500. Suffice to say, orthodoxy of thought, obedience to tradition, and Christian dogma were large and in charge, to the extent that those who diverged even in small part

---

[70] Nixey, Catherine. *The Darkening Age: The Christian Destruction of the Classical World.* Harper One, 2017.

suffered social censure at best, or burning at the stake, all manner of torment and torture, or death at worst.

An accurate portrayal of history would begin with the recognition that the dominant narrative is significantly skewed to depict Christians and Christianity as innocent victims and do-gooders, whereas the truth differs significantly. The received version of reality has gone through the hands of the dominant Christian culture, one Christian scribe at a time, over the course of millennia. It has undergone perpetual revision at the hands of religious individuals, scholars, groups, monasteries, inquisitions, and institutions, often with very specific, narrow agendas. There is a direct connection between the subsequent dominance of Christianity and the fact that an entire millennium carries the pathetic appellation it does. It became the 'Dark Ages' for a reason, and that reason was the unchallenged dominance of Catholicism and religious indoctrination.

Finally, the truthful narrative recognizes an early version of the rise of the nones, largely beginning around the end of these Dark Ages. The real story draws a direct, causal connection between the rise in secular, religion-free thinking, and the ensuing 500 years of significant human progress, beginning with the Renaissance (literally *re-birth* in French). Beginning with this transition, secular thought and atheism sit at the core of about 500 years of genuine human progress, and our discernible shift away from faith, dogma, and the supernatural, increasingly toward reason, science and the natural.

Over the ensuing years, Europe especially has continued to move slowly but steadily toward a more religion-free status. Of course, the extraordinarily powerful and dominant forces that are Islam and Christianity are not falling innocently or quietly by the wayside. Most of the rest of our world, including much of the United States, is still religious, with more than half of the people on our planet professing allegiance to one of the Abrahamic traditions.

Despite this fact, the last half millennium, particularly the last two hundred or so years, has been a remarkable and revolutionary epoch in human history, in large part as a result of the Renaissance, the Enlightenment, and the subsequent rise in secular thought in Europe and, in part, the United States, as well. Although the lineage of skeptics, atheists and agnostics extends continuously back to pre-Abrahamic, pagan, Mediterranean cultures, there was a particular lull in such free-thinking within Europe during the thousand-year long Dark Ages. Our current process of awakening can trace its origins largely back to around 1500, and subsequently includes *the enlightenment, the scientific revolution*, and the *age of reason*. In part, this more recent historical awakening consisted of the rediscovery of the freethinking of pre-Christian culture. But in large part, it was also something brand new.

Around 1500, Nicolaus Copernicus, astronomer and mathematician living in what today is known as Poland, displaced the earth and human beings from our self-appointed place at the center of the universe. His work, famously supported by one of history's most recognized early methodological scientists, Italian Galileo Galilei, was merely one manifestation of this newly secular perspective, an important freedom from religion which had begun to awaken. This important turning point in human history, this removal of god and man as the epicenter of the known cosmos, marks a symbolic beginning of our turn, away from instinct, indoctrination, pseudoscience, and faith, toward our increasingly secular, educated, scientific, and rational era, an era of true human progress.

Changing Everything. Literally.

Possibly the best example of the kind of progress I am talking about is Johannes Gutenberg's invention of the printing press. Gutenberg was a German craftsman who devised a means of printing from moveable type. His innovation made books far more widely available than ever before, eventually ushering in one of the most significant revolutions in information technology, something we in modern America are somewhat familiar with. As with our current communications revolution, Gutenberg's printing press was far more than mere technological innovation, as great and awesome as that alone may be. His creation precipitated the transformation of essentially the entire human species from illiterate to literate, all within the amazingly brief span of a mere couple of centuries.

Literate and Illiterate World Population
(among people aged 15 and older)

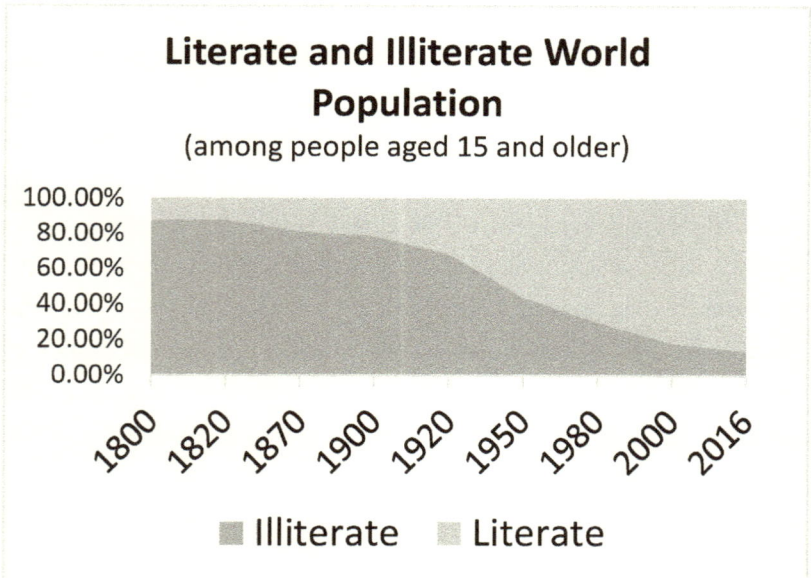

This graph shows a radical transformation in the global literacy rate. This revolutionary metamorphosis spanned the entire globe in little more than a single century.[71]

Within a mere hundred years or so, humanity went from 90% illiterate to 90% literate. That is an astounding change in a remarkably brief span of time. The subsequent alterations in the human condition, a transformation of genuinely inestimable magnitude, were all made possible, made almost inevitable, by this one, singular innovation. It is not beyond the realm of possibility that every single thing I am talking about in Rise of the Nones—our shift from the supernatural to the natural, the reality of human progress, our growth away from religious epistemology and toward increasingly naturalistic ways of knowing the cosmos—is a result of humans learning how to read.

Gutenberg's press was invented in the middle of the fifteenth century. Its impact, slow at first but ultimately sweeping in scope, *literally* changed our entire world. Literacy had been largely the province of the religious authorities, and accordingly was primarily effective as a means for increasing conformity, obedience, and submission to Christian dogma and the hierarchic power structure. Reading was like an awesome superpower, but it was the domain of the powerful elite only. For all of the preceding centuries of the Dark Ages, the vast majority of the scriptural reading and interpretation was performed by the religious authorities, for the illiterate masses.

This was often done in combination with the added power of stagecraft and theatrics, in majestic cathedrals with stately grandeur, stained glass working its magic on the peasantry as only lasers and fireworks might today, all of it performed by practiced thespians festooned in the most glamorous and breathtaking costumery, always in

---

[71] Max Roser and Estebar Ortiz-Ospina (2016) – "Literacy." Published online at OurWorldInData.org. Retrieved from: https://ourworldindata.org/literacy

highly ritualized manner and context. This added layer upon layer of mysterious and other-worldly power, a magical sense of spiritual magnitude and significance which stood in stark contrast to the mud-and-dust caked, blood, sweat, and tear-soaked tedium of your average peasant's humdrum worldly existence. But, at the heart of it all, scripture always served as the justifying foundation for the show, validating the spectacle. In the hands of the religious authorities, literacy was essential and effective as a tool for indoctrination, conformity, and control.

After Gutenberg, people all over the world, slowly but surely, over the course of several hundred years, started to read for themselves, which eventually encouraged thinking for themselves to some extent. And they started to read other things, beyond their scripture. From other peoples, other places, other perspectives. Literature and literacy, ultimately, took power out of the hands of the ruling and religious elite, and shifted our world toward democracy, secularism, liberalism, egalitarianism, and justice.

One useful way to think of the role of literacy in human progress is through analogy with contemporary changes in technology, with our recently enhanced capacity for globalized transportation, and international, multicultural intercommunication. Both increasingly enabled our ability and opportunities to experience regular encounters with *the other* – the foreign, the different. With 'them.' Sure, the short-term impact involves some friction, some tension and animosity. Surges in xenophobia. But the bigger, more long-term impact is entirely the opposite. Ultimately, the reader got to know the other, understand them better, identify with their humanity, and stimulate and grow their own capacity for empathy and understanding, along with which comes the diminution and cessation of fear and the dissolution of boundaries.

Gutenberg's creation transformed literacy into a means whereby people all over the world could cease being cognitively confined to their small, provincial lives. Being able to read and write ceased to be the province of the elite, a tool of indoctrination, limitation, and control. Increasingly, over time, literacy became a mechanism for genuine education as books went from magic in the hands of the powers-that-be, to empowering tools in the hands of the people.

These increased literacy rates also had the inevitable effect of expanding our *circles of moral relevance.*[72] People got to know the other, beyond the scope of their immediate village, the forty-mile circle beyond which your average person rarely ventured. Increasingly, people learned that their myths were not the only ones, nor were their gods. Commonalities were recognized. For more and more human beings, the differences between cultures, ethnicities, and languages began a process of slow transformation—a steady, glacial shift—away from the terrifying and threatening, toward the unthreatening, the novel, the interesting, the informative, and ultimately even the mutually life enriching, the life enhancing.

Meeting the other, the stranger, the Out Group, in a non-violent, respectful, welcoming embrace, with compassion, with empathy, as equals, as we are learning to do, is a significant step forward for our species. This process entails a synthesis of embracing and accepting difference, with recognizing and accepting elements of commonality, of sameness. This will bring us closer toward a far more fulfilling, and mutually enriching life than ever could be hoped for under the fearful, IG/OG yoke of Abrahamic insular self-righteousness. The change we are in the midst of is bigger than the mere normalization or validation of atheism, not just about the rise of the nones and our shift from superstitious and supernatural thinking to naturalistic thinking. It is also about having our lives determined less by instinct, and more

---

[72] Singer, Peter. *The Expanding Circle: Ethics, Evolution, and Moral Progress.* Princeton University Press, 2011.

determined by reason and choice. That is self-actualization, freedom, and autonomy.

As we face our instinct-based religious nature, bringing it to bear with the help of our instinct-overriding capacity for reason, so too do we face our IG/OG instincts, similarly bringing them to bear through knowledge, reason, and will. Nature is not destiny. Knowledge is power. Knowledge in this case is a far more enlightened and enlightening knowing of the other. It is an understanding radically enriched and enhanced through literature, film, music, dance, art, and multimedia, all of which are made increasingly accessible through our explosive growth in communications technologies. We stand at an historic juncture, one pivotal moment in which humanity as a whole has this golden opportunity, to collectively shift away from thinking in terms of *either-or*, toward thinking more in terms of *both-and*.

We are in a critical time, which means a time of peril, but also of great opportunity as well. Our basic self-conception is shifting, away from the dominance-oriented IG/OG of our antiquated origin mythology, increasingly toward the 'new and improved,' more scientifically accurate, post-Darwinian self-conception in which we are intelligent eusocial animals, intimately interconnected as brothers and sisters with all of the other humans on the planet.

It is no coincidence that a number of significant changes, awakenings, and manifestations of human progress follow directly on literacy's heels. Knowledge is power. This is the complete opposite of what the *Bible* attempts to instill in us. Our very origin myth itself, Genesis and the story of Adam and Eve, appears to teach that knowledge is itself a sin. While the standard interpretation is that this is specifically a reference to the knowledge of good and evil, there is nonetheless a long-standing and widely acknowledged broader distrust of thinking for yourself implied and imbued throughout both scripture and Christian tradition. As noted earlier, the general mindset of modern

American Christians is mistrusting of academia, irrationally skeptical of science, and openly hostile to knowledge. Fundamentalist Christians wage a serious war against the science of biology, hinder our intellectual and cognitive progress through a variety of means, and are in general significantly and genuinely anti-knowledge, opposing the secular nature of a university education, an experience which tends on average to produce more freethinking and disobedient students.

But, contrary to dominant Christian thought, disobedience can absolutely be a good thing. Questioning the 'received wisdom,' authority, dogma, and the status quo are all essential to a genuinely healthy, thriving, vital society. Knowledge is a really good thing, while indoctrination is generally a bad thing. The latter holds us back, prevents us from taking the former, and moving with far greater alacrity toward the inevitably just, beautiful, peaceful, and sustainable civilization which must be our finest fate and greatest goal. Christianity hinders our progress in large part through its general anti-knowledge, anti-education tone.

> Trust in the Lord with all your heart
> and lean not on your own understanding;
> in all your ways submit to him,
> and he will make your paths straight
> – Proverbs 3:5-6 NIV

The pious and reverent are definitely discouraged from thinking for themselves. As an atheist, humanist, and skeptic, I am always pleased when referred to as a 'freethinker.' I'd imagine the truly devout feel quite differently.

The Quiet Revolution

The revolutionary nature of the latter half of the nineteenth century is not widely recognized. But the truth is that this was a particularly significant time in our modern era of progress.

A lot was going on...

Not long before Darwin, Sweden's Carl Linnaeus had classified us as an animal, scientific nomenclature and all, just like all the other animals. This was a revolutionary change already. Scotland's Geologist Charles Lyell helped Darwin incorporate the fundamental geologic principle of *deep time* into his reflections, revolutionizing the way we viewed time, our planet, the development of life forms, and human existence itself. Charles' own grandfather Erasmus was already writing stuff that intimated a less developed, less scientifically articulated, somewhat more intuitive grasp of evolutionary processes.

Thomas Malthus was famously bringing to light some of the dynamic interplay between demographics and economics, all of which had a significant influence upon Darwin's own reflections on the process of selection in the origin of species. Last but not least, there were specifically like-minded fellow naturalists, working along very similar lines, on similar tracks to that of Charles Darwin. Two obvious and well-known examples would be Alfred Russel Wallace and Jean-Baptiste Lamarck. But Darwin's version of an origin story had immeasurably greater accuracy and explanatory power, was far more comprehensive and consistent, than any other origin story, from Abraham to Alfred.

But this change in understanding our biological origins, however true it may be that its implications are so genuinely far-reaching and transformational, was not the only thing happening. The 1859 publication of *Origin* was sandwiched by a mere few years between Lincoln and Marx. Abraham Lincoln's Emancipation Proclamation on one side, and the publication of Karl Marx's and Friedrich Engels' *The Communist Manifesto* on the other. Each of these were extremely noteworthy, each a sign of the times.

Abraham Lincoln, coincidentally born on the exact same day as Charles Darwin, oversaw the termination of the legally sanctioned enslavement of millions of kidnapped African citizens in the United States of America. It is important to note that these United States, the so called 'land of the free,' was neither the only, nor anywhere near the first, to outlaw slavery. Nonetheless, this was a pivotal moment in history, and a significant example of modern progress.

Lincoln did not come up with the idea, nor the courage, all on his own, in a vacuum. Other nations were well ahead of us on this. The change was all-inclusive and global in scope. Beginning around 1800, slowly but surely, slavery shifted from an accepted, legal practice, to an unacceptable, illegal practice on a global level, in every nation on earth. The demise of sanctioned, legal, morally permissible slavery was essentially a global phenomenon, a 'we' thing of the highest order, and true evidence of human moral progress.

Much like witchcraft, slavery is a practice which Americans tend to stereotypically associate with the past. Yet, as with witchcraft, it is important for us to be aware of the fact that it is still happening, and in significant numbers as well. Unfortunate, but true. Much more needs to be done. But it is genuine progress that slavery has shifted from the morally and legally *permissible*, to the morally and legally *prohibited*. It has ceased to be the norm, as it was in Biblical times, and as it is represented in the *Bible*.

It was during this same revolutionary time frame that Friedrich Engels and Karl Marx published *The Communist Manifesto*, widely recognized to be one of the world's most significant and influential political documents. Published in 1848, it was a genuinely and profoundly revolutionary work, a work of great social significance. It was a scholarly work which illuminated important concepts in economic justice, class dynamics, and class disparity. The *Manifesto* shined an explanatory light upon the problematic nature of unequal access to wealth, goods, and the means of production. The inequity, inequality, and injustice which the work decried had been, like slavery itself, accepted as an inevitability and a norm throughout much of human history. This was one of the most foundational, serious, scholarly, and seminal efforts to shine the light of knowledge and critical scrutiny upon the true nature and importance of economic injustice.

Any consideration of the progress being made within the last several hundred years must take into account our significant shift away from monarchy, away from theocratic, religiously influenced governance, and away from rule by authority, toward the more just rule of law, and the increasing relevance of liberal principles. *Philosophical liberalism* refers to an emphasis upon the fundamental rights of the individual, civil liberties embodied in the rule of law. The U.S. Constitution and the Bill of Rights are excellent examples. This was a time frame in which it became increasingly common to truly think in terms of everyday folk like you and me having the same exact rights, to life, liberty, and the pursuit of happiness, for example, as did the kings or queens; to think that laws should be applied equally to popes and princes as to we paupers and pawns.

The United States of America's Declaration of Independence famously begins with the assertion that "All men are created equal." Unfortunately, both in America and throughout world history more generally, such words have been interpreted preferentially, unequally, unjustly. Once again, to the victor go the spoils. White males ruled America, and so the rules that governed America, written or not, favored the white male. Most notably in the case of the United States, the claim did not apply to even one single female, regardless of race, ethnicity, or class, nor did it apply to the millions of kidnapped Africans or their descendants.

But American slavery was officially ended in 1863. Black men were legally allowed to vote as of 1870. And the latter half of the 19th century saw both a considerable rise in the percentage of women who were employed in the wider economic sphere, outside of the home, as well as a notable bump in agitation and conflict as women, too, sought the right to vote. New Zealand was the first nation to legislate this right into existence, in the year 1893. Others eventually followed their lead.

The women of the United States had a more prolonged struggle. Much opposition, mostly from men but also from women themselves, was fueled by religious conservativism. Christianity encouraged the desire to preserve 'traditional roles,' with that of the women emphasizing 'children, kitchen and church.' The United States, as a direct result of Christianity's influence, was far from being a moral leader in this regard, and did not allow women to vote until the year 1920, nearly 30 years behind the leader. This serves to illustrate the disingenuous and hypocritical nature of the widely accepted claim that religion and morality go hand-in-hand. Ironically, the reverse is more likely the case. The very real progress being made in terms of women's rights was and is being made *in spite of* religion, not *because* of it.

While all of this was going on, numerous scientific fields were growing by leaps and bounds, or popping anew into existence. Psychiatry and Psychology were born in this era, their early champions in the likes of Freud, Jung, and America's William James. Geology was an important contributor to our growing understanding of our true nature, and our place within the wider cosmic whole. The geological perspective was essential for bringing notions of deep time into consideration, which was of particular relevance in regard to our understanding our true origins and the evolution of species. Deep time opened the doors of knowledge to the true immensity, initiating a gargantuan paradigm shift, a major alteration in our perspective, within which we gained a more objective understanding of our true relevance and size, in terms of time, but also in terms of space. Accordingly, astronomy and the progress made in this and related fields also serve to change, transform, and progress our knowledge. In short, science was teaching us a far greater and more accurate lesson in humility than religious considerations ever could.

During this precise same time, Gregor Mendel, working a mere few hundred miles from Darwin, figured out what became the foundation for the entire scientific field of Genetics. Mendel's work was, as would later become widely appreciated, of the greatest significance to Darwin's own. As Galileo's work helped support that of Copernicus, so too did Mendel's support that of Charles Darwin. Darwin's work is considered so profoundly important in some measure due to it being extraordinarily comprehensive. It explained a great deal. But Darwin was not yet very clear on the mechanism by which selection itself took place, the 'how' of the selection process itself, be it *artificial*, *sexual*, or *natural*. Mendel's work ultimately helped to affirm the science of evolution, and to significantly improve our understanding of the nature of life.

A mere year before *Origin*, the very first Neanderthal bones had been unearthed in Germany. The first Archaeopteryx was discovered. Albert Einstein was born. Thomas Edison received the patent for the first light bulb in 1880. In the entirely figurative, metaphoric sense, and in the very literal, factual sense, all around the world, the species *Homo sapiens* was electrically charged. Somebody was home, and the lights were coming on.

It was during this time that philosopher Arthur Schopenhauer rightly observed:[73]

Religion is the masterpiece of the art of animal training, for it trains people as to how they shall think.

In a work with the genuinely fabulous title *The Gay Science*, Friedrich Nietzsche famously saw Schopenhauer's bet, and raised it, proclaiming with finality that:[74]

God is dead.

The last 500 years has been a period of great progress for humanity. In particular, the last couple hundred years have seen a great deal of change, and significant improvement in our knowledge, our wider understanding of human nature, and our sense of justice and morality, too. Increasingly, we know more, and we know better. Individuals mark important points in this process, but we must look beyond their contributions to get a sense of the bigger picture, the context, and the patterns. It is true that one extremely important contribution focuses upon the man named Charles Robert Darwin. But it is far more important to emphasize the findings than the man, to understand the true, overarching processes at play.

We are still in this period of awakening. It is of the utmost importance that we understand the true nature of this process, the truth regarding all its various elements, the different moving parts. They say that ignorance is bliss, but that's bullshit. Undoubtedly there could be some form of insane pleasure drawn from sitting in the dark in one's

---

[73] This quote is widely attributed to Schopenhauer.

[74] Nietzsche, Friedrich. *The Gay Science*, also translated as *The Joyful Wisdom* or *The Joyous Science*, 1882. – "After Buddha was dead, people showed his shadow for centuries afterwards in a cave,—an immense frightful shadow. God is dead: but as the human race is constituted, there will perhaps be caves for millenniums yet, in which people will show his shadow.—And we—we have still to overcome his shadow!"

own warm excreta, drooling on oneself, in a numb stupor. As an alcoholic and drug addict, I am familiar with this particular form of 'bliss'.

But knowledge is far better. Knowledge is sunlight and freedom. Knowledge equals the capacity for empowerment and autonomy, for self-determination. There is no god, there is no plan. No destiny. The more truth we know, the more we will be empowered to define and shape our own future, to create the kind of world in which we can all live, the kind of world in which we all want to live.

Rejecting Religion Versus Embracing Humanism

I look about me at the world of today, and regularly marvel that Americans in particular are not in a state of perpetual amazement and gratitude, constantly jumping up and down and proclaiming 'how immensely fortunate are we!' or 'what remarkable times we live in!' I mean, merely having an indoor shower, with warm water, soap, working plumbing, fridge full of food, clothing, shelter, and decent health care at our disposal – what luxuries! Far and away more so than most people that have ever lived have enjoyed. And that is, of course, at its most basic.

But, then I remember that we still have racial injustice and misogyny, trash piles in the Pacific gyre measured in cubic miles, melting ice caps, 8 billion human mouths to feed, and 8 billion asses to wipe, most of whom still believe in gods and ghosts. We also have leaders like Putin and Trump, in control of thousands of nuclear warheads still primed and ready to go.

We have problems. Very serious problems. But we are doing well in a number of areas. *Recognizing the latter does not mean denying the former.* Most importantly, in fact, it may help. Figuring out some of what we are doing right can bleed over, giving us some clues as to what we are still doing wrong, or how we might approach anew what we have been getting wrong. We are told that the answers to our problems lie in turning toward god, turning toward our *Bible* or *Quran*. But turning toward god of necessity means turning away from humanism, from science, from naturalistic thinking, and from reason, and it is precisely our turning *toward* these which has been getting us some seriously good results in recent history.

Mendel was a monk. But, most importantly, his work, his discovering genetics, founding the field, had absolutely nothing to do with religion or god. His status as a man of religion was essentially accidental to his brilliant work. The fact of the matter was that everyone and everything was associated with the church in one way or another. The reason so much of European genius, the Bachs and Beethovens, the Gregorian Chants, all that amazing artwork, the Sistine Chapel and the incredible, mighty cathedrals, the reason all of it is religious in theme has nothing to do with god or spirituality or religion as sources of inspiration, or anything remotely of that kind. It has to do with the fact that the church owned everything and everyone, with the fact that everyone was deeply indoctrinated in religious thought and belief.

If you wanted to do anything, anything at all, it went through the church. It had a religious name or theme. It came into being in religious form. The relevant religious authorities or texts or references were involved in one way or another. Every marriage took place in a church, under the control of religious authority. Every baby born needed to be baptized. Every home, every construct, every creation or project needed to be blessed. Even death itself needed official ecclesiastic sanctification and certification. When we were grateful, we gave thanks to god. Basketball superstar Steph Curry still publicly gives god credit for every shot he makes.

Even some nones and nonbelievers are prone to suspect that we might miss something of importance if god and religion should disappear entirely from the scene. This is not only a false belief, an inaccurate one, but it is one which fully hinders us, which restrains us from the full recognition and pursuit of our potential as social beings, as creative beings, as responsible, moral, just, rational, and wise beings. The more we give to god, the less we own, honestly understand, or fully take responsibility for.

Religion is required for (blank) is another of those great big lies I was talking about. What we need to get is that this is purely and entirely a sales pitch. This is something which we have been told, which we have been indoctrinated to tell ourselves. But it is not fact. It is not truth. It is only true if we believe it to be so. And we have some very good reasons to *not* believe it. We do not need religion for anything whatsoever, and continuing to believe that we do is absolutely hindering us from fulfilling our potential.

The point is that god, being a fiction, a 'man-made' thing which by definition disempowers human beings, is something which we are not merely capable of going without, but are in fact *better off* without. Consider, as a perfect illustration, the germ theory of disease. The belief that evil spirits, or bad karma, or god's will cause illness hinders our ability to recognize and build upon more accurate alternative explanations, explanations which were in fact far superior in every way. One reason that I call them superior is because, being more accurate, they can be built upon. Accretion and mutualism again. They explained things better, answered questions better, predicted better, solved problems better. In no way accidental, they did so because they had zero supernatural components. The only reason we found the cure for polio, or vaccines for Covid 19, is because we cast aside religious and supernatural explanations, and replaced them with the entirely naturalistic germ theory of disease.

For the last few hundred years, we have had a great deal of success in figuring things out, in creating things of great importance and pertinence, precisely because we were approaching things in an entirely secular, atheistic, humanistic manner. Darwin's work is genius precisely because he explained, in a very thorough and exacting manner, a whole lot about the nature of life, our own nature, without recourse to any supernatural elements or components. His genius was that his work proved god's irrelevance. Darwin made room for us to recognize, to discover, and to acknowledge, god's irrelevance. Irrelevance in value, as a causal agent? That's basically the death knell for a deity. If you don't need to make him up to explain things, he's got no reason to exist; he's dead meat.

Some Conclusions

History is written by the winners. The version we generally receive should always be taken with a grain of salt, a skeptical consideration which recognizes the probability that persons in positions of power and privilege have skewed the story line to present the version they prefer, the one which shows them and their beliefs in the best possible light, truth be damned. The historical narrative which we in modern America accept as the truth has been significantly whitewashed by Christianity.

At the same time, knowing our history also entails recognizing that some pretty remarkable stuff was, and is still happening – in terms of knowledge and our understanding of the nature of reality, and in terms of moral growth and overall progress in human rights and justice – ever since Copernicus and Galileo displaced us from the center of the universe, ever since Gutenberg invented his printing press, and we emerged from our Christianity induced Dark Ages, and stepped out into the light of the more recent eras known as the Renaissance and The Enlightenment. These were eras of progress characterized by a significant increase in freedom from religion, and a concomitant emphasis upon reason, science, and naturalistic thought.

The theory of evolution does not in and of itself so much prove that god does not exist, as illuminate his irrelevance. For a deity must be created, and for a reason. The deity of the AIC has no purpose anymore, no reason to exist. But, more than merely being irrelevant, the god of Abraham, Isaac, and Jacob holds us back from taking the reins ourselves, deciding and shaping our own destiny, owning our own choices, and being responsible and mature toward our fellow life forms, and our environment. In this sense, god does far more harm than good today.

Yet he hangs on. Belief in god and religious faith continue to dominate the human world, and all that we impact. God clings to life by virtue of cognitive biases, instinct, tradition, habit, indoctrination, and ignorance. He will continue to so self-perpetuate unless cast aside by an intentional effort, a conscious choice to stress reason over instinct, education over indoctrination, knowledge over ignorance, and facts over faith.

Human progress in terms of morality, ethics, and justice has been described in terms of expanding circles of moral relevance. Such circles expand, from the immediate or nuclear family; outward to our increasingly extended family of chance or choice; to our tribe; then to our wider community; our species as a whole; to our larger type, such as how recent laws have been passed to respect the rights of great apes and other non-human animals with certain obvious cognitive or sentient capacities. This expanding circle may ultimately encompass more. It may extend outward to become a moral regard for the wider biosphere as a whole, our global womb as it were. Possibly even beyond that at some point. Literacy and education tend to enhance this process, to nurture our capacity for developing in this way. The AIC literally do the opposite, hindering both the growth of knowledge, as well as our moral development, individually and collectively.

I enjoyed an interesting conversation with someone the other day, one that may be familiar to us all. A friend asserted the position that people are not capable of any significant essential change. This person asserted that our personalities were set by the age of three, and were not much capable of change beyond that point. I disagreed with the claim. We can change, at a most fundamental level, individually and collectively.

As a thought experiment only, consider the following scenario. Imagine a racist police officer. The stereotype will do: white and privileged, and prone to the institutionally sanctioned unjust treatment of 'people of color' (POC) which has become, unfortunately, a hallmark of modern American policing. Having been caught on camera abusing his position in an overtly racist manner, Officer White is subjected to a class or presentation. Perhaps this is a well-meaning, liberal effort to ameliorate his racist thought and belief, in order to alter his behavior on the job. Maybe this amounts to a four or five hour-a-week snooze-fest, with a little embarrassing role-play thrown in. Meanwhile, Officer White is still immersed, full time, in a social and cognitive milieu which reinforces his racist thought and belief during the rest of his life, both on and off the job. One hour a day of faking it, versus 23 hours of his real life, a life which invariably is founded upon a past clearly steeped in all kinds of racist, ethnocentric indoctrination.

So, here is the thought experiment: what if we take Officer White, and place him in a wholly immersive context? What if he lived with a black family, spent his time with black people, and studied real African American history, literature, and thought? When he wasn't studying, he was playing and partying: all with black people. What if he lived as a black man lives for a year, full time, 24/7? And what would happen if Mr. White spent 5 years fully extracted from the racist environment of his upbringing, immersed and educated in this black world instead? Is it even remotely possible that he would remain unscathed, fully and completely unchanged after an immersive and educational experience of that magnitude? I propose to you that it is fully ridiculous to so claim. Further, that this potential for change is one of the beautiful things about we human beings. Far and away, one of the top coolest things about us.

I should again stress that this is a philosophical, psychological thought experiment *only*. I am not suggesting this as a practical measure in any sense. As a philosophical thought experiment, it is solely intended to highlight the crux of an issue, the real issue at work, the spot where the heavy lifting is being done, as my college professor used to say. Would Officer White truly emerge from this immersive experience the same racist he was when he went in? *No way!* I believe knowledge on such a fundamental level, truly *knowing* something in the sense implied, can and does change us.

The point is that his behavior is a learned behavior. This means that we have the ultimate say in this stuff. Not our genes, not fate, not destiny, neither god nor the devil. This kind of positive change can happen. In fact, it is happening. It is precisely what is happening, and what this book is intended to simultaneously describe and prescribe. It is happening on a wider social scale, one that incorporates our entire species. It's just happening slowly, almost imperceptibly.

Importantly, I am not talking about indoctrination, but about education. This distinction is obviously of the utmost importance. Nor is it about superficial book learnin', so much as knowledge that runs deep. It is one thing to read all about the bugs and the plants and how they interact. But when you spend a season in the field, firsthand, combining that with real world experience, that is the more immersive educational experience which can and does change people and their beliefs.

The progress we are making is a natural result of the increasing scientific awareness of our material interconnectivity within the wider natural schema, our evolved interdependence within tribe, within environment, and as evolved animals in this complex web of life we know of as our biosphere. It is natural also in that it represents the best possible actualization of our evolved capacity for accretive, mutualistic, and applied intelligence. Anything which stands in the way of this important knowledge is a bad thing, and must be swept aside for our own betterment. It is in our own self-interest to seek freedom from religion.

Knowledge is power, while nature is not destiny. Genetics, instinct, habits, and tradition need not determine our behavior. To differing degrees, depending upon the instinct in question, human beings have the power of self-determination, autonomy, and freedom of will. Or something which, strict determinism be damned, looks, smells, feels, walks, and talks an awful lot like free will. Our future is up to us.

We have a choice over how we behave, how we define ourselves. Even what we believe to a very real extent. While we clearly cannot believe that which we do not believe, we *can* willingly choose to engage in an educational or immersive context which we recognize may ultimately change our beliefs. In this way we can realistically be said to change our own beliefs.

Mr. White had a set of beliefs prior to his immersive and educational experience. In all likelihood he had a different set of beliefs, believed something qualitatively different, when he emerged five years later from engaging in this freely chosen immersive process.

Human nature is not pre-determined. We are malleable, adaptive. In our case, nurture can override much that is problematic in our nature. This is because we are, first and foremost, the learning animal. It is 'in our nature' to adapt, to learn, to change. Knowledge of the real world, knowledge of the truth of our nature, the interdependent nature of all life within this planet's biosphere, rooted in the rejection of ignorant or instinctual errors and tangents, is the key to our making a better human civilization, a beautiful, peaceful, and sustainable system, going forward.

Chapter 6
Onus Probandi
&
The Argument from Probability

On Effing the Ineffable

The notion that god is beyond description or definition, the characterization of the Abrahamic deity as transcendent, as beyond our limited ability to comprehend, is but another of religion's many falsehoods, largely the result of propaganda, of indoctrination, intentional or otherwise. The god of the *Bible* and the *Quran* can and should be defined and described. He has characteristics and traits, all enumerated both in the scriptures, and subsequently by religious authorities, traditions, and institutions for millennia since.

This god is a powerful force which is, through his followers and their beliefs, extremely active and alive in the world. I and my fellow infidels may not believe. But billions of people *do* believe. Far more do than don't. And this belief makes him powerful, effective, and, in a very important sense, quite real. So, let's take some of that 'transcendent' and 'ineffable' smokescreen bullshit out of this very real, worldly phenomenon. Let's define the god of Abraham, Isaac, and Jacob. Let's define Jesus's daddy.

So, there are times when we encounter the fundamental question, 'Does god exist?' or 'Do you believe in god?' or some variation. I am genuinely baffled when the next thing uttered or written, on the part of either party, is not, 'What do we mean by 'god'? As in, define your terms. This is of the utmost importance. I suppose it is not overly surprising. I take a much greater interest in this stuff, and have all my life, than most people. Accordingly, I am familiar with a wide range of beliefs on the subject. But, for most Americans, perhaps his nature is safely assumed. In truth, most are going to be talking about more or less the same thing. And it is the fact that so many believe in this same kind of god that is behind how much impact this god belief has upon the world we live in. It is this impact which makes him 'real,' in this particular sense.

Nonetheless, as I mentioned earlier, if I learned at least one thing in all of those philosophy classes, it's the importance of defining your terms. Make sure you are all talking about the same thing. Getting it right matters. Big, expansive terms especially require exactitude. 'God' can mean very different things, to different people, in different contexts. Considering the real-world impact of religious belief, and of the AIC in particular, getting it right really matters. All that said, it is finally time to define what is meant by the word 'god,' in so far as it is used within the confines of this book, and by the majority of humans today.

We often tend to identify something by describing a specific set of necessary and sufficient conditions which need to be met. For example, a straightforward Oxford English Dictionary definition of god is:

> a superhuman being or spirit worshiped as having power over nature or human fortunes; a deity.

But a better way to define broad, expansive, umbrella terms - words such as *art, love, language, game,* and especially one as big as *god* - is by employing Wittgenstein's family resemblance model of identification[75], introduced in Chapter 2. The family resemblance model differs in that it consists of a list of characteristics or traits, none of which are

---

[75] Wittgenstein, *Philosophical Investigations*, 1953.

either necessary or sufficient, yet which combine in various degrees to construct a more complete picture of the thing or phenomenon under consideration. Notably, not every god hypothesis will have every one of the traits in question, nor hold to them all in identical respects.

To illustrate Wittgenstein's family resemblance model, consider the concept of family resemblance literally. So, for example, little Jamie Jones may have daddy Jones' curly hair, mommy Jones' skin in color and tone, but not auntie Jones' green eyes, nor grandma Jones' depressive personality…yet it's still very clear from a suite of traits that young Jamie is a Jones, all right.

The god of Abraham, Isaac, and Jacob, the god of the *Bible*, has billions of believers and followers, who believe in a wide range of attributes and characteristics. But they will pretty much agree on enough of the following for us to justify the claim – this is god defined:

Interventionist:

God is believed to intervene regularly in human and worldly affairs. This is an essential characteristic for *theism*. *Deism* is an alternative mode of religious faith, one in which god is believed to exist, and has several of the traits listed below, but has not in any sense intervened in the natural world beyond the original act of creation. The god of the theist, including the Abrahamic god of Islam and Christianity, is very much a hands-on, micro-managerial deity. Sacrifices, offerings, and prayers are the most common means of entreating him for specific desired outcomes. Events which cause suffering – your newborn succumbs to disease, or your home is singled out by a twister, or events such as 9/11 and Hurricane Katrina, or most famously Noah and his ark – are often interpreted *a posteriori* as being the result of god's wrath, disapproval, or disfavor over something which humans have done, or failed to do.

141

Creator:

God is believed to be the cause of the universe, of life on this planet, and of human beings in particular. This supernatural creation sits at the foundation of Abrahamic dualism: the notion that reality is divided into a lower, natural, worldly realm, and a distinct, divine, supernatural, or 'spiritual' realm. We are god's special creation, especially dear to him, and made in his likeness. We are part nature, but also partly divine, unlike the other natural beings and the world around us. This does not bode well for environmentalist concerns.

One fairly common criticism of the atheistic perspective is that we believe everything sprang forth from absolutely nothing. 'How can something come from nothing?' they often ask semi-rhetorically. Interestingly, however, they fail to recognize that this self-same criticism can be levied against their own position. If you can't get something from nothing, as they so often assert, how did god spring forth? The most common response is that he is 'self-caused.' But this is more rhetorical gibberish than reasonable response. It literally is describing what they just said cannot be done. Plus, it also opens up the problem of infinite regression. The simple cause and effect model would appear to prove equally problematic for both theist and atheist cosmology.

Plan:

We and all of nature are understood to be *created*, and god is understood to be the *creator*. He exists outside of the plan as the planner. He is the designer, and we are all a part of his design. This plan is understood to somehow be the source of meaning, purpose, and destiny in the lives of human beings, individually and collectively. Rather than recognizing this blueprint/architect paradigm as a manifestation of our instinctive predisposition to interpret phenomenon in a teleo-functional manner, the faithful followers of the AIC employ an epistemological inversion, interpreting a predisposition of the human mind as an actual trait of the cosmos itself.

Caring:

God cares about human beings, above and beyond all else, much as would a father care for his children. However, importantly, Abrahamic conceptions of god's love for his people generally take an IG/OG form, with god clearly having a 'chosen' people whom he prefers over all others. This propensity to split humanity apart along some form of lines, usually interpreted as along religious lines, has historically been employed to justify all manner of violence, crusades, wars, unjust treatments, and literal genocidal efforts, in numerous instances throughout history.

Humanoid:

Employing a similarly parental model, god is understood as humanoid in form and content. According to scripture, we are made in his image. This can be external: meaning that, in appearance, the Abrahamic god takes a predominantly male, humanoid form. Or it can refer more to the internal: psychologically, temperamentally, and behaviorally akin to an adult male member of *Homo sapiens*. This conflation of 'man' and god sits at the source of human exceptionalism, our highly problematic notion of human beings as separate from and superior to the natural realm.

Again, much of the confusion stems from what I have described as the primacy of mind, our failure to account for the primary role the brain plays as an intervening, interpretive force in the process of knowing, the manner in which *Homo sapiens* has traditionally failed to distinguish between the mind which does the knowing, and the thing being known. The devout and the pious are therefore guilty of this epistemological inversion, failing to recognize that the mode of thought itself pre-determines what is observed, known or described. Human beings need to recognize that everything which we know should be subject to careful critical reflection in light of the unavoidable fact that all human knowledge is a result of the evolved, imperfect organ we know of as the brain/mind. Accordingly, rational and atheist thinkers tend to reverse the standard thinking here. Rather than it being we who are made by god in his image, it is we human beings who conceived god in our own image.

Cosmic Caulk:

…'caulk' for injecting into the 'gaps' in our knowledge. God serves as the ultimate filler/explanation for any and all things unknown. The well-known concept of the god of the gaps refers to humanity's historical tendency to inject supernatural explanations into the gaps in our knowledge, simultaneously bringing curiosity, the search for knowledge, all science, *Homo sapiens* uniquely accretive and mutualistic kind of intelligence, and the bulk of human progress, to an unfortunate, screeching halt.

Benevolent:

God is understood to be the source of all that is *moral*, *just*, and *good*. He is the ultimate wellspring for all human morality, and the ultimate source of justice as well. Even in the realm of the aesthetic, god is considered the source of the good. Believers will often wave their arms about in splendor and wonder at a beatific sunset, breathtaking vista, or similarly impactful aesthetic phenomenon, whereas the ugly, profane, or mundane are rarely attributed or associated with him in the same manner. This has proven highly problematic in numerous regards, some I have discussed, more still to be considered. Amongst other things, it takes morality and justice out of human hands, conceives of them as supernatural and beyond our scope, dismissing the essential role of evolution in generating morality and justice as essential aspects of any species which evolves to be both eusocial and highly intelligent, and accordingly disempowering us, dismissing our species' immense potential.

Judge:

God is cosmic judge, jury, and executioner. He ensures justice and personal accountability for all human beings. Moral scales and worldly justice are all balanced out and made right, according to most Christian and Muslim thinking, upon each person's death, at the commencement of their alleged afterlife. At that point, god is in charge of all punishment and reward, according to his system. He is responsible for all karma-related, heaven, hell, and rebirth placements or re-assignments. Again, this misconception places justice and morality mysteriously 'beyond' humanity, 'beyond' our scope of responsibility.

Omni:

'Omni' is a prefix which comes from Latin and means *all* or *of all things*. God is understood to be omni-everything. So, he is:

Omni-present - meaning everywhere, all of the time.

Omni-scient - meaning all-seeing, all-knowing. He knows each of our thoughts, our hidden motivations, and everything about each of us individually. He sees you when you're sleeping, knows when you're awake. He watches you help that woman across the street. But he can also read your mind, so he knows if you are just doing good deeds in order to get brownie points with him. You brown-noser, you. And later on tonight, when you're lying in bed and masturbating, and suddenly images of that woman pop into your perverse little fantasy world - he knows about that, too.

Benevolent - God is all good. This characteristic in particular sheds some fascinating light upon the relationship between god, morality, and progress. His benevolent nature is understood differently according to the when and the where of it.

In the Old Testament, as in much of today's Islamic world, and in some of modern America's more traditional quarters, god's love is hard. As with real life fathers back in the day, the ideal was firm, inflexible, distant, dominant, with a very limited emotional range, largely emphasizing a controlling, angry temperament. Essentially, old-world stereotypic machismo. This type of father figure is held as an ideal in harsher times, but also in today's more traditional, conservative, and fundamentalist religious slices of the Abrahamic world, places where the Biblical warning 'spare the rod & spoil the child'[76] is still the predominant parenting advice, and is taken quite seriously.

Modern sensibilities have, over time, come to re-interpret god in keeping with a kinder, gentler, father-figure ideal. I describe this phenomenon as enlightening because it reflects larger societal shifts. Our changing understanding of what it means to be both *good* and *a man* walks hand-in-hand with the increasing emphasis upon the 'god is love' ideal of modern Christianity. It mirrors what I am calling human progress, and it mirrors it very precisely. Of particular interest and importance, then, is the question of causation:

Does religion itself progress independently?

or

Does secular society progress, and religion merely lag behind?

What is the true source of human moral progress?

---

[76] English Standard Version of the Bible. Proverbs 13:24 – "Whoever spares the rod hates his son, but he who loves him is diligent to discipline him."

Omnipotent – God is omnipotent, meaning all powerful, beyond the physical limitations of nature and natural law. Inevitably, combining the attribute of benevolence with omnipotence brings us to a genuinely classical philosophical argument, one which traces back through David Hume all the way to the pagans of the ancient era known as the Golden Age of Greece, and the classic argument known as Epicurus' trilemma.[77] This argument, familiar to many of today's nones and atheists, begins with the reality of evil and suffering in the world.

If god is truly *benevolent*, he must not be all-powerful, or else he would bring about an end to all of this evil and suffering in the world.

If god is truly *omnipotent*, he must not be all-good or all-loving as, again, if he were, there would not be so much evil and suffering.

Therefore, the presence of evil serves as proof that there is no god, as so defined.

Supernatural:

God is believed to be *transcendent* and *beyond* all that is natural and known. He is considered to be the cause of nature, yet somehow stands outside of, or separate from, the natural realm, which we know from experience, and of which he is the creator. His existence represents an essential duality, a schism of the cosmos into two distinct realms: the natural and the supernatural, also understood as the material and the spiritual. This religious dualism paves the way for belief in such supernatural phenomena as the eternal soul, the afterlife, god's divine judgment, heaven and hell, as well as grounding a disregard for the natural.

---

[77] Larrimore, Mark J. *The Problem of Evil: A Reader.* Blackwell, 2001.

How to Tell Truth from Fiction
Part One: Falsifiability

Many who live under the considerable influence of the AIC have been indoctrinated into the habit of thinking of scientific and religious epistemology as separate-but-equal ways of knowing. More or less comparably valuable, just different perspectives. This is a misrepresentation of reality. In truth, scientific knowledge is superior to religious knowledge in a number of very important respects. It simply represents the new kid on the block. As such, it encounters a great deal of misunderstanding and resistance. Let's revisit our Schopenhauer:[78]

> All truth passes through three stages on the way to acceptance:
> First, it appears laughable;
> second, it is fought against;
> third, it is considered self-evident.

An entirely religion-free, atheist, humanist world is possible, preferable, perhaps even inevitable. Ultimately, the secular positions which I am outlining in this work will be recognized as self-evident. For now, however, they are in the first and second stages for most people.

But the bottom line is that the more naturalistic epistemology is, simply put, *the best means for figuring things out which Homo sapiens has thus far hit upon.* Not just different. Better. Using this basic approach, the scientific model, emphasizing evidence, data, facts, and reason, any good explanatory theory, one which can be taken seriously and considered as a viable potential explanation for any given phenomenon, has to have two key things going for it. First of all, in order to be a meaningful explanation, it must be possible to disprove it, to refute it, to show that it is false. The relevant criterion so far as this

---

[78] Widely attributed to Schopenhauer.

closed end is concerned is referred to as *falsifiability*.[79] The central epistemological role of this possibility for falsification was brought to the fore by Karl Popper in 1934.

The example most frequently employed to illustrate his insight is the simple claim that:[80]

All swans are white.

This is a clear and simple example of a falsifiable claim. In order to refute this claim, all that is required is one non-contentious counterpoint. For example, one black swan could refute the claim.

Problematic religious claims are generally those which lack this characteristic of falsifiability. For perhaps the most illustrative example, consider the position of the Young Earth Creationist (YEC). In keeping with literalist interpretations of the Genesis chapter in the *Bible*, Young Earth Creationism contends that the Earth and all life were created in essentially the manner we see all about us, as is, by the will of a divine entity, specifically the supernatural acts of the Abrahamic god, approximately 6,000 years ago. Mountains of evidence have accrued to increasingly make abundantly clear that the earth is, to the contrary, several billion years old. Scientists have presented copious examples of such evidence, all of it attesting to the earth's significantly greater antiquity.

However, the YEC claim hides behind a veil of unfalsifiability. YEC believers simply assert that 'god made everything precisely as we see it,' regardless of the worldly evidence supplied. The scientifically well-versed may ask 'what about the enormous number of fossils

---

[79] Mcleod, Saul. "Karl Popper: Theory of Falsification," *Simply Psychology*. (Updated 2020). – The Falsification Principle, proposed by Karl Popper, is a way of demarcating science from non-science. It suggests that, for a theory to be considered scientific, it must be able to be tested and conceivably proven false."
[80] Popper, Karl. *The Logic of Scientific Discovery*. Julius Springer, Hutchinson, & Co., 1934.

reliably dated back in time multiple millions of years; or the geologic stratification, the layering and folding of mountain ranges and other landscape features, and essentially all of modern day geology; or the genetic patterns consistently pointing to interconnectivity and extreme antiquity in lineage; or the extensive similarities in bodily structure, the shared morphology so perfectly and consistently inter-connecting the entire, vast range of living organisms, the evidence emphasized in such popular science works as Shubin's *Your Inner Fish*[81] and Dawkins' *Ancestors Tale?*[82]

This immense and daily growing body of data would seem to be thoroughly damning to the YEC position. However, to such claims, these religious literalists merely assert that their god made everything as is, precisely as we see it, including all of these deceptive and confounding discoveries, during his singular act of creation, just as described in the *Bible*. Thus is their god hypothesis rendered unfalsifiable, and thereby outside of the realm of any rational argument or otherwise meaningful explanatory theory, regardless of the evidence provided.

The YEC position, discounting so much of modern science as it does, may seem at first glance to be rather extreme, an outlier out on the fringe. Yet it is but a stone's throw from there to the far more numerous moderates who proclaim that the fossil record alone is damningly sparse, the millions today who teach their children that the alleged problem of the missing link serves to entirely discredit the theory of evolution. This is a real thing, and far less fringe than the YEC.

Every time scientists produce precisely the fossil required to fill in the alleged gap in the record, the faithful simply cry that two new gaps

[81] Shubin, Neil. *Your Inner Fish: A Journey Into the 3.5-Billion-Year History of the Human Body.* New York: Vintage Books, 2008.

[82] Dawkins, Richard. *The Ancestor's Tale: A Pilgrimage to the Dawn of Life.* New York: Houghton Mifflin, 2004.

have just appeared, one on either side of the link provided. In addition to smacking of a confounding degree of general scientific ignorance, and in addition to ignoring entire fields of scientific knowledge such as all of genetics, this commonly expressed argument also simply dodges the falsification requirement for any viable theory.

All of which serves to make two very important points.

Religious faith often rests upon a foundation of non-falsifiable, fundamentally irrational claims;

and

Seemingly fringe, extreme religious beliefs are not always the benign outliers they appear to be. Sometimes they're just more extreme, more obviously wrong versions of widely held, common religious falsehoods.

In the end, the Abrahamic god hypothesis itself exemplifies unfalsifiability. It lacks the essential rational criterion of being refutable. The well-known god of the gaps concept offers one final demonstration. Placing god into the gaps in our knowledge was, and for many still is, considered a viable form of explanation for any and all sorts of phenomena. It may be a village-decimating volcano, earthquake, or tsunami, the psychic transformation which allowed alcoholic Uncle Barney to stop drinking for years, or the sudden and inexplicable remission of Grandma Vera's cancer.

God and the supernatural serve as ready-made, all-purpose spiritual caulk, filling in the gaps in our knowledge of causation, offering comforting answers to any and all queries. It is thereby also an answer which can never be 'disproven,' as the theist can always pull another explanatory end-around such as described or, what amounts to the same thing, simply fall back upon god's infamously mysterious ways. The common claim that "god works in mysterious ways" is in fact nothing more than an appeal to unfalsifiability. What the believer does not realize is that, inevitably, this renders such claims devoid entirely of content. They tell us nothing interesting or important about the subject in question.

Any good, viable explanatory model, intended to shed light upon worldly phenomena and human experience, such as the ten examples listed above, must be falsifiable if it is to be taken seriously. Many pivotal Abrahamic claims lack this important characteristic, and are therefore not viable explanatory or predictive models of reality in any sense.

Before I move on, however, I feel obliged to pose one technically tangential, though I think wholly unavoidable question. Regarding claims such as the YEC makes, in which god is alleged to have made everything precisely as is, with all the intentional deception and mis-direction that implies, the question which keeps bubbling to the surface for me is: why?

That is, why in hell's name, or in heaven's name, or for heaven's sake, or even for Pete's sake, would the good lord almighty play such a mind-numbingly pointless, and, dare I say, mean-spirited trick upon us? Exactly what would be his motivation for such a ludicrous act of intentional deception? Why would an omni-everything deity need to test us, and why in such a cruel and flagrantly heartless manner? No matter how you slice it, it looks bizarre and sadistic.

Perhaps if we had a broader, more populous pantheon, one which included trickster deities the likes of Loki, Anansi, or Kokopelli, it might make a little bit more sense. But, with the brooding bully of the *Bible*? Suffice to say, he was not known for his fun-loving ways, mad-cap sense of humor, or zany shenanigans.

Let's get back on track. On one end we have falsifiability. The Abrahamic god hypothesis entirely fails in this regard. Its very nature as such, as the answer to any and all questions which itself can never be questioned, proven, nor disproven, renders it entirely specious. The god of Abraham, Isaac, and Jacob is designed to be unfalsifiable. It is imagined-up in precisely this slippery, evasive, unprovable, and intentionally mysterious manner. Because it is designed so as to be the answer to any question whatsoever, it can give us a *meaningful* answer to absolutely zero of our queries. What does it tell us, to say that god made something, or caused something? It is tautological, empty, really gives us no information, tells us nothing about the thing or its relations with other things.

This connects up with the earlier arguments in which I considered the longstanding claim that god's existence can neither be proven nor disproven. Truly, god cannot be proven wrong. But not because he exists, or because his nature is ineffable or transcendent. He was 'designed' by the human brain, collectively, if unintentionally, over time, to be a much needed, all-purpose cosmic fill-all, as just the kind of thing which could not be pinned down, yet which could serve to answer all questions. He cannot be falsified because he is cosmic silly puddy. Jello? Whack-A-Mole?

How to Tell Truth from Fiction
Part Two: Probability

The second essential characteristic of any viable model for explaining the human experience is *probability*. Falsifiability, on the 'prove it wrong' side of our equation, has to be hard and fast. A clear matter of fact. One black swan. Bunny rabbit fossils in Pre-Cambrian strata.[83]

But, on this other side of the equation, the 'prove it right' side, a good theory has to be open ended. We do not want a theory that is

---

[83] Christopher Hitchens, Richard Dawkins, and others have made use of an amusing historic anecdote in which famed scientist J. B. S. Haldane reportedly quipped, when asked what he would consider sufficient evidence to cast doubt upon evolutionary theory, 'fossil rabbits in the pre-Cambrian.' Rabbits are mammals, members of the class of organisms known as Mammalia, a class of organisms which did not begin to evolve into existence until more than 300 million years *after* the terminus of the time frame known as the pre-Cambrian.

hard and fast, cut and dried, in the same sense. This is precisely because of the accretive and mutualistic nature of *Homo sapiens* intelligence, the fundamentally dynamic nature of human knowledge itself.
It has to have this vibrant, fluid character in order to stay accurate,
meaningful, relevant, and applicable.

A look at one very common linguistic misconception helps shed
light upon this very issue. Some theists, and some of the less scientifically informed atheists no doubt as well, fail to grasp the more formal
application of the term *theory*, nor do they get the need for a good,
viable explanatory model to be open-ended. People crave the simplistic finality, the stone-like irrevocability, of the irrefutable fact. So colloquial and formal usages of the term theory differ considerably in
tone.

For example, many do not understand that evolution is simultaneously both a theory, and yet at the same time it is *also* a fact. In this
context, the terms fact and theory do not have the mutually exclusive
connotations which they do in more colloquial linguistic contexts.
That is, in common usage. In spite of some confusion on the part of
the devout or the under-informed, this open-ended characteristic of a
good theory is itself a feature, and not a bug: it is an ideal epistemological approach. For human intelligence, a good theory is dynamic,
fluid, and not set in stone.

The germ theory of disease is a fine example. It is not generally
referred to as 'fact,' nor do we speak of it as 'proven'. Yet we think of
it in this manner: as fact, as truth. It is the most *probable* model for
understanding disease which we have yet to discern, based upon the
totality of all of our knowledge. It works and makes sense better than
any other model does.

Sickness was, and for many still is, widely understood to be karmic
consequence, punishment for sin or moral transgression of some kind,
or a result of other supernatural forces, such as curses or spells, or

demons in need of casting out. Even today we still feel habitually inclined to say "god bless you" when someone sneezes. The germ theory is a relatively new understanding of the nature of sickness and disease, and requires that we unlearn some long-held misconceptions. Only as we were able to question and discard enough of that mis-directional falsehood, the old models in which illness was considered the result of god's will, what many today refer to as 'karma,' or to assorted demons in need of casting out through prayer, sacrifice, or some other form of penance or supplication, were we able to begin to cultivate a more naturalistic, falsifiable, and accurate understanding, one from which our knowledge could genuinely progress.

As a direct result of embracing this new, both falsifiable and most probable theory for understanding human health and disease, we can make increasingly accurate predictions. We can clearly understand and accurately explain cause and effect. We have cured numerous ailments, discovered or created many thousands of treatments, and brought about plenty of preventative practices and procedures, from potions and pills to prophylactics and protective patchwork, a plethora of which prevent pesky parasites and pests from poisoning a patient's plasma. I have no idea what just happened there. Sorry.

Anyway, it is only within the last century or two that we have accumulated and shared enough accurate data and knowledge to even begin to make sense of the complex interrelations between *Homo sapiens* and the millions of microscopic organisms with whom each one of us lives in an entirely interdependent, dynamic relationship. Only within recent decades have we begun to discover the truly vast extent to which each human body is not so much a single organism as an actual microbiome, a biological complex. Over half of the cells on and in the human body are non-human life forms - bacteria, viruses, fungi, or archaea. The vast majority of these microbes are somehow relevant to our continued functioning as healthy, living animal beings. These are not 'bugs,' not germs we need to wash off. Nor should we wish to, even if we could.

The human body has co-evolved to exist in some kind of complex, interdependent, interactive relationship with these millions of microbes — be it parasitic, mutualistic, symbiotic, pathogenic, commensal — whose true extent and nature we have only just begun to figure out. In the not-too-distant future, humanity will receive an abundance of significant health benefits from this new knowledge, and the subsequent burgeoning scientific endeavors.

This all could have gone very differently, though. Religion could have continued to hinder our learning, kept us longer in the Dark Ages. Conversely, it is possible that we could have long ago figured this stuff out, been far further along this pathway of knowledge and understanding. Religion serves to fill the gaps in our knowledge with supernatural answers. But such tumors of the understanding are not harmless and benign. Any false answer to a question, if accepted, plugs the gap, and serves to halt further investigation, curiosity, inquiry, or reflection on that question. If one thinks a question sufficiently answered, then one is disinclined to continue investigation upon the matter. When their child was sick, the devout would pray. If the child's condition did not improve, more often than not the response was simply to do more of what didn't work. That is, pray harder, better, faster, stronger.

This is why Alcoholics Anonymous and the other twelve-step programs are, in a very real sense, more problem than solution. Members are taught to believe that the problem of alcoholism/addiction is understood. It is known, and it is a 'spiritual' problem (whatever that means). The resultant solution, the answer to their problem, is therefore also spiritual in nature. The big book, the basic instruction manual for the fellowship, strongly advocates prayer, and surrender to a higher power. As do the twelve steps themselves.

As the treatment industry is composed of a very high percentage of AA members, the general overall mindset is that alcoholism/addiction is essentially a problem solved. As they say at the conclusion of every meeting, in ritual unison, hand in hand: 'it works, if you work it.' We do not need to figure out or better understand the true nature of addiction. We simply need to apply our spiritual tools harder, better, faster, stronger. The genuine scientific cause and effect facts of the whole affair are, as a result, not the subject of sufficiently rigorous inquiry and investigation. The approximate 10% 'success' rate, generally cited by the treatment centers themselves, remains sadly consistent and unchanged.

Covid, for Example...

As I work to complete this final draft of *Rise of the Nones,* it is midwinter of 2023 here in the United States of America. The global pandemic caused by the Coronavirus, commonly known as Covid-19, just turned 3 years old. During its first year, the death toll around the world rose into the millions. Billions were in lockdown, working from home wherever possible, foregoing communal gatherings, work sites, classes, parties, events, and doing far more of their socializing 'virtually.' Most of the people I knew, the members of my community, friends, and family, all kept up 'best practices': we kept 6 feet of bodily separation, wore masks on our faces, obsessively washed our hands, and stayed home an awful lot of the time. Businesses and government required employees to follow such commonsense guidelines as well. We reaped rewards as a direct result. Such entirely empirical, scientific, secular responses, properly practiced, successfully reduced the spread of Covid-19, the rates of overall infection, the impact upon our medical infrastructure, and the disturbingly high mortality rate.

During the pandemic's first year, there was much resistance to these evidence-based best practices. Here in the United States, the greatest resistance came from the cultural nexus of the politically conservative and the devoutly religious. The antigovernment, antiregulation stance of the former merged with the latter's faith that god would protect them from this plague of Biblical proportions. As the pandemic became an ongoing daily reality, they proudly and openly asserted prayer and faith as viable safeguards, beseeching interventionist supernatural entities, Jesus and Muhammad, Allah and the god of the *Bible*, to protect them, rather than donning face masks or staying out of crowds.

By now you can probably guess how well that worked out. Despite their faith, those who refused to exercise best practices suffered noticeably higher rates of infection and death. They also irresponsibly raised the rate of infection for everyone else. Their errant beliefs put millions at risk, exposing our beloved essential workers on the front line, as well as those of us who followed best practices. They filled their churches and pews when allowed, gleefully proclaiming that Jesus was stronger than any virus, and that their god would protect them.

Many folks like myself predicted that a solution would be found within a year or two, something along the lines of a cure or vaccine. This solution would be 100% the direct result of secular and scientific efforts. Working within the framework of falsifiable, probabilistic, scientific methodology, human beings would soon bring some form of resolution to this very serious, deadly disease. This would not be like the plague or the black death, decimating a third or half of humanity, and science would be the reason why. I did not have faith in science. I trusted science. An important distinction. Trust is evidence-based. It is earned.

We also predicted that, once science had solved this huge problem, the devout and pious would come streaming out of the woodwork to praise the lord, rather than the scientists who figured out the eventual vaccine or cure itself. They would throw their hands up in exultation and misdirected gratitude proclaiming "Hallelujah! Our prayers have been answered. Praise be the Lord, for he has delivered us from this terrible plague!" For millions of believers, their faith would in fact be reaffirmed or renewed. No matter what solution came along, it could be claimed to be the result of prayer. This is an example of what is meant when saying that religious claims, such as the claim that prayer can cure, are unfalsifiable.

The predictions of those of us with a trust in science were manifested when, around one year after it all started, effective vaccines were created, immediately serving to reduce both the frightening rates of infection, and the massive death tolls. These vaccines significantly turned the tide, reducing the impact of Covid-19 all around the world. As a result of best practices and vaccines combined, our lives began to return to a sense of normalcy.

After spending over a year cooped up at home writing and working, my wife and I enjoyed our first mask-free dinner out, dining with a good friend at a fine little Italian restaurant downtown. We were very grateful to be alive and well. Millions had died around the world. Though it was still an ongoing issue in many places, humanity as a whole had essentially 'turned the corner'. The number of new cases, hospitalizations, and the death toll all began a significant decline. During the subsequent years, variants have evolved, causing occasional spikes in the numbers. But, on the whole, the vaccines did the job they were supposed to do, and continue to do so.

This could have been an epic disaster, a plague of historic proportions or worse, if it were not for science. It was bad, bad enough. Yet it could have been so much worse. Covid-19 has, essentially, been brought to heel using scientific methodology and our understanding of the germ theory of disease. This success is a clear demonstration of how human progress is a direct, quantifiable, and undeniably positive result of freedom from religion.

Sadly, however, many religious believers still attribute the win to something supernatural. As a matter of fact, the church has not suffered any exceptional or noteworthy diminution in believers. According to Pew Research, people who prioritize religion are more likely to say that Covid-19 actually strengthened their faith.[84] Confirmation Bias worked to help believers affirm prior convictions, such as the thought that prayer works, or that god protected them, no matter how irrational. Today as before, there are millions of devout who are indeed praising the good lord, thanking god or Jesus or Allah, for 'giving' us the vaccines and delivering us from the evil pandemic.

...Or Evolution, for Example

Another excellent example of a viable explanatory model would be the theory of evolution. On one hand, nothing has arisen which might falsify Darwin or the evolutionary model. There are still no fossils of bunny rabbits in the pre-Cambrian strata. At the same time, Darwin's theory of evolution explains our origins, our overall nature, our relationships with the rest of life on this planet, our long-term history, how we fit into it all, with greater precision than any other competing explanatory models.

> Every day, hundreds of observations and experiments pour into the hopper of the scientific literature. Many of them don't have much to do with evolution – they're observations about details of physiology, biochemistry, development, and so on - but many of them do. And every fact that has something to do with evolution confirms its truth. Every fossil that we find, every

---

[84] "More Americans Than People in Other Advanced Economies Say COVID-19 Has Strengthened Religious Faith," Pew Research Center. Washington D.C., January 27, 2021.

DNA molecule that we sequence, every organ system that we dissect supports the idea that species evolved from common ancestors. Despite innumerable possible observations that could prove evolution untrue, we don't have a single one. We don't find mammals in Precambrian rocks, humans in the same layers as dinosaurs, or any other fossils out of evolutionary order. DNA sequencing supports the evolutionary relationships of species originally deduced from the fossil record. And, as natural selection predicts, we find no species with adaptations that benefit only a different species. We do find dead genes and vestigial organs, incomprehensible under the idea of special creation. Despite a million chances to be wrong, evolution always comes up right. That is as close as we can get to a scientific truth.

                                                      – Jerry A Coyne[85]

In a nutshell, my own atheistic god hypothesis is all about probability. This argument from probability simply means that we take the totality of available evidence, from every department and arena, and critically, skeptically apply it to the problem at hand. Whichever falsifiable theory best explains the totality of phenomenon, whichever one seems the most probable in light of the totality of all evidence, has the best explanation, makes the best predictions based upon that model: bingo! Winner, winner, chicken dinner.

This argument I espouse is, again, functionally proof, as in the most viable model at hand. In terms of the god hypothesis, we can today offer naturalistic, scientific explanations for the ten phenomena listed above, each of which proves far more likely, more salient, more viable, by orders of magnitude, than those offered up by Islam, Christianity or, for that matter, any other religion. Here's the thought: saying, 'There is probably no god' is equivalent to saying, 'The theory of

[85] Coyne, Jerry A. *Why Evolution is True*. New York: Penguin, 2009.

evolution is probably accurate,' each of which are equivalent to saying, 'The sun will probably come up tomorrow.' Such claims may not have the epistemological certitude of claims in logic or mathematics, but they have the very probability of which the most viable empirical claims consist.

The standard conception of knowledge as a thing, a singular objective, to be attained, is less than ideal. Empirical knowledge is more verb than noun. It is less the end goal of a path, than a path itself, a lifelong pursuit, ever guided by an unattainable goal on the ever-receding horizon, the distant yet guiding point on the horizon which is *certitude*. And the horizon itself is, of course, famously unattainable, yet ever the guiding beacon, the paradigmatic ideal.

Onus Probandi

Many of today's nones and atheists take great pleasure in pointing out that, from a strictly rational point of view, the *burden of proof*, regarding the existence of god, rests upon the shoulders of the pious. 'You say there is a god. Show me the evidence.' This notion of the burden of proof, the Latin *onus probandi* from our legalistically inclined forebears in ancient Roma, is a fair point, on the face of it.

Rationally speaking, the pious should carry the burden of proof. If one is going to propose that something exists, especially something of such magnitude, something of such great significance and import, yet something which, simultaneously, is not readily apparent to the senses, it is only reasonable that one should be willing and able to provide some degree of convincing evidence in support of that assertion. Then again, we Americans today don't necessarily pay strict attention to that which is rational and reasonable. With the overbearing weight of two millennia of Christian cultural tradition and domination, reason has faded considerably into the shadowy woodwork.

For whatever reason, the burden of proof is not one which the devout feel any keen need to acknowledge or address. As a rule, it is we atheists who are expected to justify our position, even though ours is by far the more credible, reasonable, and rational of the two. The pious tend not to take the whole burden of proof argument very seriously at all. Fortunately, there is an important sense in which this particular ghosting is entirely irrelevant. When all is said and done, the evidence is abundantly and overwhelmingly in our corner at this point in history. Reality, evidence, facts, and reason are all on the side of atheism and humanism. While the words I write may seem blasphemous and heretical, the truth is that time is on my side. Yes, it is.

Eventually, the fictional and problematic qualities of Abrahamic thought and belief will be readily apparent to all, as humanity continues to grow, educate itself, and mature. In time, truth will win out. It's just a matter of when, assuming we survive long enough, and assuming we can avoid slipping backward into another Dark Age. With the advent of modern communications and technology, coupled with our growing numbers, our shift from naive provincialism toward a more secular, educated, all-inclusive globalism is all but guaranteed, our shift away from religious indoctrination, and toward a slow but steady increase in reason, in naturalistic and atheistic thinking. All in good time, my pretty. All in good time.[86]

We nonbelievers need not wait until the devout accept *onus probandi*. We can take on the burden of proof. We can do so with ease, and with confidence, if we wish to. This was not the case two thousand years ago, nor even two hundred years ago. For centuries, the claim that *the existence of god can neither be proved nor disproved* was accepted as philosophically axiomatic. But the bottom line is that this is no longer the case. Things have changed over time, sufficiently so that

---

[86] (There! Mick Jagger & The Wicked Witch of the West, together at last.)

this once self-evident claim is simply not true. God is a belief, not a being. Recognizing the truth, that religious faith is largely instinct-based human thought and belief, in combination with cultural indoctrination and tradition, is the key to us freeing ourselves from a very real imprisonment which most of us never knew we suffered.

Consider the ten characteristics of Abrahamic belief which I described earlier. This is not a god defined by logic or mathematics, a god deduced by pure reason or abstract thought. It is an empirical god, a hands-on type of god, concerned with matters of fact about the world we experience, the world we live in on a day-to-day basis. The Abrahamic god is known in terms of human experience, thought, and belief. He weighs in on moral matters, plays judge, jury, and executioner, both for the individual and for groups, and he does it all the time. He loves us like a father. He helps us defeat our enemies in battle. Or on the football field, or basketball court, where his greatness and importance are daily extolled. But, only in victory. For some reason, he only gets credit for the wins.

The faithful truly believe that god answers all their prayers. As the very devout former president of the United Sates, Jimmy Carter, famously asserted:

God always answers prayers.
Sometimes it's 'yes.'
Sometimes the answer is 'no.'
Sometimes it's 'you gotta be kidding.'

Talk about your unfalsifiability! God is the answer to entirely worldly questions, such as why this tsunami happened, or why that innocent baby had to die, or why Steph Curry is such an amazing three-point shooter. It all concerns our beliefs about life, death, and all the stuff that happens in between, the stuff of worldly experience. These are all, at their basis, empirical questions, having not to do with formal logic or mathematical theorems to which proofs apply, but with the realm of human experience and our beliefs about it. Probability and falsifiability are far more relevant than is proof. The Abrahamic God hypothesis described above should be considered the same as any naturalistic hypothesis whose function it is to best explain the phenomenon we experience. There is no justification for a special dispensation, despite religions' consistent demands for exceptional consideration.

Again, simply juxtaposing things historically, one way of seeing the last two millennia is as a shift from religious epistemology, toward a new and far better way of knowing the world, one which focuses upon reason and evidence over faith, tradition, and authority. Since the above god hypothesis is essentially empirical in its content, it must play by the same rules, must be subject to the same type of analysis as any other empirical claim or explanatory theory.

The notion of 'proof' is not, strictly speaking, pertinent to such empirical phenomenon. The germ theory cannot be 'proven.' Nor can the theory of evolution. It is more so the case that a thousand little confirmations and substantiations every day serve to verify the plausibility of that theory which is most probable, while at the same time nothing arises which can seriously be claimed to falsify it. This is precisely as the quotation from Jerry Coyne described earlier.

Just as with our theories regarding disease, or plate tectonics, or gravity, in precisely the same manner, the theory of god which I am describing is not subject to the kind of proof one finds in logic or mathematics, but a thousand little affirmations and probabilities which accumulate, every day, continually and consistently reaffirming the nature of the god of Abraham, Isaac, and Jacob as a figment of the human imagination only. This proves the most probable explanation throughout a million little tests every single day. The alternate

requirement, that something comes along on the other side which fal-
sifies the theory, this has never even once come to pass.

What Has Changed?

In a nutshell, my argument in this section is simply that much positive
change has been made since the Renaissance, particularly within the
last two- to three-hundred-year period. Enough to shift us from a
place of genuine agnosticism, in which it might reasonably be asserted
that we do not know, to a hard atheist position which confidently
asserts that all gods are fictional entities. So, what precisely is it that
has changed so much that we have made this radical transformation?

There are several interrelated factors. First and foremost is the tremendous growth in human knowledge, generally speaking. The im-
poverished, fraudulent nature of religions pseudoscientific accounts,
such as in Genesis for example, has been highlighted by the increasingly accurate, productive, falsifiable, and probable nature of findings
in a range of scientific fields. Astronomy, physics, and astrophysics
have illuminated the true nature of the cosmos – the stars which fill
our nighttime sky, our sun, our moon, our own world, and our origins
on the more cosmic level. We are, quite literally, composed of star
stuff in very specific ways which we have acquired extensive, detailed
knowledge regarding, radically transformative knowledge, all within
very recent history.

But the truth is that this has been happening across the board. This
is but one example of countless ways in which the last several hundred
years of increasingly secular thinking has brought home significantly
more accurate and explanatory knowledge of the true nature of life
itself, of human beings, and of the entire natural world, answers to the
very same questions which serve as a grounding, foundational framework in religious scripture. We are made up from dust, according to

166

the *Bible*. But science can answer the question of what we are made from, and with accuracy and details which blow religions' answers out of the water completely.

On the face of it, this may sound like a trite and superficial objection. But the bottom line is that this kind of pseudoscientific thinking sits at the foundation of these religious origin stories. It concerns entirely empirical stuff, like where did we come from, how did we get here, what are we made of. And the truth is that we do far better entrusting science with that job. Chemistry and the germ theory of disease have tremendously expanded our knowledge regarding our own body, its various functions, as well as those of all other life forms, all within the last couple hundred years.

The scientific fields have essentially taken over in these definitive arenas, rendering god and religion moot. Again, this stuff is truly central to religion: huge swaths of the religious life concern disease, illness, death, cures and miracles associated with sickness, and moral justifications for all of it: god is punishing us, or god took my 3-year-old brother Tony, we know not why, because god's ways are mysterious, but it's OK, cause it's all a part of his plan, or because Tony's in a better place now.

For millennia we answered such questions through faith, prayer, sacrifices, rituals, magic, demons, angels, more prayers, penance, and sacrifice. Sickness, illness, disease, death: this is when even the less devout turn to god and religion. All of this human mortality stuff was understood and explained for centuries through a combination of confirmation bias, group bias and peer pressure/support, tradition and indoctrination, and belief in alleged supernatural, karmic forces. Moralistic components in the traditional interpretations served as vapid, empty consolations and comforts, intended solely to ameliorate the anguish and pain caused by nature's cruel indifference.

But now, we have medicine and the germ theory, to far better address problems of illness and disease. And we have psychology to help constructively address associated issues without the burdensome complication of the moralizing lies, guilt, and judgmental deities' religion so often attached to sickness. Illness and death are hard enough to deal with without adding morality and guilt into the mix unnecessarily. Psychology and psychiatry may be in their infancy, but they have already enabled us to make great strides forward, particularly in removing god's wrath, guilt, blame, and moral judgment from issues of illness and health, physical and mental.

But, most importantly, we now have the germ theory of disease, we have knowledge, preventative practices, and medicine. As a result, life expectancy on our planet has doubled. Doubled! As a direct result of switching from religion to science. Now, take a wild guess when everything began to change, when global life expectancy began its impressive turn around? It began during that revolutionary period right around the time of Darwin, the latter half of the nineteenth century. Since approximately 1870 until today, within the last 150 years, the global life expectancy of your average *Homo sapiens* has progressed from around 35 to over 70. No more obvious example illustrating the very point I have been arguing could possibly be imagined. Despite the fact that we are well and truly overpopulated, we have doubled the human lifespan around the world, all as a direct result of shifting from religious to naturalistic thinking.

To a certain extent, knowledge and technology progress hand-in-hand. The cultivation of our abilities in microscope and telescope technology has significantly enhanced our knowledge in all of the above noted arenas. Cultivating our capacity to see through a telescope, to see microscopically, these both opened up vast new realms. They allowed us to grow immensely in terms of understanding the nature of life itself, the exact structure of living organisms, in increasingly greater detail. The telescope and microscope in particular are examples of inventions which have enabled us to radically alter our comprehension of the true nature of things, seeing back to the dawn of time, down to the ultimate building blocks and fundamental forces of nature itself. This technological advancement has caused a huge leap forward in our knowledge.

Everything happens below the microscopic level. Well, OK, not everything. But, a lot. Think about it: life on this planet was literally born in the form of invisible organisms. Their tremendous abundance and variety, then and now, dwarf the number and diversity of larger beings, from mosquito to mammoth, from blue fly to blue whale; fully half of our own bodies today are constructed of a copious variety of these infinitesimal life forms, and life has thrived on planet Earth in the form of the resilient and invisible for far, far longer than it has been large enough for the unaided human eye to perceive. If any type of organism can be said to be foundation, dominant, and essential to life on earth, it would be that life which we cannot see. Application of knowledge in optics has brought about genuinely revolutionary change in human knowledge over the last few centuries.

From the first strand of DNA, the very blueprint from which all earthly life is made, to the Covid-19 virus which so recently threatened to kill us all, the microscopic realm is the stuff of life. Knowledge of the microscopic realm is knowledge regarding the true building blocks of life itself, but also of non-living stuff, of all that is the cosmos. This sort of thing makes god superfluous, renders religion irrelevant. Chemistry and medicine today address similar questions to those of early religion, including what makes us tick, why we suffer illness and disease, what is the nature of life, and a whole range of connected, fundamental issues not unrelated to religion.

Geology and the earth sciences further illuminated us regarding similarly fundamental questions. These are central and foundational to our origin story. The pure pseudoscience of Genesis begins the *Bible*, and is quite possibly the most well-known of all scriptural passages:[87]

> In the beginning God created the heaven and the earth.
> And the earth was without form, and void; and darkness was upon the face of the deep. And the Spirit of God moved upon the face of the waters.
> And God said, Let there be light: and there was light...
> And God said, Let there be a firmament in the midst of the waters, and let it divide the waters from the waters...
> Let the earth bring forth grass, the herb yielding seed, and the fruit tree yielding fruit after his kind, whose seed is in itself, upon the earth: and it was so.
> And the earth brought forth grass, and herb yielding seed after his kind, and the tree yielding fruit, whose seed was in itself, after his kind: and God saw that it was good.

This kind of pseudoscience serves as the foundation, establishing legitimacy in origin stories for all the subsequent stuff that follows. And yet, the truth is that if you really want to know how the earth came to be, the nature of day and night, understand more about the stars, the sun, the moon? The nature of light itself? The nature of earths landmasses, its oceans, their interrelated dynamics? Wish to know how planets came to be, understand more about life forms, their origins, their development, the relationships between...

...You get the picture. Much of the *Bible* is just bad science. But, especially after the Dark Ages, we have matured significantly, improved our ability to figure out those kinds of things. Much of the *Bible* is bad history, but we got better at that, too. Much of the *Bible* is bad psychology. Ditto. This is all precisely what reasoned secular

---

[87] *The Holy Bible,* King James Version – Genesis 1:1-23

thought, including science, does, and does far better. Especially when encouraged, pursued, and nurtured.

The paramount example of what I am describing, is of course, evolution. Charles Darwin and the theory of evolution is precisely science doing a far better job of explaining things than the pseudoscience of scripture and religion. Darwin's *Origin* was, quite simply, a far better, more accurate, more useful origin story than the *Bible*. Apologists, thinkers on both sides of the divide, have famously argued that religion and evolution are not mutually exclusive, that there is no essential conflict, that the two can coexist harmoniously. As recently as Steven Jay Gould in the 1990s, such apologetics dominated the discourse.

The 'new atheists' – the four horsemen of the atheist apocalypse, as some refer to Dawkins, Hitchens, Harris, and Dennett – prove decidedly more contentious, precisely because they openly espouse atheist thought, acknowledging the fundamental either/or nature of the schism. They did not try to tiptoe around the subject. Something's gotta give, and that something is religion, no question. The truth of the matter is that this alleged tension between the Non-Overlapping Magisteria of science and religion is just another example of it being difficult to accept the truth when it comes at you raw and hard, challenging everything you'd previously held dear. The bottom line is that evolution and the Abrahamic god are indeed in direct conflict. This is just something which people don't want to hear. You won't get elected.

All of this science is happening hand-in-hand with the explosive growth of literacy. What good would all of this knowledge do if people couldn't access it? People all over the world have virtually unchecked access to the vast bulk of all human knowledge.[88] Our revolutionary

---

[88] Of the many challenges we still face in our increasingly secular future, economic injustice remains one of the more glaring. Today, while internet access has greatly

universal enlightenment is available to most all human beings. But none of our current communications and information revolution would be the case if not for the foundational fact that, between around 1800 and today, humanity went from 90% illiterate to 90% literate.

The result of all this globally spreading knowledge is a decreasing provincialism, and a concomitant growth in human cognitive sophistication. Localized origin stories have been downgraded from 'the truth' to the status of mere pseudoscientific cultural mythology. In contrast, we could begin to reflect critically, to consider the possibility that *our* story was not *the* story. Many of today's American Christians have yet to fully make this shift, this cognitive maturation. Like toddlers, there is an essential self-centered ignorance of the other, of the big picture. This is why they fail to recognize the profound nature of the erudite Dawkins observation cited earlier:[89]

> We are all atheists about most of the gods that humanity has ever believed in.
> Some of us just go one god further.

The Argument from Utility

A common objection which the religious apologist proposes at this point hinges upon god's alleged value as a useful fiction. So, they argue, the god of the *Bible* and the *Quran* doesn't exist: so what? We need him. Without him, civilization will descend into an amoral or immoral morass, life will lack for meaning, humanity will have no sense of purpose, and our values will get all out of whack. Even if god does not exist, is not belief in him a beneficial reality? Surely that is a force of great good? Might the question of his existence be entirely

---

leveled the playing field, there still remain very significant disparities based upon such factors as geography and economics.

[89] Dawkins, *The God Delusion*, 2008.

irrelevant, as his value derives not from existence, but from our belief in him? As Voltaire famously observed:[90]

If God did not exist, it would be necessary to invent him.

Perhaps there is more irony to be found in the fact that the problem here, as so often, is that this accepted truism is in fact completely and utterly false. As simplistic as it sounds, as simplistic as it indeed is, the AIC literally just lie. But because of their immense power, size, history, because of the suite of relevant cognitive biases discussed in earlier chapters, those which encourage the maintenance of faith, these lies are accepted as truth.

The truth of the matter is that the evidence does *not* suggest we need religion. In fact, if anything, it suggests the opposite. Ergo this book. That religion is necessary is a claim promoted and perpetuated by Christians and Christianity, a claim which serves to protect mother church, yet has absolutely no truth value whatsoever. The claim that we need religion is not a claim of truth, but more of a sales pitch. Not a statement of fact, but an act of coercion. As such, it is inherently true that it is itself morally problematic, as it disregards one of the most morally salient of our attributes, and that is our autonomy. You feed me false bullshit, you strip my ability to live my own life, you in effect make of me a pawn in your own chess game. That's not good. That's bad, in my book. Morally uncool, man.

Speaking merely from personal experience, anecdotally, as it were, I call bullshit. My life does not lack for meaning or a sense of purpose, nor is my moral compass in any respects broken or unfocused. As a matter of fact, I am distinctly aware of several respects in which my whole-hearted and enthusiastic embrace of atheism has served to make

---

[90] The Voltaire Society of America, "If God Did Not Exist, It Would Be Necessary to Invent Him." *The Voltaire Society of America.* Jack Iverson, Whitman College, n.d. Available at: https://www.whitman.edu/VSA/trois.imposteurs.html

my life richer, stripped away false supports, and allowed more real, more meaningful values to grow in their place. Some of the most kindly, charitable, compassionate people I know are nonbelievers. They do not behave in a morally good, prosocial manner from fear of hell, or to win god's favor, nor to earn a place in heaven. They do good because it is right to do so in principle, or because teamwork is an essential part of what it means to be human, or simply because it feels right to be and do good, whether or not anyone is watching, or keeping score.

Another anecdotal tidbit might be to consider the morality of your average citizen in some far less religious, more atheistically inclined locales, such as New Zealand, Australia, Great Britain, Germany, France, Iceland, or Japan, and ask yourself if he or she is less moral than the average American. The answer will be no. In fact, data mining either example in detail, one will find the literal opposite of what Christianity and Christians proclaim to be true. The fact of the matter is that your average, non-believing Dane or Kiwi is actually more likely to be a morally decent chap than is your average Christian American, who often appears by contrast to be self-absorbed, entitled, racist, ethnocentric, self-righteous, and inexplicably arrogant.

Setting aside such subjective, anecdotal evidence, more quantifiable data serves to tell much the same story. If it were true that atheism breeds immorality, one would expect to find huge numbers of atheist deviants incarcerated. That is, one would find that the prison population in America would be less religious than the general population of the country. Yet the percentage of prisoners who are atheists is actually far lower than a representative sampling of the country as a whole. The prison population in fact consists of less than half the percentage of atheists than the non-incarcerated population of Americans. If anything, we are in fact significantly underrepresented in US prisons.[91]

In *Rise of the Nones*, the reader will encounter more than enough pertinent facts—such as Christianity encouraging American slaves to be obedient and accept their fate; religious resistance to abolition; the abundant role of Christians in the slave trade; Catholic and religious American cooperation with Adolph Hitler; American conservative, and largely Christian, resistance to the rights of women, blacks, and LGBTQ persons; religious indoctrination for the young, as well as opposition to science education; and last but certainly not least, the truly heinous immorality of institutionalized child sex abuse and subsequent, apparently well-practiced, cover-ups – to cast significant doubt upon the claim that, without religion, we would fall into a cesspool of immoral deprivation. I'm not so sure the devout have a leg to stand on in the face of all this worldly evidence to the contrary. Perhaps they should take their own advice on the subject, from John 8:7:[92]

He that is without sin among you, let him first cast a stone…

Religion is not needed for morality, and in fact serves to hold us back, to perpetuate a state of affairs in which our moral growth and development are hindered. Meantime, in spite of the influence of the AIC, justice continues to grow and expand. The civil rights act was passed, as slowly but surely white America awakens to its legacy of extreme racial injustice, and to the fact that Black Lives Matter. Significant changes in women's rights, increasing justice for African Americans, and equal rights for the LGBTQ communities, have all

---

[91] Mehta, Hemant "Atheists Now Make Up 0.1% of the Federal Prison Population." Blog: Patheos/Friendly Atheist. August 21, 2015. Available at: https://friendlyatheist.patheos.com/2015/08/21/atheists-now-make-up-0-1-of-the-federal-prison-population/

[92] *The Holy Bible,* King James Version – John 8:7

come about in spite of resistance from religious quarters, with far greater support coming from secular and non-religious sources.

The United Nations Declaration of Human Rights is an entirely worthy example of irreligious, secular human morality.[93] I highly recommend that every atheist read this basic statement of fundamental human rights. This important and underappreciated document serves as a premier example of a reason-based, naturalistic, secular, humanist statement of moral, ethical, and legal guidelines. It alone, in just a few pages, represents a tenor of secular morality which puts the entirety of the *Bible* to shame. There is more justice, fairness, and a general 'how to treat your fellow humans' in its few pages than in the many hundreds of pages of our alleged moral guidebook. And with significantly less ambiguity as well, I might add. I can imagine that some picky atheist might find a section or sentence here or there to object to. Nonetheless, the UDHR serves as proof of my claim that an entirely religion-free, secular foundation for morality, ethics, and justice is both realistic and attainable. That we require religion to treat each other well is complete and total bullocks.

The vast majority of human beings either believe in the Abrahamic god's existence, or consider the question of god's existence/nonexistence to be a great cosmic mystery, a question of great intransigence

---

[93] On the United Nations website, we find the following description: "The Universal Declaration of Human Rights (UDHR) is a milestone document in the history of human rights. Drafted by representatives with different legal and cultural backgrounds from all regions of the world, the Declaration was proclaimed by the United Nations General assembly in Paris on 10 December 1948 (General assembly resolution 217A) as a common standard of achievements for all peoples and all nations. It sets out, for the first time, fundamental human rights to be universally protected and it has been translated into over 500 languages. The UDHR is widely recognized as having inspired, and paved the way for, the adoption of more than seventy human rights treaties, applied today on a permanent basis at global and regional levels (all containing references to it in their preambles)." Available at: https://www.un.org/en/about-us/universal-declaration-of-human-rights

and insolubility, quite probably beyond our cognitive capacities altogether. The truth is that we now know enough to assert an argument, based upon falsifiability and probability, that god, in so far as the Abrahamic tradition is concerned, Yahweh of the *Bible* and Allah of the *Quran*, is not truly the cause of creation, our master planner, or our supreme moral overlord. He is simply a belief in the mind of the animal *Homo sapiens*, and not an actual being, entity, or power in any real sense, except in so far as we have made him real through our books, buildings, beliefs, and behaviors. Recent centuries have brought about such a radical change in human knowledge and overall awareness that the question of his existence has become significantly less enigmatic, less impenetrable. The claim that he is beyond our understanding is not true, and in fact serves largely as a ruse to coerce the gullible.

The argument that this deity is a useful fiction is also little more than yet another long con, intended to maintain status quo and retain power and control. It is not supported by the facts on the ground. Belief in god hinders humanity from fulfilling its potential. His immediate retirement is highly recommended, as he causes far more harm than good. The sooner we start riding without our training wheels, the sooner we'll be able to do that Tour de France. Most of humanity either believes god is real, or else believes that he is a useful fiction. My argument is that they are wrong on both counts. But, even further, I argue that this double error serves to hinder essential human progress. Far from needing god, we are in fact held back by our belief in god. The solution is to be found in turning away, and embracing modes of thought and understanding which do not rely upon instinct, but upon reason, evidence, science, and our rapidly accumulating body of secular human knowledge.

Chapter 7
What Is Selection?

What is Selection?

Great question! So glad you asked.

It was during this same fecund and seminal epoch, the latter half of the nineteenth century, that the works of Darwin and Gregor Mendel began to come together. For his part, Darwin appears to have known nothing of Mendel's work. Mendel, on the other hand, was well aware of Darwin's. There is some evidence in extant writings which suggests that Mendel refrained from pursuing the connection between their respective bodies of work, so as to avoid making 'clerical enemies.' But their works were inevitably bound to come together. We fortunate beneficiaries have the synthesis of Genetics and modern Biology, which together shine considerable light upon the evolutionary process we call selection, the true origin story of life, of all the differing species of beings, including our own.

Selection refers to the two-step process which gave rise to every single species of organism or creature which has ever lived here on planet earth. The first step is a genetic mutation of some sort, which arises spontaneously. More often than not, such genetic mutations don't make any real difference, so they just tend to come and go, unnoticed and more or less irrelevant.

Once in a while, a mutation can cause a slight change in an individual, either in its body or in its behavior. If that mutation happens to cause a change which benefits the individual in evolutionary terms, improving its *fitness*, as in its ability to *survive and successfully reproduce*, that mutation is likely to breed into subsequent generations, to spread into the future populace of that species. This is the process of selection, how evolution happens, how species are shaped. The environment or context *selects* whether or not the mutation, and whatever little change it wrought upon the organism, either:

Is irrelevant to the ability of that specific organism or creature to survive and successfully reproduce,

or

Makes a relevant, if minute, difference in said abilities.

Darwin knew that something like this was going on. He just lacked knowledge of genetics, of the gene, which is the fundamental unit of the selection process. That is where the mutation either does or does not happen. It was the work of Mendel, which was happening right around the same time, a mere few hundred miles away, which initiated the subsequent field of Genetics. If only they'd texted each other. Or even just an old-fashioned email would have done the job.

Selection pressures are generally described in terms of three additional variables: *natural, sexual,* and *artificial*:

Natural Selection

A genetic mutation acts upon the organism or creature, and the organism or creature interacts with their natural environment. The subsequent interaction with the totality of their given natural environment and context either selects the mutation, or it does not. There is nothing random about such stringent tests, despite the under-informed critiques of the theistically minded who mistakenly accuse evolution of being pure chance. The mutation is passed on because it gives that specific organism an advantage in survival or reproduction, an advantage in passing the gene into the subsequent generation, based upon these demanding, rigorous, real-world tests.

The organism is able to pass on the mutation to subsequent generations because it is more fit, better adapted because of that mutation, better able to survive and successfully reproduce within that specific context and environment. Every species is a result of millions of these tiny mutation/interaction tests, which select whether or not the mutation stays or goes, accumulating to create significant changes according to the counterintuitive principles of deep time.

From one, teeny-tiny, little, infinitesimally small, minute change at a time, combined with huge amounts of time, significant multitudes of generations, every single type of creature, organism, plant, animal, microbe, and mammoth has been shaped. The fact that this is mind boggling - that's a feature of the theory, and not a bug. Any given thinker's failure to grasp the immensity of what evolution can do, the gargantuan changes these minute mutations and interactions can sculpt, create, or appear to design, given the considerable accumulations possible as the result of increments of deep time, simply suggests a paucity of the imagination.

In his work *The Blind Watchmaker*, Richard Dawkins describes what he refers to as the 'argument from incredulity.' The mindset of these religious thinkers, these deniers of the theory of evolution, is basically:[94]

I cannot myself understand this, therefore it must not be possible.

That the theist cannot understand how a complex thing such as a frog, a tardigrade, the feather, and the extreme diversity of feather types, the bat's echolocation, or the human eye, to name a few

---

[94] Dawkins, Richard. *The Blind Watchmaker: Why the Evidence of Evolution Reveals a Universe Without Design.* New York: W. W. Norton & Company, 1986.

examples, could have evolved into existence, is a problem not for the theory, but for the incredulous and unimaginative thinker. The immensity and grandeur and inconceivability of it all is not evidence that it is false or improbable, as the faithful sometimes proclaim. Rather is it an opportunity for awe and wonder on a scale which eclipses any theistic pretense to reverence for the supernatural. This is an opportunity to stretch and strengthen our capacity for understanding, not bemoan its limitations and shortfalls, be they merely apparent, or be they genuine.

Evolution is truly a wonder. As simple as the process is, the inconceivable magnitude of it all helps to explain why it took humanity so long to start figuring it out. That, combined with our penchant for settling, for accepting the answers on offer by mere instinct, by our willingness to believe, to obey, our sundry cognitive shortcomings and shortcuts, by our beautiful, evolved brain, and its built-in imperfections and deficiencies.

Sexual Selection

Just think peacock. Those glorious feathers appear to serve no other practical purpose whatsoever, other than simply attracting a mate. Many evolved traits do not appear to serve the straightforward, practical purpose of aiding in our procuring a meal or dodging a predator. Their value is instead in ensuring that we can get laid. The value is in successfully attracting a mate. If a shiny spot on my wing or a lilt to my song gets another member of my species, one of the opposite sex, interested in fucking, then that trait gets passed on into subsequent populations. Too crass? Sorry. Should I have said 'making love' instead?

The ensuing reproduction ensures that whatever it is that attracted him or her in the first place will then be passed on to subsequent offspring. Further theorizing along such lines often includes the supposition that something about such features – the peacock's feather, the bower bird's elaborate constructs, the copious impressive antlers or horns, the various dancing routines, Barry White's deep and sonorous voice, Prince's sexy swagger and dance – all of these are communicating something about their health or wealth status, in some species-specific form, to the prospective mate.

Artificial Selection

This refers to any selection which is intentionally caused by humans. Basically, we take two organisms, be it plant or animal, which both possess a feature we would like to see more of, to exaggerate or emphasize, and we crossbreed those two individuals.

For example, when we breed one relatively timid, non-aggressive fox with another of like demeanor and temperament, we will get kits with even more distinctively domesticated qualities. In just a few generations, the wild, non-domesticated fox evolves into an animal with notably more friendly dispositions, as well as piebald coats, floppy ears, and wagging tails.

Or we could choose to mate two mammals with longer, thicker fur, to the end of breeding long-hairs. Or two with different hair color, or two plants with sweeter fruit, or any other preferred trait. This is how we made the many species of domesticated cows, sheep, goats, chickens, and horses from wilder ancestral animals. This is how we made corn out of the wild grass *teosinte*; made apples bigger and sweeter, in over 7,000 varieties; made 30,000 different kinds of rose, in a wide range of colors, scents, and numerous other features as well.[95]

The first time we humans seriously engaged in this appears to have been with wolves. Turning wolves into dogs may have originally been

---

[95] Ratliff, Evan. "Taming the Wild." *National Geographic Magazine*. March 2011.

a synthesis of *natural* and *artificial* selection. The current dominant theory is that some wolves self-selected. The thought is that the first creatures along these lines were those who, naturally, were less skittish, less uncomfortable with human proximity, and therefore more easily tempted to get closer to human encampments, wherein they could gain greater access to yummy treats. It is entirely plausible that such self-selected wolf-dogs would benefit from, amongst other things, the scraps and leftovers of the mega-fauna creatures which our ancestors were so busy eating into extinction. And thus was born the 'doggy bag'.

Such individuals tended to get closer and closer to human encampments. They self-selected, initiating the very process which, over time, we then took so much further, becoming best of buddies as dogs and humans tend to do. Subsequent artificial selection gave us racers like salukis and greyhounds, sled pullers like huskies, bull-fighting bulldogs, and everything from Chihuahuas to Great Danes, Bull Mastiffs to Rat Terriers, Poodles to Pomeranians. Humans and canines have mutual interests, as well as similar socio-emotional natures. So, getting us together was, well... natural.

Well before I encountered the works of Darwin or Dawkins, Hitchens or Harris, before I had read a word of Arthur Schopenhauer or David Hume, and before the copious number of other philosophers, scientists and scholars from whom I have learned, there was Teddy. Teddy was the first philosopher, the first thinker, that I ever knew. She was also my mom.[96]

Teddy had many 'theories.' It was a running family joke. At least once or twice a day, Teddy could be counted on to exclaim "I have a theory...", and off she went, elaborating and expounding upon one

---

[96] Winnifred Theodora Rehand Neiblum

topic or another. About this or about that. I always paid attention, though. She was often quite insightful.

Teddy the philosopher once queried, as we were driving into view of a large, towering American city, as to why the human assemblage before us was considered *artificial*, while the ant's colonies by the side of the road, or the termites air-conditioned edifice towering above the African savannah, were considered to be qualitatively distinct, entirely *natural* phenomena. I still think this an insightful and provocative query. Why was a bird's nest or a beehive not artificial as well? Why was New York City 'unnatural'? When she posed the question to me like that, I agreed that the distinction itself seemed somewhat contrived, 'exceptionalist' in some manner. Perhaps even a tad artificial itself. Wait… Is that irony? Or paradox?

Ants like the leafcutter are in fact an excellent example of the many species which have evolved *cultivated mutualism*, which looks an awful lot like what we call *artificial selection* when human beings practice it. Cultivated mutualism is when one species evolves to practice the intentional cultivation of other organisms, from which both derive some form of benefit. We cultivate crops and herd livestock, as a part of our own unique survive-and-reproduce skillset and strategy. But, so too do the leafcutter ants.

There are a minimum of 240 species of *attine* ants. These are various forms of what we call the leafcutter type. The leafcutter harvest chunks of leafy detritus, take these back to specific rooms in their underground cities, chew them into pulp. They combine their own excrement into the mix, just as we combine various animal excretions to make our own garden fertilizers. (For my own gardening needs, my personal favorite, much to the olfactory dismay of my wife and kids, is chicken manure.) The result of all this work is a nutrient rich food source which nurtures the ants. But cultivated mutualism benefits both species involved. The fungus, for its part, benefits because that diligent and hardworking paradigm of industriousness, the marvelous ant, is entirely devoted to creating and sustaining the very conditions upon which it most prodigiously thrives.

The question which philosopher Teddy brought to the fore was this: why is theirs *natural*, while ours is described as *artificial?* The two are generally considered as qualitatively distinct. They are different things. But is this true? Or merely another example of our pseudoscientific exceptionalist bias, our bad habit of thinking ourselves outside nature. It is entirely plausible that the name, concept, and designation 'artificial' reinforces our Abrahamic pseudoscientific stereotype of *Homo sapiens* as separate from nature. The person indoctrinated in Abrahamic modes of thought has a quick and ready answer to Teddy's question: our cities are different because we are not animals, but in fact a distinct and superior type of being.

But maybe they're wrong.

Chapter 8

Gould's Second Stage:
Progress, Evolution, & Human
Exceptionalism

This chapter is an extended version of an essay originally featured in Free Inquiry Magazine under the same title (August/September 2019; Volume 39, No. 5).

Our self-conception is very important. The way we understand ourselves, as a species, here on this planet, the *who we are* and the *why we are here*, our overall sense of how we human beings fit into the whole cosmic scheme of things, it really matters. Whether subconscious or conscious, accurate or false, our subjective worldview determines much about how we live. It shapes the way we interact with our fellow humans. Equally important, it affects how we interact with the other animals, the billions of living creatures with whom we share this planet in a complex state of mutual interdependence, beings to whom we are literally related as distant cousins, if not brothers or sisters.

Human exceptionalism refers to our sense of ourselves as separate from, and superior to, the rest of nature. This view is both *false* and *problematic*. False, because it is not accurate or correct in any sense to say that human beings, or our preferred evolutionary traits, are superior to any other evolved beings or their traits. Human superiority is but a pseudoscientific claim rooted in human exceptionalist biases, not a scientific claim rooted in facts, evidence, or any particular scientific theory. By problematic, I mean that the arrogance and hubris inherent within the exceptionalist perspective may well be causally connected to such worldly problems as climate change, human-exacerbated global warming, pollution in its many forms, rising extinction rates, and our overall environmentally rapine approach to survival on this planet.

Instead of coming up with sexy plans to run off and colonize Mars, like the Mad Hatter and his retinue, racing from soiled place to clean, as if we might somehow outrun our own short-sighted, destructive inclinations, rather we should cultivate a deep and abiding appreciation for the awesome little blue, green, and white marble upon which all the multifarious forms of life which we have ever known have been born, lived, and died, and within which we ourselves sprang into self-conscious existence. Better we develop a self-awareness rooted in a more accurate, post-Darwinian knowledge regarding our animal nature, our true nature, and embrace the challenge to become a self-aware, scientifically intelligent, peace loving, social animal which lives sustainably within an environmentally and socially harmonious civilization in the here and now. This is the great challenge facing humanity in our time, and perhaps the greatest, most potentially fulfilling challenge which we have indeed ever faced. Atheism and freedom from religion are, once again, front and center, pivotal aspects of this life-or-death concern.

Our understanding of human nature is changing, and in a progressive, improving sense. It's getting better, meaning increasingly accurate, modest, and sustainable. But there are impediments. Religions like Islam and Christianity, plausibly the most significant forces propping up and perpetuating human exceptionalism, represent serious obstacles to human progress. Yet, perhaps somewhat more surprisingly, human exceptionalism rears its ugly head in entirely secular, even scientific contexts. Becoming aware of all of this is a first step toward the cultivation of a more accurate, less destructive self-conception. With new thinking, new knowledge, and new beliefs come new behaviors, new actions, new choices and priorities. Like they say, the first step in solving a problem is becoming aware of the fact that you have one. We do. We have a problem, and its name is human exceptionalism.

The Roots of Human Exceptionalism

The late, great evolutionary biologist and science author Stephen Jay Gould saw the problem over 25 years ago:

> Evolution still floats in the limbo of our unwillingness to face the implications of Darwinism for the cosmic estate of Homo sapiens...All thinking people accept the biological fact of our descent from the animal world. But the second stage, mental accommodation toward pedestal smashing, has scarcely begun...we have managed to retain an interpretation of human importance scarcely different in many crucial respects from the exalted state we occupied as the supposed products of direct creation in god's image.
>
> – Stephen Jay Gould, 1995[97]

In this genuinely brilliant and insightful passage, Gould refers to our "interpretation of human importance" having remained essentially unchanged, in spite of everything we have learned about who and what we really are. He and I are talking about the same thing. He is talking about our 'self-conception,' and he is talking about human exceptionalism. How did we get this way?

It is so easy and tempting to go for the low hanging fruit of religion. But it's possible that human exceptionalism (H.E.) cannot be entirely blamed on the Abrahamic traditions of Christianity and

---

[97] Gould, Stephen J. *Dinosaur in a Haystack: Reflections in Natural History.* New York: Three Rivers Press, 1996.

Islam. There's some viable scientific evidence suggesting that H.E. thinking, much as with mankind's instinctive penchant for superstition and supernaturalism, may be hardwired into the human brain, that imperfect, not-so-intelligently designed, cognitive-bias-infested 3 pounds of grey goop in between our ears.

The brain of *Homo sapiens* is far from the precise reality detector we like to think it. It is fraught with oddities, quirks, and biases galore. As previously noted, a cognitive bias is simply an inclination on the part of our brain to interpret and respond to reality in a specific irrational manner. H.E. is just such a quirk. There is no objective meter or measure by which human beings, or human traits, are 'superior' to any other beings or traits. Yet we continue to believe that there is. Theory of Mind may be unique, unique to humans only perhaps. But unique and superior are not synonyms.

It makes sense that we have evolved this tendency toward H.E., to bias ourselves toward our fellow human beings. Our evolutionary lineage would have come to a rather speedy demise had we truly felt that, say, for example, all things 'lion' held value equal to our own. Rather than saving our children from the charging beast, what if our evolutionary forebears had instead recognized the lion's need to eat as cosmically equivalent to our offspring's need to not become lion food? That would have been the end of team human right then and there.

But our brain did not evolve to be such an objective truth detector. It evolved to be as it is because it aids us in survival and successful reproduction. Further, it was far from intelligently designed to do so, but was rather the result of a far more haphazard, thoughtless, Mac-Gyver-style process of opportunistic jerry-rigging than most people realize or fully comprehend. Our brain was not naturally designed - i.e., did not evolve - to do science, but more so to aid us in effective survival and reproduction. Scientific thinking requires some cultivation, as well as a bit of a step back from our instinctive predilections.

We have evolved to be naturally inclined toward H.E. But that is not the end of the matter. As we have seen, some instincts are more robust, more undeniable, than others. Some cannot be overcome, some can with great effort, still others with relative ease. Knowledge can empower us to override instinct in some instances. Education consistently empowers people to overcome religion, in spite of religion's natural, instinctive roots in the human mind. That some people are atheist while others are not, that some remain celibate, or abstain from sugary foods – these all attest to differing abilities to override natural instincts. Such abilities are significantly affected by upbringing, education, knowledge, and a host of other variables. We may tend to believe the biased things which our H.E.-inclined brain tells us. Yet we are also able to counter such beliefs, to strive for greater objectivity, given sufficient reasons and alternatives. Nature is not necessarily destiny.

And knowledge is power. Knowing that H.E. represents an inaccurate view, a cognitive bias, or that it may be causing real world problems, empowers me to resist its call. Knowing H.E. is directly implicated in our rapine relationship with planet Earth likewise inclines me to be increasingly aware of such effects, and to exercise my will in response. Becoming the 'stewards' many of us understand our current role to be, it behooves us to override natural instincts which we evolved in far different environmental contexts than the present, to see our existence within earthly environs in a new and different light.

H.E. predates the religious traditions, and represents an evolved stratagem, an instinctive belief or cognitive bias hard wired into the human brain. The context in which this was particularly beneficial was extremely different from our own. Contrary to the common, new-agey, woo-woo notion that we will find a more sustainable way of living by harkening back to some supposed utopian ideal of the noble savage, at one with the birds and the bees and the rivers and the trees, through increased spirituality, the more obvious, less dubious path would actually entail its polar opposite: an enthusiastic rebuke of religion and other non-rational, instinctive predilections, such as human exceptionalism, in the name of reason, knowledge, and science.

The Human Exceptionalist Narrative

All that being said, the Abrahamic religions of Islam and Christianity do not get off the hook that easily. If they are not the cause of H.E. thinking, they nonetheless bear the lion's share of responsibility for its promotion and perpetuation. Partially this is because, when you combine the rapidly growing number of Muslims with the already immense number of Christians, you're talking about over half the world's population. Plus, it's also the case that, for a variety of reasons, these combined Abrahamic traditions have had an outsized influence upon the rest of the world.

These dogmatic religious traditions, concepts, and general perspectives have spread globally as a result of a variety of phenomena: as previously touched upon, it starts with simple geographic centrality; the success and dominance of a series of Mediterranean empires such as the Sumerian, Egyptian, Greek, and Roman; the Silk Road and over a millennium of world commerce; the missionary conversion imperative of both Christianity and Islam; the reach of modern-day petroleum powers; and last, but certainly not least, the flagrantly materialistic imperialism of Christianity-infused Europe and, ultimately, the extremely Christian and imperialistic United States of America as well.

Though the AIC may not themselves be the cause, they are nonetheless guilty of perpetuating and promoting the H.E. narrative. Embedded within this we find an overarching dualistic worldview, one which interprets and understands the cosmos in terms of two distinct

191

realms: the natural and the supernatural. This plays an essential role in the continuing historic dominance of human exceptionalism.

Such dualism is highly problematic, even for those of us who no longer adhere to these religious traditions. We associate our 'lower' traits, our fart jokes or dangerous liaisons, our bodily functions and fluids, with the natural and the beastly. Yet we are less likely to think of the 'higher' traits as equally of the animal. Justice is an excellent example. The ants have their complex of antennae touching, chemical communication, and pheromones, all of which evolved because, being eusocial creatures like us, such teamwork aids them in their survival and successful reproduction. Likewise, we human beings have justice, as well as morality, ethics, compassion, and altruism.

Justice, as astounding a phenomenon as it is, would not even exist but for the evolution of animals like us. It is nothing more than an aspect of our evolutionary repertoire. Yet we are still prone to the dualistic thought hangover of seeing poop, pee, and boogers as animal, while failing to recognize that equally of the animal is the objective rule of law, the treatment of all men and women as equals under the law, or any of the other finer embodiments of justice toward which our species genuinely aspires, even while we so often fall short of our intended mark and high ideals.

Of purely animal making are the ACLU, Amnesty International, Doctors Without Borders, the United Nations, and the United Nations Declaration of Human Rights. We lament our 'beastly' nature when we recognize the death penalty as uncivilized, yet fail to give equal credit to our animal roots when presented with the factual reality that it is we humans who have legally banned the death penalty in 108 nations so far around the world. This, too, was of the purely animal.

Similarly with the artwork of Bach and Beethoven, or Lennon and McCartney, the Sistine Chapel, The Burj Khalifa, Michaelangelo's *David*, anything by Monet, or Van Gogh, or Da Vinci, or the astounding technological marvel that is an aircraft carrier, or our landing on the moon, or solar energy, or even just our ability to cooperatively handle a four-way intersection, not to mention the collected works of Dawkins, Dennett, Hitchens, and Harris. Pick your own favorite amazing creative or brilliant person, invention, discovery, creation, and there you have it. Products of the human animal one and all.

We are a truly conflicted animal, indeed. We combine all of this within us, ordinarily interpreted as a touch of the animal combined with a touch of the divine. But the religious bifurcation which attempts to interpret our wide-ranging temperaments and talents in terms of the lowly natural versus the divine supernatural is errant nonsense and misguided pseudoscience. And how we understand ourselves matters, as I have said. We understand our true nature far less when we see our positive and negative attributes as the result of a supernatural schism. Yet, again, we understand ourselves far better when we do so in a naturalistic light, in light of evolution, and in a manner consistent with reason and the sciences.

The Great Chain of Being

Abrahamic dualism has long ruled the roost. It represents by far the greatest single source of pseudoscientific misunderstanding and problematic misconceptions of the real world, including human nature. And one of the most influential and all pervasive of these pseudoscientific misconceptions is the hierarchic concept of the fundamental structure of our cosmos known as the Great Chain of Being (GCB). For millennia, some variation on this fundamental mode of understanding has served as a model for the known universe, and for the order in which all beings have their existence.

Generally imagined as a stairway to heaven, a climbing ladder, or a hierarchic triangle, the GCB starts with the Abrahamic god at the top. Below him, yet still within the realm of the 'divine,' are the other supernatural beings, such as angels or demons (fallen angels).

Below these, on the dividing line between the two realms, one foot ensconced equally in each, is man (sexist, yes, but historically accurate). Below man is the lesser, lower, natural realm, beginning with the 'higher' animals. In the circular, tautological manner of human exceptionalist thought, animals are considered higher simply because they are, for one reason or another, considered more like we humans. Generally, the mammals. Below these are reptiles, then amphibians, down to insects, then plants, et cetera. You get the gist.

The three key points which come from an understanding of the central role which variations on this GCB played in human knowledge are:

- Those under the sway of the AIC have long understood the cosmos dualistically.
- This dualistic model is necessarily hierarchic and implies value judgment:
  - Superior: The supernatural = the sacred, the divine, the good, the higher.
  - Inferior: The natural = the profane, the lowly, the beastly, the worldly.
- In this longstanding, pseudoscientific model of the cosmos, we humans, alone in all of nature, partake of divinity.

Of significant, if slightly tangential interest, is the fact that this model, the GCB, and its evaluative, judgmental conception of everything, was also applied to inter-human relations, serving to justify all manner of social oppression and inequality. This hierarchic model served to rationalize worldly authoritarianism, as in the so-called 'divine right of kings.' It also justified and encouraged the oppression of people based solely upon hierarchic conceptions of *race, ethnicity, class, sex,* and *gender.*

For example, in many iterations, the 'man' straddling the dividing line between the natural and supernatural was, quite literally, male in gender. Meanwhile, women and other marginalized groups were placed below this all-important dividing line. They were conceived and treated as lesser beings in value, as less than human. Based upon the Great Chain of Being's hierarchic understanding of the cosmos, and of all living beings, women and assorted other Out Group members were deemed inferior to the dominant males of the In Group. Based upon entirely pseudoscientific justifications, such persons, despite making up the literal majority of all humanity, were seen as inherently inferior in one respect or another, and were treated like anything from second-class citizens, all the way down to literal 'things,' mere objects that were the property or possessions of the more elite members of human society.

Getting Darwin Wrong: Human Exceptionalism

Charles Darwin's *On the Origin of Species* represented a true and real revolution in our self-conception. Uncle Charley gave us a new and improved origin story, one rooted squarely in scientific epistemology, which had itself been producing some prodigious results for a while. And yet, using a handy-dandy little dialectic associated with his contemporary Friedrich Hegel, we can show precisely where and how a fundamental derailment occurred in our understanding of the process of evolution, and thereby of our own true nature, that of other life forms, as well as of our relationship with them.

Hegelian dialectic is a very useful tool for understanding historical progress, the kind of progress I have been talking about. It simply refers to our recognizing the three following steps, and the subsequently dynamic nature of our ideas, our history, and of human knowledge itself.

Thesis: an idea or understanding regarding the true nature of a given phenomenon, of how it works, or how it came to be, for example.

Anti-thesis: a new idea, which calls the original thesis into doubt, suggesting a flaw or weakness in the original conception, i.e., the thesis.

Synthesis: a new and original idea regarding the phenomenon under consideration, this one takes the anti-thesis into account, and reconciles it in a new, improved, better model, explanation, or understanding, a new thesis which improves upon or replaces the original.

This synthesis then becomes the new model, the new thesis. As the reigning theory, it then becomes susceptible to new challenges, new observations, new anti-theses. As such, the process continues on, in perpetuity. This is the same phenomenon which was considered in the previous chapter when I talked about how our best explanatory models are open-ended, or 'probabilistic.' This Hegelian dialectic is also another way of describing what I am talking about when I argue that our definitive evolutionary trait is our uniquely accretive and mutualistic form of intelligence.

Let's take a look at a familiar example from history to illustrate how it all works. For centuries before Darwin, it had become common to believe in the *thesis* that the sun and planets revolved around the earth. The church was very happy to perpetuate this geocentric conception of the heavens, as both equally emphasized a similarly anthropocentric perspective. The earth, ergo man, was at the literal center of the universe. Everything revolved around man, and not just figuratively, symbolically, or allegorically. Over time, however, enough worldly evidence accumulated to cast increasing doubt amongst the learned regarding the validity of the geocentric thesis.

These scientific objections and difficulties represented a growing *anti-thesis*, which served to challenge, undermine, or weaken the geocentric model. As a result of this clash between the thesis and the anti-thesis, a different theory came to mind, famously including the minds of such luminaries as Copernicus and Galileo. The new, replacement understanding they came up with represented the *synthesis*. It met the objections of the anti-thesis, and thereby offered a new, original, more cogent explanation for the phenomenon under consideration, in this case our planet, our solar system, and our planet's relations with the rest of the cosmos.

This synthesis was the heliocentric model, in which the earth and other planets all revolve around the sun. Copernicus and others helped us to grasp that we were not the center of the universe, that everything did not revolve around us. It was several hundred years down the road before Darwin essentially did more of the same, further displacing human beings from our self-proclaimed centrality, our exceptionalist assumption that we were special in god's eyes, were made in his image, and were in fact what it's all about. Darwin did with animal minds and bodies what Copernicus, Galileo, and others did in terms of the planets and stars. They all served to inform us that we were not the center of the universe, move us closer to an evidence-based, more humble and accurate understanding of humanity's standing and status within the larger cosmic schema.

Charles Darwin represented a big win for scientific epistemology, in both form and content. In form, in that his work served to strengthen the case for reason, and for naturalistic, evidence-based methods of acquiring knowledge, as opposed to religious knowledge, with its antiquated emphasis upon faith, scripture, tradition, and authority. Rather than the natural realm being one which distracted us from the superior divine, from important things like god's plan or our impending afterlife, this new approach demonstrated that naturalistic explanations held great promise indeed. In terms of content, in that this new origin story presented an extremely compelling case that we humans are 'mere' animals ourselves, related to all the others, interdependent within the greater natural whole, and neither god nor any other supernatural forces had anything to do with it all.

Still, some 150 years down the road, the ramifications of this revolutionary new self-conception have failed to crystallize in the minds of most of humanity. It is not hard to grasp why those who remain under the direct sway of the Abrahamic religions remain stuck in past conceptions, of course. But how are we to understand the millions of secular, humanist, and even scientific minds who continue to misconstrue Darwin's brilliant naturalistic explanation? The process of evolution continues to be widely misunderstood. And much of the problem stems directly from human exceptionalism. Let's jump back to the Hegelian dialectic to illustrate this important historic misstep.

The Great Chain of Being represented a longstanding thesis, a basic model of the universe. The anti-thesis to this position consisted of a growing body of naturalistic facts and data which cast increasing doubt upon our origins as described in scripture and religious tradition. Darwin's Origin's embraced these misgivings, offering explanations in such complete and total accord with observations of the natural world that their validity could scarcely be reasonably denied. His work was an act of creation, a new and complete picture of life which itself should have become the subsequent synthesis.

But for most it did not. Through a combination of entrenchment in religious thought, and the power of H.E. thinking in and of itself, the faulty synthesis which many embraced at the time, and still do today, was much more akin to that famously depicted in scientific illustrator Ernst Haeckl's *Tree of Life*.

PEDIGREE OF MAN.

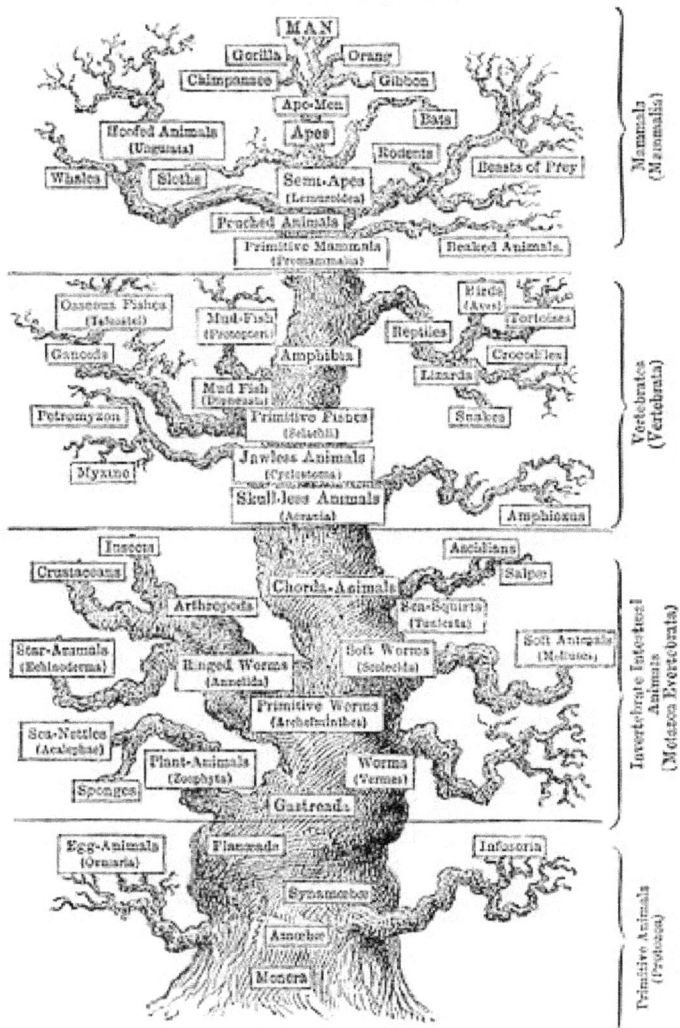

MAN

Gorilla   Orang

Chimpanzee   Gibbon

Ape-Men

Apes   Bats

Hoofed Animals (Ungulata)   Rodents

Whales   Sloths   Semi-Apes (Lemaroidea)   Beasts of Prey

Pouched Animals

Primitive Mammals (Promammalia)   Beaked Animals

Mammals (Mammalia)

Osseous Fishes (Teleostei)   Mud-Fish (Protopteri)   Birds (Aves)   Tortoises

Ganoids   Amphibia   Reptiles   Crocodiles

Mud Fish (Dipneusta)   Lizards

Petromyzon   Primitive Fishes (Selachii)   Snakes

Jawless Animals (Cyclostoma)

Myxine   Skull-less Animals (Acrania)   Amphioxus

Vertebrates (Vertebrata)

Insects   Ascidians

Crustaceans   Chorda-Animals   Salpæ

Arthropoda   Sea-Squirts (Tunicata)

Star-Animals (Echinoderma)   Soft Worms (Scolecida)   Soft Animals (Mollusca)

Ringed Worms (Annelida)

Sea-Nettles (Acalephae)   Primitive Worms (Archelminthea)

Sponges   Plant-Animals (Zoophyta)   Worms (Vermes)

Gastreada

Invertebrate Intestinal Animals (Metazoa Evertebrata)

Egg-Animals (Ovularia)   Planæada   Infusoria

Synamoeba

Amoeba

Monera

Primitive Animals (Protozoa)

Pedigree of Man, Ernst Haeckel, 1879

199

Here we can plainly see that everything takes place within an undivided, entirely whole natural cosmos, with zero supernatural beings or forces whatsoever. We have eradicated religious dualism. There are no gods or supernatural elements, no divine realm of any kind. As such, this constitutes some very real progress, and a genuine win for science.

Science: 1

Religion: 0

However, at one and the same time, the hierarchic and judgmental element, so definitive of both the Abrahamic and H.E. worldview, remained entirely intact. The gods had been rendered moot. Yet the model still retained a higher and a lower, a superior and an inferior. What remained was nothing more than blatant, undisguised human exceptionalism, untethered from its supernatural, religious moorings, but still large and in charge, still self-perpetuating through an inaccurate and judgmental misinterpretation of Darwin's theory of evolution. This is where it becomes undeniable that Yahweh and Allah had really been but surrogates for we human beings all along, much like Dorothy's humbug wizard, hiding behind his curtain in the merry old Land of Oz.

By the time of Charles Darwin, smack dab in the very center of this under-appreciated revolutionary epoch in human history, the flow of incoming evidence, combined with the increasing respect with which naturalistic explanations had come to be regarded, encouraged the growth of doubts in the minds of the learned, doubts as to the validity of the old thesis, the Great Chain of Being. Darwin's revolutionary work should have inspired us to create a new, value-neutral synthesis. But our human exceptionalist bias skewed our interpretation of Darwin toward a fallacious hierarchic and evaluative understanding of the process of evolution, one in which:[98]

> ...we have managed to retain an interpretation of human importance scarcely different in many crucial respects from the exalted state we occupied as the supposed products of direct creation in god's image.

Evolution and Progress are Not Synonyms!

One of the most fundamental expressions of this major historic misstep is our tendency to conflate *progress* and *evolution*. Though many tend to think so, the truth of the matter is that progress and evolution are *not* synonyms. This has genuinely important ramifications for our understanding of human progress itself, for the patterns within human history, and simultaneously for our understanding of the biological process of evolution responsible for all life that we know of, including, most importantly, our very own. For human nature itself.

We tend to interpret evolution as an improvement process and very much a real kind of progress, with us at its apex. This conflation represents an inaccurate interpretation of Darwin with undeniable roots in our H.E. biases. Cultivating a more accurate understanding of human nature, with an emphasis upon the distinction between evolution and progress, is an important first step toward freeing ourselves from the exceptionalist biases which separate us from the very world in which we live.

Evolution, the process of natural selection, is an immediate response to environmental variables, and as such is both context dependent and non-linear. The value of any given mutation is entirely context dependent. It may work, and if it does, it's likely to spread into subsequent generations. Or it may not, in which case it won't.

---

[98] Gould, *Dinosaur in a Haystack*, 1996.

Environment and context decide, and these are some wildly malleable and variable factors. But there is never a goal, direction or purpose to evolutionary change, no blueprint, design, or plan, contrary to common thought and belief. Governing physical laws, yes. Of course. Plan, direction, or design? No. Not for evolution.

When looking at living beings, exemplars of the evolutionary process, we have historically tended to emphasize that which supports our H.E. biases, which place us in the finest of lights. Look how big our brains are! Look how fast they got that way! Unfortunately, we human beings are known to sometimes do our science cafeteria style. If you do a little digging, you will soon notice the biases at work. For example, it is common knowledge that human beings have relatively big brains. Yet most grown adults are singularly unaware of the fact that the correlation between brain size and intelligence[99] is dubious at best. The brain of any given African elephant or sperm whale is far larger than our own.

We tend to emphasize those examples which perpetuate the idea of evolution being an improvement process, such as the increasing speed of the cheetah and impala, and their so-called evolutionary arms race. We pay far less attention to the fact that physical limitations always bring any such 'improvements' to a halt. The impala can only run so fast. The cheetah only so long. At some point the Impala shifts to zigs and zags, or leaps and bounds. The whole speed racer analogy comes to a screeching halt, so to speak. We choose to emphasize those aspects which best feed our sense of self-importance, but at the expense of oversimplifying the complex realities of the evolutionary process. And, as with religious thought, it is often at the expense of human knowledge.

---

[99] The meaning of 'intelligence' itself is also quite often the result of a great deal of cafeteria style cherry picking.

Another example. Hundreds of millions of years ago, it behooved one of our ancestors to move from the water onto the land. H.E. inclines us to exaggerate the importance of this transition in the larger story of life. There is a tendency to think of this as momentous, of great significance, to think of this as *the* path, as in the path which life took, or to think of this one step as an improvement in some important sense, a highly significant step in humanity's all-important march toward our great destiny.

But the vast majority of living organisms did not leave the water. Life merely went on as before, the vast bulk of it still in the oceans, and in its myriad, and continually evolving forms. It was an extremely small number which changed, a number whose import we overemphasize simply because they include our direct ancestors. Yet we tend to think that life started in water because it had to, but moving to land was an important *improvement*, a form of progress. This is an example of the skewed eye which we apply to the processes involved.

If evolution is progressive, why, then, are there still analogues to all sorts of 'primitive' forms, and in such grand abundance, for that matter? Because evolution is not progress. There is a tendency toward increased complexity. This is because nature is good at addition, but sucks at subtraction. But, importantly, complexity and improvement are also not synonyms, not at all the same thing. If evolution were an improvement process, we would look around us at the world today and see 'perfected' versions of everything: only the 'best' eyes, wings, feet, and brains. But this is an entirely ludicrous concept. The 'best' eye means something very different for a dragonfly and a dugong, a human versus an octopus, or a tarantula and a peregrine falcon.

What we perceive when we investigate the world around us are actually a plethora of excellent stand-ins, analogues to nearly *every stage in the evolutionary process*, be it the development of eyeballs, feathers, or intelligence. For example, current thinking on the origins of flight[100] suggests both top-down and bottom-up models of equal validity. But we do not merely have the final result of this 'perfecting process' around today.

We have a variety of top-down exemplars, literally dozens of species including mammals, reptiles and more, floating, flapping and falling slowly from their canopies and cliffsides, increasingly wide-spreading membranes stretching between digits or limbs, assisting them in their safely decelerated descent, and thereby aiding them in their subsequent attacks upon prey and/or escape from predators back up in the heights.

At the same time, we also have numerous analogues of the bottom-up theory, including a covey of quail-like birds who need but an evolutionary nudge or two more to make the jump from accelerated leapers to full-blown aerial acrobats, as their cousins the starlings or sparrows are.

Or, consider what wonderful gap fillers the hippo, the crocodile, the manatee, and the dugong would all make if we placed them in a lineup, filling in some allegedly missing link between the whales and their land-dwelling predecessors. Around our world today we can see it all, including some of the most ancient, simplistic, or microscopic of organisms. Why is that? Because evolution and progress are like apples and oranges: two very different kinds of things.

Evolution is not progress. Unfortunately, due to the exceptionalist tint upon the epistemological glasses through which we view the cosmo-scape, many people fail to recognize this basic truth. Unlike evolution, progress *is* very much a goal-oriented, linear, directional process, describing improvement. Whereas evolution is a directionless

---

[100] Ritchison, Gary. "Origin of Flight." Lecture: Bird flight, n.d. Lecture notes available at: http://people.eku.edu/ritchisong/554notes2.html

contextual response, progress entails an ideal, an end point, and thereby necessarily a direction in which to move.

For example, the move from ignorance to knowledge is a form of progress. Improving our understanding of any given phenomenon, such as our planet, the solar system, or the nature of living organisms, is an example of a kind of progress. We tend to move incrementally from ignorance toward improved understanding, under the right circumstances at least.

Empty spaces in human knowledge were for millennia filled by guess work, instinct, wishful thinking, and, of course, the supernatural, in the process famously referred to as the god of the gaps. These problematic answers which religion has systematically employed to quench our thirst for knowledge have been, and still are being, systematically replaced over time, by increasingly evidence-based, empirical, science friendly answers. As described in the previous chapters, the pace of this progress has increased over the last several centuries.

Replacing supernatural explanations with falsifiable and more probable ones represents some major improvement. Because of the cumulative nature of human knowledge, scientific explanations, which allow us to test and tweak and add to our knowledge, to build upon it, extend it, apply it, learn from it, answers which allow for anti-thesis and synthesis, are far superior to those of the ancient past. The non-falsifiable fillers of old served to problematically bring human knowledge to a standstill, because they cannot be falsified, tested, improved, or built upon in the same constructive, progressive manner. As a result, you get a 1,000 year-long epoch known as the Dark Ages.

Tellingly, this replacement of religious answers with rational, falsifiable, scientific answers never goes in the reverse direction. Scientific answers replace religious ones. But it never goes the other way around. The only thing which can replace a scientific answer, and usually does, is a *better* scientific answer. The source of humanity's progress is this unique form of accretive, mutualistic, applicable intelligence. *Homo sapiens* is the learning animal. Learning is an evolved trait which very much defines humans.

Kevin Laland, in 2017's *Darwin's Unfinished Symphony*, notes this under-recognized cumulative and mutualistic character of human intelligence.[101] What Laland calls *culture* I describe as our evolved capacity for *accretive* and *mutualistic* intelligence, but what we are talking about is essentially the same thing.

> By 'culture' I mean the extensive accumulation of shared, learned knowledge, and iterative improvements in technology over time. Humanity's success is sometimes accredited to our cleverness, but culture is actually what makes us smart. Intelligence is not irrelevant of course, but what singles out our species is an ability to pool our insights and knowledge, and build on each other's solutions. New technology has little to do with a lone inventor figuring out a problem on their own; virtually all innovation is a reworking or refinement of existing technology.

Human intelligence takes a tribe (mutualism), and it takes time (accretion). My dream '67 Ford Mustang convertible required hundreds of thousands, probably millions of incremental steps to come to fruition. Human knowledge, intelligence, and creativity, and of course progress itself, are characterized by slow, yet steady, long-term, incremental changes, somewhat analogous with our process of biological evolution in this singular regard.

None of this is limited to mere technological innovation. Rather, it is the entirety of all human knowledge which benefits from our evolved capacities for accumulating and sharing what we learn, think, believe, and know. The progress from a geocentric to a heliocentric

---

[101] Laland, Kevin N. *Darwin's Unfinished Symphony: How Culture Made the Human Mind.* Princeton University Press, 2017.

model of the solar system served as but one example. Darwin's new and improved origin story is another. But so too is our extremely important progress toward nonviolence, equal rights, justice, environmental sustainability, and the rule of law. People often describe this kind of change as us 'evolving,' which is both inaccurate and extremely misleading. It is far more accurate to describe it in terms of an improvement process, to call it progress.

Increasingly, when freed from indoctrination and focused instead upon education, it is indeed the case that we know more, and we know better. This is a genuine form of human progress.

The cumulative, communal quality of human knowledge enables us to synthesize, to create, to progress. But this is a cultural phenomenon, not a biological one. Evolution is strictly a biological phenomenon, whereas progress is cultural. Evolution endows us with specific traits, such as our brain, and human intelligence, whereas progress is a result of the functioning of such traits. Progress shifts the emphasis from a *biological* paradigm to a *cultural* paradigm.

Human and Divine intelligence

From the perspective of our species, the human mind is truly the point of it all. We are biased toward ourselves. That's all well and good. We shouldn't expect evolution would do otherwise. But it then behooves us to take this bias into account regarding our ability to know the truth of things. We *feel* like the center of the universe. But we *know* that we're not. That is an extremely important distinction. We need to identify and understand the nature of human exceptionalism in order to properly address its significant epistemological implications, to modify and adjust our response and understanding accordingly.

There are other examples of this kind of epistemological stumbling block. We do not think in terms of deep time, but instead suffer an instinctive temporal bias. We think of our now, the present moment or epoch, in a grossly disproportionate manner. Similarly, we struggle to overcome spatial biases, in which our location, or the earth, or our galaxy even, loom larger than the rest, remain of greater significance in our understanding, despite our ever-increasing knowledge of our cosmically humble status, our growing understanding that we are merely one of many, that we are not the center or the reason for it all. In terms of evolution and of life, we have only recently begun to take seriously the likely prospect that we, meaning either earthly, sentient, or conscious life, are but one of many life forms to populate the vast cosmos. It looks increasingly likely that we are but one of many differing forms of intelligence as well.

We struggle to overcome our belief that the human brain is the apex of a creative, progressive process, in some sense the best of all of nature's creations, and really, truly the whole point of it all. The truth of the matter is that we believe such things merely because of instinctive biases evolved into the human brain. We believe them despite our reason, not because of our reason.

The strictest application of our reasoning capacities actually informs us that the human brain/mind may not necessarily be the astounding, amazing phenomenon which our biases suggest, nor which the linear, improvement-model pseudoscientific mis-understanding of evolution suggests. The truth is that the human brain is problematic in multiple respects. Obviously, these include its numerous quirks and biases, the many ways in which it does not function ideally, or rationally. But problems with the human brain also include things like the huge amount of energy required to keep them functioning, and the numerous problems associated with our being post-natal, learning-based animals, including our many years of immaturity and dependence, as well as our ongoing vulnerability to such forces as indoctrination and coercion.

Our giant brain is the result of a very recent 'experiment' on natures behalf. This makes it unique, indeed. But it also makes it of dubious, somewhat untested value, evolutionarily speaking. Human brains and human intelligence may seem like the cat's meow to us, or perhaps the bee's knees? But the truth is, the jury's still out on this one.

Another instantiation of H.E., and of our tendency to adulate human intelligence, humanity has long imagined the creator of the universe to possess human-like intelligence, imagined that this is one of his fundamental attributes. Every culture has created deities which are imagined in this particular likeness, to be like us in this key respect. Even non-theists fall victim to the belief that there must be some form of intelligence behind things, an intelligence which caused or causes everything we know – ourselves, our world, this universe. Perhaps we are all merely taking place within an intelligent being's fever dream or imagination; or merely a simulation being run by an intelligent being; or it's all about artificial intelligence in some sense or another.

Thinking in this way is once again a kind of reversal of causality. Intelligence is an evolved trait of animals. It most certainly did not pre-date the existence of animals. It is an *effect* of life, not a *cause*. In yet another example of epistemological inversion, we have once again placed the cart before the horse. Intelligence, so far as all of the evidence suggests, is merely one amongst many evolved traits of biological organisms. We have no good reason to think it anything more. In fact, we think of it as so much grander and more important and essential, all entirely and merely because of human exceptionalist biases and instincts alone.

Intelligence did not precede the evolution of such beings as possess it – be they canids, rats, chimpanzees, *Homo sapiens*, marmosets, octopuses, ravens, gibbons, or those very cetaceans who were, before our recent appearance on the scene, the more intelligent animals on this planet, by far, and for far, far longer, than our brief tenure has thus far lasted. Intelligence is merely one of many traits which some creatures have evolved because it aids them in survival and successful reproduction. No more, nor less. It certainly does not predate the evolution of such beings as eventually evolved the trait.

Confusion may also stem from our understanding of complexity itself. One form of intelligence may be more complex than many other traits or organisms, perhaps more complex than the intelligence of other earthly animals. This is important because when many think of evolution as progressive, what they are really recognizing is that complexity tends to increase over time. But, as noted earlier, *complex* and *better* are also not synonyms. *Better* is a value judgment. But *complexity* is not a value judgment. Complexity is a matter of fact or, at least, should be. A given eye either has more parts than another, or it does not. The eye of the fly is more complex than that of the worm. It is a matter of fact that it has more parts, more going on, more interactive components. This does not make it *better* in any objective sense. It would certainly do the earthworm no good. It would, in fact, be quite the evolutionary handicap. Plus, an earthworm with huge, compound, fly eyes would be really, really creepy!

Why imagine that our particular type of brain would offer a bacterium, a mole, a tiger, or a starfish any adaptive advantage, would render it more 'fit'? We have no objective, rational reason to think human intelligence superior to any other evolved trait of any other being. Yet, such baseless claims continue to be asserted as if self-evident. The bottom line: *Describing human intelligence as superior is the very epitome of pseudoscience, and another erroneous manifestation of human exceptionalism.*

Advanced is In the Eye of the Beholder

H.E. is a projection of human values. The AIC's god was but a surrogate human all along, a supernatural entity which we created in our own image, and then projected across the heavens, thereby justifying human qualities, characteristics, and values on a cosmic scale. *But nature itself is entirely value-free.* We have absolutely zero evidence to think otherwise. Ramses, Rousseau, or your aunt Rose are no more nor less objectively valuable than a rhinoceros or a rhea (the ratite), raging rivers, rice or raisins, rads of radon, a rousing reception for those risqué reptiles Reese and Riley, or a regolith on Rhea (the rotating rock). Right?

Rrrrrrrr. Like a pirate. Where was I? Oh, yes…

Value requires a valuer.

What!?! What exactly does that little philosophical word salad even mean? It simply means that, for any given thing at all to have any kind of value at all, something has to value it. Superior, inferior, better, worse. Judging human intelligence to be superior or more advanced than others is a value judgment. But such words have no meaning, do not in fact exist, without a being which experiences that subjective state of valuing. There must be a valuer for any given thing to have a value.

When god, our grand, surrogate, uber valuer in the sky, is eliminated from the equation, the notion of things having objective or intrinsic value rightly evaporates. God was very useful to us. His supposed existence justified the projection of human values onto all of nature, allowed us to justify exceptionalist thinking.

Our tendency to judge human traits such as intelligence to be superior to others, or to other evolved traits, judging mammals to be superior to insects or fish: these are all values in the sense I am employing the term. They lack objective validity. They are true only in

211

the eyes of the valuer, in this case, the human animal. When we get honest about it, god's-eye values are really just human values, writ large across the cosmo-scape. No cosmic-scale valuers, no cosmic-scale values.

Think about the example I gave earlier of the eyes. The eyes of a spider or fly differ radically from the eyes of a falcon or a human being, which differ entirely from those of an octopus, from those of an eel, from those of the chameleon, etc. From the point of view of nature, none is intrinsically superior or inferior. Adaptive, evolutionary value is all about the interrelationship between an organism and its environs at a specific complex of space and time. The point of this example is that we tend to think about eyesight or eyes erroneously: 'the hawk has great vision,' 'the rhino has poor vision': that kind of thing. But the real deal is that our thinking is skewed by anthropocentrism and the imposition of self-referential values onto a valueless, value-neutral playing field. Valuing beings have values. Nature and evolution do not.

Homo sapiens traits are not self-evidently superior to the elephant's listening feet, the octopus's thinking arms, or the tardigrade's unparalleled resilience. We often think, write, and talk about human beings and our idealized traits as being more 'advanced' than those of others. Sometimes the terms *primitive* and *advanced* are used in the rigorously scientific sense, meaning simply *earlier* and *later,* respectively. But lay interpretations often problematically insert value judgment into the mix. This confusion illustrates the importance of distinguishing between progress and evolution. To think of a being or a trait as more 'advanced' than another in this sense is to apply one paradigm (the culture/progress paradigm), where it does not really apply, and where another paradigm (the biology/evolution paradigm) should in fact be employed. Round pegs and square holes.

If we wish to be accurate and truthful then, wish to have as real as possible an understanding of the true nature of things, *Homo sapiens*, and our various evolutionary traits, should be understood in the most value-neutral manner possible. Something more like this:

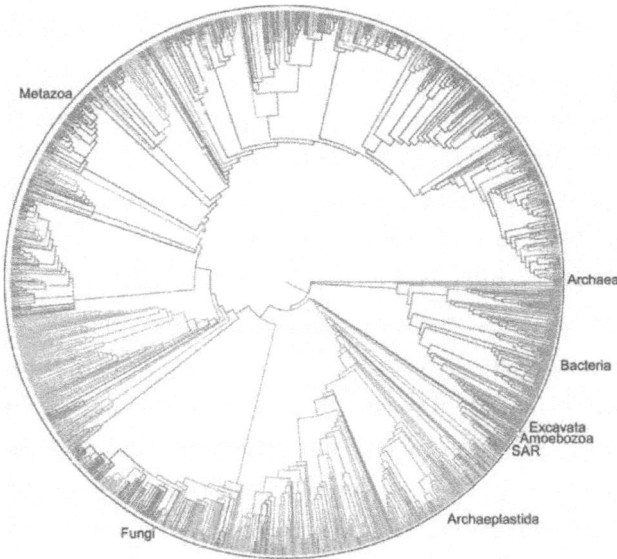

Value-neutral, nonhierarchic model of life.[102]

Clinging to Exceptionalism

In the middle of the twentieth century, we defined ourselves in part as the only creature which was capable of making and using tools. Then along came Jane Goodall. After she made popular knowledge of the fact that chimpanzees were creating and using tools, we began to see that other creatures were doing so as well.

---

[102] Hinchliff, Cody E., Stephen A. Smith, James F. Allman, Karen A. Cranston, et al., "Synthesis of Phylogeny and Taxonomy into a Comprehensive Tree of Life." PNAS 112, no. 41 (2015): 12764-12769.
https://www.pnas.org/doi/abs/10.1073/pnas.1423041112.

This was a very significant milestone in human progress, a noteworthy fissure in the mighty edifice of H.E., and a step forward in our science-based humility, our cultivation of a right and balanced view of human importance. We had been so confident in our sense of ourselves as separate and superior by virtue of our tool-making abilities that our scientists had even given one hominid branch the name 'handy man': *Homo habilis.*

Nonetheless, and even with no overt push from religion, many scientists still remained hell-bent upon defining us as separate and superior. They merely sought other avenues for the same mode of thought. Instead of tool use, there was self-awareness, which was considered the relevant attribute at one time. This led to all sorts of experiments employing the prodigious usage of red paint, brushes, and mirrors.

Some also believed that only human beings have 'genuine' emotions. Unfortunately, the central role of vague linchpin concepts such as 'genuine' render their claims somewhat pseudoscientific in nature, as they tend to inject an element of unfalsifiability into the argument. Elephant, porpoise, orca, or chimpanzee communication is similarly dismissed as not being 'real' or 'genuine' language, although again the criterion are often unclear or inexact. One problem with such claims is that we have thus far an extremely poor and under-developed understanding of their communication techniques, in all of the above examples. We lack knowledge.

A second is that those involved tend to anthropocentrically interpret their communications according to human criterion or metrics. Apparently, the bottlenose dolphin fails to qualify for the simple reason that the syntax so essential to human language is considered a requirement for all languages universally. Meanwhile the whole-body rumblings of elephants, communicated over miles, vibrations picked up by the receiver-like feet, transmitted to the brain through thick femur and tibia, these are summarily dismissed or minimized. So too are the decidedly complex songs of numerous bird species, or the thus far largely impenetrable echolocation of the various cetacean species. This despite the fact that we are largely incapable of interpreting or understanding most of it. Blue whales communicate over thousands of miles, across entire oceans, with sounds well below those our un-aided ears can hear.[103] But we know they do not include syntax. So, it can't be genuine, real language. Exceptionalist self-protection ensured.

Yet another example of our anthropocentric cherry picking is our default to *sizeism*. We exaggerate the importance of creatures within our general size range. Just as our narrow temporal focus inclines us to ignore the important lessons offered by a more deep time sensitive perspective, we tend to exaggerate the importance of creatures roughly within our own general size range, in defiance of the fact that the vast majority of life throughout the history of this planet has taken on con-siderably smaller, not to mention different, shapes and sizes indeed.

Relative to all the species which have ever existed on earth, we are actually very large. Scientists frequently refer to us as the dominant species on the planet. Our 'food chain' models emphasize sharks, wolves and other large-bodied predators. But our brains are surpris-ingly poor at gauging the relative importance of differing risk factors. The truth is that we are in far less danger from the 'dominant' lions, tigers and bears, than we are from mosquitoes or the veritable army of microscopic organisms which truly dominate life on this planet. If you wish to arm yourself before going to exotic, far-away lands, forget the gun, sword, or suit of armor: get yourself some immunization shots, pack a bar of soap, and some condoms. But, if you forget, don't worry about it. You'll just die, and then the similarly small-scaled posse of insects and microbes will come along and do their fantastically

---

[103] Yong, Ed. *An Immense World: How Animal Senses Reveal the Hidden Realms Around Us*. New York: Random House, 2022.

thorough cleanup job. With no help required from the lions and tigers and bears. Oh my!

Cultivating a less exaggerated sense of our own importance can only help us to better understand the true nature of things, including ourselves. An improved understanding of deep time and the principles of geology helped Darwin to move in this more accurate and objective direction. Our present circumstances, our 'Anthropocene'[104] epoch here on this one little planet, is but a very tiny blip in space and time. Contrary to being the point of it all, as the AIC have for so long told us, we are but an infinitesimal speck of stardust within the grand scheme of things. We well might have never even come into existence in the first place. Like it or not, we are but a happy accident.

Putting things in their proper perspective, then, we should recognize that the dinosaurs were anything *but* a failure, evolutionarily speaking. As with our flawed yet ever-popular conception of Neanderthals as knuckle-dragging brutes, the narrative which ignores the 200-plus million-year success of the dinosaurs falsely portrays them as lumbering, mindless failures, and serves not to inform or educate us, but merely to promote and perpetuate human exceptionalist thinking. If not for that random bolide which hit Earth out of the blue 65 million years ago, our planet would probably still be covered in dinosaurs, and not just the little air-borne versions we feed seeds to in our backyards.

For a proper view of things, then, one which, as best as possible, emphasizes objectivity and the truth of things as they stand, independent of our beliefs, instincts, thoughts, and feelings, we need to cultivate a new understanding of human nature. This one clearly starts with the rejection of the pseudoscientific, mythological misconceptions of old.

---

[104] Smithsonian Magazine, "What is the Anthropocene and Are We in It?" Smithsonian.com. *Smithsonian Institution*, January 1, 2013. Available at: https://www.smithsonianmag.com/science-nature/what-is-the-anthropocene-and-are-we-in-it-164801414/

At least half of our world has yet to get there. Then, the foundation for a new and improved origin story is to be found beginning with the work of Charles Darwin and the theory of evolution.

After this, we must be on guard against human exceptionalism. We are animals, and share a great deal of common ground with the rest of life on this planet. What we do not share, what is unique to us, that is also a part of who and what we are. But it is no more, perhaps even somewhat less, what defines us. That which distinguishes us is but a small part of human nature. In addition to that, it is *only within our minds* that it makes us better, or superior to others. No matter how we feel about things, there is no objective measure by which our traits or our species are superior to, or better than any other species or its definitive traits.

You Don't Know What You've Got, Until it's Gone

Human exceptionalism is both *inaccurate* and *problematic*. Inaccurate, in that nature does not value human intelligence or theory of mind over bottlenose echolocation, elephantine emotional intelligence or memory, the falcons' 200-mph dive speed, or the octopus's astounding camouflage or problem-solving skills. No skillset or specific trait has decontextualized superiority.

Problematic, because it inclines us toward hierarchic thinking, encourages environmental irresponsibility, inhibits our capacity to change in the face of human-exacerbated climate change, the ever-increasing rise in extinction rates, and other human caused problems. Human exceptionalism serves to encourage the rapine lifestyle which the 'developed' world has enjoyed for a while, and which everyone else on the planet now wants to enjoy equally. That would doom us all, and in fairly short order.

But we are the learning animal, problem solvers par excellence. Our kind of intelligence grows exponentially, building and transforming with each passing day, year, and generation, encouraging many of us to come up with sound, naturalistic principles of sustainable thinking, principles for sustainable living. It doesn't merely allow us, but ultimately requires us, to work together to come up with solutions to our problems.

But we cannot count upon destiny to get the job done. We are not a part of a big plan. We do not have a cosmic purpose. We do not even get a second chance after we die. We are simply not that important. The scriptures lied to us when they told us that we had value and importance on a cosmic scale. We have to unlearn that, to replace it with a scaled-down, right sized, more humble way of giving our lives meaning and purpose. Our contemporary notion of ourselves as cosmically valuable, still separate from and superior to nature, has to give way, because the truth is that we are no more nor less important than piggies or penguins, plums or paramecium, and, when we see that, things will go better for all concerned.

What *is* important is that we recognize this cosmic insignificance and accept it. At the same time, we must embrace our context dependent value. We do have importance and purpose. But our purpose and meaning have a far more localized, context-specific reality than scripture suggests. We are valuable as members of a community, of various communities, communities comprised of fellow valuers. Our worth, meaning, and purpose are, much as evolutionary adaptations themselves, contextually localized, interdependent within the environmental and social context wherein we live and move and have our being. We are very important: to our family, our community, the animals and environments with whom we are interacting on a daily basis.

Our true nature is one which recognizes that we are not separate individuals but, as the evolutionary sciences inform us, deeply interconnected, environmentally ensconced, eusocial, communal organisms, living beings defined and shaped by our multiple relations in the natural realm, utilizing our evolution-given unique brains to learn and know more and more, and thereby to solve problems for all in need, and to pursue the long term goal of creating a viable, sustainable, beautiful civilization for all.

Chapter 9
Getting it Right:
Darwin & Human Evolution

This chapter is an adapted version of two essays originally featured in Free Inquiry Magazine under the titles, "Getting it Right: Darwin & Human Evolution-Parts 1 and 2" (December 2020/January 2021; Volume 41, No. 1 and February/March 2021; Volume 41, No. 2).

Getting it Wrong: Abrahamic Dualism

As mentioned previously, one of the primary characteristics shared by our origin myths is that they are hierarchic. They emphasize an understanding of the universe which makes a value-laden distinction between natural and supernatural realms. Whether it be the God of Abraham or Plato's essentialist *Forms*, our origin stories reinforce this fundamental qualitative distinction between the natural and the supernatural. This is the key thing to recognize about these pseudoscientific origin myths, be they Pagan, non-theistic, or Christian – according to them, we are both *separate from* and *superior to* the rest of nature.

According to the AIC, which have of course been historically, and oppressively, dominant over both pagan and atheist thought and belief for well over a millennium and a half now, we are part natural, and this is bad, a stain upon us, our original sin. At the same time, unlike the other natural beings, 'man' is allegedly part supernatural, part divine. We are the whole point of things, according to this long-dominant perspective. The world was made for us; we are the central components in god's plan. We are the lead role, in fact the whole point of the play. The rest of nature is mere backdrop, here for us. Supporting cast only. Extras.

The religious are by no means the only guilty attendees at the soirée, however. There are secular positions depicting *Homo sapiens* as distinct and superior. Popular science magazines and videos today frequently refer to us as the *dominant* species. Our language is replete with this inherent bias. We refer to our cities, our products and creations, as artificial rather than natural. Body/brain is considered to be distinct from mind. My anti-theistic father pontificated on human genius, arguing that the minds of people like Mozart, Beethoven, or Einstein were somehow preternaturally extraordinary.

Consciously or not, many today still imagine a hierarchy, composed of the superior spiritual and the inferior material. But by far the most influential of these enduring pseudoscientific origin stories continue to be those of Christianity and Islam.

Getting it Wrong: Human Dominance

Pseudoscientific thinking continues to overshadow purely rational, naturalistic, or scientific accounts. Belief in *human dominance* is an excellent example. It permeates popular thought, amongst theist and nonbeliever alike. Dominance is a central feature throughout Abrahamic scripture. According to this prevailing understanding, we are to dominate over infidels, nonbelievers, blasphemers, pagans, and to dominate over the natural realm as well. This concept of human dominance itself still permeates the pages of scientific journals and secular works over the last 160 post-Darwinian years. But, what does it mean? In what sense is our species dominant? When we try to pin down a scientific claim of this sort, it proves elusive...

In Biblical times, admonishing us to be fruitful and multiply seemed like a good idea. *Homo sapiens* had often faced hard times, with genetic bottlenecks even threatening extinction. But, as everyone today is painfully aware, the problem of human reproductive fecundity is now the precise opposite of what it used to be. We have been fruitful. We have multiplied. And multiplied some more. Yet surely this notion of teeming throngs cannot be what they had in mind?

There are certainly more insects, both in number and in weight, than there are humans. There are more ants in my backyard than there are humans on this whole planet. In terms of sheer numbers or overall mass, humanity does not even hold a candle to the plants, whose nuts, seeds, and burrowing roots regularly sprout amidst 12 lane super-highways, immediately after nuclear explosions, or following millennia desiccated in Egyptian tombs or the icy Siberian permafrost. The biomass of land plants alone is 1,000 times greater than that of *all* animals combined.[105] That cannot possibly be what is meant by human dominance.

Water covers over 70% of Earth. That's where life got started. For the vast majority of Earth's history, life has been largely a water thing. Today, 78% of animal biomass still lives in the sea.[106] The microscopic krill are amongst the most abundant living organisms on earth. Meanwhile, the behemoth whales which thrive on them certainly have us beat in the weight and size department. It's hard to lay claim to being dominant when you're a land animal on what is essentially a water world.

---

[105] Bar-On, Yinon M., Rob Phillips, and Ron Milo. "The Biomass Distribution on Earth." *Proceedings of the National Academy of Sciences* 115, no. 25 (2018): 6506–11. https://doi.org/10.1073/pnas.1711842115.

[106] Ritchie, Hannah. "Oceans, land and deep subsurface: how is life distributed across environments?" *Our World in Data*, April 26, 2019: https://ourworldindata.org/life-by-environment

In terms of species survival as the metric for dominance, *Homo sapiens* does not even compare to the sponge, jellyfish, or horseshoe crab, each of which has been around for hundreds of millions of years. We, on the other hand, have maybe 1 or 2 million years in our current form to claim, at best. The truth is, we would not even rate near the top 1000 in this particular category.

Then how about individual longevity? Might that be the way in which our dominance is demonstrable, measurable, falsifiable? While humans have been known to make it to 120 years on occasion, there are Galapagos tortoises alive today who top that, and probably even a few who personally met with Charles Darwin when he blew through 160+ years ago. Bowhead whales often exceed 200 years in age. Scientists are currently speculating upon the longevity of the even colder water Greenland shark, whose age may well be greater than that of the Bowhead.[107]

Of course, we have only recently begun to understand that there are organisms, such as certain polyps or jellyfish, which have a functional immortality going on.[108] And, if we are willing to step outside of the animal kingdom, there is a vast range of other awesome and wonderful evolutionary creations for us to marvel at. Some members

---

[107] Nielsen, Julius, Rasmus B. Hedeholm, Jan Heinemeier, Peter G. Bushnell, Jorgen S. Christiansen, Jesper Olsen, Christopher B. Ramsey, et al. "Eye Lens Radiocarbon Reveals Centuries of Longevity in the Greenland Shark (*Somniosus Microcephalus*)." *Science* 353, no. 6300 (2016): 702–4. https://doi.org/10.1126/science.aaf1703.

[108] Berthold, Emma. "The Animals That Can Live Forever." *Curious.* May 24, 2021. Available at:
https://www.science.org.au/curious/earth-environment/animals-can-live-forever#:~:text=To%20date%2C%20there's%20only%20one,stage%20of%20their%20life%20cycle

of the species *Pinus Longaeva*, the Bristlecone Pine, have been alive since the Egyptians built their first pyramids.[109]

A very beautiful aspen forest in America's Rocky Mountains is actually one singular, giant living organism, which humans have named Pando. Just below the surface is one individual root body with one unique DNA signature. Pando is several thousand years old. So, we can confidently state that *Homo sapiens* does not win the individual longevity prize. Pando is also approximately 110 acres in size, so if you still had any hopes about us winning the biggest critter category, you can cross that one off your list as well.

How about overall adaptability? The urban myth is that the rats and roaches will be in charge come the pending post-apocalypse. There may be some truth to that. But they will have plenty of competition from a vast coterie of other, similarly smaller-sized models: multiple kinds of insects, as well as the various microorganisms who thrive when larger organisms like us face mass extinction.

The lowly little tardigrade is a common favorite. The infamous water bear can do the vacuum of outer space, sans space suit, then come home and lay viable eggs upon its return; survive the Himalayas butt-nekkid, as well as the scalding insides of geothermal hot springs; thrive under the extreme high pressure at the bottom of the ocean; and survive radiation levels fatal to we 'dominant' hominids. Clearly, they have us significantly outclassed in the resilience category. Plus, they're really fuckin' cute.

There is a very definite sense in which the dominant life forms on planet earth are those which are microscopic in size. We are merely hosts to these uncountable millions of microbes and bacteria living on,

---

[109] Welch, Craig. "What's the Oldest Tree on Earth – and Will It Survive Climate Change?" Environment. *National Geographic.* May 31, 2022. Available at: https://www.nationalgeographic.com/environment/article/whats-the-oldest-tree-on-earth-and-will-it-survive-climate-change?loggedin=true

around, and within our very bodies. Many of these came before us. Many we could not survive without. In some very genuine respects, our bodies are more accurately described as ecosystems than as individuals. We're certainly not self-evidently dominant from this perspective.

Perhaps what we have in mind concerns our ability to manage or control the environment. Ironically perhaps, given the current state of environmental crisis in which we have placed ourselves and other life forms with whom we share the surface of this planet, this more definitive, self-evident version of 'dominance' may be the most laughable of all. It brings to mind a veritable slideshow of environmental degradation and destruction, calving glaciers the size of Delaware, entire island nations swallowed beneath the ocean's rising tide, or, at best, strip malls, McDonald's, Taco Bell, cookie-cutter condos and filling stations, concrete, glass, and steel, stretching all the way to the smog-shrouded horizon.

I would like to propose another thought experiment, the purpose of which is to meditate upon, and cultivate a heightened awareness of what precisely we mean when we say 'dominate.' Essentially, a Socratic query: what is 'dominance'?

Imagine a community of, say, 15 or 20 African elephants. Now, picture that grouping of beings confined within a limited space, say, the size of a football field or rugby pitch. At first our pachyderm parade will experience stress and anxiety. However luscious and verdant that little strip of land was to begin with, it will quickly become overrun, downtrodden, and fully decimated. It will be trampled, consumed, and completely despoiled. This is what it looks like when an animal 'dominates' its environment.

What elephants need in order to thrive is a vast area in which they can continually roam. They will certainly consume vast swathes of greenery, knock a tree or two over. But then they will move on. That's what they do. That's how they roll. While they meander, a wide variety of other flora and fauna, which have adapted specifically to survive and reproduce within this particular dynamic, will thrive within the niches created by the elephantine wanderings.

Properly balanced in space and numbers, the environment will have time to regrow before they cycle back in their wide-ranging ramblings. This is long-term interdependence. Dominating an environment is not the same as living sustainably, interconnected, in an established interrelationship. Our beloved elephants will be much happier, too, once they get out of that pen and stop dominating. This is another lesson we have yet to learn from Darwin: the benefits of being interdependent organisms rather than dominating lords.

Looking back to the previous chapter, then, let us take a second look at Stephen Jay Gould's insightful observation regarding human exceptionalism:[110]

> Evolution still floats in the limbo of our unwillingness to face the implications of Darwinism for the cosmic estate of Homo sapiens...All thinking people accept the biological fact of our descent from the animal world. But the second stage, mental accommodation towards pedestal smashing, has scarcely begun...we have managed to retain an interpretation of human importance scarcely different in many crucial respects from the exalted state we occupied as the supposed products of direct creation in god's image.
> - Stephen Jay Gould

Smashing the pedestal which Gould describes begins with us recognizing that none of the above examples of alleged human dominance serve to properly justify our claims of human superiority, exceptionalism, or importance. In fact, there is no sense in which *Homo*

---

[110] Gould, *Dinosaur in a Haystack: Reflections in Natural History*, 1996.

sapiens is unarguably dominant. Neither is dominance something to which we should even aspire. Human dominance is, just like *Genesis* in the Christian *Bible*, 100% pure, unadulterated pseudoscience.

Pseudoscience refers to anything which claims the validity associated with good science, when in fact it is neither earned nor deserved. It is non-science masquerading as science, dubious claims seeking an unwarranted cloak of authoritative validity. Claims of human dominance are merely pseudoscientific assertions which serve to demonstrate nothing more than our *subjective sense of self-importance*.

Getting it Right: Human Value

For millennia, Christianity had held us aloft as creations finest achievement, its apex, its goal, its purpose. After Darwin, we were no longer creation's raison d'être. We were being cast in a new role. Apparently, however, the folks over in central casting didn't get the memo. Instead of being genuinely reconceived in light of the totality of the new data, we were simply recast with a slightly adjusted script: no longer *god's* finest creation, we were *evolution's* finest achievement, its apex, its goal, its purpose. Before Darwin, and still for the devout, we were the *crown of creation*. Afterwards, we retained our seat at the head of the table, yet were now considered the *pinnacle of evolution*.

But the truth of the matter is that, as paleoanthropologist and curator emeritus at the American Museum of Natural History Ian Tattersall rightly observes in *The Rickety Cossack* (2015):[111]

We are the pinnacle of nothing.

As previously noted, nature itself is value neutral. There is no good reason to think a mountain, river, planet, galaxy, bonobo, mosquito,

---

[111] Tattersall, Ian. *The Strange Case of the Rickety Cossack and Other Cautionary Tales from Human Evolution.* New York: St. Martin's Press, 2015.

bacterium, or human has intrinsic value. Valuing is a state of mind. As such, it necessarily requires a mind to exist, and necessarily exists only within the mind. Not necessarily a human mind, of course. Just a mind capable of valuing. All value resides in and only in the valuer, within the organism which has evolved the capacity to experience value or valuing in some sense. Like 'beauty is in the eye of the beholder,' only a tad deeper. Once we remove judgmental interpretations, such as human exceptionalism, from our model of the cosmos, only then do we take our more appropriately humble place within the grand schema.

But there is no viable, evidence-based justification for thinking that human beings have purpose, meaning, or value above or beyond that of any other evolved organism. We are of no greater or lesser importance than is the long-whiskered catfish, the old-world swallowtail, or the African forest elephant. We, and they, exist simply because we have evolved into existence. There are no grounds for thinking that any of this happened for a reason, or has a purpose. We do not exist for a reason, or toward an end. We simply exist.

This grates upon our sensibilities primarily because we have evolved a *sense* of purpose. But it is nothing more than that: a sense, an instinct, a gut feeling. Perhaps even a form of cognitive bias. If you have a sense that we have a purpose, and all of the above stated bothers you, well, you are not alone. It is a sensation with which evolution has certainly endowed our species. But it is misleading, and another example of epistemological inversion, to think that the entire natural world is here to serve us, or that we serve some higher purpose, are more important somehow, and all as part of god's ever-mysterious master plan.

We have an innate sense, another cognitive instinct, to think teleofunctionally: we think, see, and interpret things in terms of purpose. Religion, as our origin story, teaches us that everything is here for us, to serve us. We have this huge, universal importance in the Christian mind, this cosmic purpose and value. Religion gives us something to pin our instinctive hunger for such thinking to. But we are doubly mistaken when we believe that a trait of our mind, of our thought, is itself a real, separate, existing force in the world, or that our legitimate purpose is grandiose or of cosmic-scale import.

We may think and interpret in terms of purpose, but we do not *have* a purpose, or even any kind of value, in any sense that is either preordained or objective, nor in any sense that is universal, or vast and important. We're just hardwired to think that way. But, fortunately for us, meaning and purpose in a human life do not require the AIC's grandiose conception of human importance. We experience fulfillment, have meaningful lives, we value, and are valued in return. In other words, we are more than capable of satisfying the itch for purpose, entirely without AIC notions of godly plans or grand designs. Thinking that we are special elements within a divine blueprint is neither accurate, nor beneficial. On the contrary, it would appear to be leading us entirely astray. Our heads are too big. 'Too big for our britches,' as Mama Teddy used to say.

Our species values teamwork. Tribe. Community. We have never existed as lone, singular entities, but always as family members, first and foremost. Members of team human. We value our fellow humans, and we value how they also value teamwork. This brings our lives a sense of purpose and meaning. But this form of worth is less sweeping and universally significant, less grandiose, and far more humble, more localized, more contextual, than it is in the traditional stories of old. Good science, accurate and objective origin stories, these can tell us a great deal about who and what we truly are. But they will never place us back at the center of the universe. Nor should they.

Purpose

As previously observed, *Homo sapiens* has evolved an instinct to interpret the world teleologically, that is, in a teleofunctional manner. These terms simply refer to our instinctive predilection for thinking *in terms of* purpose. A small child sees an apple, and instinctively thinks the apple is *for* something. The apple does not simply exist. It exists *for* the deer to eat, or *for* the person to bake some apple turnovers.

This teleofunctional form of intelligence has obvious evolutionary value. The inclination to, upon seeing a piece of wood, think, 'We could *use* that, to catch food, construct a shelter, ignite a fire, carve out a canoe,' would result in greater fitness, make human beings who are more likely to survive and successfully reproduce. Thus was teleofunctional thinking hardwired into the human mind. That's how we evolved to think and interpret the cosmos before us in a teleofunctional manner, and how the gods became planners, creators, and designers with a grand destiny for their favorite creations, human beings.

However, we place the cart before the horse when we believe anything was, or is, placed here for our use. This is another example of an epistemological inversion, wherein we juxtapose *a way of understanding* with the true nature of the *thing in itself.* We do not *have* a purpose. Nothing exists *for* a reason. We just think in terms of things having purpose. Like a tinted filter on the pair of glasses with which we view the world. Teleological thinking may be evolutionarily useful, but it does not meaningfully answer questions such as, 'Why does X exist?'

As previously observed, all value requires a valuer, a valuing entity of some kind. To extend this thinking, then, it is also the case that nothing has intrinsic purpose. For any given natural thing to have a purpose, there must be something which conceives of that thing in that way. In other words, for X to have a purpose, there must be something which conceives of X as having a purpose. Purpose is, in this sense, a form of value.

When we kill off god, we end that objective, outside source of purpose, of value more generally speaking. This is why atheism is a very big deal. No river, mountain, planet, animal, nor person has value, other than in the eyes of a valuer. And without god, there is no separate source of value, no other source of purpose, other than the evolved organism or being which experiences that sense of value, be it purpose, or any other form of value.

This is the deep thing about atheism, and why it must be understood intelligently and seriously. God is gone, and with him, our naive, simplistic notions of morality, justice, purpose, meaning... of value. Now, we get to identify the true and real source of our particular values, what it has been all along: *Homo sapiens* and its primate brain. We merely made up god, in our image, as a surrogate: a valuing placeholder.

But, it's all good. No reason to panic. Subjectivism, relativism, nihilism, reductionism, materialism: we need fear none of these bogeymen. It's merely as if we are being commanded to 'grow up!' to face reality in its true form. Sure, it maybe sounds a bit scary. At first. But, in the end, it's absolutely freeing, fulfilling, right, and doable. And, in the end, we will need to embrace the atheistic truth in order to grow up, to mature as a species, and to create a peaceful, beautiful, natural, genuinely sustainable human civilization.

Neither the apple, the protozoa, the water bear, the deer, the cetacean, nor we humans exist for a predetermined, set reason, for a purpose. We are not that important. Purpose is a cognitive phenomenon, a characteristic of thought only, not a characteristic of nature, of things in and of themselves. All of this stems logically from an understanding of Darwin's work. This modern, scientific understanding differs from that of the old, pseudoscientific origin stories, and helps us to better understand our true nature, as well as our relationship with the rest of the cosmos.

The modern, post-Darwinian perspective suggests a far more scaled-down, localized, humble account of value, meaning, and purpose than the old anthropocentric stories. Yet this stacks up nicely with our subjective experiences. In our daily lives, most humans tend to know purpose less in terms of god's plan or other such lofty theological or metaphysical abstractions, and more so in terms of family, friends, and immediate projects of import. It may be true that, in the big, cosmic picture, a key point of the atheist POV is that we are each of no greater importance than any given earthworm or paramecium. But my family and friends, perhaps one or two readers, they hopefully feel otherwise. As I feel toward my tribe, my communities, my projects, and relationships. Well, at least I think my dogs do.

Evolution & Progress Revisited

Our brains did not evolve to be objective reality detectors. They evolved to be good at helping us survive and reproduce. Parsing out that which is true from false? Not so much. This is why religion dominates, while such objective-minded pursuits as science, truth, and justice lag and require so much more effort and training, why being 'objective' or dispassionate is so challenging to us. As a student and teacher of philosophy, I have often been frustrated by my immersion in a discipline based largely on the use of reason, when 90% of humanity's beliefs and behaviors are determined not by reason, but by such irrational forces as instinct and emotion.

As a result of our instinctive exceptionalist inclinations, we have long tended to misinterpret Darwin and the theory of evolution. As I have argued, one of the most telling examples of this is our tendency to conflate *evolution* and *progress*. From religious literalism and creationist thinking to the more secular minds of scientists and atheists, most of us interpret Darwin and the theory of evolution as a progressive, improvement-oriented process. This is a significant historical misstep and an erroneous understanding of this all-important natural process.

To briefly recap: Evolution is the word we use to describe the process whereby organisms which survive and successfully reproduce, within a complex relationship with a specific set of environmental variables, pass on to subsequent generations the genes and traits which enabled them to do so. Traits are 'good' – read: adaptively beneficial – in, and only in, relation to a given environmental context. There are no intrinsically adaptive traits, no traits which are good independent of context. Tentacles would not help an ostrich, nor feathers an octopus. Increasing complexity happens, sure. But more complex does not necessarily mean more 'good'. Our preference for human beings over other animals, for human traits such as intelligence, or theory of mind, or empathy or altruism, all of it merely comes down to an instinctive bias to like our own, our own kind, our own qualities and characteristics, regardless of objective or rational justification for so doing.

For a perfect illustration of this under-appreciated point, consider the evolution of the modern whale. Today there are more than 80 extant species of cetacean. Humans tend to place a significant emphasis upon the moment when our ancestors climbed out of the water, out of the wellspring from which all earthly life appears to have originated. Well, the creature that did so, which was probably very much like Ichthyostega, or the recently identified Tiktaalik, was common to both of our lineages. To all mammals, for that matter. This was around 400 MYA. Primates and cetaceans share this common ancestor. We shared common ancestors for many millions of years after that, as well.

The lineage which eventually led to the cetaceans, and that which was to become the primate, eventually diverged, but not until approximately 70 MYA. This was just before the arrival of the extinction-causing Chicxulub bolide, the one which crashed into the Yucatan Peninsula and the Gulf of Mexico around 65 million years ago, obliterating most life on land and sea, famously including the large dinosaurs.

A number of smaller creatures, variations on the mouse/rat/shrew/squirrel template, survived and thrived, including our ancestors, who scampered amongst the forest canopies and eventually gave themselves the name *primate*. But the lineage we gave the name *cetacean* to, they took an entirely different route. Fossil evidence of such creatures as *Pakicetus* (52 MYA) and *Ambulocetus* (50 MYA) offer evidence of specific creatures who, making their living along lake-shores and similar such borderline environments, slowly but surely evolved to become underwater creatures.

Well before we upright, tool-making, intelligent apes came along, multiple species of dolphins and whales had evolved to fill Earth's green and blue, clean and bounteous seas with communication, 'song,' family, teamwork, cooperation, intelligence, and probably some rudimentary culture as well.

So, our common ancestor started out in the water. They left the water and lived on land for a long time. Then we split lineages, but our ancestors continued to live on land. Then we climbed into the trees, while their lineage went back into the water.

Here, then, is the question:

Which part is the 'progress'? In the water? Out of the water? Onto the land? Back into the water? The out? The back in? Land or sea? Fins or feet?

The lineage of cetaceans includes the development of hind legs, enabling ambulation upon dry land. Millions of years later, the precise opposite proved beneficial for this lineage as they returned to the sea. This process – from fins to legs, but then back to fins again later – this *IS* evolution. Devo is not a real thing. Well, they're a cool 70s punk band. But the bottom line is that 'devolution' is pseudoscience. The cetacean lineage was not devolving. In both cases, they were evolving. The misconception is rooted in the faulty assumption that evolution has a linear, progressive, improvement quality. This would mean that moving in the opposite direction, for example, back into the water, would be a *negation* of that process, a 'de-evolution.' But it's not. It is evolution, both coming and going. Our base assumption, that evolution and progress are one and the same, that is the error.

Evolution is the term used to describe a continuous biological process whereby species adapt, changing in a nonlinear, nondirectional manner, in response to specific environmental conditions. *Progress*, on the other hand, describes a specifically linear, unidirectional process characterized by movement toward a specific goal, ideal, or end point. They are not the same thing. The linear progress of human beings is about culture and our accretive and mutualistic brand of intelligence, the root of all creativity and human progress. Evolution is a specifically value-neutral *biological* process, whereas progress is a specifically *cultural* phenomenon, requiring a valuer and something valued.

Despite what Abraham or Aristotle may have believed, human beings are not the reason for everything, for the world, for the universe. Nor are we necessarily the standard, the metric, by which good or bad, superior or inferior, should be measured. In fact, there is no such standard, so far as evolution, science, or objectivity are concerned. The cultural conception of movement toward an ideal does not apply to biological change, which neither has goals, nor ideals.

Progress is not a concept which maps onto biology. We and our brains are not a result of a biological process of improvement, just as we are not a result of a special divine creation. We are simply another animal. Biological change is always context dependent. Life just happens. It's not a part of any master plan, not going anywhere, not headed toward an end goal, toward some ultimate climax or fruition. That stuff is all in our heads: the brains of one singular species of animal, brains with proven quirks and biases, mere bodily organs within one limited hairless ape species, an animal which thus far has caused the extinction of hundreds and thousands of others, despoiled its own nest, and has yet to stand the test of evolutionary time scales. A species which may well yet go extinct, as have 99.9% before us.

The form and content of *Homo sapiens* is merely the result of evolution, organisms adapting to survive and successfully reproduce within a specific context, just like the dragon fly, the snapdragon, or the Komodo dragon. Conflating progress and evolution is itself merely a result, and perpetuation, of our fallacious and problematic exceptionalist self-conception. Overcoming human exceptionalist thoughts and beliefs, in all their various forms, is a goal for us. It is one which would represent some real progress on our behalf, in so far as doing so would move us closer to a respectful interdependence within our natural environment and, ideally, would represent a solid step toward the creation of a genuinely sustainable human civilization here on our beautiful blue, green, and white marble in the sky.

Getting it Right: Human Uniqueness

I became deeply interested in all of these issues for several good reasons, one of them being my frustration with the depiction of *Homo sapiens* in the popular media. It became increasingly bothersome for me to encounter these constant references in popular science, contemporary magazines and books, as well as in common screen and radio presentations, in which we humans were described and depicted in terms of the aforementioned pseudoscientific dominance. These popular portrayals of human nature more often than not started with something like, "What separates us from the animals…"; and, "What makes us human…" with the assumption that the two were essentially addressing the same question. The ensuing focus would be placed upon that which differentiates, to the complete and total exclusion of that which is held in common. But what makes us human, our true nature, is only in small measure that which is unique to our species.

Popular science depicts us as separate and superior, though we are neither. The Abrahamic tradition promotes and perpetuates this tendency to think, understand, and interpret in this way. H.E. and Abrahamic thinking both incline humans to identify ourselves entirely in terms of that which *differentiates* us from other animals. In spite of Darwin, we still tend to ignore or misinterpret a great deal of shared, common ground. Tool use, emotion, culture, language, ensoulment, self-awareness, intelligence, Theory of Mind: each of these and more have taken their turn as that singular trait which allegedly distinguishes us from the merely animal, lifts us above them, and in so doing, defines us.

But understanding human nature solely in this way is a delimiting, inaccurate, and highly problematic understanding, one perpetuated and promoted by religious tradition and indoctrination. We do not define something simply by observing what it is not. We can unequivocally assert that an apple is not an orange, a potato, a piece of charcoal, a '67 Mustang, a forest of quaking aspens, a spleen, or a supernova, right? And yet, having done so, are we not still a long way from saying precisely what an apple *IS*? Distinguishing and defining are not synonyms. Understanding what distinguishes us from chimpanzees, bonobos, dolphins, tsetse flies, gingko trees, and turtles will only give you a partial picture of human nature. Much of what we are consists precisely of genes, traits, attributes, and qualities which we do indeed share with other forms of earthly life.

What makes us human beings is also, in large measure, that which is shared between us and the various other forms of life. And that's not a bad thing, contrary to popular, Christianity-influenced belief. The differences are real and important. But they are not the whole picture, not by a long shot. Note that this smacks of Abrahamic hangover again. The old origin story hangs on beyond its usefulness, continuing to separate us from the natural realm of which we are in fact integral, interconnected, interdependent components. The human and dolphin genome are basically the same. We share 99% of our DNA with chimpanzees. We remember like elephants, play like otters and dolphins, fly like eagles, fight like lions, sing like birds, and fuck like bonobos.

A few decades back, the Unites States government's Speaker of the House recommended to all members of congress, particularly the newer members coming in, that they read primatologist Frans De Waal's *Chimpanzee Politics*. De Waal has written dozens of works which offer compelling evidence of our similarities, the common ground upon which we and other animals walk. Despite our pretensions to the contrary, *Homo sapiens'* true inner motivations, behaviors, impulses, needs and wants often differ little from those of our animal kindred.

We may dress in fancy attire, work in shiny, clean, metallic offices, drive exquisite cars to fancy restaurants, museums, plays, or concerts, along with our darling, highly coiffed, beloved spouse. But behind it all, whatever façade we may concoct, is just another hungry animal. An evolved life form, a creature with desires, fears, preferences, instincts, and impulses driving much of its behavior, if not all. Behind the mask, we are animals, seeking to fulfill our desires, wary of threats, possessive and protective of what is ours, looking to eat, have sex, or defend our territory, protect our offspring. Being a highly eusocial, highly intelligent pack animal, we're also always seeking the welcoming embrace of our kindred and kind, ever aware of and concerned with our status and standing as parts of a larger whole, with the nature of our relations within a tribe, team, family, community, pack, or pod.

It gains us nothing, in fact throws us significantly off track, to understand our more lofty, ideal traits in similarly misanthropic ways. Whether it's Steph Curry's three-point shot or another attempt by Uncle Bernie to get sober in Alcoholics Anonymous, we miss out on an important opportunity for learning when we interpret failure as our fault, yet attribute the win to god. Win or lose, genius or failure, Bach or bum, we need to recognize that it is all *of the* human, *of the* natural, *of the* animal. Only then can we appropriately own it, fully understand it, and ultimately learn from it. And only then can we build upon it, can we progress.

Altruism and love, compassion and peaceful coexistence, brilliance and creativity; these, too, are entirely animal things, entirely within our nature as the kinds of animals we are. Genius of the loftiest kind, also pure animal. Utilizing our brain's evolved capacity to reason, to cooperate and learn from the past, to change and work peacefully together with former enemies, in order to build an environmentally stable and beautiful human civilization? This, too, is entirely, completely, 100% all-natural animal behavior. Be it glorious or gutter, it is natural, it is of the animal. Darwin himself recognized this common ground when discussing that most quintessential of human traits: intelligence. He famously observed that the difference between us and other mammals, such as the chimpanzee, is "...certainly one of degree and not of kind."[112]

---

[112] Darwin, *The Descent of Man and Selection in Relation to Sex*, 1871. (American Home Library, 1902).

In spite of Darwin, intelligence is still commonly understood as a wedge, separating us from nature and from other living beings. Our super brains enable us to make increasingly complex tools and toys; practice intensive cooperation and team work; manage complex tasks and social structures; learn from mistakes, from experience, from others; imagine and perform symphonies; create satellites and global communications; cure diseases; build cities; feed the world; fly to the moon, then return home, alive; act against our own self-interest when we have good reason to do so; even step outside of our instincts; express boundless love and compassion; learn, share, synthesize, create, transform, and progress; all these and many more amazing, unique things.

Clearly, there is a sense in which *Homo sapiens* is unique. But we are not as unique as we tend to think, and our uniqueness does not make us better nor superior. We need to acknowledge the fundamentally value-neutral nature of biological uniqueness. In order to understand the cosmos and ourselves more accurately, and reap all the benefits of so doing, we will need to cultivate an understanding of the distinction between what I have been calling *value-laden uniqueness* and *value-neutral uniqueness*. This is what we tripped up on when we misinterpreted Darwin, allowing our hubris and arrogance to warp our understanding of the true nature of things.

Every species is equally, and literally, unique, by definition. But unique and superior are not synonyms. Nothing about *Homo sapiens'* unique qualities makes us in any sense self-evidently superior to any other species and its given traits. To know the truth about human nature, we must recognize and acknowledge precisely how we are different and unique, as well as precisely how we are not, how we are in fact comprised of shared characteristics and traits. Finally, we must cultivate some degree of objectivity, some ability to free ourselves of the biases, prejudice, and blinders imposed by religion and the human exceptionalism built into the Abrahamic tradition.

The End of Dominance

Our problems are increasingly mutual, our borders increasingly irrelevant, our fates increasingly intertwined. Examples of this mutualism begin with the recognition of our exponentially swelling numbers as problem numero uno. Yet moving down the list we see a number of other problems which have a similarly shared, mutualistic character: climate change and environmental pollution; resource availability and management, like water, or petroleum; migration, immigration, and xenophobia; epidemics and pandemics; the military-industrial economy; religion and other anti-science and anti-education forces; over-consumption, poverty, and economic injustice; misogyny and gender inequity; and, of course, violent, armed conflicts of any and all kinds.

All of these border-crossing, international problems are growing concurrently with our increasingly globe-spanning technologies in communications and transportation. This serves to drive home the reality that our old tool kit is in desperate need of repair or replacement by one which is simultaneously more accurate, more in keeping with our current needs, and more guided by where we want to go. Scriptural admonitions to dominate the other, to conquer nature, to convert the other to our way, or even kill the other if they do not accept our view, are clearly not benefitting humanity in today's global context. We are burdened with an *IG/OG* mind, yet no longer live in an *IG/OG* world.

The domination mindset inherent to ancient texts like the *Bible* and the *Quran* tend to set us at one another's throats, perpetuate age-old adversarial relationships, and promote a decidedly rapine approach to the natural environs within which we are immersed, and upon which we depend for our very survival, not to mention our quality of life. A self-conception which rejects dominance thinking, and instead defines us as intricately interdependent, both within our complex natural surroundings, as well as with our fellow species members, is both *descriptively* more accurate, and *prescriptively* more advisable. Utilizing what evolution has gifted us, our uniquely learning capable brain, let us reshape our self-conception in accord with the truth and, simultaneously, with who and what we wish to become on this Earth.

An accurate, post-Darwinian self-conception, freed from pseudoscience and H.E., rooted in a morally preferrable, autonomy-respecting emphasis upon education over indoctrination, will enable us to more accurately recognize our true place, and to live with greater humility. We are not the product of divine creation. What we are is an interdependent organism, intertwined on multiple levels, and quite literally interconnected with the billions of microorganisms in and on our bodies, the food we eat, the air we breathe, the land we live upon, and more. Both we and our shared global environment will only stand to benefit from embracing such a new, more accurate origin story, one firmly rooted in scientific reality. We're all in this together. Spaceship earth.

Fortunately, not all of our instincts are out to screw us over. Some of our deeper predispositions and instincts work to our real long-term advantage. We are hardwired by evolution to experience pleasure when we engage in things like cooperation, teamwork, helping others, living peacefully, making justice happen right now in our world. We get joy from love and affection, shared between ourselves, between us and other non-human beings as well. The truth is that when we immerse ourselves in pro-social thoughts and behaviors, when we make dinner with our friends, when we make peace with our enemies, and when we experience the nurturing, rejuvenating connection with pure, wild, unadulterated nature, in all of these contexts, the human brain has evolved to produce the bio-electro-chemical changes which cause us to feel joy, pleasure, and contentment.

If we simply allow the wrong instincts and cognitive biases to control our minds, we will continue to be ruled by the dominance mindset and H.E. We will continue to try and dominate the environment and other humans, rather than live sustainably and cooperatively within the bigger whole. Rather than dominance and exceptionalism, we can choose long-term viability through the primacy of reason, reason rooted in real knowledge. This would help us to not merely avoid extinction, but also to cultivate a genuinely sustainable, just, and beautiful human civilization. This would enable us to thrive. Let us reshape our self-conception in accord with the truth, with a full knowledge of our instincts and the importance of knowing when and how to override them, in accord with who and what we wish to become.

We are extremely fortunate to be in this moment, this tiny window wherein we are aware that we have only just evolved into self-consciousness here on the surface of this absolutely amazing, gorgeous blue, white and green marble, situated right next to a nice, warm, yellow fireball, all of us together on this tiny sanctuary of life, so many of us learning to gratefully and responsibly appreciate what an awesome and truly irreplaceable oasis our Earth is.

Chapter 10
The Wolf in Sheep's Clothing

Where questions of religion are concerned,
people are guilty of every possible sort of dishonesty and
intellectual misdemeanor.
– Sigmund Freud[113]

Bamboozled

When I first saw the subtitle to Christopher Hitchens' 2007 book, *God is Not Great: How Religion Poisons Everything,*[114] I was genuinely taken aback. 'Oh, come now, Mr. Hitchens,' I thought. 'I may be with you on the whole atheism thing, but…isn't that a bit much? Literally *everything*? Rhetorical exaggeration much?!'

I'm sure glad I stuck with it, read the book anyway. Today, well over a decade later, I am obliged to say that the Hitch was spot on. The majority of people believe that hardline atheists such as Hitchens or Dawkins overstate things, make mountains out of molehills, are simply obsessed for some reason, and should be dismissed outright.

The truth is that very few people have read enough, learned enough, unlearned enough, or reflected seriously enough upon these specific issues so as to fully grasp the enormity and depth of the impact which religion has had upon human society. Not to the same degree as these fine, under-appreciated gentleman scholars. As a result, very

---

[113] Freud, Sigmund. *The Future of an Illusion.* Hogarth Press, 1927.
[114] Hitchens, *God is Not Great*, 2009.

few grasp how all-pervasive and problematic religion's reach is, and the serious importance of seeking freedom from religion. The vast majority assume falsely that people like me are merely obsessed, have a chip on our shoulder for some reason, or are generally speaking just off track. But the truth is more so that it is they who are missing something. Most Americans have blinders on and remain naively ignorant of religion's true reach and impact, past and present.

One of the biggest hurdles which humankind must eventually surmount is religion and religious thinking. Their composition is a surfeit of falsehoods. Religion lies. It lies big, and it lies a lot. Islam and Christianity have presented us with lie after lie, deception after deception, fiction upon fiction. And they have done so for century upon century. Billions of people, swayed by a powerful amalgam of evolutionarily inculcated instincts, cognitive biases, and powerful learning in the form of indoctrination, have been, and still are, seriously swayed by these lies. Hoodwinked. Duped by a very large wolf in some very convincing sheep's clothing.

The Abrahamic religions of Islam and Christianity are the cause of thought control, coercion, and manipulation, beginning at formative and vulnerable early ages, affecting both our belief and our behavior. No conspiracy required. As a result of cruel or kind intent, by evil or by compassion, through intentional coercion or genuinely benign concern, whether systematic and institutionalized or merely as the cumulative result of one kindly but misguided priest at a time, one well-meaning but ignorant pastor at a time, falsehood upon falsehood has warped the understanding and the lives of billions of human beings, with cumulative, long-term, and highly pernicious results.

Perhaps the clearest example which serves to prove my point would be the child- and sex-abuse scandals within the church, which have garnered so much attention since the turn of the 21st century. Unfortunately, this obvious, low-hanging fruit is such a glaring example of how the problem manifests that it cannot be avoided. The problem is not merely a recent, nor in any sense an isolated one. Prior to our time, it is quite safe to assume that similar practices pervaded the church – the hypocrisy, the abuse, the secrecy, and the fraternal collusion as well – the primary difference simply being that they remained relatively unrecognized by the wider public, escaping such widespread attention as the modern media offers, and they did so for century after century.

This means that the church simultaneously represented itself as a place of sanctity and security, a sacred sanctuary and safe zone for all, while at one and the same time acting as the most singular perpetrator of heinously immoral, criminal, and sinful practices, the very worst kind of devious and deceitful predator. The church is supposed to be the very place one goes in the event of abuse, specifically to escape it, to find sanctuary, to find safety, to heal. A more glaring example of hideously immoral misrepresentation and duplicitous hypocrisy cannot possibly be conceived. What's worse than a child being sexually abused by an adult? A child being sexually abused by an adult who is supposed to be the very embodiment of trustworthiness, a man of god, a holy man, one of god's special envoys.

In modern times, even with communication and transparency at their historic heights, the disturbingly widespread, fiendishly hypocritical, heartbreakingly normalized abuse of the church's many victims is still widely dismissed, minimized, hidden from view, and even blamed on the Jews (of course: what isn't?). The guilty have been shuffled from diocese to diocese, the problems kept largely in the dark, victims consistently and methodically disavowed and silenced. Catastrophic and mounting harms have been systematically denied or minimized, victim counts ever increasing, allowing the wound to fester, to metastasize, and the guilty to go unpunished, justice thwarted, presumably to be found in an alleged afterlife. And yet the pews are still lined with future victims every week.

My argument is that this is not an aberration, a departure from the norm. All of this is simply business as usual for Christianity. This is merely one example of the kind of thing which has been going on for millennia. The sexual abuse, the physical, psychological, and emotional abuse of women and children. But, far more than even that. This abuse of power, broadly speaking, coupled with the perpetual promotion of harmful fictions, all compounded by the doubly immoral duplicity of the wolf in sheep's clothing – these are all systematic and ongoing, not random nor isolated.

Going beyond that, Christianity and Islam are founded upon actual falsehoods. Born of lies, bringing forth the fruit of lies. Fictions tend to compound and breed. The more lies told, the more lies needed to perpetuate the fraud. The more lies told, the more lies needed to cover up the lies. The more lies told, the easier it gets to tell more lies. And, of course, as one who believes the truth is both intrinsically and instrumentally valuable, I argue that the more lies told, the more harm caused.

One of the primary reasons that we generally fail to recognize how religions like Christianity and Islam consist of a pack of lies is precisely *because* they have twisted our brains with their profusion of lies. And they are very good at it. In other words, one very significant reason we fail to acknowledge that religion depends upon propaganda is because religion is good at propaganda. Propaganda simply means disseminating information of a misleading, biased character, intended to promote a specific cause or point of view; to coerce; to manipulate. Christianity and Islam both survive and thrive in large measure due to propaganda and indoctrination.

Faith undoubtedly brings comfort. But it does so as the fix comforts the junkie. It comforts at great expense. And the victims, those most harmed, are often the most enthusiastic and vehement defenders and advocates. Christianity creates or exacerbates fears with one hand, then offers comfort and the alleged cure with the other. It keeps the faithful coming back for more by *creating false needs*. The need for salvation is caused by the inculcated interpretation of human nature as evil, caused by indoctrination in an ideology of 'original sin.' Manufacturing evil in this way entails a great deal of disingenuousness and insincerity.

The good done by the Abrahamic religions of Islam and Christianity overall has been systematically exaggerated, while the harms they have caused, and continue to cause, have been surreptitiously downplayed, seriously underrecognized, systematically underreported. Freedom from religion is an important goal for humanity to pursue. In order to achieve this goal, we will need to more honestly and openly acknowledge some of these many misrepresentations, inaccuracies, deceptions, lies, and propaganda, which have for so long gone largely unquestioned by the substantial majority of our species.

The Asymmetric Dialogue

The church enjoys a unique dispensation, an exemption from criticism far exceeding that which any other significant social institution enjoys. Beneath the protective canopy of this special privilege, religion gets away with far more than would otherwise be the case, indeed should be the case. For centuries, religious authorities have been able to say and do things without having to endure even the most basic public scrutiny. Sins and crimes the likes of the contemporary 'scandal' of sexual abuse would have long ago been made public, with genuine, lasting change being far more likely, but for the undeserved sanctity of the ecclesiastic.

Perhaps, if saying no to your pastor or priest was a more viable option, the problem would never have grown to such endemic, widespread, and systemic proportions, would never have become a literal tradition in its own right. Examples of a similar nature are not the exception, but in all probability characterize the hidden history of these religious institutions and cultures.

Importantly, this taboo against criticism does not go equally in both directions. There is a fundamental asymmetry to the dialogue, an unjust imbalance between norms. We who believe in reason, free-thinking, and rationality above faith, comfort, and conformity, have been vilified and denigrated, in the pages of allegedly holy books, from the minbars and pulpits, and from the wagging tongues and talking heads of the pious and the faithful, loudly, proudly, with passion and impunity, for century upon century. Criticism of the heathen has long been socially acceptable, and religious authorities themselves have long been openly on the attack. It has been open season on atheists for mil-lennia. Meanwhile we are morally, if not mortally, obligated to keep our thoughts to ourselves, our mouths shut. Another 'don't ask, don't tell' situation. Another reason to hide in the closet.

For centuries, European Christianity methodically nurtured this strong proscription against criticism or opposition of any kind. It was not so very long ago that anyone attempting to openly criticize the church was ostracized or oppressed; that blasphemy, heresy, and free thought resulted in various forms of torture, often followed by death, toward the end of fully eradicating any element of dissent, doubt, or criticism. While this sort of flagrant rule by terror is no longer a main-stay of European or American Christianity, the century upon century in which this was the norm has clearly had lasting effects.

In spite of this, there are millions of potential atheists, agnostics, and nones sitting in the pews today. If asked a few significant and pointed questions, a surprising proportion of these average church-going Americans, with a decent foundation of secular education and reasoning, would come to more or less the same conclusions as we infidels and nonbelievers. Perhaps they do not believe, for example, that Jesus walked on water, or that his mother was a virgin. Many no doubt recognize the basic scientific reality that, when people die, they don't go to heaven or hell. We probably just cease to exist, become but fond memories and worm food, one and all.

In the contemporary United States, a significant number of church goers self-define as Christian, even though they may not have given much serious thought or reflection to the subject. Millions today call themselves Christian largely out of social habit, a self-perpetuating momentum of tradition. They have not studied or reflected upon it as we nones and atheists have. Religion has not been a subject of much serious reflection on their part. Many self-identify as Christian merely as the result of cultural and social impetus, a general self-perpetuation of beliefs, associations, identifications, and practices, a generation-by-generation pattern.

> Many Americans consider themselves 'Christians' with extremely limited knowledge of the beliefs and practices…simply because of their parents, peers, and/or popular culture.
> – David G. McAfee[115]

Pew Research finds atheists are relatively better informed, better educated specifically on the subject of religion, than the average Christian.[116]

---

[115] McAfee, David. *Disproving Christianity and Other Secular Writings.* Hypatia Press, 2022.
[116] Pew Research Center, "Who Knows What About Religion," Washington D.C., September 28, 2010.

How Religious Groups Performed on the U.S. Religious Knowledge Survey

	Average # correct out of 32	% with 17 or more correct
Total	16.0	47
Christian	15.7	45
Protestant	16.0	46
White evangelical	17.6	56
White mainline	15.8	45
Black Protestant	13.4	28
Catholic	14.7	40
White Catholic	16.0	48
Hispanic Catholic	11.6	20
Mormon	20.3	74
Jewish	20.5	73
Unaffiliated	16.6	52
Atheist/Agnostic	20.9	82
Nothing in particular	15.2	42

PEW RESEARCH CENTER'S
FORUM ON RELIGION & PUBLIC LIFE May 19-June 6, 2010

At first this may seem surprising. But, upon reflection, it makes perfect sense. Those who are well read and studied tend toward non-belief. The 'atheists in the pews' are comprised of people who by and large have two things in common with one another:

- They are not particularly knowledgeable about religion, nor especially critical or skeptical. They are also not especially curious. It is not a topic which interests them much. Going to church is more of a habit, a tradition, a family or social obligation.

- They are the beneficiaries of a reasonably good secular education. The widespread literacy and K – college lifestyle we enjoy in America differs from other times. This secular education, the common sense, the reason, and even some science – absent any serious effort made at religious indoctrination – serves as a foundation for the rise of the nones.

The bottom line: if we wanna make an atheist world, it's not gonna be that hard to do. One generation of solid, secular education, minus any and all religious indoctrination. No book burning required. No babies need be eaten.

Yet there still remains the significant stigma associated with atheism and irreligiosity. This represents a small but potent element in the general program of Christian indoctrination, propaganda, and dogma. The millions of 'atheists in the pews,' with their solid secular foundation from their average American public school education, maybe a little college, fully literate, with little if any serious concern or curiosity so far as the subjects of religion, faith, or god are concerned, will still be reticent to lose the title of 'Christian.' Such folks may never call themselves atheists, and would in fact recoil from any such suggestion. These potential atheists cannot openly acknowledge their nonbelief, either to themselves, or to friends and family, as to be labeled an atheist has been freighted with such weighty, negative associations.

Contrast the linguistic undertones of *atheist, infidel,* or *nonbeliever* with those of *faithful, devout, pious,* or *reverent.* For most, the latter have generally positive insinuations and associations. Only amongst the 'free-thinking' is this order reversed. Many an atheist leans toward thinking infidel a compliment, while we come more and more to associate faith with the deluded, the misled, the naive, and the sheep.

Our atheism often entails a significant component of unlearning, shedding the cloth woven of religious indoctrination which shrouds most Americans.

Throughout America's history, particularly relevant during the Vietnam War, conscientious objectors were allowed to opt out of violent armed conflict. But this was true only if they claimed to believe in a supreme being. Atheists had no such recourse. Apparently, the thought has long been that atheists are incapable of having a conscience. This is a very real kind of prejudice.

It is important for me to acknowledge that the daily life of a white male American atheist, particularly one who lives in a liberal enclave such as myself, or a 'don't ask don't tell,' closeted-type atheist, is not even remotely as poisoned by the many faces of prejudice as have been those of genuinely long-suffering oppressed persons in America: particularly Native Americans, African Americans, other POC, women, or the latest hated immigrant group, to name a few. No one is profiling us, choking us out in acts of flagrant police brutality, systematically passing us over, or paying us less. In no way am I claiming that the current situation in the United States is even remotely as fraught with immediate perils. Nonetheless, the statistics still speak loudly about a certain more subtle, long-standing prejudice against the atheist of any color, sex, or stripe, about the dominance of the Abrahamic religions of Islam and Christianity, and about the importance of freedom from religion.

The prejudice may not be as flagrant or overt as misogyny or racism, but it is nonetheless ongoing, systematic, and real in its own right. Statistics have repeatedly illustrated that the average American will vote for someone who is a woman, homosexual, black, or even Muslim long before allowing anyone labeled 'atheist' to hold public office.

As an example, consider the make-up of the Unites States of America's Senate and House of Representatives. In the year 2023, the 116th congress of the United States of America consisted of 471 Christians out of a total of 534 members.[117] This comes to just over 88% of total members. This is some noteworthy over-representation. In 2007, 78% of Americans identified as Christian. But this number dropped below 65% in the subsequent decade and a half. The flip side of the rise of the nones. Such numbers clearly affirm the noteworthy overrepresentation of Christians in the U.S. government's legislative branch.

In 2017, 16% of Americans identified as non-affiliated with any religion. This has almost doubled since then. We non-affiliated represent fully 29% of the US population. As for the congress, a total of 19 members took no stance. Rather than claim non-affiliation, this is more like a 'no comment,' or a 'none of your business.' A grand total of two took a stance closer to atheism: one was brave enough to out herself as 'non-affiliated,' while another self-identified as a Humanist. That's 2 out of 534, which comes to well less than 1% representation. Nearly a third of the US population, yet less than 1% representation. This is some serious and extreme under-representation.

I am again rightly loathe to contrast atheist's current conditions here in America with the pervasive, institutionalized, historic oppression which, for example, women or African Americans have had to endure. But it is noteworthy that African Americans are currently right around equal: their percentage of representatives is very close to their percentage of the general population. Women have been making considerable strides, and the current make-up of congress, at around 25%, is well better than anything in the past. They are still grossly underrepresented, however, as they constitute fully half of Americas population. But the under-representation of atheists is vastly greater than that of any other historically mistreated groups.

---

[117] Pew Research Center, "Faith on the Hill," Washington, D.C., January 3, 2023.

The atheist point of view is the most under-represented category of them all, statistically speaking. It is highly probable that there are more atheists and humanists in public office in the U.S., perhaps even a truly representative number. But if so, no matter how many such closeted nonbelievers there may be, they are unwilling to out themselves. Even in America's more accepting, increasingly diverse social climate, even with the widely acknowledged rise of the nones, and in spite of our constitutionally protected rights to both free speech and religious freedom, not one member of congress is openly atheist. Not a single one. I think that is because the word is still so heavily freighted, due to centuries of genuine oppression, from the virulent to today's less so, and due to centuries of religious indoctrination. They may be there, but they are still afraid to say so.

This particular form of prejudice is not unique to our times, nor is it unique to America. The demonization of atheism, representations of us as beings without principle, as morally evil, depraved, dangerous, even literally demonic, have been a consistent theme of both Christian and Islamic teaching and preaching since the very beginning. For two thousand years, this has been drilled into our heads.

This ongoing propaganda has painted a clear picture of us as the worst kind of human being imaginable. But this significantly false and self-serving depiction of reality is just the tip of the iceberg. The Abrahamic religions of Islam and Christianity are guilty of spreading a surprising number of other lies and misrepresentations. Once I fully opened up this Pandora's box, I was surprised to see the extent to which our beloved religious traditions have systematically and consistently twisted the truth. Just as surprised as I was to realize that Hitchens was absolutely right, and right on track: religion truly does poison everything.

Let's take a brief yet informative walk through the history of Christianity, the last two millennia of European history, the history of the

United States of America, and Christianity's wider impact upon the world as a whole. Let's strip away, much as the archeologists and historians must do, the layers of self-justifying narrative which the victors have etched over the truth of the past. Let's take a different route, one of those 'roads less traveled,' and see if what I claim has any merit to it.

Progress 101: Knowledge is the Key

Rewriting the narrative of history is a familiar process to us all. When I was a child, single-digit age, growing up white and middle class in 1960s America, Native Americans were called "injuns," and were shown on the tv trying to scalp white-hatted good guys, and the Lone Ranger was the hero of the wild west, along with his subservient sidekick Tonto. Tarzan was swinging through the jungle, showing up all the ignorant black-skinned natives, schooling them on how to survive in the wilds of Africa. Sesame Street was banned in Mississippi for being 'too integrated,' while African Americans were still being depicted as servile, subservient, bowing and scraping Aunt Jemima, Sambo, or Step-n-Fetchit types.

Not until decades later did I learn, primarily within university contexts and through reading, that Tonto translates roughly into *moron* or *fool*; Columbus was less adventurous hero than opportunistic conqueror; Tarzan was flagrantly racist and ethnocentric; my family's household 'maid,' Bobbie, was the descendent of kidnapped Africans, whose direct ancestors had all suffered actual enslavement, followed by a century and a half of injustice and servitude still central to the lives of her family and friends; 'Redskins' were not 'uncivilized savages,' but rather the original natives of this land, the victims of both land theft on a continental scale, as well as attempted genocide. Not merely religious and cultural, but genuine, literal genocide.

As we progress, our numerous IG/OG stereotypes and prejudices are slowly whittled away and over-written by increasingly sensitive, increasingly accurate knowledge. This rewriting is not an intrinsic or natural consequence of time, of aging in and of itself. Insular or xenophobic cultures, such as ancient Egypt, Japan, or China during certain periods in its long history, tended not to change much despite the passage of time. The same is true in microcosm for the individual human being. Be it merely the individual person, any given culture or nation, or be it the entire human species, progressive change results not merely from the passage of time, but more so from exposure to knowledge that is new, to alternatives, be they real live ones, or depictions in literature or, even more recently, film and multimedia.

Gutenberg's printing press was a central contributor to this progressive process, to the beginnings of our contemporary secular revolution, our increasingly rapid rate of movement away from antiquated beliefs, away from the supernatural and instinctive, toward nature, evidence, and reason, toward education and science. We are undergoing a similar boost in egalitarian access to knowledge and information with today's technological equivalent to the printing press of its time: personal computers in a variety of forms, in combination with access to the internet. We tend to change, to progress, as a result of exposure to the new, the different, the very 'other' which we so often fear. This transformation is often slow, measured at the pace of succeeding generations. Grandpa won't change much. But his grandkids are different in some important respects.

I grew up in the 1960s and 70s, primarily in the Northeastern United States and the West Indies. In those decades, American life was characterized by some long-dominant social strictures. Anything in the LGBTQ range was publicly outcast and socially taboo. Anyone not in the closet suffered significant social censure outside of their own insular, secretive, inner circles. My peers used 'fag' as the very worst kind of insult, and any such inclinations were strongly discouraged. Heterosexuality was the dominant accepted norm. Most people were of a distinct ethnic or 'racial' group as well. You were either black, white, Asian, or Hispanic, and that about covered it. The mixing of the so-called races was depicted by many as a dystopian horror – we would all be one uniform shade of dull, unattractive, monotonous grey. Concerns that inter-breeding would dilute inherent Caucasian superiority no doubt lingered just below the surface in the minds of many Europeans and Americans. Mixing the races was taboo, and extremely rare.

My own children, growing up in California during the 1990s and the beginning of the 21st century, have lived in an entirely different world. A large number of people in that generation dabble in bisexuality before settling, if ever, on a preference. They are familiar with, and comfortable with, male, female, and even nonbinary partners. Their many friends and acquaintances include a wide range of mixed-race persons, shades of beige and brown skin that are completely unrecognizable and uncategorizable. With talents, intelligence, and beauty in representative samplings the likes of Barack Obama, Stephen Curry, Kamala Harris, Bob Marley, Derek Jeter, Jimi Hendrix, Dwayne 'The Rock' Johnson, Jason Mamoa, Sade, and Halle Berry, it's starting to look undeniable that, rather than oppose mixing things up, perhaps we should have been encouraging it all along! In fact, unsurprisingly, science suggests that mixing the 'races' would appear to be good for humanity, making us smarter, healthier, and more generally fit than ever before.[118]

Exposure to the other rests at the heart of human progress. Improvement is hampered when we merely stay in the same place.

---

[118] Solomon, Scott. "The future is mixed-race," *Aeon*, February 2, 2017. Available at: https://aeon.co/essays/the-future-is-mixed-race-and-thats-a-good-thing-for-humanity

Literacy acts as a surrogate for genuine encounter, as can the arts. Not so much, of course, if we read only one book repeatedly.

> As a reader, I could put on someone else's shoes and live through his adventures, borrow his individuality and make choices that I didn't have at home.
> The moral dilemmas I found in books were so interesting they kept me awake.
>
> – Ayaan Hirsi Ali[119]

This kind of real education and exposure is the key to our path forward.

> Education is a human right with immense power to transform. On its foundation rest the cornerstones of freedom, democracy and sustainable human development.
>
> – Kofi Annan[120]

The following is an excellent example which clearly illustrates the type of process I am referring to, a kind of change which must be copied on an international, global, comprehensive scale. This example is culled from that venerable and highly esteemed mainstay of popular culture, *National Geographic Magazine*, the February 2021 edition, from an article titled *Preserving Paradise*.[121]

The gist of it concerns the people living in the jungles of the Osa peninsula, in the southwestern corner of Costa Rica. The people living off of the land, hunting and seeking gold, eventually denuded and poisoned the landscape, and decimated the incredible natural diversity of plants and animals who previously inhabited this particularly

---

[119] Hirsi Ali, Ayaan. *Infidel*. Atria Books, 2008.
[120] Annan, Kofi. "The State of the World's Children (Foreword)." UNICEF. 1999.
[121] Shreeve, Jamie. "Preserving Paradise." *National Geographic Magazine*, February 2021.

fecund spot on our world. In other words, they essentially enacted, in their little corner of the world, a microcosmic version of the very rapine approach characteristic of the 'go forth and dominate nature' mindset, the dominance mindset so characteristic of the *Bible* and of Christianity in general, which has placed us all into our current global environmental crisis. But the Osa peninsula has since become a model of the turnaround, of progress, away from ignorance and irresponsibility, toward a far more knowledgeable, sustainable, enlightened lifestyle. In this particular example, the

> ...transformation was wrought through necessity—there wasn't enough employment for everyone—but its direction was determined by education. In 2002, Ureña and 14 other villagers ranging in age from 14 to 60 took an intensive course in forest biology. The students learned, among other things, how peccaries function as "ecosystem engineers." They disperse seeds, create habitat for aquatic life with their wallows, and alter the structure of the forest by eating the seeds of common plants, allowing diverse rarer ones a chance to compete.
>
> With the understanding that the biodiversity surrounding them was a natural draw, residents also learned how to set up ecotourist operations. Now the village monitors peccary movements, conducts bird counts, maintains camera traps, collects tree seeds, and offers forest hikes and educational programs for children. Hidalgo has helped guide and encourage this change of heart but takes no credit for its success.
>
> "They took the tools and changed themselves," he said. [122]

The first and foremost tool amongst them all? Knowledge. Of the environment, of the organisms and animals, their complex inter-relations. Scientific knowledge, of the details of the environment in which they lived, and of the big picture, how everything was literally,

---

[122] Shreeve, Jamie. "Tourism loss threatens Costa Rica's Osa Peninsula." *National Geographic*. May 3, 2021.

scientifically interconnected. Including we members of the *Homo sapiens* family. Knowledge changes everything.

> It isn't inevitable that human beings degrade these systems; we simply have to understand them. It is our understanding, our consciousness of these systems that determines what they look like. What I've noticed is that degraded landscapes are coming from human ignorance and greed. If you change that scenario to one of consciousness and generosity, you get a completely different outcome.
>
> – John D Liu[123]

To the precise same degree that we move away from indoctrination, toward more genuine, secular, and science-friendly education for all human beings on the planet, will we progress toward a more peaceful, abundant, egalitarian, and sustainable civilization. This should be our top priority and focus.

All of the warning signs are becoming increasingly difficult to ignore. There is no denying the fact that the quality of our lives, and of the lives of the many other beings with whom we share this planetary surface, all depend upon how we understand our nature and our place, and thereby how we behave, how we live, how we relate to our fellow *Homo sapiens*, and how we relate to the wider natural world. We have clearly arrived at the point where we can see that we are all in this

---

[123] Groome, Alexandra. "Meet John D. Liu, the Indiana Jones of Landscape Restoration." *Regeneration International.* August 12, 2019. – "John D. Liu, ecosystem restoration researcher, educator and filmmaker, has dedicated his life to sharing real-world examples of once-degraded landscapes newly restored to their original fertile and biodiverse beauty. Liu is director of the Environmental Education Media Project (EEMP), ecosystem ambassador for the Commonland Foundation and a visiting research fellow at the Netherlands Institute of Ecology of the Royal Netherlands Academy of Arts and Sciences." Available at:
https://regenerationinternational.org/2016/03/07/meet-john-d-liu-the-indiana-jones-of-landscape-restoration/

together and, to put it bluntly, one should not shit where one eats. How do we change? Knowledge is power. And nature is not destiny.

Somewhere around 1980, historian and scholar Howard Zinn's revolutionary work *A People's History of the United States* initiated a popular wave of historical revisionism, for me and for many other Americans.[124] Though considered radical both then and now, his work eventually became required reading material in a number of academic settings, as an antidote to outdated falsehoods, propaganda, and the standard top-down narrative which ordinarily shaped our understanding of history and the world around us. Editing the narrative, becoming increasingly skeptical, aware of how history is written by the winners, sensitive to propaganda and prejudice, as well as to America's history of immoral, unjust, and historically rapine pursuits, has been an extremely important process, an essential reality check, in my life, and in the lives of many others. Learning means challenging the known, and it means unlearning much 'knowledge' with roots in the past.

Our history books generally represent the early Christians in a sparklingly pure light, as the innocent victims of significant religious and political torment. Americans imagine Jesus's persecution, as he's nailed upon the cross by evil Roman soldiers. We proudly display the hideous torture device of the era, the crucifix – in jewelry, on our walls, hanging from rear-view mirrors, tattooed upon our very flesh – as a regular reminder. We imagine large numbers of innocent Christians being mauled by lions in Roman arenas, for fun, blood sport, and pre-television pagan entertainment of the most brutal sort. Bread & Circuses. Yet the idea that these early Christians were the entirely blameless victims of ongoing systematic oppression is highly exaggerated.

---

[124] Zinn, Howard. *A People's History of the United States*. Harper & Row; HarperCollins, 1980.

The truth of the matter has been largely skewed, if not wholly expunged and obliterated from the historical record.

As ever, history is written by the victors. If you look around the world today, fully 1/3 of all human beings are Christians of one kind or another, while more than half of all *Homo sapiens* are members of the Abrahamic tradition in one form or another. At the same time, how many genuine, practicing pagans do you know? How did everything change so significantly, away from a world which, 2,000 years ago, was almost entirely pagan?

Is it because Christianity has the true word of god, is in fact the superior message? Is it a result of a natural progression, religious belief developing from animism and polytheism into an allegedly superior monotheism in due course, as I was taught? Is the monotheistic tradition of Christianity somehow *superior* to the pagan, tribal and animist traditions which it has methodically displaced and all but eradicated? Is it the case that monotheism is the more advanced state of affairs, or perhaps even that Christianity is the true word of god?

Or are these simply more lies promulgated by Christianity? Is the current state of things merely another example of 'to the victor go the spoils?' Yet another instance of the historic reality that the winners get to rewrite the history books, and inevitably do so with a mind to self-justify, to skew the record so as to display themselves in the finest light?

Turning Off the Lights

Christianity—including the many different churches and sundry institutions, the billions of adherents and practitioners, their various assorted businesses and artistic works, the countless books, films, and public representations—generally presents itself as a force for good overall throughout history. But, is that truly the case? I am going to make a claim which should in fact be self-evident to any student of

European history, and yet which raises the hackles of the faithful and the devout: *Christianity caused the Dark Ages.*

It was the dominance of Christianity which caused a full millennium characterized by stagnation, indoctrination, superstition, conformity, and ignorance – plain and simple. Describing the cause as the 'fall of the Roman Empire' is disingenuous, inaccurate, and misleading in the extreme. In *The Darkening Age: The Christian Destruction of the Classical World*, journalist and author Catherine Nixey, herself the child of a former nun and former monk, helps us to cultivate a far more realistic understanding of the early centuries in our Gregorian calendar.[125] Much as Zinn did in his *People's History*, Nixey points to a significant body of data which counters the dominant narrative. But her work also makes the compelling point that it is the *absence* of data which is particularly telling.

In the early centuries of our Gregorian calendar, the citizens of the Middle East and Mediterranean regions were mostly what we would today describe as *animist* and *polytheist* in their various beliefs and practices. They paid regular homage to a pantheon of local gods, some as familiar as family members. They erected shrines and places specifically devoted to regular worship, sacrifices, and general communing with their numerous deities. Some of these many gods are recognizable in name to this day. We are at least passingly familiar with Greek and Roman mythology, naming discovered planets, moons, and stars, our sea and space-faring vessels, our composers' symphonies, our manuscripts and movies, even our very own children after these gods, with respect, and in homage.

But Christian efforts to eradicate dissent and create conformity began with a passionate objection to, a literal demonization of, such pagan deities and the associated heathen practices, as well as all of the

---

[125] Nixey, *The Darkening Age*, 2018.

related shrines, sculptures, temples, architecture, and artwork. These early Christians were hell-bent upon eliminating the touchstones of faith which had been so essential to others, to our beloved forebears of classical Greece, the pyramid-building Egyptians, the Empire-building Romans, to all the great cultures of the Mediterranean, as well as all that would later become Europe.

Well before Christian missionaries went out on their more recent, more infamous imperialist quests, hand in hand with Western European 'explorers,' to conquer and convert all of Africa and the Americas, their proselytizing sites were set far closer to home. Of more immediate concern were the pagans who constituted the population of the Mediterranean region, including ancient Greece and the Roman empire, as well as the tribes toward the north and west, the lands which were later to become the familiar cultures and nations of France, Spain, Germany, England and the like.

In Chapter 4, *Knowing More & Knowing Better*, I described the focus in god's ten commandments upon intolerance, proselytizing, conversion, and what was essentially cultural genocide. Recall that nearly half of god's divine commandments, still considered by many Americans to be the genuine word of god and our true moral and legal compass, clearly demonstrate god's possessive wrath, and a jealous need for the pious to demonstrate their devotion to him and him alone through proselytizing and conversion. Four of these ten allegedly divine moral commandments stress only one thing: the importance of eliminating even a scintilla of alternative belief, be they animist, polytheist, pagan, atheist, literally anything other than their god, their way.

The pagans themselves were relatively tolerant, pluralistic, and accepting of differing faiths, deities, and diverse practices. But the Christians were unwavering in their assertion that they alone possessed the right way to please the one and only true god, and that all others were wrong and in need of salvation, lest they be doomed to spend eternity in hell. They were similarly unswerving in their opposition to much that was of value in Greek, Roman, and neighboring cultures more generally. In short, they were an obnoxious, extremely arrogant, and highly intrusive bunch.

As with the Islamic extremists who occasionally populate our modern news cycles, the early Christians engaged in religiously motivated acts of violence and destruction. Fully convinced that they alone knew the truth, that they were justified in their course, they set about destroying any and all divergent views. They defaced and smashed art and artifacts, destroyed architecture, annihilated altars and representations of other gods, and appropriated or repurposed the structures of the ancients for their own needs.

The early Christians destroyed or defaced any artifact or monument associated with non-Christian belief and practices. Any tribal, animist, or pagan representations, altars, or artwork which they encountered were subject to historic revision, such as with the addition of crude crosses on the foreheads of statues, the lopping off of arms or heads, even outright obliteration. These Christians genuinely believed that they were doing god's work by defacing pagan art and architecture, eliminating alternate faiths, and thereby saving souls from eternal damnation.

The history of Christianity and Islam are both replete with this rampant insecurity and intolerance, characterized by consistent efforts to quell dissent, vanquish doubt, eradicate criticism, and demonize the 'other.' Thus were any alternative forms of belief, including nonbelief itself, which was far more acceptable within pagan contexts, branded as morally wrong, as sin, according to fully 40% of Christianity's divine commandments. To not be a Christian was a sin, punishable even by death in some instances.

This destruction, perpetrated by the early Christians upon all the peoples of the Mediterranean region, had its desired knock-on effects upon the citizenry.

> ...the violent destruction of a temple resulted in almost
> instantaneous conversion among locals
> – C. Nixey[126]

The subsequent centuries of Christian proselytizing and missionary work ultimately resulted in the eradication of alternative beliefs and practices of any kind – a thorough religious and cultural genocide which essentially obliterated some extremely significant pagan cultures from the face of the planet. As a direct result of this ongoing persecution, today we have only a small fraction of ancient literature, estimated by scholars to be at best around 10%, but possibly as low as a mere 1 or 2%. This ruthless intolerance eventually resulted in the eradication of not merely all paganism within reach, but eventually the old schools of philosophy and education as well, along with the freedom and diversity of thought which they had for centuries served as bastions of.

Far from being tolerant of alternative faiths, of pluralism or diversity, these Abrahamic interlopers were zealously afire with this relatively newfound religious imperialism, with the mission to convert, to save souls and, most significantly, impose their notions of sin and redemption upon others. Christians created a need for a salvation which no one knew they had. Subsequently, they pushed the belief that their god alone could meet that need. First, they sold you on the notion of an eternal soul. One which was broken at that. Then they sold you on its requisite repair kit. All Americans are familiar with this particular form of coercion. This is the one-two punch of modern advertising,

---

[126] Nixey, *The Darkening Age*, 2018.

which seeks to create within the consumer a false need, and then subsequently to offer the only product which could satisfy this newly invented need.

Christianity introduced a new sense of misanthropic self-loathing, a uniquely joyless conception of human nature, in which many of the fundamental pleasures of Greek, Roman, and pagan life were rewritten as immoral, branded as sins which angered the one and only true god. This new, misanthropic religion was very critical of the much beloved traditional pagan festivals, of joy and happiness themselves. Their ideology emphasized an austerity and asceticism in direct conflict with both the eudaimonia of Golden Age Greece, and the 'joie de vivre' which constituted a genuine ideal in the lifestyles of ancient Rome.

> He is a monk...who does violence to himself in everything....eat straw, wear straw, sleep on straw...Despise everything...claimed the ancient monastic traditions.
> – C. Nixey[127]

This growing emphasis upon austere values cast a considerable pall upon much that the Greeks, Romans, and the numerous other diverse Mediterranean cultures considered of value. Important aspects of life were portrayed in a new, far darker light, including freethought, philosophy, theater, the arts in general, and human sexuality in particular, once celebrated, now repressed. That which was widely considered natural, normal, healthy, even good and right by the standards of numerous cultures throughout human history was now rendered vulgar or obscene by the Christian faith. The early Christians made human nature itself into a sinful, evil thing, and then sold us on the package deal containing the one and only cure, salvation and redemption, only

---

[127] Nixey, *The Darkening Age,* 2018.

available through the one true god of the *Bible*. Order now! Supplies are limited!

Over time, as their mission to convert grew in scale, they took to burning literature, and eventually began the systematic oppression of scholars and intellectuals. By the time of Constantine in the 4th century, Christians were in significant positions of political power. Philosophers, teachers, and academics were being silenced, physically abused, and, as in the famous case of Hypatia, torn limb from limb by crowds of angry Christians. The rest of humanity was watching, and these often violent coercive actions had ripple effects, eventually successfully discouraging the teaching of anything which conflicted with Christian doctrine.

> ...philosophers were beaten, tortured, interrogated and exiled and their beliefs forbidden...intellectuals set light to their own libraries in fear...a story that is told by absences: of how literature lost its liberty; how certain topics dropped from philosophical debate...a story of silence.
> – C. Nixey[128]

Much of the centuries-old, widely revered intellectual and philosophical work of the ancient Greeks was methodically plundered, eradicated, and lost forever. The freedom and heights of intellect which gave us Pythagoras, Sophocles, Heraclitus, Plato, Aristotle, Socrates, and Lucretius had been simplistically rebranded as sin. Philosophy itself was doused as if water upon flame.

The reason we have so few of the works of antiquity, of the numerous creative geniuses of ancient Greece, the Middle East, or of Mediterranean civilization in general, for the entire amazing millennium *prior* to that, beginning with Thales and Democritus, running a full

---

[128] Nixey, *The Darkening Age,* 2018.

thousand years up until the time of Constantine, the first Christian Emperor of Rome, is because of this systematic intolerance, plunder, and wanton destruction of that which the early Christians deemed profane.

By 529, the philosophers were no longer legally allowed to teach. By that point, we are well into our descent, the early stages of 1,000 years eventually known as the Dark Ages, commonly described without mention of Christianity or its influence at all, and only a passing reference to a vague worldly 'decline.' Nixey's valuable, yet predictably underappreciated work helps bring a far more accurate historical picture to the fore, in which the cause of this widespread deterioration is not some vague, secular decline, but in fact the very success, and the subsequently increasing dominance of, the imperialistic, proselytizing Christian religion.

The squelching, hindering impact which Islam and Christianity have on the world is still happening today, and all across the board, from science and technology to issues in morality and social justice. The difference between the Dark Ages and our own time is only a matter of degree.

The Work of the Saints

Sainthood is yet another lie. Ordinarily we think of saints as being... well, saintly. We like to think that canonization is conferred posthumously upon those who lived their lives in a sufficiently holy or virtuous manner. But what we think of as virtuous today differs from what the seriously devout Christians, especially those of two millennia back, thought virtuous. Today the saintly are popularly understood to be those who exemplify such virtues as compassion, kindness, selflessness, charity, and humility. But the truth of history is that the saints were not always 'saintly' in these regards.

Our contemporary emphasis upon these virtues is a result of humanity's overall secular progress, a post-enlightenment, post-scarcity re-prioritization of values which is not a result of religion, is in no sense internal to the church, or caused by the church, but has in fact been imposed upon the church *from the outside*, from bigger changes in the wider, more progressive, secular culture. These decidedly more modern values are a result of humanity's overall maturation – a secular, atheistic growth toward more just, enlightened, egalitarian, democratic, liberal, pro-social, and genuinely moral values.

The Christian position has essentially been that one is saintly who promotes the Christian cause, in one way or another, by hook or by crook. The end apparently justifies any means. One of Christianity's most significant falsehoods consists simply of blurring the distinction, erasing the distinction even, between that which is 'good' and that which is 'godly,' between what is moral and what is merely obedient. This conflation was more widespread in the past. It has become increasingly the mindset of only the more serious-minded, true believers in more recent times. Secular progress imposed upon the church has increasingly changed human society over the successive centuries. People today are beginning to better understand that what is good or right is not the same as what is religious.

Take a look again at the ten commandments: only some of them have to do with morality as we understand it today. Again, much of what is commanded has to do with furthering the Christian agenda in some form. If it were reason, or genuine morality, which were in play, the ten commandments would differ considerably. Instead of promoting faith in the Christian god, or even an authoritarian, blind obedience to parents, perhaps a commandment that said, 'Thou shall not make of thy neighbor a slave' would have been nice. Or perhaps it would have been genuinely moral to proclaim a 'thou shalt not rape' principle as one of humanity's guiding rules, until such time as this obvious tenet should be emblazoned directly upon the human heart, so to speak, arising spontaneously from the rational and compassionate mind of the matured *Homo sapiens.*

Saints were regularly canonized for destroying any and all things deemed pagan or idolatrous, from art and architecture to actual human beings themselves. In all cases, the goal was roughly the same: proving the Christian god's existence and his might, eradicating every possible alternative form of worship or belief, increasing their foothold. As in the example of the more modern missionaries of Africa and the New World, well before the sword-wielding crusaders to come, or the example of Mother Teresa in our own time, as Hitchens points out in his scathing work titled *The Missionary Position*, the early saints knew a single-minded mission: to evangelize.[129]

Nixey describes the systematic and ongoing destruction of anything and everything related to the pagan gods – the copious shrines and statuary, the art and architecture, the books and scrolls, entire libraries. This was the kind of thing for which the early Christians were ultimately canonized. Saint Benedict of Nursia, the patron saint of Europe, was revered in part for being a "...*destroyer of antiquities.*" Not being kind or helpful. God was not so caring or kindly back in the day. He was angry and jealous.

Many earned the title merely for taking the ever-popular path of martyrdom – simply dying in some manner which was interpreted as promoting Abrahamic religion. This is the precise same saintly martyrdom which millions of faithful today associate with the 19 Muslim extremists who transformed four commercial jet airliners, filled to the brim with both human beings and highly explosive petroleum-based fuel, into the equivalent of four enormous suicide vests, and subsequently

---

[129] Hitchens, Christopher. *The Missionary Position: Mother Teresa in Theory and Practice.* Verso, 1995.

used them to murder three thousand 'infidels' in New York, Washington, D.C., and a grassy rural field in the quiet Pennsylvania countryside on the morning of September 11, 2001.

The average Christian thinks of this memorable event as a heinous act of the utmost barbarity. Millions of Muslims feel and think precisely the same thing, as a matter of fact. I personally agree with them both on this singular assessment. But the truth is that there are also millions of devout Abrahamic believers today who think these 19 men and their actions holy. They believe it was god's will. Those 19 are all supposedly in *Jannah* now, the Qur'anic equivalent of heaven, enjoying their reward for a job well done, a life well lived. For doing god's will. The bottom line is that this was in fact precisely the kind of thing for which ancient Christians were canonized. From a fundamentalist religious point of view, these men were supremely devout – the equivalent of Christian saints.

Too much? Not at all. Heinous deeds such as those perpetrated on 9/11 would litter the narrative of Christian history if the truth were told. Consider the words of the well-known and respected Saint Augustine, a prodigious and highly revered Christian writer, around the dawn of the 5th century. In a classic example of the destruction described by Nixey, Augustine scraped and defaced one of the last copies of Cicero's *De re publica* known to exist at the time, and made it his own by writing over it. Augustine became a saint after a career which was characterized, amongst other things, by his arguments in defense of violence and murder in the Christian cause. He asserted that it was *"merciful savagery"* and that *"Where there is terror...there is salvation."*[130] Nixey herself justifiably concludes that *"The intellectual foundations for a thousand years of theocratic oppression were being laid."*[131]

---

[130] Nixey, *The Darkening Age*, 2018.
[131] Ibid.

These above words we might well imagine Bin Laden himself uttering as he watched the first plane make impact with the north tower on that fateful Tuesday morning. With all due respect to the victims, families, and loved ones, indeed to all who suffered as a result of the barbaric events of that well-remembered day, the victims of 9/11 are the victims of religion itself, not merely of extremists. This noted historical event was merely the latest in an ongoing line, a long-standing tradition of death, murder, and mayhem associated with these Abrahamic traditions, stretching back uninterrupted for 2000 years.

The truly devout were encouraged to fully embrace the belief that nothing was more important than their god, nothing mattered more than acknowledging, believing in, and worshipping him. They had little concern for human lives or human laws. In their minds, they were obedient to a higher law.

> There is no crime for those who have Christ.
> – Saint Shenoute [132]

When you grasp the enormity of this kind of commitment, its implications are frightful and disturbing. Faith for such believers is so fervent that they hold the view that their religious 'law' supersedes mere human law, and that non-believing infidels are better off dead than living as nonbelievers.

> To turn on, hound and hunt your fellows…was not to harm them. No, [Saint] Chrysostom reiterated, it was to save them. To punish a sinner violently, to flog them, beat them, make them bleed—this was not to harm them but to help

---

[132] Ibid.

them…[Saint] Shenoute worried that if he didn't beat the monks in his care then he was offending God.[133]

        – C. Nixey

Biggest Bully on the Playground

Religion is ubiquitous. Owing to causal factors touched upon in the preceding chapters—such as instinctive proclivities toward superstitious thought and belief, the creation of supernatural agents, gods, and similar belief instincts, like pseudoscientific efforts to understand and explain the cosmos and humanity's place within it – thousands upon thousands of religious traditions have arisen all around our world, everywhere that we brainy hominids migrating from Mother Africa eventually settled.

Animist, polytheist, tribal, and pagan traditions flourished, in every far-flung corner of the globe, in full profusion, a true splendor of diversity in its own right, before the emergence of Christianity. Once this ruthlessly intolerant, misanthropic, moralistic, and missionary religion was established, every one of these local traditions encountered was inevitably doomed to fall, like thousands of dominoes, all stacked in a row, one after the next.

Even being raised as a relatively well-educated atheist, I grew to adulthood in the United States of America thinking that the provincial polytheist, pagan traditions were replaced by monotheistic traditions because the latter were somehow superior. I came to believe, as I suppose many others did also, that there is a natural progression which characterizes civilization, one which entails that primitive, inferior polytheistic traditions ultimately, and ideally, grow up to become superior, more advanced monotheistic beliefs, given sufficient time and the requisite development.

---

[133] Nixey, *The Darkening Age*, 2018.

Americans, and many others, have been indoctrinated to think of polytheism as primitive and false, whereas monotheism is the more advanced belief, and that this is why the latter ultimately devoured and obliterated the former. There is a far better, far more plausible explanation for the dominance and ubiquity of the Abrahamic religions. This has less to do with their inherent value, whether that be truth value, or the value of utility.

The ultimate dominance of Christianity in particular owes not to any such inherent superiority, but merely to their specifically intolerant, self-righteous, proselytizing, conversion-oriented character. Christianity seeks to convert, to coerce others to join, to eliminate the competition, and to sell us on the misanthropic lie of original sin and redemption. The pagan cultures were as wholly unprepared for this onslaught as the native Americans were for the small-pox infested blankets so generously offered up by their European conquerors. Their ultimate dominance owes to their true ultimate goal, the ideology's endgame as it were—to erase the competition and ultimately be the biggest, baddest bully, having vanquished all comers, in full possession of everybody else's lunch money, dominant, standing solo, tall, proud, and all alone, astride the playground.

Chapter 11

In Spite Of, Not Because...

Retrospective

The first 500 years in our Christ-centric Gregorian calendar can be seen, in historical retrospect, as a transitional period. In the beginning, there were but a handful of Christians. But by the 4th century, the Roman Emperor Constantine the Great himself became one. The learned, having run afoul of dogma or doctrine, might well find themselves torn limb from limb, right there in the public square, under the full illumination of the noon-day sun, by followers of the so-called Prince of Peace. By the beginning of the 6th century, the bulk of Mediterranean Europe was Catholic, and it was spreading like the plague to come. Suffice to say, alternative beliefs and practices, such as paganism, animism, local beliefs and traditions, and most certainly atheism, were rapidly becoming not merely rare, but actual sins.

This doctrinal intolerance is, of course, the ultimate source of Christianity's dominance. Between 500 and 1500, rounding out the numbers, Christian religion, tradition, authority, and conformity dominated European life. Its tendrils spread deep and wide. They were woven into the very fabric of our daily lives, the births and deaths and marriages, all the way up to politics and policies, all the way down into our bathrooms and bedrooms.

The beginning of the transition from the supernatural to the natural, away from faith, slowly towards reason, can be placed somewhere around 1500 A.D. Much of this radical change no doubt has to do with Martin Luther, and what came to be known as the Protestant Reformation. The Catholic church had been large and in charge up until this time. But this movement created the space for a variety of reforms. Independent branches of Christianity came into existence, alternatives to Catholicism. These came, in time, to be major religious traditions in their own right. Today only about half of the world's Christians are Catholic. The other half consists of a range of differing denominations and sects under the umbrella of 'Protestant.'

But entirely secular factors were also increasingly in play. Copernicus removed humanity from its narcissistic self-placement at the center of the known cosmos. Galileo followed suit, in a manner which characterized and exemplified scientific methodology and freedom from religious dogma and tradition. Da Vinci was inventing flying machines and solar power. And Johannes Gutenberg invented movable type, a minor technological innovation with major implications. At first, it simply meant more *Bibles*. But in time, it brought about a significant revolution, one of the first communication revolutions, which played a significant role in pushing forward secularism and human progress. Since around the beginning of the 19th century, human civilization has undergone a truly radical transformation: we progressed from a literacy rate of around 10%, to a literacy rate of nearly 90%. And we're not just reading scripture anymore.

So, in retrospect, this last half-millennium can be interpreted as a transitional one as well: a transition out of religiously imposed darkness of the human mind, toward increasing enlightenment, reason, science, atheism, and knowledge. This is what I have referred to as our shift from the supernatural to the natural, our progress away from religious epistemology, increasingly towards scientific epistemology. As a result, we have a far more accurate understanding of the nature of human life, of life in general, of the cosmos, and of our true and decidedly humbler place within the grand scheme of things.

This growing body of knowledge and understanding walks hand-in-hand with significant progress in terms of worldly and practical applications. As a result, we have experienced major improvements in the general health and welfare of all humans, as well as in terms of morality and social justice. Harvard's Steven Pinker famously describes this progress in *Better Angels of Our Nature* and *Enlightenment Now*, as does Michael Shermer in his work, *The Moral Arc.*

With all of this knowledge comes empowerment. Specifically, the power to choose our future and make our own destiny. Knowledge increasingly means rejection of the ignorant and instinctive beliefs which constitute the bulk of religion, including the disempowering belief that god has a plan for us and that our destiny is not in our own hands. Instead of having passive faith in god's mysterious master plan, we get to take responsibility for our own lives in the here and now.

Atheism is a message of empowerment, about humans learning the truth about our nature, and about that knowledge guiding us to become 'right-sized.' The more people get this secular, humanist, atheist message, the sooner we will all remove the blinders caused by religion, and work together intelligently to build a peaceful, genuinely sustainable civilization on planet Earth. We can choose our path forward. We are not fated or predestined to have it chosen for us by the eschatological lies of Christianity.

We are experiencing all of this good stuff as a species, all around the world, and in spite of some significant hurdles. Some of the problems we face today – global warming, overpopulation, and economic injustice, to name a few – these are what one might call 'luxury problems.' That is, they are either partially or in full the result of the current state of human knowledge overall, and the resultant material abundance. We know how to feed, clothe, shelter, and give basic medical care to everybody. But we are not doing so. Some of us are getting too fat, some too rich, and some are making a big old mess of our playpen. But luxury problems can be fixed. We can learn. We can change this.

The biggest problem is actually religion itself. It is still large and in charge. Indoctrination perpetuates religion, just as abusive patterns of behavior, genetic predispositions, racism, or blood feuds get passed down from one generation to the next. Hardwiring inclines us toward superstition and supernatural belief and thought, to the easy answers which they offer the human brain. And as long as they continue to dominate, we will remain embattled, ignorant, disconnected, naively poisoning ourselves and our beautiful little planet.

We will only know in retrospect if today's 'rise of the nones' is but a flash in the pan, or if it is a genuine turning toward the light, a legitimate awakening. The worst possible outcome would be that our secular revolution dies on the vine, that it gets turned back by a rising tide of religious revival. This, in my view, creates a *moral imperative* to advocate for science, reason, secularism, humanism, and, yes, atheism.

Some claim such promoting atheism is tantamount to religious proselytizing, and thereby makes us 'just like them.' This 'soft' atheist position suggests that we should simply 'live and let live'. But the differences between religious proselytizing and the promotion of atheism are highly significant, both in terms of *form* and *content*. In terms of form, religious proselytizing shoves down the throat whereas atheist promotion lays before one's feet. Religious proselytizing takes the form of coercion, whether overt or covert. Overt would be the torturer's dungeon or the blade of the crusader's sword; perhaps somewhat more covert, the Salvation Army with a much-needed meal in one hand, a *Bible* in the other; or the multiple references to 'He' and 'Him' in AA's 12-steps. But, ultimately, the force at work coercing people into buying Christianity's message sits at the very base of the whole operation: the manufactured need generated by the fictitious 'original sin/salvation' model of human nature.

Religion famously emphasizes indoctrination over education. By its very nature, indoctrination seeks to coerce people into holding a set of beliefs, and to downplay or deny facts and realities which run afoul of the attendant ideology. This, however, goes against human autonomy, and the fulfillment of human potential.

> Education either functions as an instrument which is used to facilitate the integration of the younger generation into the logic of the present system and bring about conformity to it, **or** it becomes "the practice of freedom," the means by which men and women deal critically and creatively with reality and discover how to participate in the transformation of their world.
>
> – Richard Shaull
> From the Foreword to Paulo Freire's *Pedagogy of the Oppressed*[134]

In terms of content, *atheism is not itself an ideology, but the elimination of false narratives and their corresponding ideologies.* The atheist position concerns the truth value of what is being communicated. 'The truth will set you free' (Ironically, this is from the *Bible*, specifically John 8:31 - 32 ESV). As such, it places trust in human autonomy: given the truth, human beings will believe and do good. They need not be bullied or coerced with carrots and sticks. The truth speaks for itself.

The simple act of telling the truth itself can be interpreted as promoting atheism. When one is promoting truth as a good, seeking to convince others that religious or pseudoscientific narratives are false,

---

[134] Freire, Paulo. *Pedagogy of the Oppressed.* New York: The Seabury Press, 1968.

or problematic, then one is advocating atheism. Religion is fictitious, and does not consist of replicable, scientifically verifiable truths. Promoting one and promoting the other are not synonymous.

Merely teaching science is promoting atheism. You are offering evidence which has the intentional effect of dislodging false views, and these most certainly include religious views. Plain and simple. The one is promoting falsehood while the other is promoting verifiable truth. If one is teaching science, then one is necessarily debunking false pseudoscience. Teaching Earth history and evolution is calling *Genesis* a pack of lies. And rightly so.

This distinction is at the heart of Ricky Gervais' pithy response on the subject:[135]

> ...Science is constantly proved all the time. You see, if we take something like any fiction and any holy book...and destroyed it, ok, in a thousand years' time, that wouldn't come back just as it was. Whereas if we took every science book, right, and every fact, and destroyed them all, in a thousand years they'd all be back, because all the same tests would [produce] the same result.
>
> – Ricky Gervais, *Professional Wit*

Our progress is the direct result of us freeing ourselves from the mental enslavement which is religion, from supernatural and superstitious thinking, and instead embracing the atheistic, secular, and humanist life, emphasizing knowledge, truth, reason, and human autonomy. What progress we have made, the difference between the Dark Ages and the vastly improved conditions of today, and the fulfillment of the positive dreams and aspirations we have for a brighter tomorrow, are all the direct result of the accretive, shared, and applied secular

---

[135] Ricky Gervais speaking with host Stephen Colbert on 'The Late Show with Stephen Colbert' on February 2, 2017.

knowledge within the animal minds of our species. We can continue to progress toward a more peaceful, just, and sustainable human civilization, a world in which we are living up to our immense potential for good. What progress humanity is making, is being made *in spite of* the influence and dominance of the religions of Islam and Christianity, not *because* of them.

Chapter 12

In Spite Of, Not Because:
Christianity & American Slavery

Human progress is real. I did not realize this for the bulk of my life. I was a fully committed cynic, proudly proclaiming misanthropic despair as I perceived humanity going to hell in a handbasket all around me. I believed that what appeared to others to be my pessimism was in fact my insightful realism. I believed that I was seeing things as they really were, without the blinders so many wore.

I lived a half century in this manner before I discovered Steven Pinker's, *The Better Angels of Our Nature: Why Violence Has Declined*.[136] I have read thousands of books in my lifetime. Of those, maybe a dozen would rate as having a profound and lasting impact upon my life. *The Better Angels* was amongst the tops on that list. Pinker single handedly cured me of my naive misanthropy, seemingly overnight.

I am still a pretty skeptical person, as are most atheists. And I still tend toward the cynical. After all, it's not easy to erase one's upbringing, nor 50 years of habitually cynical thinking. But, thanks in large measure to *Better Angels*, followed by other works in a similar vein,[137]

---

[136] Pinker, Steven. *The Better Angels of Our Nature: Why Violence Has Declined*. New York: Penguin Books, 2011.

[137] Michael Shermer's *The Moral Arc: How Science Leads Humanity Toward Truth, Justice, and Freedom* (2015), and Steven Pinker's follow up work, *Enlightenment Now: The Case for Reason, Science, Humanism, & Progress* (2018), are both excellent works which are similarly optimistic in tone.

my outlook on humanity became significantly less despairing, less pessimistic, and more hopeful. I cultivated an ability to see some of the good stuff, to recognize some of humanity's genuine progress, to acknowledge what we were getting right. I began to see more of the patterns behind our successes.

One of the more obvious examples of our progression is the institution of slavery. Yes, it still exists. And nothing that I say is intended to impugn or make light of the severity of modern instances of human trafficking and bondage. But, on the whole, humanity is making significant progress. Slavery in Biblical times was thoroughly normalized. It was accepted as an aspect of everyday life all around the globe. In some places more than half of humanity was enslaved to others. By far the majority of peoples either were slaves, traded slaves, owned slaves, or lived some combination of the three.

Conceiving of a world without slavery, the norm for Americans and most others today, would have been beyond most people's capacity. Undoubtedly such a world was beyond people's imagination at the time; it would have seemed a remote, utopian fantasy, just like a world without war, rape, or religion sounds to us today. The best they could hope for was no doubt something far more plausible to their time and place. Perhaps the dream was simply to live ever on the *master* side of the *master-slave* dynamic, rather than on the *slave* side. But a world without slavery? Impossible!

Yet, slowly, incrementally, we have progressed from slavery as a norm, an accepted aspect of everyday life, to a situation wherein slavery is universally recognized as a moral and legal wrong. Recalling the pivotal distinction discussed in Chapters 8 and 9, this positive historical change is not a direct result of evolution, but of a very distinct process of cultural development. We are not 'evolving' away from slavery. It is *progress*, not *evolution*.

And we have made this progress. Far from it being acceptable to have half of society in chains, our whole nation goes into an uproar if we find out that three young women were kidnapped and kept locked away in an Ohio man's basement for ten years. Trafficking in humans is no longer business as usual, but rather, seriously illegal, morally wrong in the extreme, and very rare. By a significant margin, most human beings in our time are neither enslaved, traffic in other humans, nor own any slaves.

Certainly, more work remains to be done. Perhaps it is the case that for we human beings, justice will ever remain a distant point upon the horizon: forever our guiding light, though its full and absolute attainment may ever remain elusive. Nonetheless, a more obvious, fundamental, and important illustration of human progress than the slow but steady demise of the institution of slavery is hard to imagine.

What is the role, if any, of the AIC in all of this? It could well be argued that Christians or Muslims were no more nor less guilty than any other peoples of their time, that time and place are far more determinative of beliefs and practices then religious affiliation, that the situation was the determinative factor. Everyone was doing it, so why expect believers to be any different?

One problem with this is that religions like the AIC are supposedly where we get our morality, our values, our sense of what is right or wrong from. Rather than excusing the devout from liability, shouldn't the fact that they behaved precisely the same as everyone else suggest that religion's claims to being the source of human morality are empty, are thoroughly devoid of merit? The truth of history is that these major religious traditions serve more so as the proverbial albatross hanging round the neck of humanity, anchors tethering us to the morality of the ancient past, than as moral spearheads, the avant-garde of humanity's moral progress and social justice.

286

The common claim is that religion is required for morality, and that, without religion, society would descend into chaos and anarchy. The reality of history, as the example of slavery illustrates, suggests absolutely zero causal connection whatsoever between moral progress and religion. There is no link between these world-dominating theistic traditions and our genuine moral improvement and maturation, nothing to suggest that they were in any respects the cause of our collective movement toward an increasingly moral and just state of affairs. What connection there is in fact suggests the opposite: if anything, religions such as Islam and Christianity act in service to the status quo, operating as socially conservative forces, standing in *opposition* to progressive change as a rule, and thereby serving to promote the conservation and perpetuation of antiquated beliefs and behaviors.

Famously, the *Bible* is filled with slavery. It normalizes slavery, presents it as morally acceptable. As odd as it may be upon serious reflection, the *Bible* does not list slavery amongst god's sins or commandments. Quite the contrary, in fact there is not one word in the *Bible* or the *Quran* to condemn slavery, yet vast swathes of the books serve to justify, rationalize, and normalize the practice of holding one's fellow humans in bondage and servitude, so long as they were not god's favorites.

Those were Christians and Muslims who packed the cargo holds of their ships with Africans, crammed together like sardines in a can, marinating in their own bile and urine, their sweat and shit and blood and tears. It was Christians who sailed those ships to the Americas, raping the women and girls en-route, unceremoniously dumping the dying and the dead overboard along the way like so much chum in what came to be known as the middle passage.

Those were Christians who brought kidnapped and chained human beings to the markets of the Caribbean and the Americas, who bought and sold them like appliances, who brought them to their plantations and put them to work under the most unjust, inhumane, and brutal of conditions. And per chance one of your slaves were to run away and seek freedom, you could always pray to St. Theodore. If one slept upon the tomb of St. Theodore, he would supposedly come to you in your dreams and show you where your slave was hiding.[138]

Those were Christians who stole the land from the natives, murdered them en masse, corralled the survivors onto parcels of the worst possible land, and took the best land for their slave plantations. Those were Christians who engaged in ruthless buck-breaking, Christians who routinely raped, and often impregnated, the women and the young girls as well. Those were Christians who tore families apart, who practiced cultural, linguistic, religious, and literal genocide.

And those were Christians who filled their coffers to the brim, exploiting the cheap slave labor in order to attain the morally dubious goal of accumulating massive wealth and power. The overall history of American slavery tells an unflattering story, when told accurately and in full, in relation to the morality of Christians. Importantly, the *Bible*, with its IG/OG ideology, its normalization of slavery, its intolerance of pagan, animist, or tribal religions, and its claim to religious superiority, served merely to spearhead an *apologist, justifying mythological narrative* instead.

The White Man's Burden

Slavery is rampant throughout holy scripture. Both the *Bible* and the *Quran* serve to normalize it. But race, as we know it today in America, the white versus black thing, did not exist per se in the *Bible*. Today, when your average American thinks 'slavery,' they also tend to think 'race' in this sense. Yet slavery did not originally have the racial component it does for us in America, not until a full millennium and a

---

[138] Nixey, *The Darkening Age*, 2018.

half after Christ, Caesar, and Cleopatra were all dead. And their slaves, too. (OK, sorry. Jesus did not appear to have slaves. But, the other two did, as did Muhammad several centuries on.) By the 16th century, however, the American institution of slavery was very much conjoined with a pseudoscientific racism, and a distinctly ethnocentric and rapine ideology of white superiority. Both America itself, as well as American racism and race-based slavery as we know it, are relatively modern phenomena.

Christian missionaries, regardless of their individual motivations, some of which were no doubt quite benevolent, understood their religion as superior, their god as the one and only true god. By the 16th century, this dovetailed with the growing ethnocentric belief that the white-skinned people of Europe were inherently superior, as well. Along with that came a natural, God-given right to dominate the dark-skinned savages of Africa and the Americas. Many of America's towns, churches, streets, historic missions, institutions of higher learning, even entire towns and cities, are still named after such missionaries to this day. I have lived most of my life beneath the eschatological and torturous shadow of Christianity's crucifix, from Saint Croix in the US Virgin Islands, to Santa Cruz, California. At the core of this ethnocentric Christian/European narrative was a belief that the Europeans were doing the dark-skinned savages of Africa and the Americas a favor, improving their lot by bringing Christianity and civilization to a barbaric, savage, and inferior peoples.

The Christian belief in religious superiority, the European imperialist hunger for expansion, power, and wealth, and the increasingly dominant narrative of white European superiority all intertwined most conveniently. The missionaries served as either the vanguard or accompaniment to the conquering, imperialist forces, hell bent upon theft of land, property, and goods.

Slave traders, *Bible* in hand, missionaries by their side, claimed, whether they believed it or not, to be doing the Africans a good turn by salvaging them from their allegedly horrid tribal existence, and bringing them to civilization and Jesus Christ. What they were really doing was making astounding profits by destroying families, torturing, murdering, and enslaving human beings under the most brutal and dehumanizing of conditions. The dominance of Euro-American economic, military, and political nations during the subsequent centuries, up into our own time, owes itself in large part to the blood, sweat, and tears of the African peoples who were kidnapped and forced to work as slaves upon the lands stolen from the original inhabitants of the Caribbean and the Americas.

The developing narrative justified all engaged in these joint imperialist pursuits as benevolent and superior, and actually burdened by a commitment, a covenant with god, to civilize inferior savages and save their souls. Most of the medieval missionaries, conquerors, slave traders, and plantation owners claimed to be doing 'gods work.' They were doing the inferiors a favor, bringing them Christ and civilization, taking on the 'white man's burden,' as it eventually came to be known.[139]

The phrase 'white man's burden' was an expression of this extremely ethnocentric, self-justifying, racist narrative, which served as a major component in an effort to rationalize religious, political, military, and economic imperialism, and the enslavement of both dark-skinned natives in the Americas, and kidnapped Africans by the millions. Perverse as it may sound to most of us today, it expresses an underlying belief which pervades Euro-American thinking, an understanding related to the notion of manifest destiny, and the dominant, and intensely arrogant, belief that it was Euro-American white male's

---

[139] Kipling, Rudyard. "The White Man's Burden: The United States & The Philippine Islands, 1899." In *Rudyard Kipling's Verse: Definitive Edition.* Garden City, New York: Doubleday, 1929.

burden of responsibility to bring civilization, and Christianity, to the non-white peoples of the world.

This dominant narrative served as a justification for an entrenched, systematic white privilege. Obviously pivotal components in this process of 'civilization' were Jesus Christ, the *Bible*, and the Christian religion. In a classic example of syncretism, the blending of influences, Jesus Christ and God themselves were increasingly interpreted as Euro-American and, most importantly, white-skinned.

Religious propaganda, in the form of indoctrination and 'false' narratives (i.e., lies), has inclined us toward a far more generous interpretation of the missionaries and their works. To this day, it keeps the focus primarily upon their allegedly beneficent deeds. Whatever good may have been done, however, it always went hand in hand with efforts at the conversion of infidels and the damned over to Jesus and the supposedly one true god; the reformation of inhuman savages into morally upright, European-tongued, properly attired and shorn, civilized citizens; the eradication of paganism and false gods; the spread of the gospel; and the all-important saving of souls. In other words: complete cultural genocide and assimilation.

By the 1600s, slavery in America was ideologically merged with the pseudoscientific concept of race, whose invention was in large measure an effort to dehumanize dark-skinned Africans in order to justify their being treated like things. Historically, efforts to rationalize or justify brutal and oppressive practices such as slavery or genocide have gone hand in hand with a specific dehumanization process, intended to create association between the oppressed or enslaved peoples, and some form or other of non-human animal. This process confers upon them a lesser value, makes of them a 'thing' to be owned or used.

History affords us with ample illustrations of this dehumanizing process, countless examples in which indoctrination and propaganda associating an Out Group with one non-human animal or another served in an effort to pave the way for overtly oppressive, if not fully genocidal practices. In the 1930s, Hitler and his Nazi propaganda perpetuated the image of the Jewish peoples as flea-ridden rats which carried contagion. In Rwanda during the 1990s, members of the Hutu majority sowed the seeds for a machete-wielding genocide by characterizing members of the Tutsi minority as snakes and cockroaches. This process continues on to this day in Christian America. A huge proportion of songs in contemporary popular music refer to women, long subject to devaluation in the AIC's hierarchic view, as bitches, the pejorative term for a female dog. Those who believe this history is all in the past merely fail to recognize the many ways that this is all relevant today, in one way or another, often in forms more subtle than in the past.

But not always. This dehumanization is also at times surprisingly overt. In the Euro-American slave trade, the dark-skinned Africans were characterized as monkeys or apes. In some quarters of American society there has been little if any change. In 2016, emboldened by the election of overtly racist entrepreneur and game show celebrity Donald Trump to the presidency, a government official in West Virginia famously perpetuated the simian references by publicly proclaiming that, "It will be so refreshing to have a classy, beautiful, dignified First Lady back in the White House. I'm tired of seeing a ape [sic] in heels."[140]

This comment was in reference to Michele Obama, President Barack Obama's dark-skinned wife. The ironic reality, widely recognized by many decent Americans, is that this comment, in addition to being a flagrant example of ignorance and racism, is also the complete and total opposite of the truth. Michele Obama was, and is, a woman

---

[140] Browning, Lexi and Lindsey Bever. "'Ape in Heels': West Virginia. Mayor Resigns Amid Controversy Over Racist Comments About Michelle Obama." *The Washington Post*. WP Company, October 26, 2021.

of great class, dignity, intelligence, education, and character, whereas Trump's third mistress/wife is none of the above. She was, in fact, best known for her work in pornography. The government official's comments would indeed be laughable but for the unfortunate fact that so many Americans share her misguided and bigoted point of view.

In Spite Of, Not Because...

Suffice to say that, by a significant margin, most of the perpetrators in the above examples were Christians. The slave traders, the millions of contemporary racists who constitute a disturbingly high proportion of the population of the US, and the many often well-meaning whites, at varying stages of wokeness, but all enjoying levels of underacknowledged privilege, freedoms, and rights regarding which they are relatively insensitive or unaware: all Christian. Again, this may all be correlation without causation. Nonetheless, we should always keep in mind that it is the AIC who loudly and proudly assert their status as the bastions of the moral high ground. An accurate rendering suggests otherwise. A legitimate historical narrative plainly exposes the truth: that moral change and improvements in social justice in the real world have come about *in spite of* the influence of the AIC, and not *because* of them.

American racism is, in a very real sense, a Christian invention. One glaring illustration of this concerns American Christians who interpret the Biblical stories regarding the curse of Ham, and the mark, or curse, of Cain, as justification for racism and the dehumanization of Africans and their American descendants. The founding fathers of the Mormon church believed that the darker skin of those kidnapped predominantly from west central Africa represented this Biblical curse, and that this marked them as inferior beings in god's eyes. The Mormons made an especially virulent point of this interpretation, limiting access of these cursed, black-skinned peoples in their Church of Latter-Day Saints, a ban which was not lifted until god apparently told them to do so, which was not until 1978.

So, it is abundantly clear that this sort of rationale for race hatred and racial discrimination is alive and well in today's Christian-dominated United States, both within some American churches, as well as within the cultural tradition amongst racist white congregations and denominational communities, particularly within the rural and southern areas of the United States. Modern white supremacist movements, riding a wave of nationalistic populism and retroactive politics in America and several other nations around 2016, proudly assert Christian and Biblical justifications for their racist agenda, as did the Nazis before them, and the KKK before that.

Where things have progressed away from this decidedly immoral and unjust historical narrative, they have done so as a result of what was imposed upon Christianity from *outside* of the church, its institutions, and communities, rather than from the *inside*.

Credit where credit is due: William Lloyd Garrison was one of the loudest voices clamoring for the abolition of slavery when that time eventually came in America. He read his *Bible* regularly and was a devout Christian. There were other Christians, famously the Quakers for instance, who also took up the cause of abolition when the time came. But they did so no more than did the deists, nor the secularists, agnostics, or atheists of the time.

A significant voice calling for the abolition of American slavery, so far as the white-skinned community was concerned, was that of Northern freethinkers, rather than the church. Humanist and freethinker Thomas Paine, who argued vehemently against organized religion in general, and against Christianity in particular, was one of the more prominent anti-slavery voices of his time. His *Rights of Man* was founded entirely upon secular considerations, and upon enlightenment principles of the natural rights of all humans.[141]

Moral progress, social progress, and improvements in justice are the result of forces outside of the church more so than inside the church. This is the precise opposite of what they would have us believe. Such improvements have been disproportionately thanks to those who have fought for justice, but often against the interests of the church, progressing in spite of, and not because of, religion. In many cases Christianity has served, as does modern Islam, to indoctrinate people in conserving outdated and long-antiquated traditions, which are themselves highly problematic, and in direct conflict with the human need for social progress and the perpetual, natural thirst for improved justice in human society.

Progress is the inevitable result of our natural talent for learning, acquiring knowledge, accumulating, sharing, and applying that knowledge, and learning some more, in combination with our native instincts for pro-social, cooperative, peaceful, In Group living, our rational thought, and concomitant principles of universalization and abstraction. All of this together ultimately gave birth to the rule of law, all in the light of a human world shifting away from scarcity, and toward a paradigm in which the needs of all are increasingly satisfied.

---

[141] Whittington, Keith E. *American Political Thought: Readings and Materials*. New York: Oxford University Press, 2017. – "That some desperate wretches should be willing to steal and enslave men by violence and murder for gain, is rather lamentable than strange. But that many civilized, nay, Christianized people should approve, and be concerned in the savage practice, is surprising; and still persist, though it has been so often proved contrary to the light of nature, to every principle of Justice and Humanity, and even good policy, by a succession of eminent men, and several late publications.
Our traders in MEN (an unnatural commodity!) must know the wickedness of the SLAVE-TRADE, if they attend to reasoning, or the dictates of their own hearts; and such as shun and stifle all these, willfully sacrifice Conscience, and the character of integrity to that golden idol." –Thomas Paine

The hunger for justice and for moral, pro-social human relations burns deep within the breast of all mentally healthy *Homo sapiens*, and does not require religious piety, devotion, worship, faith, nor indoctrination.

Chapter 13

In Spite Of, Not Because:
Christianity & Hitler's Germany

Paradigmatic Evil

The bloodiest and most destructive war in all of human history, World War II, presents us with more opportunities to recognize the fallacious nature of the assertion that religion serves as a source of peace, as well as to acknowledge that freedom from religion, and our movement toward reason and humanism, means a more peaceful, non-violent world for us all. For example, it is not widely recognized that millions of Christian Americans opposed and delayed entering the war against Hitler's Nazi Germany not because they held pacifist, or even isolationist, concerns, but because they actually appreciated Hitler's anti-Semitic agenda.

The overwhelming majority of the citizens of Nazi Germany were Christian. When Hannah Arendt wrote about the 'banality of evil,' the banal she was referring to were, according to the 1939 German census, 55% Protestant and 40% Catholic, with 3.5% merely claiming to 'believe in god' in some other form.[142] 95%: that is an extremely significant majority. Christians made Nazi Germany work, filled out the forms, in triplicate, signed for the deliveries, manufactured and erected the barbed-wire fences, around the ghettos, around the

---

[142] Gailus, Manfred. *Zerstrittene "Volksgemeinschaft": Glaube, Konfession Und Religion Im Nationalsozialismus.* Göttingen: Vandenhoeck & Ruprecht, 2011.

concentration camps. Those where Christians, who pressed the buttons and pulled the levers, drove the trains, filled the gas chambers, the 'showers,' with live human beings, and then removed the still warm, lifeless corpses minutes later, wheeled them out by the score, dug the graves both large and small, then came back and did it again, and again.

The Pope at the time, Pope Pius XII, leader of the Catholic world, had some very real and significant concerns. Unfortunately, the pope's priorities were off. Skewed. Immoral. What the pope was primarily concerned with were the perceived elements of paganism in Hitler's Third Reich. He was not as concerned with the welfare of the millions of Jews and other non-Catholic peoples whose lives and well-being were threatened by the Nazi regime.

But intolerance of paganism aside, it was intolerance of alternative Abrahamic denominations, which was a far more determinative factor in World War II. Anti-Semitism was undeniably one of Nazi leader Adolph Hitler's primary motivations, if not itself *the* singular, overriding obsession. Far from opposing or even remaining neutral in the face of obscene and atrocious levels of immorality, injustice, and ruthless oppression to the point of genocide, the leading Christian authority in the world was largely on good terms with the Nazi leader.

> On the big question, it's clear: Pius XII never publicly criticized the Nazis for the mass murder they were committing of the Jews of Europe – and he knew from the very beginning that mass murder was taking place. Various clerics and others were pressing him to speak out, and he declined to do so.
> – David Kertzer[143]

---

[143] Kertzer, David. *The Pope and Mussolini: The Secret History of Pius XI and the Rise of Fascism in Europe.* Random House Publishing Group, 2014. – Pulitzer Prize for Biography or Autobiography (2015).

Adolph Hitler, that infamous paragon of human evil, was himself a Catholic by upbringing:[144]

I am now as before a Catholic and will always remain so.

Hitler claimed, on a number of occasions, to be doing God's will:[145]

Hence today I believe that I am acting in accordance with the will of the Almighty Creator: by defending myself against the Jew, I am fighting for the work of the Lord.

World War II was, at its core, yet another holy war. In the eyes of Christians and Muslims, Judaism is first and foremost a religious category. So, even if Hitler's words embracing the faith were merely another example of that famously effective Nazi propaganda, keep in mind that those words were intended to mollify an audience composed almost entirely of pious, church going, god-fearing Christians. Either way, it was a war with religion at its core, an ongoing battle between Abrahamic sects.

Religious Lie #420: Hitler was an Atheist

The facts conflict directly with contemporary popular conceptions, in which this major conflict is understood as being of an entirely worldly, secular nature. Hitler himself is even sometimes argued to have been an atheist. The evidence suggests otherwise. But, of course, if he was, that too bodes ill for religion: if he only pretended to be Christian in order to stir up genocidal hatred of the Jew (and it worked so exceedingly well!), does that truly make for a better look, so far as Christianity is concerned?

---

[144] Toland, John. *Adolf Hitler: The Definitive Biography*. New York: Anchor Publishing, 1992.

[145] Hitler, Adolf. *Mein Kampf* ("My Struggle"). Houghton Mifflin, New York: Hutchinson Publ. Ltd., London, 1969.

The bottom line is that WWII was in significant respects a religious war, like so many others. We understand it as secular because the winner writes history, and depicting it otherwise would not have been a good look for Christianity. It is indoctrination, propaganda, lies, and falsehood. The truth is that World War II was a conflict with pivotal economic, political, and military factors, but with significant religious elements also playing all-important roles: stirring people up, playing upon and encouraging their predisposition to interpret and understand the world in IG/OG terms, complete with a dehumanized other, inspiring war fever, and establishing the supposed spiritual high ground. Abrahamic religion was either a genuine cause, or at the very least a significant source of justification. In this respect it was precisely the same as the hundreds of other religious wars which have been raging over the centuries since the 'prince of peace' was born.

After World War II, there was significant hand wringing and critical self-reflection on the part of much of humanity. People all around the world, faced with the tremendous destruction, casualties, and horrors, asked themselves *"How?"*; asked themselves *"Why?"* Social Psychologist Stanley Milgram's famous studies shed considerable light upon the 'banality of evil.' While the implications of his work are still being debated to this day, one result which is fairly straightforward supports the notion that humans tend to be very obedient to perceived authority. We are, to a disturbingly large extent, followers. For every single Jesus, Gandhi, or Martin Luther King, there are millions or billions of religious sheep ready and willing to be led, awaiting direction, prepared by a lifetime of following commandments to sit, to stand, to bend the knee upon command.

Another fiction perpetuated by the AIC is that religion and god are the source of morality. This claim relies upon a fundamental conflation of two distinct human phenomena: *being moral* versus *obeying commands*. But these two are not synonymous. What the AIC idealize is compliance to orders, the follower who is 100% obedient to god's commands, who does not question the orders which are handed down to them, but follows them compliantly, faithfully, devoutly, as Abraham did when told to murder his beloved child. These sorts of stories in the *Bible* or *Quran* are, if not taken literally, alleged moral allegory intended to impart an ideal toward which all of humanity should aspire.

This training in obedience to command and authority is surprisingly similar to the goals in military training. Don't think; just follow orders. The 'negation of self' is presented as an ideal and a goal to aspire to, both in religious and military indoctrination. For both monks and marines. The message is the same, from Abraham and Isaac; to the banal Nazis 'just doing their jobs'; to the My Lai Massacre in Vietnam; to the justifications in the hearts and minds of every suicide bomber, and every one of the 19 terrorists on the morning of 9/11. To the atheist and humanist mind, on the other hand, faithfully following orders is a far cry from being a morally developed human being.

An accurate reading of the narrative of history tells us that it is precisely such order following, the obedience training that is religion, which produces banal evildoers by the millions. It was not Adolf Hitler who pressed the buttons that released the gas, who pulled the trigger to shoot small children in their mother's arms, who dug the mass graves, or shoveled the bodies into them, and then went to church on Sunday. It was every day, god-fearing, Christian citizens.

Through either explicit lies, or in more covert forms, the AIC are responsible for a vast coterie of falsehoods and deceptions. Here and now, these diverse and widespread fictions remain widely believed and trusted, and thereby essentially intact: Christianity is a worldwide force for peace; the early Christians were the entirely innocent and peaceful victims of ruthless oppression; monotheism reigns supreme because of a natural historical progression and an inherent superiority; the Dark Ages of Europe were caused by secular forces; Christian Americans were abolitionists and the church helped end the institution of slavery; Christian Americans opposed Hitler; Hitler was an atheist and World War II an entirely irreligious affair; and if Americans just read their *Bible* more and went to church, we'd have fewer school shootings and less gun violence. The list of flagrant lies goes on and on.

These and other misrepresentations of reality continue largely unabated in our time, along with their ongoing ramifications. Even when outed, religious falsehood continues to have lasting effects. It is increasingly clear that the path forward, toward a truly moral, rational, and humanist civilization, begins with a fundamental need to unlearn religion, to forego religious indoctrination, whilst simultaneously becoming more genuinely educated, about the wider world around us, about our true nature, and about the history of misconceptions, their many and diverse forms, and their enduring impact upon humanity.

Christianity, Americans, and Violence

I came not to send peace, but a sword.
– Jesus Christ[146]

American parents have long obsessed over their kids playing video games. They are anxious lest such games deaden kids' sensitivity to real-world violence. They wring their hands over the possibility that the games have the effect of normalizing or even encouraging violence, worry that their son or neighbor may be the next news cycle's school shooter. Despite the fact that both the *Bible* and the *Quran* normalize interpersonal and even genocidal violence, devout Americans still have

---

[146] King James Version – 10:34-35

faith that a steady diet of Biblical teachings would somehow turn this current tendency on its head, solving the problem of fever-pitch gun violence in contemporary America.

Addressing America's scourge of gun violence, one time governor, presidential candidate, right-wing journalist and staunch supporter of the NRA, Mike Huckabee, speaking on behalf of many devout Christians, claimed that a decreased connection with god is causally related to the mass shootings which plagued the United States.

There is in fact no data to support Huckabee's assertion, yet a great deal suggesting the contrary. The problem here is the reliance upon fiction and faith rather than facts and reason. Huckabee, representing a perspective shared by millions of Americans, believes that the *Bible* and Christianity will reduce gun violence, but his faith is not based upon any credible evidence whatsoever. Such beliefs are entirely devoid of factual content. Despite a total absence of supporting evidence, they assert a causal connection and, in so doing, demonstrate the worst kind of pseudoscientific thinking.

The AIC promote themselves as forces for nonviolence. History, told honestly, suggests otherwise. Religion does not cure our violent tendencies. It may in fact be more cause than cure. The emphasis on self-righteousness, proselytizing, and conversion, on obedience to command, hand-in-hand with a distinctive *IG/OG* mentality, what I have also referred to as the dominance mindset, strongly suggests that violent, armed conflict is ultimately inevitable in a world in which anyone's views differ from those of the AIC's.

The *Bible* and *Quran* are additionally responsible for indirectly leading to more violence, because they serve to normalize, exacerbate, and justify violent conflict against infidels, idolaters, or nonbelievers. In this sense, these traditions are responsible for far more of this world's violent conflict than the average believer generally cares to acknowledge.

Homo sapiens, particularly the male of the species, is by nature violent and warlike. But we are famously conflicted. In addition to having such natural tendencies, we also have instincts which incline us in the precise opposite direction. We are naturally compassionate, tender, kind and forgiving equally so. Yes, even we males.

This is true, though it does not tend to make the evening news with the same frequency. After all, "If it bleeds, it leads," as they say. The truth is that both ordinary gossip and daily media content of all stripes will emphasize the violent rape that occurred, or the school shooting, so many killed in the latest battle-scarred region, or the princess who died in a car crash, but will say nary a word about the million peaceful interpersonal interactions that 'go without saying,' quite literally, every minute of every day, all around our world.

This is the norm of human society, the scoreless acts of kindness, benevolence, or even the non-violent discord peacefully resolved that went down at one and the same time. *Homo sapiens* manages the co-operative complexity of four-way stop signs, intense frustration, not getting what we want, disappointment and disillusion, rejection, and even meets anger and hatred with patience and kindness millions of times a day.

The vast majority of human beings today, as ever, have a strong desire to live in peace and harmony. But the AIC exacerbate our violent tendencies by placing a significant emphasis upon dominance or IG/OG thinking, inclining us to see and interpret the world around us in a comprehensively divisive manner. At one and the same time, they also nurture a false front, an image of themselves as promoting peace, love, and understanding. By the millions, Christians genuinely attest that 'God is love,' while Muslims cling to the belief that Islam is the 'religion of peace.' All the while, both are guilty of encouraging, exacerbating, enflaming, perpetuating, and normalizing our tendencies toward conflict.

In *The Curse of Cain: The Violent Legacy of Monotheism*, Professor Regina Schwartz argues that these monotheistic traditions, with their jealous and demanding deities, command an exclusive allegiance which is so central to a people's shared identity that it is causally implicated in violence, pitting one group of humans against an 'other,' as an essential component in a given people's self-identity.[147] Her work argues that the...

> ...Bible is filled with narratives of division and exclusion, scarcity and competition, that erupt in violence. Once these narratives were appropriated and disseminated by western religious traditions, they came to pervade deep cultural assumptions about how collectives are imagined—with collective hatred, with collective degradation, and with collective abuse.

The result of this long-lasting legacy of intolerance, conversion, and conquest is a world which is currently suffused by an inherently oppositional perspective, a basic way of thinking which inclines most humans to interpret all relationships as essentially conflicts or battles. Through the divisive lens of this dominance mindset, this IG/OG weltanschauung, this fundamentally antagonistic, oppositional mode of thought and belief we are inclined to create more enemies than friends, to erect boundaries rather than eradicate them, to build walls rather than bridges, from bedroom to boardroom to battlefield.

Abrahamic scripture is replete with carnage, mayhem, and slaughter galore. The *Bible* and *Quran* equally prioritize, emphasize, and normalize violence, from the simple act of killing someone who does not share the same ideas about how to pray, to the wholesale genocide of Out Groups in the name of god. This is not merely an ancient issue but, as the news cycles regularly portray, continues unabated into our

---

[147] Schwartz, Regina. *The Curse of Cain: The Violent Legacy of Monotheism*. The University of Chicago Press, Chicago, 1997.

own time. Be it steady trickling stream, or flash flood of epic proportions, this continuous river of human blood has been flowing steadily, 24/7/365, quite literally, since the time of Cleopatra, Caesar, and Jesus Christ.

The bottom line is that a more contemporary, post-Darwinian, science-friendly understanding of *Homo sapiens*, one which considers our unique capacity for accretive and mutualistic intelligence, would emphasize our nature as the learning animal, and our resultant post-instinct, non-genetic, cultural malleability. Both the religious notion of us as subject to god's divine blueprint and masterplan, and it's more contemporary variant in genetic determinism, fail to properly acknowledge the significant uniqueness of the *Homo sapiens* brain on this particular score. To a degree apparently never before seen in life on Earth, we are the result of an evolutionary process which, in our case, resulted in a species with a singularly unique capacity for learning, an unparalleled ability to adapt based upon knowledge and culture rather than genetics and biology.

More so than any other organism or animal, we are a result of nurture over nature. We are what we learn. We are the learning animals. For better or for worse. Religion ensures the 'for worse'. Religious indoctrination exposes the downside, the weakness, of the intense emphasis upon nurture over nature. We will have to take this bull by the horns. We will have to intentionally choose our own destiny. An entire generation of non-violent human beings would be the inevitable result of a well-educated world: teaching people about one another, not to fear the other, teaching them science, the evolutionary sciences and more, in a comprehensive, well-balanced education, and teaching non-violent conflict resolution from an early age. These are all ways in which significant reductions in violence can happen, and in fact are already coming to pass.

I have described several examples of ways in which we are genetically predisposed to beliefs or behaviors that are all natural or instinctive – religious belief, prejudice, superstition, and supernatural thinking – any of which are fairly easily overwritten by a solid general education. That is, with a genuinely comprehensive general education, importantly skewed away from indoctrination, and incorporating important elements of skepticism, science, and reason, we would go a long way, if not all the way, toward creating a non-violent world, a world characterized not necessarily by bliss or total unanimity, but by peoples matured enough to resolve their disputes in a non-violent manner. And, in the end, who would not prefer to resolve our seemingly inevitable conflicts over a cup strewn coffee table than over a battlefield strewn with the dismembered bodies of our sons and daughters.

Chapter 14

In Spite Of, Not Because:
Christianity & Misogyny

Gender & Justice

Whether we are talking about earning only 79 cents to every male dollar;

Or the fact that only 5% of Fortune 500's CEOs are female;

That today's U.S. Congress has more women members than ever before, yet that amounts to a mere 27%, well below the genuinely representative ideal of 50%;

Or that Saudi Arabian women only recently were allowed the right to drive;

Or that Afghani women cannot leave their homes unless covered head to toe, and even then, they must be in the escort of a family male;

Or we are talking about blaming females when they are raped or assaulted by males;

Or the massively underreported numbers of such instances;

The predominantly patriarchal Christian and Islamic legislative bodies passing laws regarding women's control over their own bodies;

The bilking of billions of hard-earned dollars by convincing girls and women that they are imperfect little playthings who must 'put on' their faces every day, flawed toys seriously in need of cosmetics, dyes, perfumes, hairstyles, shaves and waxes, the latest costly fashions, a little nip here and a tuck there;

Or the fact that Americans still think it is normal and morally permissible for women to unthinkingly take on the names of their husbands, becoming 'Mrs. John Smith', upon entering into marriage;

Or denying girls the most modest of educations or business opportunities;

The history of sexist, misogynistic, patriarchal injustice is enduring and universal. The scope of this ongoing imbalance is beyond measure. I am ill-suited to do this issue justice as I am a privileged, white American male. But as it is one of the most insidious and virulent evils perpetrated by the AIC, it must be recognized and outed as the real problem which it is.

Islam and Christianity have perpetuated an understanding of humanity which places women below men in a hierarchy of value. They have created origin myths which standardize metaphysical and ontological justifications for the subjugation of women by men. They codify it within scripture and our very origin stories themselves, presenting women's secondary status as a natural and innate feature of human existence. They establish this gendered injustice as a norm. Misogynistic inequity has been normalized and institutionalized to such a degree that many believe it to be both an integral aspect of human nature, and entirely morally justified.

The AIC are not merely sexist and misogynistic. They are *extremely* so. They do not practice and preach mildly sexist philosophies and agendas, but rather virulent and intense versions. These religions have long been patriarchal in the extreme, sexist and misogynistic forces hindering women's rights, and perpetuating the second-class citizenship of girls and women for centuries. The sexism promoted and perpetuated by the AIC is truly Biblical in its dimension, scope, and proportion. As such, Islam and Christianity combined serve as one of the greatest impediments preventing genuine equity for women and girls.

So far from woman owing what liberty she does enjoy, to the Bible and the church, they have been the greatest stumbling block in the way of her development.

— Elizabeth Cady Stanton[148]

Our Abrahamic ancestors were no more nor less guilty than most peoples, be it two hundred, two thousand, or ten thousand years ago. In the pagan culture of classical Greece, women were legally considered to be just another part of the household: initially under the father's thumb, later under the husbands. They were but mere possessions. So, we cannot fault the *Bible* as uniquely misogynistic. It represented the general perspective of many folks at that time and in that general cultural context.

And yet religion and apotheosis hold us all back. Considering the *Bible* as holy scripture, holding its words, depictions, and conceptions as divine and of paramount significance simply hinders progress toward social justice and a more ethical state of affairs. Outside of religious influence, much of the rest of humanity has matured some since those times and is progressing.

Might Makes Right

No doubt, for millennia, well back into our more tribal and simian lives, might made right. Physical dominance was what mattered, and this was just the way of nature. Sexual dimorphism simply means some species have evolved to have different morphology between the sexes —i.e., shape, color, ornamentation, or simply size. Female spiders are often significantly larger than their male counterparts. The female black widow can be as much as 10 times larger. In mammals, females tend to be smaller. In the case of *Homo sapiens*, as with many other

---

[148] Stanton, Elizabeth Cady. "The Degraded Status of Woman in the *Bible*." Free Thought Magazine, September 1896.

mammals, the male has been the larger, faster, and stronger of the two. Physical superiority in this sense quite reasonably determined much, more often than not, including who was in charge of the family, tribe, and village.

But we are no longer in a pure state of nature. In a very real sense, we appear to be the first species of organism on this planet to have evolved into a qualitatively distinct state, one in which nature can be differentiated from nurture; culture can and often does override what is natural. We have something very much like freedom of choice; and nature alone does not determine what is good, right, or ideal. We have crossed a line. For us, it's not all about biology. We are also part culture. Sexual dimorphism is far less relevant than it was 50,000, 2,000, or even 200 years ago. When Alexander the Great or Julius Caesar pulled the 'might makes right' card, it played OK at the time. When Adolph Hitler tried it, not so popular anymore. Increasingly, for much of humanity, might no longer makes right.

Today, we are instead guided by principles of justice, determined largely by use of reason, theoretically to be applied equally regardless of class, wealth, position, skin color, sex, or gender. Instead of systematically raping all the girls and women, as the *Bible* describes in such an off-hand, casual, normalized manner, victorious armies today will instead sometimes build schools and hospitals, attempt to win over 'hearts and minds.' Not all. But some. We fail to live up to these standards much of the time. But they are standards which we have or aspire to. While the results of our justice system are often disconcertingly unjust, we achieve genuine results that point us in the right direction, while the interventionist deity of the Abrahamic tradition has a truly horrid track record by comparison. We still have a long way to go, but, at the same time, we most certainly have progressed away from strongman politics, increasingly toward genuine rule of law.

In the 18th century, the declaration of human rights in the *Preamble to the Declaration of Independence* stated:[149]

> We hold these truths to be self-evident, that all men are created equal, that they are endowed by their Creator with certain unalienable Rights, that among these are Life, Liberty and the pursuit of Happiness.

These lofty principles were the gift of a divine being, although it was more of a deist model which held sway for a number of our nation's Founding Fathers at the time. More to the current point, 'men' in this context was meant entirely literally. Women simply did not count. In fact, American women did not even achieve the right to vote until well into the 20th century, well *after* black men did.

In the middle of the 20th century, almost two centuries after the *Declaration of Independence*, the *United Nations Universal Declaration of Human Rights* states:[150]

> Article 1
> All human beings are born free and equal in dignity and rights.
> Article 2
> Everyone is entitled to all the rights and freedoms set forth in this declaration, without distinction of any kind, such as race, colour, sex, language, religion...
> Article 3
> Everyone has the right to life, liberty and the security of person.

---

[149] "The Constitution of the United States: A Transcription." National Archives and Records Administration. Available at: https://www.archives.gov/founding-docs/constitution-transcript
[150] "Universal Declaration of Human Rights." United Nations, https://www.un.org/en/about-us/universal-declaration-of-human-rights
– The United Nations Declaration of Human Rights is an excellent example of an entirely secular approach to morality, justice, and human rights, and a quintessential example of human progress as well.

The two documents are not equivalent in impact. The *US Constitution* represented the founding document for the government of a nation. Relatively speaking, the *UN Declaration* had, and still has, considerably less bite. Nonetheless, it expresses and illustrates our changing priorities and values, our secular progress. Evidence for this claim comes from the simple fact that interpretations of the US document have moved, over the course of that 200 years, more and more in these precise same directions. Black men received the right to vote in 1868, all women in 1920. Neither group receives truly equal, fair or just treatment to this day in the United States, but it tends to get better over time. Albeit slowly. With a great deal of struggle involved. This is what progress looks like.

Like slavery, huge swathes of humanity no longer consider misogyny morally permissible. Still, the deeply antiquated *Bible* presents the ancient past as normalized. Nowhere in the *Bible* will you find guiding principles, appropriate instructions, or even a single thought regarding the status of women as equal partners, as morally, legally, ethically, intellectually, socially equivalent to males. The *Bible* advocates, of course, for the treatment of women precisely as it did in centuries past. The *Bible*, the church, Christian traditions and long-standing practices, not to mention religions' conservative emphasis upon seeking truth and wisdom in tradition, in the past, all serve collectively to reinforce patriarchal culture, and to hinder the healthy course of social progress.

Religion stands directly in the path of us moving from a place in which women and girls are but things in 'a man's world,' to a position in which genuine moral equivalence is the accepted and normative state of affairs. What change has been made, has been made *in spite of,* most certainly not *because of,* Christianity or Islam. All whilst they continue to assert the claim that they are the ultimate source of morality.

313

We have encountered versions of this same story in previous chapters. Earlier chapters pointed out how, according to both Abrahamic dualism and the Great Chain of Being, women have often been considered separate from 'mankind,' an adjunct, a spare rib, a possession, a mere part of the household. They have often been associated with the natural, below that fine line which 'men' straddle, one foot in the natural realm, the other in the divine. This is not dissimilar from the ways in which black people were dehumanized, associated with the lesser, 'animal' realm, and thus accorded an inferior status in the imagined cosmic hierarchy. This process of dehumanization serves in this archaic mindset to validate grossly immoral inequity.

In Spite of, Not Because

By way of analogy, consider the subject of LGBTQ rights. The greatest stumbling block to equal rights for the lesbian, gay, bisexual, trans, and queer members of the community that is the United States of America, resistance to the belief that LGBTQ persons should be accorded the precise same moral and legal status as everyone else, has far and away come from religion, specifically the Abrahamic religions of Islam and Christianity. Often to highly pernicious, offensive, even violent and life-threatening degrees.

It is through secular and humanist efforts that so many have ceased to think of LGBTQ people as morally reprehensible at best, at worst as egregious sinners. Within very recent history, American laws and those of many other nations have changed to reflect this increasingly enlightened perspective. American congregations and churches have begun to increasingly avow more tolerant, open-door policies. But these institutions are latecomers to the party. As is generally true regarding issues of social justice, the religious tend to be the followers, not the leaders.

The suffragist, feminist, women's empowerment, women's liberation, and gender equality movements have played a vital role in moving the human world ever closer to the ideal of equal rights for all persons. Arguably, no nation can claim to have achieved the goal of genuine social justice for women and girls as of yet. But some communities and nations are clearly doing better than others, and those are the ones with a rising number of nones, more atheists, and solid divisions between church and state.

Islam and Christianity are not the sole cause, nor the lone perpetrators of patriarchy. If there is any place on Earth that is actually outside the sphere of the influence of AIC, I am confident that there, too, one will find women enduring the yolk of second-class citizenship. In America today, business, social, and governmental institutions and traditions of long standing are also guilty of perpetuating patriarchy.

However, it is important to acknowledge the ways in which the AIC bear a disproportionate burden of responsibility for promoting this unjust state of affairs. The AIC have codified it in scripture, which serves to normalize and justify the errant beliefs and practices on some deep psychological levels. Antiquated traditions tend to self-perpetuate, generation by generation. It takes a real, concerted effort to change the direction of such things. But being the self-appointed source of what is moral, should not these institutions and traditions be *leading* the pack toward social justice and equity, rather than pulling up the rear or, even worse, having to be dragged towards social justice, kicking and screaming all the way, by godless heathens?

It's in the Book!

All of us in Christian America are familiar with the story of Adam and Eve. Your average atheist actually has an even better understanding of this foundational origin myth than does your average believer.[151] And yet, it cannot be said that we are equally so 'all familiar' with, say, evolutionary theory, for example. In other words, despite the passage of over a century and a half of professional acceptance and ongoing affirmation, more people are aware of the fictional, mythological origin story, than the factual, evidence-based, scientifically undisputed origin story, the one which far more accurately and genuinely describes our true origins and nature.

This speaks to the power of religious indoctrination, and its broad reaching, ongoing effects. In essence, most people are underinformed and undereducated. They are trained, instead of educated, running on a combination of instinct and learned ignorance. They have learned what they were taught, but they have often been taught some very questionable things. That 'we all know the story of Adam and Eve' is basically saying 'we have all been indoctrinated.' And, of course, a significant part of indoctrination requires negating or denying opposing views. The more indoctrinated, the less educated.

Unfortunately, the indoctrinated rule. *'What people generally believe'* has more impact upon our world than the more accurate, falsifiable beliefs of the well informed, rational, or educated. So, rather than acknowledge that we are long past the days when might made right, when sexual dimorphism alone justified inequity in gender relations, we are still stuck with billions who take their advice from an ancient book of tales written in all probability entirely by males, misogynist males with a clear vested interest in perpetuating extremely sexist norms, in maintaining their privileged status.

---

[151] Fahmy, Dalia. "Among Religious 'Nones' Atheists and Agnostics Know the Most About Religion." Pew Research Center, Washington, D.C., July 23, 2020.

Wives, submit yourselves to your own husbands as you do to the Lord. For the husband is the head of the wife...wives should submit to their husbands in everything.
                    – Ephesians 5:22 - 24[152]

'If it's in the *Bible*, it must be so.' These are our origin stories, codified and deified through the process of apotheosis, still causing billions to think that this inequality is an integral aspect of god's divine plan, a part of the structure of the cosmos itself, hardwired and written into our very natures. Women's inferiority is understood to be natural, god-given, preordained, and an important part of the cosmic blueprint.

Scripture ensures that this prejudice is passed from one generation to the next, this belief that women are innately inferior, that women are rightfully men's possessions and play things, that they are but the property of males, even that females are evil and sin-saturated temptresses. The AIC may not be the initial cause of this rampant misogyny, but they are entirely responsible for elevating it to the point of normalcy, and for seeing to it that this understanding remains largely unchallenged and self-perpetuating from one generation to the next.

The combined impact of religious institutions, traditions, and culture, and the billions of individual believers passing these beliefs down to innocent, vulnerable children, results in the perpetuation and normalization of misogyny through the ages, and its grounding in allegedly sacred scripture, in god's own word. Women and girls are inferior to men, the property of men, and, as the mere spare ribs they are, are to be savored as the spoils of war, as booty for man's enjoyment. Yes. That's right—Booty.

---

[152] New International Version – Ephesians 5:22-24

But the women, and the little ones, and the cattle, and all that is in the city, even all the spoil thereof, shalt thou take unto thyself; and thou shalt eat the spoil of thine enemies, which the LORD thy God hath given thee.

– Deuteronomy 20:14[153]

There it is, right there in the book. Women are just spoils. In addition to these origin stories and fundamental myths, the religious institutions themselves also perpetuate this ongoing injustice internally, bolstering it up with each successive generation, each appointment, each hire, each assignment. Women are simply not allowed to be religious authorities in the vast majority of Christian congregations and sects.

According to Catholic and Orthodox Christian traditions, women are not allowed to be priests at all. There are a couple hundred, though. Out of about 400,000 total priests around the world, there are about 200 female priests.[154] So, women comprise 50% of human beings, but merely .05% of priests. It's a little hard to say if this is an example of progress or not. Regardless, the role of women inside the church is slowly responding to the growing pressure for change and social justice impinging upon religion from the outside, although, in this respect, there is clearly still a long way to go.

Fortunately, we are in an era of unprecedented historical progress on this whole matter. The changing status of women, perhaps most of all, indicates that this progress is not just a temporary thing, another swing of the pendulum that will reverse itself in time. It is too widespread, universal, deep, and genuine. It is hard to imagine women stepping back into the shadows, allowing the shackles to be snapped

---

[153] King James Bible – Deuteronomy 20:14
[154] Pearce, Valeria Perasso and Georgina. "Excommunicated: The Women Fighting to Be Priests." BBC News, December 13, 2022. https://www.bbc.com/news/world-63923460

back in place. My daughters, and their friends of all sexes and genders, accept women's fundamental equivalence as a given, and are not disposed to cede their well-earned rights. And this significant historical change we are enjoying stretches well beyond American shores.

Brutal & Bigoted

Back again to the garden. Once Eve was tempted by Satan, and ate from the tree of knowledge, we were no longer pure. We were cast out of Eden. That is the source of original sin, according to the *Bible*. God said, 'You guys suck; you're outta here, and you're going to suffer, and it's all Eve's fault, because she let Satan compel her.' Though subject to a wide variety of interpretations over the centuries, Adam and Eve is a memorable fable with some fairly clear, though dubious, morals. There are at least three clear messages which your average Jane and Joe Faithful take home, and which indoctrinated children grasp early on in their religious 'education':

- Knowledge is a dangerous thing, primarily something which Satan uses to lure us away from faith.
- We should feel ashamed of our bodies, nudity, and indeed our natural selves.
- Women are the reason everything is fucked up, and they deserve to suffer.

Clearly, we are no longer talking about moral exemplars when we justify locking girls and women behind closed doors; deny them education at any and all levels; deny them driver's licenses; deny them even the most rudimentary degree of human autonomy and basic human rights; mangle their bodies, or indoctrinate them to self-mangle their own bodies with paints and primers and perfumes and Prada and prosthetic procedures aplenty; train them in self-loathing, make them complicit in their own internalized subjugation; cover them from head to toe in oppressive black cloth; and call them the problem.

The AIC and their scriptures, alleged moral authorities so many believe them to be, actually serve to reinforce and justify misogyny, rather than question its moral validity in any way. Foremost amongst the reasons that the misogynist traditions of both highly patriarchal religions are morally bankrupt is the obvious fact that they simply fail to treat women as true persons, as autonomous human beings. Far from being a source for morality, the AIC in fact serve to prevent men from taking responsibility, and from cultivating their own capacity as moral agents. Islam and Christianity infantilize men. And women pay the price. Of the utmost importance, we must recognize the need for individual moral development. These ancient sexist traditions allow men to remain morally immature and underdeveloped, shoving responsibility for the problem onto the primary victim.

> ...the Quran is not a holy document. It is a historical record, written by humans....
> And it is a very tribal and Arab version of events. It spreads a culture that is brutal, bigoted, fixated on controlling women...
> – Ayaan Hirsi Ali[155]

This culture she is describing is not specific to Islam nor today's Middle East. It is the same culture as that which is normalized and codified within the *Bible*, the central scripture of Christianity. The genuinely devout males of Islam or Christianity are not expected to develop, to mature, neither morally nor emotionally. Women are expected to adjust their own behavior, conform their choices, in deference and subordination to the desires of men. Men must have that which sexually tempts them sequestered away, hidden from their

---

[155] Hirsi Ali, *Infidel*, 2008.

hungry eyesight, their grasping, desirous hands, much as we keep temptation from a small child.

In this and in numerous other ways, religious tradition and scripture, and religious strictures, impede individual moral development, emotional maturity, and social responsibility. Genuinely religious men remain emotionally, sexually, and socially immature. The oppressed, underclass of women and girls is required to warp their lives in accord with both religious commands and the desires of their overlords, the religiously pious and faithful males.

Lest we Americans, westerners, or Christians mount up upon our high horse, let us pause to acknowledge that this supposedly 'Islamic' issue is simply a different version of a very real problem still plaguing Christian culture and the west today. Women in Islamic theocracies may be forced to hide beneath Burkas, but at least they do not willingly part with approximately 50 billion dollars (Yes, that's billion with a *B*!) every year, in order to purchase and consume cosmetics, and then turn around and claim that they choose to do so 'freely.' Both these holy books have been used for millennia to beat women down, to impede justice, and to maintain women and girls in varying positions of dehumanized servitude to the dominant male.

Double Trouble

By the year 2023, the U.S. Senate had a total of 25 seated women senators out of the total of 100. As noted, this is both good news and bad news. It is actually a high-water mark in American history. In fact, the recent relatively progressive elections have almost doubled the total number of women Senators over the 200-year span of American history. There have been only 59 since our inception, *including* today's 25. Representation at 25% is exceptional, and the highest it has ever been. But a genuinely representative body should be twice as many. Still, today we are witnessing some noteworthy improvement.[156]

Importantly, this change has come not from the allegedly more 'moral,' highly religious, center/right-wing of American politics. Rather it has come from the opposite, the decidedly more secular, humanist, left/moderate wing of American society. The current composition of women Senators is majority Democrat by a wide margin, with a total of 9 Republican women, 15 Democrat, and 1 Independent. Of course, knowing their true religious affiliations is unrealistic, given that self-acknowledging as an atheist equates to immediate political suicide. Apparently, given the off-term elections of 2021, for many Americans, storming the Capitol in a violent insurrection makes one worthy of elected office, whereas admitting you may not fully believe in a 2000-year-old Middle East deity renders one unfit to lead.[157]

The AIC historically serve highly conservative functions in America and around the world, hindering rather than encouraging forward movement on vitally important social and moral issues. Far from generating the social movement of women and girls (of all people, for that matter) toward a more just and equitable state of affairs, the church actively perpetuates and defends its boys' club-style membership. To this day, wealthy, old, white males only need apply.

If religions like Catholicism change at all, it is extremely slow. The Catholic Church, Christianity's largest branch, with just over half of all the world's Christians, recently offered a formal apology to Galileo. Unfortunately, the poor old guy has been dead for 350 years. Perhaps it was appreciated by his great, great, great, great, great, great grandchildren. But many feel this sort of gesture, flagrantly too little too

---

[156] Center for American Women and Politics. "Women in the U.S. Senate 2023." Available at: https://cawp.rutgers.edu/facts/levels-office/congress/women-us-senate-2023

[157] Center for American Women and Politics. "Women in the U.S. Senate 2023."

late, speaks very poorly of religion's alleged moral and ethical authority.

The church was feeling conspicuously contrite in the 1990s. It was around this time that Pope John Paul II also apologized for Catholic participation in the slave trade, the holocaust, the crusades, the Inquisition... Oh, and for their historic mistreatment of women, as well. These long-overdue words were not accompanied by any significant discernible change in either theory or practice. Clearly this represented some much-needed P.R. work, as the church is facing a noteworthy diminution in interest over recent decades. Systematic child rape will do that. Kinda puts the kibosh on the whole recruitment process.

It is truly a heinous offense when a male adult abuses a child sexually. But the offense is doubled when the perpetrator is a man of the cloth. There is supposed to be a level of trustworthiness inherent to such a position. This is analogous with being a parent. The parent, or priest, bishop, imam, uncle, grandpa, is taking on the role of proxy. This means they are supposed to be representatives of the child's best interests, as children are presumed to be not fully capable of seeing to their own needs and healthy interests.

When we take on such a morally weighted responsibility, we are not merely another adult in the child's world. We are essentially deputized as that person's representative, the guardian of their health, welfare, and interests. It is one kind of moral wrong, a form of evil, when a person abuses a child. But it is double so if that person is a trusted proxy, such as a family member. Religious authorities claim such trustworthy status, they claim the moral high ground. In fact, they claim to be *ALL* of our proxies, our shepherds, as they say. As such, their sins are at least doubly egregious.

If Christians were truly our moral exemplars, the church our actual locus of what is good and right, we should be able to look to them to exemplify moral good, expect them to be leading the charge. They

323

should set the standard on such crucial issues as equal rights for girls and women. It is all the more appalling, therefore, that they have failed miserably in this regard.

Far from being a leader on this issue, authorities from these religious traditions are, to this day, amongst the most active, loud, and vociferous defenders of their antiquated Biblical vision of women's place, a vision which is obsolete, unjust, and wrong. At this very moment, 'round the world, there are literally a billion young women and girls, from toddlers to twenty-somethings, reading their *Bible* or *Quran*, going to church, being trained by their parents, being inculcated into these old views in one way or another. There are women of 50 or 60-something, who have been absorbing these messages for half a century and more. They are being trained to think that god is a gendered male, with the appearance, the demeanor, and the psychology of a male, being taught to believe that such maleness is the norm, that this is what it means to be human, and that as females they are a mere off-shoot, a by-product, an extra, toss-away rib, inferior to males.

Girls are taught that they are inherently evil and dirty, that they caused our fall from grace, should be ashamed of themselves, their sexuality, their vaginas. They are being taught that menstruation and vaginas are shameful things to be hidden, embarrassed by. They are channeled onto the pink track, forced to navigate the schizoid terrain between Madonna and whore. They are being taught that their purpose in life is subservient to men's, that they are to serve men, serve 'his' offspring, and that their lives have less value than the lives of their brothers. At this very moment they are, by the multiple millions, being brainwashed into believing that their lives have meaning only in relation to the males to whom they are in service.

All the while their brothers are being inculcated with this same poisonous indoctrination. Men and women are both victims of antiquated religious sex and gender roles. But just as it demeans and diminishes the importance of the claim 'black lives matter' to counter it with 'all lives matter,' so it is with the claim that men, too, are victimized by Biblical indoctrination in antiquated gender roles. Surely, both are diminished by the pressure to conform. But males are placed in a position of privilege by this process, whereas females are cast into a subservient role. In this very important respect, the two are not synonymous.

Secular gender liberation will ultimately be a boon for both men and women, as the master and slave are both demeaned by the master-slave dynamic. Of course, the price we pay differs considerably. But it would be fallacious to depict feminism and equal rights as a scenario in which *men lose* and *women gain*. Rather this is a scenario of transcendence, and when we achieve true gender equity, it will be a win/win scenario for all.

It is not *because of,* but *in spite of,* the allegedly moral teachings of religion that Americans have come to increasingly embrace the moral, just and, politically speaking, entirely constitutional, patriotic ideal that people's race, sexual orientation, or gender status should have no bearing upon their moral status, or their legal rights or responsibilities as citizens. At its core, the essentially secular, humanist founding documents of our nation expressed a recognition of the fundamental moral and legal equality of all persons.

It just took time, and is still taking time, for these high ideals to manifest for *all* American persons, for the descendants of American slavery, for the indigenous of this continent displaced by the invading and conquering Christians, and for LGBTQ persons. And so must it be for girls and women, as well. That the church is so far behind speaks particularly ill of religion, particularly as the alleged source for what is morally good and right.

Chapter 15

Manufactured Need
&
Human Autonomy

This chapter is an amended version of an essay originally featured in Free Inquiry Magazine under the title "Manufactured Need: What Capitalism Learned from Christianity" (October/November 2022; Volume 42 No. 6).

Capitalism is, in many respects, an offshoot of Christianity. As capitalism developed, it borrowed significantly from the most successful sales model in society at the time: Christianity. In earlier Euro-America, during the entire time frame in which what we know of as capitalism emerged and developed, Christianity was the dominant paradigm in terms of mass marketing, public relations, indoctrination, hierarchic construct, management, political influence, and, of course, sales, as well as in the cultivation of what today is known as brand loyalty. Capitalism clearly mimics Christianity in numerous respects.

But the fact that they *are* structurally similar is perhaps less fascinating than the specific *ways* in which they are similar. These common traits have themselves become so definitive of the American experience that living with them is as natural and unreflectively familiar as is water to the fish. I found it enlightening to step back and observe these common characteristics at work, in my own life and the lives of

Americans generally, and in the lives of many others around our world today.

Capitalism & Manufactured Need

Manufactured need refers to creating a need where none exists naturally. It means coercively generating wants and desires where there are none, and elevating wants and desires to the psychological status of genuine necessities.

Manufactured need is manipulating young persons to believe that one of Joe Camel's cigarettes, dangling from the corner of their mouth, makes them look cool. It means coercing them to 'put on' their face, confident that, with the right combination of eyeliner, face primer, foundation, concealer, mascara, eye shadow, lip color, highlighter, setting spray, and perfume, they will win a valued place within the social hierarchy, or meet that Mr. or Mrs. Right. It means convincing your average American male that he needs a new car, one that is better, faster, and stronger, to win his valued place within the social hierarchy, be accepted by his peers, or get laid, all to the tune of 20, 40, or 60 thousand dollars in debt.

The number one priority of modern capitalism is to ever increase profit and sales. Utilizing a combination of marketing, propaganda, sales, and indoctrination, it invents that hard-to-reach itch, then sells you the perfect backscratcher. As can be discerned from the fact that 'planned obsolescence' is a thing, capitalist enterprises thrive when one purchase is followed by another, then another, and another, ad infinitum.

Ideally, that backscratcher breaks down shortly after purchase, or is followed by a sales pitch which convinces you to buy the accompanying foot scratcher, knee scratcher, the right-hand scratcher (for your left), and the left-hand scratcher (for your right). Perhaps the new and improved hi-tech 'smart' scratcher.

Under a well-developed, corporatized capitalist system such as our own, and the consumerist identity it has cultivated, sales is no longer considered a *means-to-an-end*. It has increasingly become an *end-in-itself*. Philosopher Immanuel Kant distinguished between the two types of value, between what in Kantian parlance are considered *instrumental* and *intrinsic* goods. Capitalism inclines persons and institutions to think of profit and sales as *intrinsically* valuable, meaning valuable as *ends-in-themselves*. We consumers, on the other hand, are reduced to the status of *instrumental* goods. We are mere *means-to-an-end*, i.e., the end of making the sale.

This current economic mindset rewards and encourages thought of sales and profit as the ultimate ends, regardless of whether or not they meet the consumer's genuine, autonomously determined needs. This is, of course, entirely and completely ass-backward.

Generally, capitalism is considered to be an a-moral, or morally neutral, economic system. But in reality, capitalism is inherently immoral. I readily acknowledge that capitalism is partially responsible for the abundance which is an integral component in the progress of the last two centuries. But this does not give capitalism a pass on any of its less positive characteristics or manifestations. The reversal of values at its core demeans human beings. It commodifies us, devaluing human autonomy, our fundamental right of self-determination. As entrenched and productive as it may currently be, it is not a sustainable, long-term ideology or ethos for human civilization, going forward.

Christianity & Manufactured Need

It's easy to see how capitalism relies upon manufactured need. A tad less obvious would be my claim that it learned this from Christianity.

Christianity, too, thrives upon the manufacture of needs where, if not for its efforts, none exists. It relies upon the same strategy of manufacturing needs. But it has done so for far longer than capitalism has even been a word.

The Christian religion works, at the most rudimentary level, to create a misanthropic self-conception, a pessimistic understanding of human nature which introduces and fosters a belief in original sin. Human beings are indoctrinated to believe that we are essentially corrupt. Being of the flesh, we are, by our very nature, understood as inherently weak and wicked beings. A flaw is built into the original design, and we are in constant need of repair, straight off the assembly line. Indoctrinated into the Christian understanding of reality from birth, billions of human beings are sold this bill of goods, emphasizing these two primary ingredients:

Each human being is allegedly an eternal, immaterial, 'spiritual' entity, known as a soul. This soul is bound into a material body upon conception, and lives within the natural world, the empirical realm of matter and energy, until that body's death.

This is a crystal-clear example of Abrahamic dualism - the fundamental distinction between a superior supernatural and an inferior natural realm. According to the AIC, we have one foot in each realm. When our natural body dies, our true self, or 'soul,' does not. It continues on in the supernatural realm, a domain separate from and superior to the natural.

Upon this earthly demise we are judged by god, a human-like, yet supernatural being who is the creator of all nature, of life itself, and of human beings. We are judged based upon how fully we surrender ourselves to him, or based upon how well we behaved in accord with his scripture during our natural lives. We then go on in a state of either eternal reward or eternal damnation, as decreed by the creator.

These foundational origin myths have been dominant in Christianity-influenced culture for millennia. Theologians make it all far more complex; apologists emphasize its allegoric or metaphoric nature; fundamentalists take it all far too literally; and even we nonbelievers and nones absorb much of it by osmosis. But if one is raised as a Christian, the basics of the above doctrine are not up for debate. This self-conception is integral to Christian thought and belief. It should be noted, however, that, as has become increasingly apparent within the last several centuries of enlightenment, such mythic origin stories are entirely pseudoscientific constructs, devoid of even one scintilla of scientific content.

Nonetheless, millions of Americans continue to understand human nature in this primitive, mythological manner. In 2014, Pew Research[158] findings indicated that 83% of US citizens were either 'fairly certain' or 'absolutely certain' that god was a real thing. 70% self-defined as 'Christian'; while 77% of US citizens claimed that religion was either 'somewhat important' or 'very important' in their lives.

Asked if it was necessary to 'believe in god in order to have good values,' a 2011 survey split the citizens of the United States down the middle, placing us just below the world average of 55%. We were far less religious than such nations as Uganda, Pakistan, or Indonesia, where the faithful constitute more than 90% of the total population, but we were far more religious than most of the other so-called 'developed' nations, such as France, Germany, Australia, Japan, or South Korea, where the percentage of self-proclaimed believers dwindles from around 25% down to less than 10%.

Ask the same question regarding values today, however, and you can see some real progress in the United States. By 2019, approximately

---

[158] Theodorou, Angelina. "Americans Are in the Middle of the Pack Globally When It Comes to Importance of Religion." Pew Research Center, Washington, D.C., May 30, 2020.

54% of US citizens, when asked whether or not it was necessary to believe in god in order to have good values, replied that it was 'not necessary,' with only 44% still holding that it was. This change of around 10% means over 30 million Americans, almost as many people as the total population of California, our most populous state. Nonetheless, despite this comforting shift toward the rational, there are still tens of millions in this country, billions around the wider world, who continue to understand our existence in the old way.

It is this mythic hierarchy of religious dualism which sets the stage for Christianity's version of manufactured needs. Christian belief creates a need where there is none, and that is a need to be saved, forgiven, redeemed. We are indoctrinated to believe that we need salvation, in the eyes of our lord and 'savior.' These alleged needs are predicated upon belief in our fallen, sinful nature. Without indoctrination into this particular mythological interpretation, and the attendant cynical, misanthropic beliefs, the need would never arise in the first place. According to the Christian faithful, we are in constant need of god's forgiveness, resulting in perpetual dependance upon his worldly institution, the church.

Capitalism effectively convinces many of us that we need that shiny new thing. Christianity creates a sense of fundamental lacking, too, manufacturing a need in order to sell us *their* product – redemption. Salvation. An alleged solution to a problem *which never really existed in the first place.* Christianity invented manufactured need.

Sin & Misanthropy

Even non-Christians are familiar with the seven deadly sins, also known as the seven Cardinal sins. One common listing is as follows:

Lust

Gluttony

Greed

Sloth

Wrath

Envy

Pride

We can all recognize how this represents a fair descriptor of us at our worst. But the Christian view is exceptionally cynical and misanthropic. My claim is that, when not carried to their extreme forms, each of these is, at root, something entirely normal, an essential and definitive human trait, an aspect of human nature which is perfectly laudable, indeed morally admirable in many instances.

Perhaps the best example of this is the so-called sin of lust. Christianity teaches us that lust is a heinous sin, and an afront to god almighty. Yet, generally speaking, it is perfectly natural, morally permissible, healthy, and indeed quite beautiful, to desire physical intimacy with another person whom one finds sexually attractive. There is nothing inherently wrong with that. Human lust is inextricably interwoven with this thing called love (speaking here only of the romantic form of love, not any of the many other types). The supposed 'sin' of lust, and the other Cardinal sins, highlight the problems associated with religious dualism, causing us to feel repelled by our very own animal nature.

But what is human being without the passion and zeal of lust? Consider, for example, how lust is a considerable part of all art, and of everything we call romance. The truth is that many of the highest heights of human creativity, artistic expression, even ecstasy itself, owe in some measure to we mere animals in rut. Even religious ecstasy has been recognized as akin to sexual ecstasy, with evidence ranging from the famously passionate nun Teresa of Avila, to recent scientific findings that both religious and sexual ecstasy generate activity in identical areas of the human brain. We prefer to gussy it up, because we have long been indoctrinated to think of romantic love as ethereal and pure, whereas lust is but a gross necessity of animal bodies, shameful, vile, and a sin. Lust is distinguished from love. But it's a disingenuous move. Lust and romantic love are inextricably interwoven, and religious dualism is a lie.

Without lust you get no *Iliad* nor *Odyssey*, no Rembrandt, no Picasso, no Van Gogh, with or without his ear. No Beatles. Certainly no Prince. No love songs whatsoever. We'd lose at least half of all literature. Neither *Pretty Woman* nor *Casablanca*, almost zero Hollywood. No Bollywood either, for that matter. No *Romeo & Juliet*, nor *West Side Story*. From John Lennon's *Oh Yoko!* to the Taj Mahal itself, lust/love is directly responsible for a huge proportion of humanity's creative expression.

Without the hard penis or the wet vagina, you get none of this.

Too much? Have I gone too far? Only if you've been immersed and indoctrinated in Abrahamic misanthropy. In other circumstances, including some of the classical Mediterranean cultures obliterated by early Christian imperialism and intolerance, the hard penis and the wet vagina have themselves been the subject of worship and veneration. They would not have the shock value so endemic to the Christian-influenced mind of today. But calling lust a sin amounts to excessive demonization of sexual desire itself. Lust, which is natural and healthy, tends to be thought of as defilement almost by definition. No shades of grey involved.

The act of sweeping these all into the category of 'sins' is a problematic exaggeration. It illustrates the flagrant, even hostile self-loathing of the maladjusted, which is at the root of Abrahamic belief. It's a fundamentally cynical turn of mind, one which characterizes the natural and the human as universally flawed and evil. The original version of what became capitalism's 'manufactured need' begins with this. It is a two-part pitch. Part one: we are all born sinners. Part two: only god can save us, repair us, or forgive us.

But…Does it Work?

A religious apologist might argue that, imperfect though religion may be, at least it serves to keep humanity in check. They ask, without the commandments, without the carrot of heaven and the stick of hell, where would we be? It may not all be ideal, or even true, but… Does it work? Does religion keep us in check?

The belief that all of this – the characterization of humans as fundamentally flawed, immoral sinners, and the accompanying obedience training that is religion – serves to make us better, more inclined to be good, is entirely naive and scientifically inaccurate. We could do *far* better, simply utilizing reason, knowledge, science, and education. Nones, atheists, freethinkers, and infidels of all stripes do just that every day, regularly disproving the assertions and beliefs of the devout. The victims of Christian programming are less inclined toward genuinely moral, pro-social behavior than they are toward a kind of arrested development, a moral and ethical immaturity characterized by obedience to authority, scriptural commandments, the church, and religious tradition.

How does it benefit us to be 'god fearing,' to feel guilt, shame, or self-loathing for our inherent sexuality? Should we be judged or do penance for experiencing lust? Should we burn in hell for all eternity? Should we consider our very nature as evil? Quite to the contrary. In fact, these are amongst the most psychologically and socially harmful of all possible responses.

The Abrahamic approach actually keeps us from developing psychologically, as individual moral agents. It hampers our capacity to actualize our potential as morally mature, eusocial beings. Religion encourages stagnation and moral immaturity. It tends to recreate generation after generation of people who may be obedient to authority, but remain simplistic, immature, and inflexible in terms of their ability to address moral, psychological, or emotional nuance. As with 'spare the rod and spoil the child,' Christianity starts with poor pseudoscience, and turns it into highly problematic, but widely accepted naive truisms. These in turn tend to perpetuate dysfunctional relationships and community dynamics. All this is discretely concealed, and cast as profundity, its often-heinous outcomes swallowed whole as just another aspect of god's ever mysterious plan.

This religious warping of our nature into something ugly is the case with other so-called sins, as well. The problem is not with our nature, with the so-called sins. It is in their excesses, their inappropriate, selfish, or anti-social expression. Ironically, the response which Christianity cultivates actually tends to *cause* the very problem itself. Denying, self-loathing, repressing – these don't address the problem in a healthy way. They are, in fact, precisely the opposite of embracing our true nature, and consequently practicing the skillsets required to handle these natural inclinations and instincts responsibly. As an inevitable consequence, we have the result that religious repression, the teaching of the 'sin and salvation' model, works to make human beings *less* morally responsible, *more* likely to err… *more* sinful.

Like everything else, learning how to live with these instincts and impulses requires practice. It is a skillset which must be cultivated over time. You get to responsible, mature moral agency the very same way you get to Carnegie Hall – practice, practice, practice!

The process of learning the difference between the good and the bad is an essential part of what we mean by growing up. In many respects, this moral development is the very essence of maturity. Those who must have holy commandments or laws above them, who must have the carrot and stick of heaven and hell to do good, are not, strictly speaking, behaving morally. Due to their over-reliance upon indoctrination and authoritarian commands, they are less likely to have developed the capacity for moral agency, including moral reasoning, reflection, and the cultivation of sensitivity and conscience, of which all mentally healthy humans are capable, and which is ultimately requisite for a psychologically mature human populace. Psychologically, socially, and morally, the truly devout and pious tend to remain children in a very real and serious sense.

Our concern should be with the cultivation and development of mature moral agency, a process which takes place throughout our developmental decades as we mature into adulthood, and is something which is 100% possible without any religion. Christianity perpetuates childish beliefs that a god imparts morality from somewhere outside of nature, from the ever-mysterious 'beyond,' that humans are inherently wicked, and that we require a process of indoctrination in order to live well.

Are human beings fundamentally good enough to be trusted with the opportunity to develop our ethical sensitivity and capacity for moral reasoning? Christianity has been telling us no for 2000 years. Do you buy it? I am not making the usual counterclaim: the hippie dippy, Rousseauian notion of the noble savage, that we are 'born good,' that we are all born atheists until 'the man' indoctrinates us. This was carefully considered in Chapter 2, *Are We Born to Believe?*

What science, common sense, and everyday experience tell us is that we are born neither good nor bad. Or, perhaps more accurately, we are naturally inclined towards both the good and the bad. The point is that we have the capacity to swing either way. We are the learning animal. We are what we are taught, trained, or learn to be. Nurture and context determine whether humans are bad or good far more than does nature. The cynical and misanthropic take on human nature promulgated by the Abrahamic religions has set us on this path of negativity, misanthropy, and generalized destruction. We can do much better. We *are* doing better.

Coercion & Human Autonomy

Christianity and capitalism both encourage the notion of people as 'things,' as objects to be manipulated, controlled. Coercion is a fundamentally disrespectful form of human relationship, a morally dubious mode of interpersonal dynamic. It devalues human beings. The entire premise of manufacturing needs, so essential to both the AIC and the capitalist perspective, rests upon a foundation of coercion as good, a fundamentally disrespectful, anti-social mode of relationship which demeans the autonomy of the 'other,' devalues their capacity for self-determination.

The idea of 'commandments' itself seriously misses the whole point of human moral agency. The bottom line is that the AIC do not make moral agents so much as they train people to follow commands. So, I am arguing that this commandment approach is highly problematic in *form*. But I would also argue we should have a serious problem with Christianity's specific commandments, the *content*, as well as the form. As previously observed, rape and slavery are conspicuously missing from the Biblical list of no-nos. I am not alone in my thinking. Atheists and freethinkers aplenty have long recognized the various and sundry shortcomings of the ten commandments, frequently arriving at similar conclusions. For example, in 2012, author David McAfee penned the following:[159]

> When you etch your moral code in stone, you leave no room
> for editing. You leave open the possibility that, as our ethical

---

[159] McAfee, David, Facebook post, November 14, 2012. Available at: https://www.facebook.com/AuthorDavidGMcAfee/photos/a.1099072350125094/4 92033577495644/

views evolve, your code becomes less relevant. You could find yourself with four of ten divine moral laws describing how to treat god and zero that prohibit rape or slavery.

But, one reason why slavery and rape are morally wrong is precisely because they dismiss, demean, and deny our fundamental right to human autonomy.

So, how about this one as well:

Thou shalt always respect the autonomy of persons.

Respecting autonomy does not mean that people get to do whatever they want without regard to consequences. Rather, they get to own the consequences of their actions, whatever they may be, rather than have them 'forgiven' by an imaginary uber-judge. Autonomy is an intrinsic good, whereas coercion is intrinsically bad. This is absolutely true, *regardless of our intentions*. Coercing someone is an inherently cynical treatment of the other as either incapable or unworthy of learning and knowing. Both capitalist sales as well as Christian proselytizing and conversion stress a patronizing disrespect for the basic autonomy of human beings.

Being bound in chains is an obvious denial of our freedom. But the impingement upon personal autonomy through coercion and manufactured need is in a sense even more insidious. This is because the egregious wrong is itself compounded by a sweet-sounding lie. When you are in chains, you know you are a slave. You usually will have some idea of who or what enslaves you, of what stands between you and freedom. But when the more subtle means of coercion are in play, people are not necessarily aware. Those who are coerced are controlled and manipulated, yet they believe they are free. This may be more subtle, but it is equally wrong.

Coercion is an immoral mode of interpersonal relationship which demonstrates indifference to human autonomy, to human beings more generally. And yet it's the bedrock upon which capitalism is founded. It has become fully institutionalized and grown, like a cancer, to become an accepted norm of social relations in modern America. Coercion in service to sales or profit is considered intrinsically good – with the concomitant reduction of human beings to mere instrumental goods. This is a doubly wicked moral wrong.

Americans are famously proud and protective of their much-vaunted 'freedom.' No other buzzword will whip Americans into a defensive frenzy or patriotic fervor with greater alacrity nor intensity. But the truth of the matter is that they are not *really* free when they are coerced into buying this or that product, nor when their manhood requires a bigger truck or when the latest fashion determines what they buy, which in turn determines their social status.

In the same manner, Christians are coerced out of their freedom when they are taught that sex is defilement, that forgiveness comes from some supernatural source, that they are forgiven for all sorts of truly heinous atrocities great and small while the rest of us are going to burn in hell, and that humans are inherently sinful. Such thoughts and beliefs do not represent examples of a well-informed and meaningful free choice.

Money Makes the World Go Around...

While it is not news that capitalism idealizes the almighty dollar and a decidedly materialistic version of the good life, it is generally thought that this pursuit of the worldly, and the attendant focus upon profit and wealth, runs entirely counter to the religious life. The religiously devout are, in theory, less interested in the worldly pleasures associated with wealth. The face of Christianity is Jesus Christ, a character famously understood to be austere and opposed to the accumulation of wealth and the worldly pleasures associated with it. But, as ever, the truth is that Christianity is rife with hypocrisy and duplicitous insincerity. Behind the scenes, the pious, both the religious authorities and their congregants, have historically been far more enamored of wealth, power, and their attendant rewards than the Christ ideal would suggest. In the United States today, there are more than 22 million people who are millionaires,[160] and over 700 billionaires.[161] 70% of these are, allegedly, disciples of Jesus Christ.[162] What's wrong with this picture?

But it's ok because Christianity emphasizes absolution, restitution, and forgiveness. The stress is not really upon worldly privation, austerity, or even the cultivation of self-discipline, so much as redemption, salvation, and forgiveness for perpetual sinfulness… *after* the fact. Christians aren't perfect. Just forgiven. The rest of us? Not so much.

The Catholic tradition of granting 'indulgences' is a perfect example of the covetousness and greed which thrive under Christianity's protective umbrella. 'Indulgence' is precisely as bad as it sounds. Essentially, it was absolution for sale. Those sinners who could afford it could buy their way out of punishment and into god's good graces. Religious authorities were empowered to dispense forgiveness and absolution. In practice, this generally involved some element of religious penance, such as confession or prayer, combined with financial or material compensation of some kind. But it was essentially just a thinly veiled bribe.

The practice of offering (read: selling) indulgences was officially sanctioned in 1095, then officially rescinded in 1567. But bribery itself was taking place well before, and continued well after, on into

---

[160] Wold, Charlotte. "The Number of Millionaires Continues to Increase." *Investopedia*, July 13, 2022.

[161] Collins, Chuck, Dan Petegorsky, Bella DeVaan, and Helen Flannery. "Updates: Billionaire Wealth, U.S. Job Losses and Pandemic Profiteers." Inequality.org, November 21, 2022.

[162] Pew Research Cetner, "Religious Landscape Study," Washington D.C., 2023.

today. The granting of indulgences should not come as a major surprise because it merely applied the time-honored practice of bribery to the notion of an afterlife. But the truly heinous bottom line is that these alleged moral exemplars are really just 'in it for the money,' much like all we worldly sinners.

Just as many churches and clergymen are hypocritical when it comes to their religion's teachings on wealth, the Christian ideals of humble privation and service to one's fellows fail to be reflected in many Christian institutions themselves. For example, the Catholic church is abundantly wealthy well beyond necessity, being the third largest owner of real estate in the world. This fact points us towards yet another one of those lies which religion tells, another sense in which Christianity is two-faced and hypocritical: the church may *preach* such ideals as self-denial, simplicity, even poverty, but they often tend to *practice* something else entirely, both individually and collectively.

... And Around...

Religion has its long and storied history of providing shelter to all manner of money-grubbing charlatan and creep, of every shape and stripe, the many "Chaucerian frauds, people who are simply pickpockets" who "prey on the gullible," in the words of the venerable, if slightly outraged, Christopher Hitchens.[163] Although church attendance is down in many parts of our nation and our world, at least one branch of Christian endeavor appears to be thriving: televised evangelical preaching and the newly minted 'mega-churches.'

This new breed of mass-marketing missionaries reveals starkly that modern Christianity is not above the flagrant greed and self-seeking

---

[163] Christopher Hitchens, speaking with reporter Anderson Cooper, on the occasion of 'Reverend' Jerry Falwell's death.

more commonly associated with capitalism and the unapologetic materialism of the broker and banker. A relatively large number of these Christian preachers are multi-millionaires. Their ministries generate tens of millions in personal income and profit, and they enjoy the exact same benefits as the rest of today's one-percenters, including vast estates, mansions, personal jets, suites of limousines, and expensive lawyers on retainer to safeguard their abundant wealth and squeaky-clean personal image.

Modern televangelists, a demographic with more than their fair share of covetous, acquisitive swindlers and 'Chaucerian frauds,' nonetheless have the faithful, cash-contributing devotion of multiple millions of ardent believers. These popular, public Christians continue the long-standing tradition of wielding significant political influence. Church authorities have historically lived lives of power and prestige, much as the 'successful' of mercantile capitalism do today. Kings, Queens, and presidents may technically rule, but they do so only at the behest of a coterie of allies and assistants. As with our chimpanzee brothers and sisters in the wild, as well as with a number of other species, we humans gain power by forming alliances. Religious authorities have always constituted essential elements in such coalitions.

The televised preachers of the twentieth and twenty-first centuries are by no means exceptions to the rule. Earlier evangelists like Billy Graham, Oral Roberts, Pat Robertson, and Jerry Falwell demonstrated considerable power over millions of American citizens, voters, and consumers with their vast and far-flung congregations. They have often had the personal ear of politicians, including presidents. These preachers can be counted upon to sway their audience consistently and considerably toward the conservative end of the political spectrum. They can also be counted upon to generate huge sums of money. And, contrary to literally everything which Christ allegedly advocated for, the vast majority of these theistic performers and proselytizers enjoy the profuse products of their power with profligate passion.

The 'prosperity gospel' is an increasingly common means by which Christian preachers pursue their self-serving and covetous ends. They preach that god's will, for both themselves and for their congregants, is to have material abundance and wealth. The vast congregation on the receiving end of the broadcast is encouraged to pray for worldly gains, and to believe that god is fine with multi-millionaire preachers. They are encouraged to give some of their newfound prosperity to this particular millionaire preacher, to believe that this is precisely what god wants them to do. It's all god's will and their Christian duty: make money, get wealthy, and contribute to the televangelist's wealth in the process.

Not merely a North American phenomenon, the megachurch, televangelism, and the prosperity gospel are becoming increasingly popular all around the globe. Cash Luna has made millions for himself running one of the largest megachurches in Latin America from his homeland in poverty-stricken Guatemala. Billionaire Alph Lukau is the richest prosperity gospel preacher in all of Africa, and quite possibly the world. The megachurch and the televised preacher have become a mainstay in modern Christianity on an international scale.

Capitalism makes no qualms about its aggressive self-interest. Christianity has historically preached the very opposite of this greedy acquisitiveness, self-seeking, and excess. Through the personhood of Jesus Christ, Christianity preaches humility, self-sacrifice, and service to others. Yet here it is, in as flagrant a form as any capitalist board- or boiler-room. From the Pat Robertsons and Jerry Falwells to today's Copelands and Osteens, the Creflo Dollars, the Lunas and Lukaus of the world: all are guilty. They are twice guilty. By preaching prosperity gospel they are attempting to justify, and to draw their congregation into, their own genuinely immoral lifestyles. They are guilty of genuinely immoral greed, but also of some gargantuan-scale hypocrisy. To harm others in this manner is a particularly wicked form of duplicity, parading as it does under saintly guise.

...And Around!

Thou Shalt Not Suffer a Witch to Live
– Exodus 22:18[164]

The persecution of those accused of witchcraft in Europe and America's recent past was very good business. While it was generally disguised as something far more spiritual or noble, it actually was fueled in large part by earthly, economic factors. The simple greed which fueled the persecution of witches has been obscured by religious lies and falsehoods.

As Carl Sagan points out in his excellent *Demon-Haunted World*, witch hunting, with all of the attendant torture, suffering, and burnings, was whipped into a frenzy in part as a result of the publication of the *Malleus Maleficarum*. This work served to help turn witch-hunting into a religious crusade, an essential defense of Christianity, and an extraordinarily lucrative business, as well. The witch craze caught fire, in part, because it was extremely profitable. The religious authorities vested with the task of playing judge, jury, and executioner benefitted greatly from the hysteria, as did a number of peripheral participants. As Sagan points out, much of it was motivated by:

> ...the greed of the inquisitors who routinely confiscated for their own private benefit the property of the accused...It quickly became an expense account scam. All costs of investigation, trial, and execution were borne by the accused or her relatives - down to per diems for the private detectives hired to spy on her, wine for her guards, banquets for her judges, the

---

[164] King James Version – Exodus 22:18

travel expenses of a messenger sent to fetch a more experienced torturer from another city, and the faggots, tar and hangman's rope. Then there was a bonus to the members of the tribunal for each witch burned. The convicted witch's remaining property, if any, was divided between Church and State...In Britain witch-finders...were employed, receiving a handsome bounty for each girl or woman they turned over for execution.[165]

Huge sums changed hands, especially as this beneficial scheme shifted over time from the few and the poor, increasingly to more and wealthier victims. Witch hunting was extremely profitable and lucrative, both for the church prosecutors, and for other members of the community. Locals could profit by simply suggesting victims to the inquisitors, even make a buck accusing those whom they simply disliked, mistrusted, resented, or envied.

The infamous abuse and torture, the state and church sanctioned murder of 40-60 thousand humans, primarily women and girls, over hundreds of years, serves to further testify to the fact that the Christian church – the institution, its employees, and its congregants – has always been far more interested in wealth, material abundance, and the worldly pleasures which riches command, than is commonly acknowledged or readily admitted.[166]

Into the Future

If you have lived long in America, as have I, chances are you have been heavily influenced by Christianity and capitalism. These two traditions and associated institutions influence us in a variety of ways, both flagrant and subtle, and it would be an unusual, or unusually

---

[165] Sagan, *The Demon Haunted World,* 1996.
[166] "Witchcraft." Encyclopædia Britannica, June 21, 2023. Available at: https://www.britannica.com/topic/witchcraft

disconnected, person indeed who could maintain complete separation and autonomy in the face of their countless influential tendrils. I am aware, both in myself and in other nones and atheists, of numerous beliefs and behaviors with roots in one or another of these two extremely dominant ideologies. One goal of this book is, accordingly, that we should each become sensitized to that inner liar, that source of false narratives and deceptive beliefs which lead us astray, from objectivity, from truth, or from that which is ideal in some other respect.

Unfortunately, another feature which the two have in common is their complete and total indifference toward the future of our species in the natural world, here upon planet earth. Neither Christianity nor capitalism offer us much by way of cultivating a constructive vision of human civilization, living peacefully upon a beautiful and healthy planet Earth. One approaches our little blue, green, and white orb as a resource to be exploited for profit, and the other as an inferior place from which we should all be planning, working, or praying for our inevitable escape. Neither serves as a proper foundation for the cultivation of a sustainability ethos for human civilization going forward.

In American Christianity, there is a 'stewardship' concept which has gained some traction, generally in direct proportion to America's growing environmentalist concerns. In spite of some growth, its numbers could be literally buried beneath an avalanche of doomsday and millenarian believers, watching movies about being 'left behind,' and generally clinging to their faith in life after death in one form or another. Hitchens famously decried this eschatological feature, this cornerstone orientation toward death and the 'better' world to come in an imagined afterlife, the supernatural 'beyond.' Concern with the future is in fact a major part of the Christian mindset, but it is not a real future. Scientific and secular knowledge acquired within the last few centuries has made it abundantly clear how fallacious and problematic the pseudoscientific religious vision of our future is. It alone may get us all killed.

One ideology cares deeply about what is to come, yet pays no attention whatsoever to reality; the other is well attentive to material reality, but is not the least bit concerned with the future. As a rule, capitalism's focus is on profit and sales in the present, a competitive frenzy of acquisitiveness which leaves very little room for such sentimentalities as our impact upon the environment, other living beings, or even our own grandchildren, for that matter.

However, some would argue that not all businesses or persons are as coercive, grasping, and greedy as the stereotype suggests. There are, after all, 'enlightened capitalists.' We read about the billionaire philanthropists who agree to give away 50% or more of their prodigious booty.[167] Then there's Rusty down the way, a local small business owner who has kept the family cars in good working order for decades, always with honesty and integrity. And then there is the proverbial Ben & Jerry's, or whatever big company is currently recognized for being genuinely green, or for paying a decent, living wage.

But, in truth, these are the exceptions which prove the rule, standing as they do against a backdrop of selfishness and short sightedness. This grows increasingly problematic as we shift from small, family-run, community-oriented businesses to the type of massive, impersonal, international, organizational behemoths which have come to dominate the economic landscapes of the world marketplace more and more. Big business serves to make the coercive model of interpersonal dynamic into humanity's everyday bread and butter, the 'new normal,' as it were.

---

[167] "About - the Giving Pledge." Giving Pledge. Accessed June 23, 2023. Available at: https://givingpledge.org/about – The pledge, launched by Bill Gates and Warren Buffet in 2010, is a campaign that encourages billionaires from across industries to commit to giving away at least half of their fortunes to charity during their lifetimes.

Capitalism and Christianity both indoctrinate their audience, be it market or congregation, in disdain toward the natural world and the future of humans on Earth. Both teach their audience indifference, if not real disrespect and disregard, for the life-sustaining, natural biosphere upon which we depend for our very existence. One teaches us to use it for all we can in the here and now, while the other teaches that a far, far better, more beautiful and perfect place awaits those deemed worthy, 'beyond' the mere natural. The common roots of these two ideologies are readily apparent in this dysfunctional orientation toward humanity's natural future. Capitalism acquired its irresponsibility, its disdain for our future on this planet, from its parental ideology, the Biblical notion of the earth being here for human use and exploitation.

Our first step in switching pathways onto something less bound for destruction is to reject such ideologies, and the fallacious answers handed down to us. In other words, embracing a sustainability ethos for human civilization requires first embracing atheism, which is fundamentally the rejection of false and pseudoscientific beliefs regarding humanities origins and humanities fundamental nature. But it does not end there.

At the invitation of the Capital District Humanist Society, I presented a slide show based upon the content of this chapter. A YouTube video of this talk can be found at:
https://www.youtube.com/watch?v=OLrGZ-lapE8&t=3142s

Chapter 16

As it Really Is

For me, it is far better to grasp the universe as it really is
than to persist in delusion, however satisfying and reassuring.
– Carl Sagan[168]

Instinctive Versus Rational Mind

Unaided, unbidden, the human mind interprets and understands the
world primarily through what I would describe as instinctive mind.
This mindset is what creates the ghosts and goblins, the scary monsters
hiding in our childhood closets and beneath the beds. Instinctive
mind is equally so the source of our protective angels and playful spirits, not to mention the thousands and thousands of gods and god-
desses who create us, protect us, manage our crops, the weather, the
seasons, and all of the hurricanes, tsunamis, volcanoes, and such. Instinctive mind is where we meet Zeus of Olympus, Quetzalcoatl of the
Aztecs, Odin and Osiris, Jahweh and Allah, Yama, Rama, and Shinje,
the Tibetan Buddhist god of the dead, Kaang, Anubis, Shango, or any
of the thousands of other African gods.

This is where we find Masaw, Unetlanvhi, and Wakan Tanka of
the Native American tribes, the leprechauns, ogres, fairies, and spirits
springing forth from the human mind since time immemorial, in
every culture which has ever existed. This is where we find the omens
and curses, the witches and spells, the sacrifices and offerings, our

---

168 Sagan, *The Demon Haunted World*, 1996.

349

lucky socks or pendant or angel pins or hat, our pregame rituals, our superstitious knock-on wood, or cross your fingers, our ancestor worship, and our ever-hopeful belief in life after death.

Instinctive mind is pre-rational, meaning the way we see, know, and understand *prior* to developing our capacity to think critically, rationally, and analytically, or simply becoming better educated. Rational mind, on the other hand, is responsible for the all-inclusive secular progress which is itself a core theme in *Rise of the Nones*. While both *Instinctive Mind* (IM) and *Rational Mind* (RM) are 'natural,' in the sense that the human mind has a hardwired, evolved predisposition to think in these ways, IM thinking comes with relative ease to the undeveloped human mind, indeed, even the child's mind, and haunts us all universally. Rational mind is more of a potentiality within each of us, requiring some measure of cultivation, development, and cognitive maturation. We're born with an instantaneously active IM, yet our RM may or may not ever be developed.

In this chapter, I will consider several of the central issues involved in the radical transformation which our species is undergoing, the revolutionary change which is a central theme at the core of *Rise of the Nones*, in light of this basic epistemological distinction between IM and RM.

From Adam and Eve in the garden of Eden, famously exhorted to be both obedient to god and indifferent to knowledge, to the modern American mistrust of science, of academics, intellectuals, and even mere 'facts,' Christianity famously emphasizes disdain for our reasoning capacity, for empiricism and worldly data. Indeed, for science itself, as the recent struggles with the Covid pandemic have so clearly demonstrated.

RM, on the contrary, emphasizes and trusts reason and rational thought, emphasizes data and evidence. It idealizes the concept of objectivity. RM does not create gods, demons, ghosts, or spirits. Instead, it shines the vanquishing light of truth upon them, dousing them like the problematic flames of primordial mind which they are. RM is suspicious of belief, intuition, and faith. RM trusts science and reason, but it does so because they have proven track records. As noted earlier, *trust* and *faith* are not the same thing. RM is a skeptical state of mind. It is ever cognizant of the primacy of mind, that what we believe and know is shaped, warped, and limited by the mind/brain, an imperfect bodily organ cobbled together by the jerry-rigging, opportunistic, survival-focused process of biological evolution.

An excellent illustration of the distinction between rational mind, and our more immediate, intuitive, or instinctive mind would be the Flat-Earthers—those people who believe that the earth is not a roundish globe but is in fact a disk-shaped object. These are people who derive their understanding from immediate experience and IM. Assume that the person did not receive much education on the astronomical or earth sciences. They step outside their door, and everything appears flat. They walk around their neighborhood, or drive on roads that, apart from the odd hill or dale, do not suggest we are all residing upon a giant sphere. In terms of ordinary, day to day perception, the earth appears flat. Ignoring or mistrusting accumulated scientific knowledge, and simply focusing upon an unreflective, intuitive, instinctive, immediate, under-our-feet subjective simplicity of experience—it's flat.

Deep Time: The Counter-Intuitive Nature of Objectivity

No man is an island. Darwin needed help to do what he did. And he got lots of it. Before him came Swedish botanist Carl Linnaeus, who developed the system for classifying living beings still in use today. Linnaeus placed us right alongside all of the other animals, within our own kingdom, phylum, class, order, family, genus, and species, just like every microbe, mite, mosquito, Mosasaurus, mastodon, mouse, mudskipper, malamute, or blue-footed Booby. Darwin's own grandfather Erasmus was a significant enlightenment thinker, a physician, philosopher, and naturalist whose own work presaged that of his grandson Charles. The works of Thomas Malthus famously got Darwin thinking in terms of large populations and the pressures to survive.

But one of the most significant contributions came from the works of geologists Charles Lyell and James Hutton before him. Their works cultivated Darwin's ability to think of biological organisms developing within the context of *deep time*. Our brain has evolved to emphasize the localized time frames relevant toward aiding our immediate survival and successful reproduction. Once again, the brain does not instinctively give us the most accurate, objective picture of reality, but that which is most adaptively beneficial to us as certain kinds of animals, intent upon survival and successful reproduction, fully embedded within a specific environment and context.

And so we think in terms of the present, and more specifically the time frame in which large, eusocial primate lives are lived. The time it takes to hunt, to build a fire, to soothe a baby's cry, or to woo a mate. The passing of day into night into day, the seasons coming and going, the cycles of the moon or menstruation, the duration of a pregnancy, a child's life. If we are lucky, we may get to experience two or three generations passing slowly before our aging eyes. We live our lives in minutes, hours, months, years, and hopefully decades, if we are fortunate. When we encounter times or distances in the thousands or more, our mind has less of an immediate, intuitive grasp. Deep time is counter intuitive. Science itself often requires counter-intuitive thinking.

Reason and science require us to work against our own nature.
  – Laura Joy Lamkin [169]

For the vast majority of our evolution, we never had cause to develop a cognitive capacity to think in terms of micro- or nanoseconds, nor ponder the speed of light or light years; nor to count the age of a species of animal, a mountain range, or an ocean. Our IM immediately grasps and understands days, months and years, numbers like 10, 20, maybe 100. Purely as anecdote, I recall reading once that, throughout the bulk of history, your average human rarely traveled more than 40 miles from the place of their birth.

RM has enabled us to understand what such counter-intuitive time frames as millions or billions could possibly mean, in miles to another star, or years since our last shared ancestor with a member of another species, be it *Pongo abelii, Loxodonta africana*, or *Octopus bimaculoides*.[170] The changes wrought by our modern lives, including increasing scientific awareness, growing hand in hand with technology such as the microscope and the telescope, have likewise encouraged the continuing development of RM.

This subjective temporal limitation makes absolute sense, in terms of the adaptive and practical. Yet it challenges our ability to see and understand reality *"as it really is,"[171]* to know the world rationally, to be truly objective and scientific. Learning to think in terms of deep time is an essential step away from IM, and toward the more objective understanding of RM. Thinking and knowing in this different way is yet another example of the progress humanity has made within the last several hundred years. The more people cultivate their ability to

---

[169] From a conversation held in April of 2022.
[170] The Sumatran Orangutan, African Bush Elephant, and California Two-Spot Octopus, respectively.
[171] Sagan, *The Demon Haunted World*, 1996.

think along these lines, the more human existence is placed within an accurate and objective perspective.

Deep time is an intentional effort to overcome our instinctive predilections, to grow beyond our innate bias toward our own immediate and exaggerated bubble in space and time. It was by thinking in terms of these counter-intuitive time frames that Darwin was able to initially conceive of things in the more expansive, objective manner required to understand our true origin story, the theory of evolution, and how we came into existence through incremental changes, over multiple millions of years. Even the longest human life exists in but the blink of an eye, when contrasted with the inconceivably slow processes of such geologic phenomena as seafloor spreading, mountain uplift, or continental drift.

Deep time is an example of the different kind of thinking which serves as a foundation for human progress, our secular awakening, and the rise of the nones. It illuminates several important points. First, it illustrates the primacy of mind, the manner in which the human brain naturally imposes serious constraints upon the kind of knowledge we acquire, on what we know and how we know it, on what we believe. It also demonstrates the value of RM over IM: the notion that some kinds of extremely valuable knowledge require us to cultivate less immediate and instinctive ways of perceiving, thinking, understanding, and knowing. Finally, it is an example of a specific means by which we can use RM to overcome the limitations of IM. Deep time requires effort, the development of a practiced way of thinking and perceiving the world. The payoff is a kind of big-picture knowledge, one essential to science itself - be it astronomy or biology, earth history or evolution - and one which is decidedly more objective.

A thought experiment on this concept employs the use of metaphor, with the history of planet Earth and all of life as we know it broken into the instinctively familiar format of one year – one rotation of the stars, twelve full moon cycles, the passing of the annual seasons, the cyclical return of life-giving rains or animal migrations. This is just one example from a variety of pedagogical techniques we employ in order to translate concepts into a format more familiar to our Instinctive Mind, and thereby more easily grasped.

January 1: Origin of the solar system and Earth (4.54 Ga)
January 4: Formation of the Moon (4.5 Ga)
January 12: Oldest known mineral grain (zircon from Australia) (4.4 Ga)
February 13: Oldest known rock (Acasta Gneiss, Canada) (4.0 Ga)
March 1: Oldest chemical evidence for life (3.8 Ga)
March 25: Oldest known fossils (bacteria, Australia) (3.5 Ga)
June 14: Major increase in atmospheric oxygen (2.5 Ga)
August 25: Oldest complex cells (eukaryotes) (1.6 Ga)
November 13: Oldest animal fossils (600 Ma)
November 18: Major diversification of animals, including the first trilobites and mollusks ("Cambrian Explosion") (540 Ma)
November 26: Oldest terrestrial fossil (fungi) (440 Ma)
December 3: Oldest four-limbed animals (tetrapods) (360 Ma)
December 11: Worst mass extinction (250 Ma)
December 12: Oldest known dinosaur fossils (240 Ma)
December 13: Supercontinent of Pangaea (225 Ma)
December 17: Oldest known mammal fossils (180 Ma)
December 21: Oldest known flowering plants (130 Ma)
December 26: Extinction of most dinosaurs (65 ma)
December 31:
12:25 pm: Human and chimpanzee lineages diverge (6 Ma)
11:25 pm: Origin of Homo sapiens (300,000 years ago)
11:58 pm: Domestication of the dog (14,700 years ago)
11:59 pm:
22 seconds: Oldest writing (5,518 years ago)
29 seconds: Great Pyramid of Giza (4,578 years ago)
57 seconds: The Copernican revolution (475 years ago)

59 seconds: The Darwinian revolution (159 years ago)

In this framework, all of the historical events of the past ~150 years—from two World Wars, to the discovery of the structure of DNA, and invention of the airplane, microprocessor, and Internet—have happened in the final second of the geological calendar – one breath and a wink over the span of a year.[172]

This calendar-year metaphor helps us to understand deep time, to mitigate our instinctive localizing bias, and cultivate our capacity for greater objectivity. The same change in perspective concerns our understanding of space, countering the inches, feet, acres, and miles of our immediate and instinctive understanding, with the millions and billions of miles, the truly incomprehensible light years, required to grasp the real magnitude of the cosmic expanse, or equally so the infinitesimally small world of atoms and molecules, the preponderance of life forms too tiny to perceive, yet which truly rule life on our planet.

Contrary to the pseudoscience of scripture, microscopic life was the only kind of life on this planet at first, and for billions of years thereafter. Multi-cellular, macroscopic organisms developed much later, and have not yet been around for an equivalent period of time. We larger organisms are even more juvenile than that, mere newborns in the grand scheme of things. We pop up somewhere during the next to last month, November, on the one-year calendar above. This dominance of microscopic life forms is not merely a thing of the past, either. Life on earth is either microscopic, or is partially composed of microscopic organisms in a form of symbiosis or mutualism, as is the case with us.

---

[172] "Geological Time." Digital Atlas of Ancient Life, September 13, 2021. Available at: https://www.digitalatlasofancientlife.org/learn/geological-time/

All macroscopic life, including we large animals, consists of, and depends upon, microscopic organisms, without which no life forms would inhabit planet Earth today. If any type of organism could be said to be large and in charge on planet Earth, it would be the invisibly small. The mysterious realms of the micro and the nano are inconceivably important realities which exist entirely beyond our capacity for unaided perception or ordinary comprehension. The telescope and the microscope opened up titanic and elemental vistas which had previously been wholly inaccessible to us, leaving gaps which we tended to fill with gods and the similarly supernatural caulk and spackle of instinct and imagination.

Utilizing reason, we are getting closer to, gaining more and better knowledge of, such mysterious, yet vast and essential domains – the microscopically small cosmos which resides within, and the macroscopically vast cosmos within which all resides. RM has gained enough of a foothold to stimulate *Homo sapiens* toward a far more intelligent and self-aware place than ever before. Despite religious intransigence and resistance, RM has grown in influence over the last few centuries. Should our secular education and freedom of knowledge continue to thrive as much as they currently do, RM will continue to grow in influence and relevance, its fruits offering us unknown and inconceivable bounty.

This kind of change in thinking has made the rise of the nones possible, perhaps even inevitable. Of course, many have yet to make this shift, despite the fact that Darwin's work is well over a century and a half in our past. *This problematic reticence can be laid directly at the feet of religion,* the dominance and intolerance of the AIC for anything other than its own narrow perspective.

Our brain evolved to think in terms of single and double digits, be it miles, people, pieces of fruit, animals in a herd, tribe members, harvests, years, days, or months. The more subjective IM, in terms of localized time and space, goes hand in hand with our problematic hubris, with human exceptionalism. We exaggerate our own subjective bubble in space and time, its size, its importance. RM, on the other hand, thinking in the counterintuitive ranges of deep time, of the microscopic or the macroscopic, this all requires practice and cognitive development. Deep time is less immediate and less natural to us. Thinking in this more objective way takes a little effort, takes thought experiments, mnemonics, metaphor, and the like.

RM represents a shift away from religious epistemology, and towards a mode of thought which encourages secular progress. Deep time, and its relevance in shaping our new and improved origin story, represents a significant *paradigm shift*, and a huge step forward in human progress. As a result, we have come to better know and understand the macro and the micro beyond our ordinary senses, and to accordingly understand the cosmos and our fit within it far better than we ever could under the auspices of scripture, religion, and IM alone.

First Cause

How did the universe start? The answer for most of humanity, for most of history, has been god or gods. Such supernaturalist belief systems are universal, often complex structures, all resting upon a foundation provided by IM. But, as comforting as some may find such answers, they offer us nothing of substance. Plugging god into the gap of 'first cause' tells us nothing about the first cause, gives us no information, answers no questions. How are we then better off or more informed? How does this answer illuminate what happened, what it was like before, or after, or what will happen in the future?

Most significantly, what it *does* tend to accomplish is the immediate cessation of further investigation, of curiosity, exploration, research, learning, or any progress toward a fuller, more accurate understanding. If we are satisfied with the answer 'god,' we will probably never find out the real answer. God is an answer without content, value, or meaning, and one which squelches human curiosity, bringing a diminution of the human will in its wake.

> What worries me about religion is that it teaches people to be satisfied with not understanding the world they live in.
> – Richard Dawkins[173]

We currently possess zero data regarding what happened before the big bang. Accordingly, RM can say very little of substance on the subject. It is currently just a mystery, with any and all gap-filling answers merely representing IM untethered and unmoored. Yet we are learning more and more about the beginnings of the universe, the big bang, each and every day. The answers are not simple and easy, because the evidence is so slight. But what answers we do have enjoy the important qualities of being evidence-based, rational, cumulative, and non-fiction.

When we look into the nighttime sky with our telescopes, we are not merely looking very far into distant space, we are also looking backward in time. Light travels at about 1 billion KPH, or 670 million MPH. A 'light year' is the measurement of the distance light travels in one year. Doing the math, that would be over 9,000,000,000,000 kilometers, or about 6,000,000,000,000 miles. That's *trillions* with a T. These are numbers which are essentially incomprehensible to our instinctive mind. As with deep time, some form of thought experiment, metaphor, or mnemonic-type aids in comprehension are required for the human mind to even begin to understand such magnitudes.

---

[173] Dawkins, Richard. "Heart of the Matter: God Under the Microscope." BBC. 1996.

The star we circle, our sun, is so very far away that, even at the inconceivable speed of light, the rays, beams, and photons take a full 8 ½ minutes to reach us. Technically, therefore, when you look at the sun, you are seeing the sun as it looked 8 ½ minutes ago. When we look at the second nearest star to us, which we call Alpha Centauri, we are seeing a star which is so very far away that it takes the light emanating from it about 4 years to get here.

With the launch of the unprecedented James Webb telescope (on December 25, 2021) we can now see farther back in time, by orders of magnitude, than any earthlings have ever seen before.

The James Webb Space Telescope's mission is:[174]

> ...to help scientists understand how we got here—how, from the tangle of molecules, stars, galaxies, black holes, and planets that populate the universe, the ingredients necessary for life emerged and combined to make this place called Earth. Are the conditions that favored this thriving, noisy biosphere common among the millions, or perhaps billions, of rocky planets populating the galaxy?

The Webb telescope is approximately 100 times stronger than was the Hubble before it. This is a stunning example of human progress, one which will inevitably change human knowledge considerably, and permanently. We will be able to look much more closely at galaxies 5 or 10 billion light years or more into our past, closer and closer to the big bang which appears to have happened about 14 billion years ago. We will effectively travel a very long way to that starting point, and most certainly learn more about it, its after-effects, and accordingly the differing stages of our universe's development, the development of other worlds, and of our own world, as well.

---

[174] Drake, Nadia. "The James Webb Space Telescope Will Transform Our Understanding of Alien Worlds." Science. *National Geographic*, December 15, 2021.

The mutualistic and cumulative nature of human intelligence reminds us that our knowledge of the first cause of the cosmos may start out like tiny baby steps. But it will build, and it will transform radically over time. With each succeeding generation, we will learn more and know more. Eventually, what was a mere rickety wooden chariot will be transmogrified into something like a baby blue convertible '67 Mustang. OK. Not a very good example of the holistic progress I am idealizing. I get it. But you get the idea. Scientific methodology points to the big bang as the theory which is the most probable, and the skeptical thinking at the heart of good science, utilizing our rational mind, ensures that we will continue to hone in on, and build progressively upon, the facts of the matter.

Our True Origin Story

The most succinct account of the revolutionary transformation in self-conception which lies at the heart of *Rise of the Nones* is this: *We are animals. We human beings are no longer the exceptional result of divine creation, but quite simply an animal, neither separate from nor superior to the rest of nature, 100% explicable in terms of evolutionary science, and related as family to every other animal, indeed every living organism on Earth, and through this, to the very Earth itself.*

Charles Darwin was, of course, central to this genuine revolution. Others were in the ballpark, but Darwin's theory of evolution explained in exacting detail what an animal was, how it came to exist, and precisely how it came to have the exact characteristics which defined it. After Gregor Mendel and genetics were identified as the significant missing component, with the gene being the vehicle for the mutations which were at the heart of the selection process, the theory of evolution came even more so to explain it all.

But Darwin's revolutionary new understanding all happened over a century and a half ago. Why am I harping on and on about it in the here and now? Two reasons:[175]

One, primarily because of religion's influence, millions of Americans are ignorant or unaware of this revolution. The slowest fucking revolution in history, that's what this is.

Two, because even those who do understand evolution and this scientific conception of what human being means, are not all entirely cognizant of its revolutionary implications.

These are some inconvenient truths. Most significantly: evolution *does* successfully challenge the religious worldview. This is a fact which the bulk of Americans refuse to acknowledge, many through the familiar 'science-denial' generally associated with the Christian faith. Others, as we encountered earlier with Stephen Jay Gould, struggle to fit science and religion onto the same page, to find some way in which we could 'have our cake and eat it too.' The bottom line is that science renders religion moot. Science points towards that which is right and true, while religion is little more than an erroneous, problematic hangover from times long gone.

Education and the cultivation of RM will help encourage this important transformation in human understanding, a change to which religious influence and human-exceptionalist thinking both serve as an impediment. For example, we tend to exaggerate the differences between us and other animals, differences which pale in comparison with the common ground and the similarities. We are more alike than different, more interconnected than disconnected. Knowing evolution and animal nature goes an extremely long way toward knowing a great deal about our own nature, about human beings.

---

[175] This essay from Pew Research Center lends support to my assertions: "Darwin in America. The evolution debate in the United States." Washington D.C., February 6, 2019.

Unlike the 'first cause' of the universe, which indeed remains largely a mystery to us, we actually do know a great deal about evolution today. In this case, the evidence is far more abundant, by orders of magnitude. It is literally both all around us, and all within us, as well. We currently have a massive base of knowledge regarding animals, life on earth, the differing species, and the animal *Homo sapiens* in particular. Yet we still struggle to fully appreciate all of the common ground.

The truth of the matter is that we animals are far more alike than different. Our day to day lives are less about our much-vaunted intelligence, or the mystery of our allegedly unique consciousness, than they are about hunger, desire, comfort, about arms, legs, mouths, anuses, our skin and our hair, our whims and emotions. They're also about the things which bring us pleasure or pain, pursuing one, avoiding the other; about the microscopic entities which make us well or not well, inside us and all around us; about our shared need for oxygen and water, our mutual need for, and love of, the sunlight.

We are just as obsessed with sex, with securing our social position, with finding the perfect nesting spot on the cliff and the right stuff to make the nest with, with feeding and protecting our kids, with fitting into the social fabric, responding to basic instincts, or with finding a mate. We tend to exaggerate and emphasize that which reinforces our sense of ourselves as separate and superior, but the fact is that every bower bird struggling to make the perfect nest differs little from every human being going through all the diverse motions to buy or build a home. Solving our problems will boil down to embracing a new self-conception in which we lose that sense of discontinuity which has got us in so much hot water.

Richard Dawkins warns about 'the tyranny of the discontinuous mind' in *The Ancestor's Tale*.[176] This important concept emphasizes how we have evolved to instinctively think in terms of discrete units, to compartmentalize and categorize the world, when in actual reality, underneath the surface, continuity and inter-relationship are more so the order of the day. RM can help us to see through this cognitive bias, to better comprehend the connections and relationships which are, in a sense, more definitive of human nature than are the discontinuities.

Dawkins uses the concept of species to help us gain a solid grasp on this important insight. He rightly observes that there is in fact no clear dividing line between any two species in most cases. Dividing two species of creatures is largely arbitrary. The line which distinguishes the two is essentially a human construct.

Imagine any two species. At some point, they shared a single common ancestor. Were you to visit the point in space and time which we imagine was the separating point between these two species, what would we find? Only one mother giving birth to one child, or perhaps a litter of them, with no species dividing line at any point.

There is no real place in space and time where chimpanzees and bonobos became two different species. Likewise, there is no clear dividing line between *Homo habilis* or *Homo erectus* and *Homo sapiens*. Nor for that matter between us and the other great apes. If we wish to follow the connections back and see what they tell us, just as Dawkins, Shubin, and others have done, we can learn a great deal about ourselves. That's because we are related by an unbroken chain to the lemurs and lorises, the rodents and rabbits, the mammals as a whole, and before that the sauropsids. Then the amphibians. Before that, our ancestors slide back into the water.

---

[176] Dawkins, *The Ancestor's Tale*, 2004.

Ultimately, our so-called species is continuous with the very kind of multi-cellular, water-borne organisms which we could probably find sufficient analogues for *inside of* our very own bodies today. But if you look at any alleged dividing spot between the differing species which we have invented, when you try and find it, all you will find in the vast majority of cases is one single type of organism present: one mom, along with some number of offspring – all of the same species. Our brains have evolved to see the world around us in this cloven, divided manner, even though the interconnectivity behind the scenes is far more determinative, is far more objectively true.

> If a time machine could serve up to you your 200-million-greats-grandfather, you would eat him with sauce tartare and a slice of lemon. He was a fish. Yet you are connected to him by an unbroken line of intermediate ancestors, every one of whom belonged to the same species as its parents and its children.
> – Richard Dawkins[177]

Neil Shubin's *Your Inner Fish*[178] does an excellent job of making it clear how our bones and bodies are continuous with the rest of the animal kingdom. This is an awareness of great importance for us to cultivate in our time, as it has significant ramifications not merely for medicine and our basic physical self-conception, but for our concerns regarding our planetary environment, climate change, the so-called Anthropocene epoch, and the mass extinction event which is currently being caused, in large part, by our naive ignorance of our fundamentally interconnected, interdependent, continuous nature.

Thought experiments and reflection upon scientific truths can help us break down the illusion of discontinuity. We can counter the IM's

---

[177] Dawkins, Richard. *Science in the Soul: Selected Writings of a Passionate Rationalist.* Bantam Press, 2017.
[178] Shubin, *Your Inner Fish*, 2008.

'tyranny of discontinuity' with thought experiments based upon reason and scientific truth. Consider, for example, how each of us is literally composed of earth stuff, all of which is composed of star stuff. Consider how each step in our evolution is a step shared with numerous other creatures. Our shoulder is essentially the same complex evolutionary creation as is the bird's shoulder, even more so that of the blue whale, and again even more for the brachiating gibbons of Madagascar. Forensic specialists can read old bones and fossils, finding out where the bones grew up, which region, what they ate or drank, as well as a whole host of genetic information, which they can use to trace migratory patterns and complex familial ancestry and relationships. Our body is literally composed of multiple other living beings, and non-living stuff, as well. In this sense, we are in fact more complex ecosystem than individual.

In a nutshell, the revolution in our understanding caused by Darwin's *Origin* consists of us recognizing and understanding that we are animals. Not merely in abstraction, but in measure of detail, understanding precisely what 'being an animal' means. There is continuity between us and all other life forms, between us and our world. This helps us understand a huge amount about human nature. Even in trying to grasp those aspects of our nature which are in some sense unique, such as our specific kind of intelligence, it is important to know it as a natural phenomenon, to study it in terms of how this evolved, what role genetics played, and how the complex environmental factors interact and weigh in to explain the evolution of the trait. Emphasizing our superiority or separateness leads to more misconception than self-conception.

Soul & Self

Supposedly, everybody has a soul. According to some believers, that is what ultimately distinguishes us from the rest of nature, from the lowly natural realm, from the 'mere' animal. Our soul is considered to be our true self. It exists in a 'spiritual' form. Our bodies? They are but material vessels, inhabited upon conception by our eternal souls, exited upon their demise. That's when our spirit departs the flesh. Then we are judged by god, going on to heaven or hell as our eternal reward. Or some believe we are then born again into another body.

Bullshit. Pseudoscience, plain and simple. We have massive evidence informing us regarding our animal nature. The mind, the subjective experience of self, consciousness, thought and belief, are all the direct result of electro-chemical activity within the animal organ we call the brain. The soul is another example of an entirely fictitious concept which, due to the extremely problematic combination of instinctive mind and religious indoctrination, has notorious popular acceptance and centuries of sticking power.

The truth of the matter is the soul as ordinarily conceived is really just one more example of a fictitious religious invention. We are not inanimate meat which some supernatural force magically breathed *elan vital*[179] into. We are not dead matter, inhabited by a soul, eternal or otherwise. The soul is merely another example of a god of the gaps filler, a pseudoscientific non-answer which does more harm than good. When our body dies, we die. Just like every other animal which has ever existed. There is no evidence whatsoever to support belief in an afterlife. On the other hand, there is lots of evidence to support this claim: the animal *Homo sapiens* has an instinctive penchant for creating just such comforting misinterpretations of reality.

---

[179] French for 'life momentum' or, more commonly, 'life force.'

The conclusions I have drawn are completely supported by the totality of all available evidence, the best possible explanations in light of the body of pertinent facts and data. To say that we do not know what happens when we die, that no one knows, is to completely downplay the importance of science, as well as the overwhelming body of data which clearly tells us of our continuity with the natural realm. As with the earlier claim that 'we can neither prove nor disprove the existence of god,' it is simply an outdated belief which inappropriately dismisses human intelligence, knowledge, science, and reason. When the heart stops beating and the brain waves cease, we go right back to how we were before we were born. Precisely as has every single animal or organism before us. Nothing. Non-existence.

The self is not the same thing as the soul. The self is not a product of religion. It is a cognitive-biological phenomenon, as hardwired as the deepest of instincts. The self is a non-conscious internal narrative produced by the human body as a whole.[180] Our brain has evolved to have this sense of personal coherence. It is like another instinct, something our brain does with no effort on our behalf.

The dendrites and neurons and axons all work together to create the perception of continuity over time, so that I am the same 'me' at 6, 16, 26, 42, and 63 years of age, and have that same sense of personal integrity with which we are so familiar. So, I am *me* despite being part my mother and part my father, part New Yorker and part Californian, as well as part basketball lover, writer, cook, gardener, and much more. We could hardly function well without this cohesive internal cognitive narrative. It is evolutionarily advantageous for us to have the sense of personal integrity which we know as the self. While it is more instinct than reality, the self is not a fictional creation of religion as

---

[180] The brain/mind are in fact a part of our body. So 'whole body' technically includes the brain/mind.

pseudoscience, so much as a semi-fictional creation of our instinct-driven, non-conscious animal brain.

However, just as language is a hardwired instinct which can manifest in widely divergent ways as a result of culture and context, so it is with our own self-conception. Unfortunately, our conception of the self is significantly influenced by the longstanding Christian belief that the self *is* the soul, an eternal spirit which inhabits or possesses an otherwise lifeless body composed of mere stuff. Mud, perhaps. Or a spare rib. Today's understanding of what comprises the self is largely borrowed from Christianity's concept of the soul. The facts suggest that what we think of as dead, inert matter, is actually something a tad more curious, and perhaps just a little bit amazing. What we do know for sure is that, when nature puts all the right kinds of matter and energy together, in just the precise right manner, life is the result.

We know that some forms of life evolve brains, concentrations of specific kinds of cells, because doing so aids them in survival and successful reproduction. Amphibians, reptiles, dinosaurs, birds, fish, cetaceans, marsupials, and every single mammal rely heavily upon their brain for survival and successful reproduction. Such brains naturally evolve a propensity to generate this personal narrative, this story of individualized integrity, but one which obviously differs somewhat from species to species. The self is a story our brains have evolved to tell us because it makes us 'fit' to do so. It aids us in survival and successful reproduction. And that is what the self is: this naturally generated, semi-conscious internal narrative which helps us survive and adapt and be 'fit,' in the Darwinian sense.

But the self – just as was the case with justice, morality, and art – is 100% entirely natural. All animal. Composed entirely of matter and energy. To understand the self, we must first recognize and reject religious dualism, and the simplistic, inaccurate understanding of matter and energy as dead stuff requiring supernatural forces to imbue it with life. We must reject all explanations and understandings which rely upon pseudoscientific stuffing and detritus such as spirit, soul, or any other variations on the supernatural theme.

Exceptionalist instincts incline us to believe that mind exists separate from brain, or that we have an eternal soul. But, in light of the tremendous bank of knowledge which we currently possess regarding animal nature, these are irrational beliefs to hold onto. When a rat dies, it is dead meat. Period. Same with gorillas, chimps, bonobos. Same with us. Human consciousness, self-consciousness, may seem super impressive to us subjectively, but it's just not nearly as magical as we like to think it is.

A great deal of life is associated with a deceased human – from the bugs and microbial life forms which will break you down into reusable bits, to the cherished memories or emotional scars you leave in your wake, perhaps a song you wrote or sang, or a law you helped to enact. Much of the microscopic life within us continues on, some aiding in decomposition, some merely leaching into the soil. You live on in your communities, in the bodies of your offspring, in the memories of those whose lives you impacted. But that self you thought of as you? You're gone.

But don't worry about that. The truth is that you also won't be around to notice it at all. That chimp and that bonobo? They are gone. Forever. Just as they did not exist before mom's egg and dad's sperm came together, they ceased existing when their heart pumped the last blood, and the final pulse of oxygen left their brain. It is the same with all animals, and we have not one single good reason to think otherwise. To believe anything else is either a result of exceptionalist hubris, or of religious indoctrination. In either case, it falls short of the objective facts.

In his brilliant and seminal work *Lack of Character: Personality & Moral Behavior*, philosopher John Doris synthesized social psychology and ethics in an analysis of *Situationism*.[181] The chief take-home point was that our moral behavior is determined less by robust character than by situation and context. We like to think our moral character determines whether or not we lie, or cheat, or help another in need. But science suggests that it is not our imagined robust character which determines the morality of our actions. Far more than we tend to be aware, it is the situation we are in which shapes and determines our choices, our behavior.

The self is similarly malleable and shaped by context and situations. My emphasis here is analogous. The self we think of as a robust being, which transcends time and space and context, which has individual identity and integrity, is actually far less 'real' than we think. We can counter the falsehoods and fictions caused by IM with thought experiments generated by RM.

There are any number of thought experiments which can help me to better know the counter-intuitive truth that the self is but a cognitive construct, a semi-fictitious narrative of personal integrity in time and space. As with the earlier example of deep time, the idea here is that knowing reality as it really is can be an epistemological challenge, a challenge to think and understand differently than we ordinarily do.

If 'you' were born into the Mongolian plains, in a yurt, in the year 500, with the radically different family, food, microbes, and weather, would you actually be *you*? Cultural context would be completely different. Education and experience would differ as well, altering your 'self' significantly. What if 'you' were born in any significantly different time and place from the one you now know? Your identity would be shaped by the genetic contributions of your mother and father, who themselves were also different, a product of their parents' genetics,

---

[181] Doris, John. *Lack of Character: Personality & Moral Behavior*. Cambridge, UK: Cambridge University Press, 2002.

each generation comprised of beings who evolved to survive and thrive within that context. After the genetic contribution, it all comes down to experience, your 'self's' personality shaped by tribe and context and environment. The bottom line is that nothing which you currently think of as your true self would be the same as it is now.

The implications of this particular post-Darwinian re-conception of the self are that the religious story is rendered entirely fictitious. The belief in the soul or the self as an animating force embodied in an otherwise lifeless body is rendered childish by the progress we have made in our understanding, in our body of knowledge. In light of these facts, it strikes one as all the more wicked that innocent African housewives are infected with AIDS by their equally infected husbands, who bring the sickness home from their city life, because the church teaches them that condoms are forbidden; and likewise all the more atrocious that young American daughters are forced to surrender the rest of their lives to unwanted parenthood, for which they are extremely ill-prepared, because safe sex, condoms, birth control, and abortion, are deemed morally forbidden, heinous sins by the family religion. These are very real, not uncommon scenarios, as is today's massive overpopulation problem, all significantly exacerbated, if not outright caused, by the religious myth of the divine human soul.[182]

On the flip side, educating the next generation as to the realities of their animal bodies will empower them to enjoy their sexuality

---

[182] Many people whom I know are starting to question this emphasis upon saving life at any cost, which is itself a direct result of Christian ideology. Increasing numbers are having doubts about being kept alive without regard to quality of life. In fact, some of us think that we should have the right to choose the when, where, even the how, of our own demise. We want to have the freedom, the autonomy, and indeed even the right, to say, 'If, or when, I get to such-and-such a state, pull the plug.' This is not only considered morally wrong, placing you on the express escalator straight to hell, but is in fact very often illegal as well. Why is it illegal? Because our legislators themselves are overwhelmingly Christian.

responsibly and knowledgeably, and avoid unwanted pregnancy and disease in the process. It will also empower them to eat better and take better care of their bodies. Knowing that there is no afterlife will motivate them to live this life to its fullest. Knowing that there is no god to handle matters of justice and morality will empower them to take responsibility for justice amongst humanity here and now, empower them to raise their children as responsible, autonomous moral agents, as opposed to command-following sheep. Knowing that we are the kinds of animals we are, interdependent within this biosphere, interconnected with all of the other living organisms and the planet itself, on a literal, physical, and material level, will empower them to take responsibility for themselves, and for their impact upon other organisms, and upon our planetary environment as a whole.

Getting it Right: Darwin & Difference

Darwin grasped this fundamental continuity and connection with the rest of the natural order. As stated previously, he famously asserted that the difference between human intelligence and the intelligence of other animals was a question entirely of degree, and not of kind. Darwin was seeking to overcome religion's long-asserted perspective of human dominance, and to break down the exceptionalist bias which had for so long permeated Euro-American and Abrahamic thought. His position is clearly and simply stated in this famous quotation from *The Descent of Man*:[183]

> ...the difference in mind between man and the higher animals, great as it is, certainly is one of degree and not of kind.
> – Charles Darwin

---

[183] Darwin, *The Descent of Man*. 1871. p. 105.

When it comes to comparing we humans with the rest of animal kind, it is important to be aware of the fact that we are not made of a different cloth, but we are all of a kind, woven from the same basic materials. Our intelligence, arguably the single most distinctive trait of *Homo sapiens*, is continuous with that of these other animals. Bridging the gap between us and what is considered the natural realm was a critical step in healing our problematic misconceptions of old. Essentially, we were not qualitatively different, according to Darwin. This was, at that time, a very bold and progressive assertion, and an essential component in a revolutionary remake of our basic self-conception, shifting us a notch or two away from our historically problematic anthropocentric bias, what I have criticized as human exceptionalism.

When dealing with the genius of old, however, we often must walk a fine line between acknowledging what they got right, which was truly revolutionary for their time and place, while still pushing the analysis to a whole new level. Such additions generally come about only as the result of the passage of time and the accumulation of further knowledge, which their initial advances themselves made possible. It is in such a vein that I offer a critical observation on this most fundamental of Darwin's insights. In fact, it is less critique than addendum, a 'taking it further,' if you will.

Consider the bottlenose dolphin. This particular cetacean has an intelligence very similar to our own, and one which has morphed into its current form as a result of very similar evolutionary forces. Eusocial in the extreme, they are skilled at teamwork. Living in an environment rife with dangerous predators and all sorts of prey, they are able to handle both as a team, if not as individuals, in large part due to their intelligence and communication skills. Communication is extremely vital to both of our team-oriented, eusocial species. The most significant differences concern *life under water* versus *life on the land*. In order to effectively thrive in water, they have evolved the capacity for complex echolocation. As a result of this divergence in our comparative evolution, the actual anatomy of the bottlenose dolphin brain has evolved differently from our own.

The most recent common ancestor shared by humans and cetaceans was more than 65 million years ago. Somewhere between then and now, a huge portion of their brains evolved to utilize echolocation and undersea communication. Meanwhile, at some point along this same timeline, our brains also underwent significant evolutionary changes, ultimately becoming what we are today. Both species evolved pivotal eusocial communication skills, but in very different contexts and environments. Indeed, in an entirely different medium. They echolocate; we speak. More to the point, it is less about the behavior, more about what causes the behavior: our brains are shaped and constructed differently, evolved to do different things. They are literally and physically different. They are different in kind.

This difference is written into our brains, quite literally, into the specific synapses and folds, into its actual shape. Our divergent evolutionary paths have led to differences in morphology, even to differences in the brain's structure itself. They either have evolved an entirely different part of their brain, or the same part has been modified in some significant sense which ours hasn't as a result of divergent evolutionary pressures.

One consequence of all this would be that measuring other animals by our standards, using our form of intelligence as the metric, is rendered an empty and uninformative pursuit. Even further, it is shown to be the arrogant, pointless act of vanity and insecurity which it always was. The bottlenose dolphin and the chimpanzee are not lesser versions of us, not 'inferior' beings. Neither species is superior nor inferior in abstraction, i.e., outside of environment or context. That there is a difference in kind must be understood in a nonvaluative, nonhierarchic manner. We are not 'more' intelligent than they are. It's like comparing apples and oranges.

Consider our hands, with the famously opposable thumb, our grasping, tool making and tool using digits, all freed up by our equally famous bipedal locomotion. Our brains have evolved a specific kind of intelligence, one which enables us to conceive, craft, and utilize a wide range of tools. Not only has a dolphin no hands, its brain has evolved with less of a 'hand held tool use' type of skillset. So, for example, dolphins probably think less teleologically than do we humans. There was no evolutionary pressure to evolve the 'hand tool making and using' type of intelligence. The key point is that there are multiple kinds of intelligence, not one single kind of which we are the shining example.

Evolutionary traits do not exist in a vacuum. Their value is completely dependent upon environment and context. Each species has evolved to be unique, and none is superior nor inferior *in abstraction*, but all have their value within environmental context only. If I were suddenly morphed into a bottlenose dolphin body, my allegedly lofty super brain plugged into a dolphin life, it would be a disaster. First of all, it would be immediately crushed under the literal physical pressure changes of oceanic life. But it would also be wholly incapable of even the most rudimentary cetacean communication.

Human intelligence grows and changes as we learn more. Science progresses. It accretes and is shared and grows, and this dynamic is of the utmost importance. Things have changed since I was a young child, when the IQ test was widely understood to measure a singular trait: intelligence. During the 1970s and since, different scientists in the relevant fields have proposed differing analyses and theories of multiple intelligences. Some say there are 4, others 9, others 12 differing kinds of human intelligence. This is how it is when an understanding is still nascent. We are learning more and more about the psychological reality of 'multiple intelligences' day by day. This fundamental shift in understanding allows us to treat differences amongst types with greater mutual respect.

In similar fashion, we need to recognize that differing animals have evolved to employ differing techniques for survival and successful reproduction. We have therefore evolved differences in kind. Even intelligences differ in kind. The other intelligent animals are not underdeveloped versions of us. We are not the metric by which all intelligence can or should be measured.

We should be highly reticent to place other creatures on a comparative metric with our own uniquely evolved type of smarts as the standard. This is more pseudoscientific exceptionalism than actual science. Besides, it still remains to be seen whether or not our fledgling species can successfully survive beyond the small family tribe, hunting and gathering format at which we were successful for hundreds of generations. Can the brain which worked so well as we strode from oasis to oasis across the African savannah, up into Europe, across southern Asia, down into Australia, out into the Pacific islands, across the icy Bering Strait, with our heads full of gods and our bellies full of extinction-bound megafaunal BBQ, survive the transition to thrive in the developed, civilized world we have created?

Perhaps thinking ourselves the be all and end all, the very raison d'être of the whole project, is not exactly ideal. Perhaps we should embrace a humbler, more science friendly, evidence-based self-conception, one in which we are but an apple within a very large bowl of fruit containing not just apples, but also pears and plums, pluots and purple grapes, pomegranates and passionfruit.

Chapter 17
Natural to Our Species

Atheism will need to be combined with something else,
something more constructive than its opposition to religion,
to be relevant to our lives. The only possibility is to embrace
morality as natural to our species.
— Frans de Waal[184]

God to be Good?

Many people believe that, without religion, civilization will suffer a
crisis of values. This belief is widespread and genuine. Even many who
are inclined to skepticism and nonbelief suspect there is truth to it. Is
there any merit to the concern? Or could it be the case that, far from
being the solution, religions like Christianity and Islam are more so
the very problem itself? What is the real story with regards to religion
and such values as morality, justice, purpose, meaning, awe, and wonder?

When we Americans look to religion, we are encouraged to think
of exceptional people, such as Jesus Christ, Mahatma Gandhi, or Martin Luther King, Jr. However, just as those who dream of being ballers
might imagine Kobe, Lebron, or Curry; as those who dream of capitalist riches idolize Buffet and Gates; as every young girl singing into
her hairbrush imagines she is the next Taylor Swift or Beyonce; such

---

[184] Tvolimport. "Primatologist Frans de Waal Responds to His New Atheist Critics"
This View of Life (thisviewoflife.com), March 30, 2013.

exemplars are far more exception than rule. They are not a fair representation of what it means to be an everyday Christian. The vast majority of devout are followers, not leaders. The heroes present us with a false face.

Instead, a significant proportion of Christian Americans are more likely to be ordinary folks, unremarkable in their virtues. Not moral ideals, nor warriors for justice. Rather, they tend more toward the paper-pushing, clock-punching, fast-food eating, occasional church attending, sin-confessing, absolution-enjoying, members of god's In Group. Not perfect. Just forgiven.

When I was still somewhat religious, I tried to have a forward-thinking kind of spiritual belief. I idolized characters – for me it was Buddha, Jesus, and Saint Francis, as well as Gandhi and MLK – as human ideals, as role models. Being of the 'atheist in the pews' variety, I thought of these role models as entirely natural human beings, yet true benchmarks for us all. Accordingly, I placed their icons about, in my car, hoping Buddha would help me to the calm and equanimity I craved while driving three squabbling children to school in early morning traffic. Or, as one-foot-tall stone statues placed artfully amongst the ferns, foxgloves, and forget me nots in my little garden, where I go daily for my own psychological battery recharge, my little escape to nature moment amongst the concrete, buses, sirens, and horns.

I do not currently believe in anything which could be described as supernatural. That has pretty much always been the case for me since becoming an adult. I simply respected and mimicked these imperfect, yet morally exceptional beings, whose lives I could seek to emulate in some measure. But the truth of the matter is that, for a variety of reasons which I could not see at the time, yet can see now with great clarity, religions like Islam and Christianity do not incline us toward the kind of self-fulfillment such people embody. In fact, they tend to *prevent* us from becoming the best we can be, from fulfilling our potential, and ultimately reduce our overall moral accountability.

The Evolution of Morality & Justice

For the last several million years, our ancestors were more likely to survive, thrive, and successfully reproduce as members of a coherent, unified, cooperative group, than as individuals. Actually, we were never really individuals at all. But current thinking amongst evolutionary biologists is that group selection, the idea that natural selection can act on whole groups of organisms, causing the evolution of group-advantageous traits, is a misconception, and that the individual organism itself is far more so the determinant of selection. Group selection is an unpopular notion. It is the gene itself which mutates, causing the change which is or is not selected by the wider environment. It is the individual's genetic makeup which is either selectively 'fit' or not.

While I have no quarrel with this current interpretation, I do believe, as described in previous passages, that humans have a tendency to draw a hard and fast line between the individual and the group which does not really exist, per se. We humans suffer the tyranny of the discontinuous mind, drawing firm distinctions where a more nuanced, interconnected dynamic is actually at play.

Suffice to say that the paradigmatic human, the old school picture of 'man in a state of nature,' the single young male standing alone against the elements, is, from the standpoint of evolution, totally unrealistic, not to mention totally screwed. We have never been soloists. We are, first and foremost, team human. Isolation = extinction. Morality and justice are best understood as naturalistic, prosocial traits which evolved because they served to make humans more evolutionarily fit, to bind the tribe together. These components are as essential to human nature as are pheromones and antennae tapping to the ants.

A million years ago, on the African savannah, striding as a team among the grasses and the sporadic Acacias, those individuals with a genetic predisposition to work well as a team would be more likely to survive and successfully reproduce than those who did not. Such individuals would have been more likely to be naturally selected, within certain specific environmental contexts, meaning not just the natural environment, but also the tribe, troupe, or community. Many species of animal have evolved in this eusocial manner. We do not understand the social animals when studying them alone, as individuals.

But, from the point of view of evolutionary science, the group is not the vehicle for selection. It is the individual organism and its genetic construct which is being selected, selection for those traits which enable the individual to thrive as a part of a larger whole. The individual's ability to be a group member, a valuable part of a team, is relevant to their selection by nature to survive and reproduce, or fail to survive and reproduce as the case may be. If being a team player in one way or another makes her more likely to succeed, specifically by making the group more successful, then the genetic element at work, the hardwired predisposition to be a cooperator in that specific way, factors into her selection *as an individual.*

For example, a mother within the tribe who was willing to care for her teammates babies as well as her own, thereby freeing hands to do more work, would personally benefit. But the group itself benefits from such social reciprocity, too. Another example would be food sharing, such as when a skilled hunter is willing to share his kill, benefitting both the group and the individual in the long term, thanks to our evolved penchant for social reciprocity (the wellspring from which Instinctive Mind generates belief in divine or cosmic karma).

Morality Versus Obedience

People today still fail to recognize that morality and justice are entirely the result of evolutionary processes, fully natural in their origins, explicable entirely in naturalistic terms. The commonly held belief is that morality is ultimately dependent upon the supernatural in some manner, comes to us somehow from the preternatural beyond, or that we need god in order to be good.

The truth behind this ubiquitous and entrenched falsehood is that Christianity and Islam function more as obedience training, and as a means of *a posteriori* validation, a justification after the fact, than as genuine fonts for morality, justice, or pro-social, compassionate beliefs and behaviors. The AIC conflate morality with obedience. More accurately, they *reduce* morality to mere obedience. The reverent and the faithful are led to believe that morality is synonymous with obedience to religious doctrine and obeying the words of particular religious authorities. This confusion, conflating obedience to scripture with moral goodness, helps shed light upon the historic reality previously described, in which the so-called saints of Christianity earn their canonic stripes not by virtue of their virtue, but owing entirely to their skills or accomplishments as recruiters. But obedience to religion and being moral are not the same thing.

What, then, is morality? As renowned primatologist Frans De Waal stated at the outset, what we need is a naturalistic accounting of the entirely human traits of morality and justice. These good traits are natural, evolved characteristics of the animal *Homo sapiens*, and seeking outside of us or outside of nature to understand and explain them is simply misanthropic, demeaning not only to human beings, but to nature itself. Supernatural explanations are unrealistic, irrational, and unscientific. Morality and justice, as well as awe, wonder, gratitude, meaning, and purpose, are all 100% completely natural phenomena and, ultimately, explicable only as products of the process of evolution.

As with other evolved traits—such as language, for example—these human characteristics are part nature and part nurture. They are qualities and skills with biological/cognitive roots, hardwired into our species, natural and instinctive to a certain degree. These traits and characteristics are rooted in genetics, and can therefore be transmitted to subsequent generations via evolution, via the process of selection.

But we are also the learning animal. Post-conception learning is central to our nature and our species. We have these moral instincts and emotions, morality in nascent, undeveloped form, from conception and birth onwards. But they must necessarily be cultivated, practiced, or developed to some extent as well. It is in this latter respect that religious indoctrination and good secular education differ so.

Nature provides the seed; learning, practice, and development takes it from there. Humans are hardwired to hunt, to socialize, to raise babies, just as we are hardwired to speak a language. Nonetheless these are learned skills, skills which we must be taught. Human beings are born with team human pro-social instincts such as the 'conscience,' instinctive or emotional pre-dispositions toward altruism, compassion, sympathy, empathy, our natural proclivity for caring, kindness, and cooperation.

But to be truly good, moral members of a community, these emotions and instincts must ultimately work within a framework provided by worldly development and acquired skills resulting from years of experience, knowledge, reasoning, and with lots and lots of practice leading the way. Ideally, in order for humans to become fully realized, mature and responsible moral agents, instinct and learning must work harmoniously together.

Reason is a very important part of the picture, aiding us in developing the ability to successfully navigate all of these impulses, often clashing with other impulses, in the complex natural and social world. What is reason? As with moral instincts and emotions, the capacity for reason itself is also an adapted trait with genetic roots, and therefore a trait which is subject to the process of evolution. Humans appear to be the only living beings to have developed this particular capacity to its current, relatively complex state.

A reason means a good, valid motive or cause for doing, thinking, or believing something: One reason MLK embraced Gandhi's model of non-violent resistance is because it had the pragmatic effect of garnering compassion and sympathy among the white community. Yet reason is also a process: Malcolm X reasoned that white America would never recognize blacks as dignified citizens, and that a form of separatism was therefore necessary.

Learning how to juggle all the differing moral claims which arise in everyday human life is an acquired skill. It requires the practice of combining moral impulses and instincts with the capacity to reason, requires the understanding and juggling of conflicting reasons. It requires us to develop our ability to think abstractly and objectively. Reason empowers us to attend to the well-being of conscious creatures, universalize principles of empathy, compassion, and care, cultivate moral sensitivity and awareness and, in short, be good. Not follow orders. Be good. Sometimes the two are worlds apart.

Lying is always wrong, commands the *Bible*. Yet, if I tell Aunt Jenny her hat is awful, her feelings will be hurt unnecessarily. That appears to be a good reason to tell a small, seemingly harmless lie. This is a simple example to illustrate that strict obedience to commands is inferior to moral reasoning and cultivated moral agency. For a more hard-hitting example: should I tell the truth, as the *Bible* commands, or should I lie to the slavecatchers at my door, and keep secret the fact that my basement harbors an innocent, freedom seeking family on the Underground Railroad?

A well-developed moral agent acts in accord with intelligible, universal principles of equity, treating all persons according to objective standards. The mature moral agent recognizes the importance of such principles, of objectivity, impartiality, and equity. But s/he learns to synthesize these principles adeptly with, and ground them in, such moral instincts as sympathy, empathy, compassion, altruism, and simple kindness. Learning how to blend and balance these traits is far more in line with human autonomy, and with human potential, most importantly. This issue is at the heart of the matter: religion actively diminishes us and keeps us from approaching our potential. Certainly, we are capable of more than developmentally stunted, misanthropic, and ignorant adherence to rules, to the *Bible* or the *Quran*'s 2000-year-old, proselytizing-heavy, insufficient, warped, yet purportedly divine, commandments.

Human beings are born with the potential to be morally good. But becoming a fully realized, responsible moral agent requires development and cultivation, on top of our basic moral instincts. More is known about these natural, scientific facts today, about the processes involved, than 20 years ago, much less 200 years ago, and even less, 2,000 years ago. The moral development of humans is a psychologically and socially scientific reality which religion ignores to its own detriment, making itself moribund through an excessive conservative intransigence and fundamental disdain for knowledge. No wonder, as it is a truly ancient and outdated rule book, and learning about the psychological and social importance of moral development is a historically recent rational and scientific phenomenon, coming into its own only after the quiet revolution of the late 19th century.

As with language and sundry other skillsets, moral development is ongoing throughout our lives. Ideally, we are never done learning. Nevertheless, the most sensitive, critical stage in human development, with regards to language acquisition most famously, but also moral development, would be during childhood. This is why Richard Dawkins is both justified and decidedly admirable for his virulent opposition to the religious indoctrination of children, described by the devout as religious education or training, but by many of we nonbelievers and none's as a kind of child abuse. Such religious training, and the truly immoral disregard for human autonomy which it represents, is indeed one of the greatest evils perpetrated by the AIC.

Moral Development and the Individual

[Children's]…ability to extend concern to others improves with development, much like numeracy and literacy skills do. This suggests the penny drops at multiple points through a child's moral development as their understanding of the moral needs of others becomes more nuanced.

– Neldner & Crimston[185]

A great deal of this moral development happens in ordinary life. Children learn to set the table, or learn a language, how to dig and prepare yams, how to make their bed, or write a love poem to woo a mate, or simply how to wipe their own butts, all in the course of daily life as human beings. We are never really individuals. We are eusocial animals, always in various forms of social interaction, learning from others, learning with others, teaching or modeling for others, always. But learning something as complex and vital as how to be a morally good and decent person is a little more complicated and ongoing than, say, that last example, as important as it may be. Moral development is a lifelong project, one which is all too often derailed by religious training, which generally begins at a very early age.

---

[185] Neldner, Karri and Dan Crimston. Moral Development: Children Become More Caring and Inclusive as They Age. *The Conversation*, 2018.

But moral development can also be nurtured, encouraged, or furthered by education and exposure to difference, to otherness. For example, *"having more contact with an outgroup member can help foster liking and feelings of similarity in both adults and children."*[186] Our natural instinct for IG/OG thinking is mitigated, just as religiosity is, by good secular education, and by the inherent exposure to diversity and difference which it entails. This sort of thing supports the argument that literacy, in addition to our technological improvements in both communication and transportation, even our problematic overpopulation itself, are all contributing factors to the human condition today, to the progress and the awakening of which the rise of the nones is but one manifestation. We are becoming more moral because we are becoming more secular, but we are also becoming more secular because we are becoming more moral. Freedom from religion is happening as we become more mature and morally developed beings.

> For example, "…reading stories to children containing main characters with a disability decreases prejudice in children towards disabled people….By giving children the opportunity to engage with a wide range of people from diverse backgrounds, parents can help build tolerance and compassion in children."[187]
> – Neldner & Crimston

Zero reference is being made to supernatural powers, to a grand plan or design, to humanity's exceptional nature, to punishment (hell) or reward (heaven). No mention of original sin, of our inherent sinfulness either. 100% all-natural human stuff. For the human animal,

Knowledge is power

and

---

[186] Neldner and Crimston. *Moral Development*, 2018.
[187] Ibid.

Nature is not destiny

Knowledge and understanding of human psychological development inform us regarding our instinctive potential, for 'tolerance and compassion' in this case. Humans can choose to be good, to emphasize the better, pro-social, nurturing instincts and inclinations. The learning animal can choose its destiny, choose to be good, by stimulating and focusing this inherent moral potential, cultivating it through knowledge, intelligence, will, and practice. This picture makes far more sense, and is far more respectful of human autonomy, respectful of humanity's potential for good, than the religious picture ever could be, with its ideal of the flock being cajoled into a state of docile, submissive conformity.

Finally, here are some further evidence-based examples, for the future of a humanity struggling to deal with diversity and difference in a rapidly shrinking world. From the same fine essay, these are strategies for assisting children in the cultivation of pro-social abilities and mature moral agency:

- emphasize similarities between groups, not differences.
- read children stories with a diverse range of human and non-human main characters.
- Explain why something is wrong, rather than just stating it's wrong

By doing this, we can all help to foster the moral development of our future generations.

     – Neldner & Crimston[188]

About one hundred years after the publication of Darwin's *Origin*, in the year 1958, a graduate student at the University of Chicago named Lawrence Kohlberg began to take the study of moral

---

[188] Neldner and Crimston. *Moral Development*, 2018.

development in human beings seriously.[189] This was a relatively uncommon area of focus at the time. Expanding upon work initiated earlier by Swiss psychologist John Piaget, Kohlberg went on to cultivate a theory of stages in moral development. This represented a genuine paradigm shift in psychology, indeed in humanity's overall self-conception more generally. It is also a clear and fine example of the kind of secular progress at the heart of *Rise of the Nones*.

Kohlberg helped us become aware of the simple fact that people must *develop* as moral agents, and introduced his concept of the differing stages in such psychological development. As an example of rational mind, atheism, secular thought, and a purely naturalistic understanding of human nature, freed entirely from supernatural and religious baggage of the past, his work represents a clear step forward. This is all about how the learning animal becomes a moral animal, a moral being, and is not magically made so by divine fiat, god, Allah, church, faith, nor higher power. One hundred years after the publication of *Origin*, Lawrence Kohlberg's stages of moral development rest upon the foundation laid by Charles Darwin, a foundation of naturalistic thinking, evolutionary biology, and the use of rational mind. According to Kohlberg, human morality develops in stages:[190]

Preconventional Stages (3-7 years of age): Morality based on rewards and punishment - fear of consequences, self-interest

Stage 1 – Avoiding Punishment

Stage 2 – Aiming at a Reward

---

[189] Sanders, C. E. "Lawrence Kohlberg's stages of moral development." Encyclopedia Britannica, June 8, 2023. Available at:
https://www.britannica.com/science/Lawrence-Kohlbergs-stages-of-moral-development.
[190] Ibid.

Conventional Stages (8-13 years of age): Morality based on external ethics - law, authority, obedience to social order and consensus

Stage 3 – Good Boy and Good Girl Attitude

Stage 4 – Loyalty to Law and Order

Post-Conventional (Adulthood): Morality based on personal ethics and reasoning - social contract, universal ethical principles

Stage 5 – Justice and the Spirit of the Law

Stage 6 – Universal Principles of Ethics

We learn, given the opportunity to do so, increasing our abilities as moral agents, in stages of psychological development. This picture of how we become virtuous and good contrasts sharply with the religious understanding, characterized by original sin and divine forgiveness, by the tempting carrot of heaven and the threatening stick of hell. Religious morality—emphasizing obedience to commandments, reward and punishment, and authority—sits at the bottom of Kohlberg's model, at the underdeveloped, 'preconventional' stages. This is the morality of the pre-school playground.

Many of us, theist and atheist alike, look around at the world, and sometimes wonder why we humans are so screwed up. Are we just naturally bad animals? But the truth is that human *nature* is not the problem. It is human *nurture* which is out of whack. It is our indoctrination which is the problem. We are not wrong or bad *naturally*; we are merely being *nurtured* wrong. Without practice and cultivation, humans cannot knap a proper stone spearhead, find a hidden source of food in a particular environment, properly care for an infant or child, sexually please a mate, play a simple sonata, dance a tango, or even properly speak and use our own native language. A young toddler's incoherent babbling, from the very start, is in fact a child practicing language. Young children also practice being moral. Sharing food, taking turns, soothing another being in distress – be it another child, an adult, or a non-human being—these are all examples of 'practicing' morality.

It stands to reason that the learning animal cannot be successful at something as challenging as being a mature and moral member of a community, without practice, experience, and learning. Indoctrination does not fill this need, whereas a full, balanced secular education, in combination with everyday life lessons, is far more likely to do the job. Moral development requires real learning, meaning trial and error, grappling with challenging concepts and scenarios, as well as significant elements of exposure to the new and the different.

Because of this power of otherness exposure, literacy, education, travel, the arts, all come to play an important role in human progress, in terms of our knowledge and in terms of morality and social justice. They all have a part to play in helping us to grow from an insular, myopic provincialism, increasingly toward the cultivation of greater empathy and a stronger understanding of self and other, as sisters and brothers all in the same In Group or tribe.

What is required is that each and every human being be recognized as a potential moral agent, a being capable of moral reasoning, from the very beginning of each life. Only then will they become so. Autonomy and the capacity for moral development should be among humanity's highest priorities. It is in this sense that religious indoctrination of young persons is rightly considered a most heinous transgression, a right and proper 'sin,' if you will. The development of autonomous, knowledgeable, and sophisticated moral reasoners is a far cry from indoctrinating people to follow simple commandments or fear authority.

The idea is to respect human autonomy and the latent potential for mature moral agency which the species *Homo sapiens* has evolved, the potential to develop and cultivate as good, moral, pro-social beings who, raised and educated properly, will know, care, and understand the importance of doing the right thing. Science, reason, and evidence support this basic secular position. Science, reason, and evidence can help us to live up to our true potential as moral, eusocial, intelligent animals with a deep and abiding passion for justice, and the mutual fulfillment inherent within a truly just society.

Moral Development and the Community

With all of this evidence, it starts to look a lot like religion rather hinders than helps human morality. But this is not merely true on the individual, psychological level. It is also true on the group or community level as well. Christianity systematically impedes movements for social justice.

An honest appraisal of the historical record, washed free of the lies and misdirections sewn into the Christian dominated narrative, informs us that Christianity actually serves to thwart or fully hinder movements for social justice, in spite of their vociferous contentions to the contrary. As I have argued repeatedly, the truth is that Christianity is a very conservative phenomenon, emphasizing tradition, idealizing the past. Far from aligning with the avant-garde in movements for social justice, the church and the pious tend instead to ally with the conservative voices of the status quo.

Let's take a quick look at a significant contemporary example to illustrate. Many American churches in our time, the early 2020's, display the rainbow flag and express solidarity with LGBTQ persons, proudly proclaiming 'all are welcome.' How quickly we forget...

New York's Stonewall Riots of 1969 were the jumpstarting origin of a genuine revolution in what eventually came to be known as the issue of LGBTQ rights. But, from the very beginning, Christian involvement in the cause took the form of significant, virulent opposition. As many readers can no doubt recall, this enthusiastic opposition to social justice was famously championed by passionately Christian individuals and organizations such as Anita Bryant, Jerry Falwell, and his misnamed *Moral Majority* (because it was, in fact, neither). In a blatant effort to instill terror into the hearts of American families, subsequent iterations of this ultra-pious opposition were launched under such fear inducing monikers as *Focus on the Family* and *Save Our Children.*

Whereas the narrative of the status quo pushes the 'all are welcome,' rainbow flag waving ideal to the front, the truth behind this 'false face' is that Christianity opposed social justice for LGBT and Q persons vehemently and vigorously. Here is yet another example of *in spite of*, and not *because*. The bottom line: the Christian religion hinders moral development, keeps us from reaching our potential, and slowing the pace of human progress, not just on the individual, psychological level, but equally so in terms of our collective struggles for social justice.

Human Autonomy & Moral Responsibility

Celebrate guilt. Embrace shame. Be thankful for those feelings of remorse. Healthy persons, psychologically speaking, should consider such 'negative' mental states as friends. Sure, they suck. They're no fun. But they are doing really important work. These unpleasant feelings have evolved as components in our eusocial package. They are essential to motivate us, incline us to be better people. Far better to suffer remorse, and let it be a catalyst for change, than to be forgiven by an imaginary parent figure or divine entity, yet continue on unchanged, neither learning to be better as a moral, pro-social member of a community, nor making reparations or amends.

Just as the ants have evolved pheromones and antennae tapping as essential characteristics in their eusocial repertoire, we, too, have developed traits which aid us in being eusocial, making the team function smoothly. Justice and morality are just such phenomena. So, too, are negative feelings like guilt, shame, and remorse. These traits have evolved as an essential component in our social fabric.

I should acknowledge that not all such discomforts necessarily lead to change. Many of us, myself included, can easily go overboard with these negative emotions, subject ourselves or others to this destructive pain in a psychologically unhealthy, dysfunctional manner. But this excessive, dysfunctional kind of remorse is not what I am talking about. I am referring to the healthy, 'right-sized,' constructive element which people experience. Positive personal change, when it does come about, is more often than not motivated by some element of emotional discomfort.

But Christianity, as a rule, stresses forgiveness and absolution. In essence, such a response amounts to *removing our motivation for change.* The fundamental position of the Christian religion is that Jesus died for our sins, meaning he died so we are absolved of guilt. Then what is to motivate us to become better people? By emphasizing god's forgiveness, the church is shifting in a mentally unhealthy direction. By absolving you of your uncomfortable feelings, the church is essentially removing a primary reason for psychological growth and pro-social maturation.

Religion causes moral and social irresponsibility. By placing the stress upon forgiveness rather than psychological maturation and growth in pro-social or moral behavior, the church inclines us toward social irresponsibility. Further, belief in an afterlife makes our one and only real life, this single go around which available evidence suggests is all we get, seem less significant. This cannot help but decrease our innate hunger to maximize our accomplishments, to make right our relations, to fight for justice in the real world, in the here and now. Belief in a moral overlord, with a plan for us, even further inclines us toward a reduction in our sense of urgency and personal responsibility. *This whole package deal cannot but inevitably lead to a disempowering moral lassitude.* Far from making the world a more moral place, religions like the AIC incline humans toward increased moral irresponsibility.

The ideal response to our own anti-social, immoral, or unjust behavior is that we correct it, not to feel absolved of responsibility for it. If we have really 'sinned,' if we have done something which we rightly feel guilt or shame over, and as a result we feel remorse for good reason, we do not need random forgiveness. What we need is to acknowledge, understand, make reparations or amends for, and change the behavior.

Fortunately, such psychological and social growth brings about a more genuine, internal sense of absolution, positive feelings grounded in human autonomy, emotions indicative of mentally healthy, pro-social, morally mature relationships. *Doing the right thing morally, socially, carries in its wake the very absolution we crave.* But it's an absolution grounded within the real world's social fabric, and has far greater integrity than religion's mere caricature. When we change our immoral or socially problematic behavior, we are inclined to experience a lightening, a sense of forgiveness with depth and weight, which has integrity and meaning, as in genuine moral heft.

This feeling of moral well-being is less likely to take place if we are absolved of responsibility by an authority figure to whom we have ceded power. Being forgiven in this way makes us less responsible. In these ways, religions like Christianity not only hinder our self-actualization, but are responsible for immeasurable degrees of moral indifference, laziness, and stagnation. This is not only true on the psychological level, but on the social level, as well.

395

Justice as Natural to Our Species

Justice is *only* explicable in naturalistic terms, as an evolved trait of a eusocial, intelligent animal. Much like language, we are born with the natural elements in place. Concern with equity and fairness is universal among our species. Very young children demonstrate an instinctive awareness of injustice, a discomfit when things are not equitable.[191] Interestingly enough, they are naturally inclined to be more concerned when it impacts them in a manner which they deem negative. Nonetheless, they have a rudimentary impulse, a sensitivity and awareness of matters of fairness and equity. That it skews a little toward the selfish should come as no surprise to anyone even remotely familiar with the human animal.

But then, as with morality and other human traits, a great deal also depends upon the subsequent experience, the nurture side of the nature-nurture dynamic. This can result in anything ranging from the simple, common religious indoctrination which teaches us to 'accept the will of god,' and the subsequent passive irresponsibility, all the way to the opposite end of the spectrum, with fine secular examples like Sonia Sotomayor or Ruth Bader Ginsberg, those human beings who dedicate their lives to learning the law, working tirelessly to bring about greater justice in the real world. Recognition that we alone are responsible for justice upon this world is important, and religious faith generally stands in the way of this recognition.

We humans evolved the suite of psychological traits which give rise to what we refer to as justice. They are essential elements in the adaptive repertoire of intelligent, eusocial animals. Frans De Waal and other noted primatologists have observed that behaviors in other primate species, such as the chimpanzee and the bonobo, our closest

---

[191] Bloom, *Just Babies*, 2013.

living relatives, are strongly suggestive of the nascent roots of morality and justice.

Humans neither invented nor discovered justice. Nor was it bequeathed unto us by supernatural forces or deities. Justice itself is an evolved trait, a eusocial adaptation. This is a rather remarkable, and extremely optimistic, humanist observation: *the animal Homo sapiens is the sole source of justice in the known universe.* This is a rather hefty antidote to our poisonous misanthropy.

What an amazing claim! This threw me for a loop when I realized it. I still struggle with misanthropic, cynical thinking, despite the influence of more positive and optimistic thinkers like Pinker and Shermer. Justice is such a beautiful, incomparable, and exquisite phenomenon. Yet we alone of all earthly creatures can fully and truly appreciate it. We alone can choose it as an ideal, recognize when it is wanting, and champion it as a goal.

But, also, we are responsible. Justice is 100% up to us. We need to make it happen. If we do not, no one else will. Cause there is no such thing as god. It is an awesome responsibility. A bit frightening, perhaps. But it is true, nonetheless. If a wrong needs to be made right, if the rules are going to be genuinely fair, and are going to apply to us all in the most just and equitable manner, we need to make sure that job is done. Religion does us a huge disservice by encouraging humans to give away this extremely important power.

Comfort versus The Cold, Hard Truth

Many factors conjoin in the creation of something as vast as Christianity or Islam. But one clear factor in the development of Abrahamic faith is our hunger for comforting beliefs, a source of psychological appeasement, a means of pacifying peoples who were subject to heinous, entrenched, and systematic injustice, yet could do little to nothing about it. With a painfully familiar irony, it should be noted that the church has often been complicit in creating, promoting, conspiring, or concealing a portion, large or small, of the very inequities in question.

For thousands of years those on the lower socio-economic rungs have suffered injustice and abuse. The *haves* have always abused the *have nots*. Human history is replete with examples. They could always get away with all sorts of unfair, often cruelly unjust behaviors and practices. This sort of 'might makes right' injustice has long dominated human affairs. It still does. Religion did not change this. In fact, religion often simply piles on, adding its own particular abuses of power to this surfeit of human misery, and offering little more in return than vacuous pablum, disempowering consolation, and emotional appeasement.

One significant sign of human progress is the increase in the rule of law, as well as the increase in laws which are genuinely just and good. The Civil Rights Act of 1964,[192] which prohibits discrimination on the basis of race, color, religion, sex, or national origin, is one such example. And yet, much work still remains to be done. In the USA, despite our constitution and bill of rights, despite our efforts to emphasize the rule of law, people of color, in particular the displaced and decimated native inhabitants of North America and the dark-skinned descendants of American slavery, have *always* suffered injustice, and still to this very day continue to endure unjust laws, or the unequal application of just laws, on a systematic basis.

Where can all of these millions go for justice in the face of a social construct which, for thousands of years, enforced unequal applications of power, and unjust perversions in the rule of law? When the realistic

---

[192] "Legal Highlight: The Civil Rights Act of 1964." United States Department of Labor.

answer is 'nowhere,' as has so often been the case, belief in god can seem increasingly attractive. Faith feels essential for people living with gross, well-established, systematic, or inevitable injustice. People turn to their imaginations, and convince themselves, with help from the church, its leaders and authority figures, the scriptures, and their fellow believers, that all will be made right in the afterlife to come. Everyone will get precisely what they deserve, guaranteed. The evil will suffer in hell, the good will be blessed eternally in heaven. All will be balanced, and justice will reign supreme.

Sounds great. Even some atheists and nones believe in this kind of moral order, a faith in an inexplicable force which promises to balance everything out based entirely upon human moral values. Now, there is no doubt that social reciprocity is a real thing, and an important thing, in human society. But it is one thing to recognize the profoundly essential nature of reciprocity within the fabric of the human social order, and quite another to imagine some supra- or supernatural moral force. There is zero evidentiary reason to believe in any form of afterlife or divine, cosmic-scale justice or karma, whereas there is plenty of evidence suggesting we are cognitively biased to interpret and read things in that way.

But for many, for those who have little to no recourse, no hope of acquiring worldly justice, some form of psychological consolation has long been attractive, and been found in their faith in god's divine benevolence, and in some form of afterlife. This is more than simply sad. It is a crushing blow to human autonomy and self-actualization. We are giving away power which should rightfully be in our own hands. It is inevitable that such belief diminishes human autonomy and has a dampening effect upon our fight for justice in the real world. Religious faith is disempowering, keeping us from reaching our potential. Religion takes the fight out of us. Religion allows injustice to go unchecked.

'Morality and justice? That's not my job. That shit's above my pay grade. God takes care of that. He balances everything out.' In the face of the scientific and social fact that we human beings are solely responsible for justice in the real world, this is a most heinous and sinful consequence of religion. Quite possibly this is the worst of them all. *Religion keeps us from recognizing and actualizing our potential as the only known sources of justice and morality.*

It's important to nurture human autonomy, but religion does the very opposite: strips it away, particularly when it comes to justice in the real world. The religiously faithful are taught to abrogate this self-same autonomy and personal responsibility, essential characteristics of the human life well and fully lived. In so disempowering humans, religion is the single greatest insult to human potential in our world.

This is a heartrending waste of humanity's boundless latent good, an abject abjuration of our highest potential, a turning away from the fullest possible realization of our most exquisite human possibility. But, beginning with an acknowledgment of the basic truth of atheism, that, regardless of beliefs, there is no god to take over the moral reigns, that justice is up to us here and now in the one life we know we get, humans can embrace and celebrate their autonomy, can accept the full weight of their moral responsibility, and can begin to approach and achieve something far closer to our innate potential for good.

The Other Values

Morality and Justice, as important as they are, are not the only values which matter in the life of Homo sapiens. But one important moral of the story is going to be the same in all cases: the AIC claim to be indispensable sources of human value, but these are simply bald-faced lies, propaganda, and the stuff of indoctrination. Other human values also have secular causes, and are best understood in secular terms, as entirely natural phenomena.

In addition to ethical concerns, such human values as purpose, meaning, and humility, as well as awe and wonder, are also 100% natural. Long claimed to be essentially religious or spiritual issues, these are all values which are woven into the very fabric of humanity by the process of evolution, and are therefore better understood in light of science and rational mind, than religion and instinctive mind.

For example, consider humility. Humility is ultimately about us being right-sized – neither too big nor too small. At several points in Rise of the Nones, I have proposed that humility, long championed to be a religious or spiritual value by the devout, is in fact better off in the science camp. Strong science education encourages a healthy, balanced, and humble account of human importance (or the lack thereof) and serves as a genuine antidote to the human exceptionalism fostered by Abrahamic indoctrination. Rational Mind over Instinctive Mind.

Science, rather than being an expression of our hubris, as the pious have historically claimed, is all about putting us in our proper perspective, neither too big nor too small. It is about finding out the truth regarding human nature, and understanding how we fit into the wider cosmic schema. The genuine humility brought about by increased scientific knowledge and the use of rational mind is in fact indispensable toward humanity erasing the exceptionalist arrogance fostered by Abrahamic beliefs, and the flagrant harms caused by our dualistic understanding of ourselves as separate from, and superior to, the rest of the natural order. This rational, empirical humility is itself indispensable toward the end of us eventually, hopefully very soon, cultivating a wiser self-conception, and through that a more environmentally sustainable civilization.

Awe and wonder have also long been associated with religion and spirituality. Even powerful aesthetic experiences are often misunderstood in this way. Not having the proper words to account for a psychologically or emotionally moving experience, people will slide easily into the default language of the god of the gaps. This is merely a variation on the argument from incredulity: it's too much for me to explain, so it must be [fill in the blank with your preferred term in spiritual-ese].

The religious perspective on our values is demeaning to humanity. Whether it be the Second Movement of Ludwig van Beethoven's Symphony #7, or coming over the pass to discover the Yosemite Valley spread before you, gently overlain by winter's first dusting of snowflakes, awe and wonder are entirely human in all their aspects, and any supernatural account is simply misanthropic, and fails to give human nature its proper due, whether as creators of the awesome and wondrous, or as those beings capable of fully appreciating that which we find awesome and wondrous.

Imagine you're seeing through the Hubble telescope, or the James Webb. Imagine actually seeing such faraway wonders as the Horsehead Nebulae, 1500 light years distant from earth, or coming upon Machu Pichu, the pyramid at Tikal, or watching Mt. Saint Helens erupting, your first view of a microbe, some pollen, or a snowflake, through a scanning electron microscope, or being the first to stumble upon the paintings in the Lascaux or Chauvet caves. By flickering firelight, the lions of Chauvet, drawn over 30,000 years ago, would have given off the frightful appearance of real, live movement. The first moving picture show! But these are just some of the things which I personally find awesome and wondrous. You no doubt have your own personal list.

So, try this thought experiment: imagine you are on a tropical beach, your feet are bathing in the gentle, warm, lapping waves, your toes digging into the pure white sand. You are enraptured by a slowly developing sunset, several flitting clouds changing color and hue before your very eyes, above a sparkling ocean vista.

The sunlight is hitting our atmosphere, causing within our perception and cognition an experience of transcendent beauty, and the question at hand becomes this: is this wonderment and awe diminished, made less in any sense, when we add to it our knowledge that it is not the moon goddess putting the sun god to sleep for the night, but in fact a fiery caldron of hydrogen and helium molecules, as vast in its totality as a million Earths combined, our globe rotating around it, spinning upon our tilted axis? Does it reduce the beauty to understand how all the myriad organisms on the planet have evolved the ability to utilize the constant inflowing energy which the star bathes us in, in countless differing ways, drinking it in like water, evolving brains which can detect it, using it to read the environment within which they exist? Not only is it the case that nothing is lost, but so much is gained, as well. Losing our religion is a win-win for Homo sapiens.

In the religious mind, this majestic phenomenon, our experience of astonishment, our sense of transcendence even, are all misinterpreted, and once again skewed anthropocentric. The religious mind reverses causation, placing us naively at the center of everything, thinking that all we perceive is magically arranged, literally designed by a designer, created by a creator. And all of this is ultimately for us, specifically for human usage, consumption, and habitation. This synchrony and order and apparent perfection, this appearance of design, is all understood as evidence of god's existence. Indeed, it is often presented as proof that there is a god. But such thinking is not merely naïve, but itself an expression of scientific ignorance.

There is, at the very least, one thing upon which the theist and the atheist have traditionally tended to agree: everything in nature seems exquisitely attuned. In many respects all the physical world appears to fit, and to fit perfectly, just like the proverbial hand in glove. Even the tarantula wasp's evil and sadistic ways seem exquisitely attuned, ordered, even beautiful, in their complex synchronicity. Nature is characterized by this appearance of perfect attunement, this sense of delicate design and remarkable craftsmanship.

The pious tend to believe that this apparent craft could only be brought about by a craftsman of some sort. It is all interpreted as design, and so the thought is that a designer must exist, as well. God designed it all; that is why it all fits so perfectly, because he is a master craftsman, of course. And this is why everything appears so exquisitely tailored and attuned. Furthermore, he designed it all for us. The pious consider this not merely evidence of god's existence, but in fact solid proof of the same.

This is the argument from design or, as it is now more commonly known, the teleological argument for god's existence. As old as the hills, this traditional belief is simply that the appearance of complex functionality suggests design. Therefore, an intelligent creator, as designer, must exist. But this longstanding belief fails to take into account two things:

First, this notion fails to account for the primacy of mind. The order and telos we perceive is in our minds. I am not saying there is no order, but that order and disorder are cognitive phenomena only. States of mind. We have a mind which works in this way, which is teleofunctionally oriented. We have evolved to see, interpret, and think in this way. We perceive everything through this teleological filter.

The second is that all earthly life forms evolved precisely so as to fit perfectly within the natural environment in which they had to survive and successfully reproduce. Each tiny step in the process of selection, each 'choice' made by the perpetual interaction of gene and environment, conforms the organism to its environs in exquisite detail. This atmosphere, this landscape, this environment. All of life on Earth evolved, as if we were the hands, growing to perfectly fit into the shape of the glove. The hand grows into the glove, fitting itself to it. Every life form is a result of a process of evolution, meaning it is crafted by the cold, hard reality of necessity, of the selection process, evolved to fit perfectly within its very specific earthly environment, including all of its aspects: air, water, temperature, predator, prey, climate, etc. The design we perceive is a result of 'survival of the fittest.'

Why would evolution not perfectly attune us to our environment? If you understand how nature works, then it explains the exquisite, perfect attunement (evolution), as well as the subsequent appearance of design and even intent (teleological cognitive bias). At each step, natural organisms only evolve traits which attune them to their environment. That's precisely what evolution does. In retrospect, it is really not that amazing how perfectly aligned and matched and coordinated and 'designed' it all appears. That is how evolution works. It couldn't be otherwise.

Living beings are quite literally shaped to fit their environment, their group, their predator/prey relations, through the process of evolution, through sexual, artificial, and natural selection. This process has all the time in the world, so some of its many manifestations can get pretty complex. Non-living nature is governed by principles with similar scales of economy and efficiency, producing equally elegant results, e.g., picture planetary formation, a river's immense watershed, or a snowflake forming as it falls toward us from above our heads.

As with humility, morality and ethics, with justice, and with gratitude, our sense of meaning and purpose, the bottom line is always the same. None needs be grounded in, or in any sense relies upon, faith in god or the AIC. God does not make us good, nor give us purpose or meaning. He does not even exist. Religious belief is both wrong and bad, and it also nurtures a highly problematic misanthropy which may indeed one day be the death of us all. To best understand and foster these important human values, we need an atheistic humanism, we need science and reason. We do not need god. We do not need religion.

But it is not merely the case that religion is pointless and unnecessary. It is in fact a diversion, a delimiting and restricting phenomenon. It lies when it tells us it is needed, and it hampers, thwarts, and poisons our minds, training us in the evil art of squandering our tremendous potential, and keeping us from living up to our true value. Religion actively keeps us from living together in harmony. We are not simply good without god. We are better.

Chapter 18
Doctrina animalium

Re-Branding

It's time for a new name. Time to update the brand. *Homo sapiens* – 'wise man' – just doesn't cut it anymore. Inherent within it is the misogynistic bias of millennia of patriarchal dominance. After all, only half of us are actually men, i.e., *Homo*. The flagrant exceptionalism and anthropocentric biases of human arrogance oozes forth, as well. Looking around at the world today, it is fairly easy to recognize that calling us wise is a bit of a stretch.

In search of what would be a more fitting name for our species, in place of *homo*, I first tried out *primate*. This sounded good. Right up until I asked the *Oxford English Dictionary (OED)* what the actual definition of *primate* was, and got this as part of the reply: the chief bishop or archbishop of a province.[193]

Being the rabid atheist I am, *Rise of the Nones* being the tour de force in blasphemy that it is, I could hardly go with that one, could I?

How about *Simians*?

Simiae cognita—the learning ape.

Close…But no cigar: That *Simiae* is prone to perpetual mispronunciation. Back to the drawing board.

---

[193] "Primate English Definition and Meaning." Lexico Dictionaries. Available at: https://www.lexico.com/en/definition/primate

One of the main problems we've inherited from our religious past is that, through the AIC, we've essentially separated ourselves from the rest of the animal kingdom, conceived ourselves qualitatively distinct. Remember Abrahamic dualism, and the Great Chain of Being, and even our exceptionalist misinterpretation of Darwin? So *Animalium* seemed appropriate. Put us right back in there with the rest of them. After a few more tries, I stumbled upon this one:

Doctrina animalium: learning animals

Not singular. Plural. A team animal, like so many other species of animal. Not wise, so much as capable of learning. That is a far more honest, decidedly less arrogant option. If we are to choose the singular characteristic which exemplifies us, it would be how we are more nurture than nature, relative to the rest of life on earth. We are *Doctrina animalium*. Recall our considerations of humanity's uniquely developed capacity for accretive, cumulative, mutualistic, applied intelligence, and the subsequent capacity for culture, creativity, and progress which have been such central themes in *Rise of the Nones*. We are learning animals.

Not Another -ism

More than merely our name needs to change. We need a new and better way of understanding ourselves, the greater cosmos, and our tiny place within it all. We are, in fact, cultivating just such a thing, all the time, as our knowledge and awareness grows. Science and reason have helped us make significant leaps and bounds in that direction, reshaping our understanding of ourselves, of life on earth, of the cosmos as a whole, and of how we fit into that whole. This process of cutting loose the anchor of religion which serves to hold us back, and the positive implications of so doing, are major aspects of this new awareness.

I do not advocate for the devout to switch horses, to become believers in an ideology of atheism or humanism. What we do *not* need is another -ism to replace the old -isms. We do not need one more religion, philosophy, system, one more ideology to war over. There is very real and warranted concern that atheists can be as entrenched, uninformed, faithful, and myopic as the most doggedly devout. This is atheism as an ideology, as yet another belief system. This is not at all what we need. Atheism, ideally, should be a rejection of ideologies, specifically religious ones. Humanism at its best is not just another -ism to cling to, either. More so it is what happens when science and reason rush in to fill the vacuum left by the demise of religion.

We gain little if we simply indoctrinate people to have faith in atheism or humanism. We do not need mindless sheep, who simply believe what they are told by authority figures, scriptures, and traditions. Rather than teach people *what to believe*, people need to learn *how to reason critically*, how to intelligently decipher good reasons from bad reasons. Belief based upon instinct, including our numerous irrational biases and our religious faith, must all be discarded if we are to continue on the path of holistic progress which we are currently enjoying, if we are to even begin to approach our potential.

How can we tell the difference, then, between a genuinely new and improved understanding, versus just another -ism? Certainly, truth content matters. Belief in the supernatural is one criterion for disqualification, for example. But there is more to it than merely fact versus fiction. An atheist ideology may be superior for getting its facts straight, yet still be just another -ism standing in the way of genuine progress. Fortunately, there are other key characteristics which can be identified.

Enlightenment and freedom from religion require good education, as distinct from indoctrination. At the heart of the distinction lies respect for human autonomy. The difference is not merely about content, but also about how information is conveyed, the method by which learning takes place. The acquisition of real knowledge must be a process freed from coercion. Genuine education, as distinct from indoctrination, requires honest and full disclosure of information, delivered through non-coercive practices.

Concern about coercion ranges widely: from medieval thumbscrews, inquisitions, and witch hunts, to manufactured need, and the stick of original sin, or hell, versus the carrot of redemption, or heaven. Coercion at its core demeans human autonomy. As such, it is a violence against personhood. Violence, the threat of violence, and violence's kid brother coercion should all be off the table for real education to occur. Freedom of choice, and respect for autonomy, are paramount.

To avoid getting stuck in another mere "-ism," we must emphasize reason. Faith, be it faith in god, or faith in atheism as an ideology, is problematic for the very same reason: it is belief without reason. The answer lies in us cultivating and developing our ability to think, to reason. This is a non-ideological capacity. In fact, it is a defense against the threat of ideology, faith, and -isms.

This primarily concerns form, but content also matters. Our knowledge and understanding of the universe should be as full and accurate as humanly possible. Education matters both as training in critical thought, but equally so it must consist of as much truth as there is available. This means content must include what we learn from science and history honestly told, regarding not merely humanity but all of life, and the natural laws which govern it. Supernatural stuff is right out. The idea is simply that the better educated we are, the better off we are, the less we will be tempted to embrace the vacuous comfort of belief systems such as the AIC.

Ideally, the goal is not to fill people's minds with a specific point of view, so much as to remove problematic points of view. We should reject the AIC because they are simultaneously wrong and bad, not because an ideology says to do so, or because we were raised to be atheists. We should do so because rational thought and knowledge clearly establishes that godlessness is a reality, and that religious faith can be highly detrimental to human beings, both collectively and individually. Acknowledging this fact about the universe is the best next step toward self-fulfillment and being the best *Homo sap*...er, *Doctrina animalium* we can be.

The result of a world filled with human beings who are freed from falsehoods, from faith and ideologies, religious or otherwise, with a solid, general, liberal arts education – not over-specialized experts, but well-rounded, well-informed, autonomous thinkers – will be an increasingly secular, rational world. It will also be a more peaceful, intelligent, creative, aesthetically beautiful, artful, interesting, cleaner, and genuinely sustainable world than ever before. Freedom from religion is only the beginning. The rest, as they say, is history.

Choosing Our Future

Religions like Christianity imbue humans with a strong sense that we have a destiny, a planned future which is somehow already scripted for us. For centuries we have been trained to believe that god has a plan for us, over which we do not have much, if any, say. But that's ok because god cares for us as a father does his children, so, in a typically American, Hollywood, 'happy ending' fashion, his grand design ensures all will be well. At least for those of us who are appropriately pious and faithful, in the right way, in the right religion, and the right sect, of course.

But the preponderance of worldly evidence suggests that this is merely another comforting religious fiction. Accordingly, one key take home message from *Rise of the Nones* is that there is no god, no blueprint, no plan for we human beings, nor for any of it. There is no evidence whatsoever of a scripted destiny for our species of animal, just as there is no grand design or plan for any other evolved organism.

There is widespread faith, meaning belief without evidence, in a god that is a designer, with our species being an important part of his design. We are exclusively important in that version of the cosmos. This belief is not merely entirely fictional and intensely naive, it is also highly arrogant. But, most importantly, this message is necessarily disempowering. It leads to irresponsibility. It takes the steam out of human efforts to fulfill their potential, to accomplish goals, to even have goals, be they personal or political, large or small, individual or collective, short or long term. The abrogation of responsibility caused by handing the future over to a fictional entity with a nonexistent plan is extremely dangerous thinking, and as such it is immeasurably harmful.

Human autonomy and responsibility have been grossly underappreciated and underdeveloped as the result of millennia of religious dominance. The good news is that we get to choose our own future. Once we reject the belief that our fates are pre-ordained, this can create a new self-conception founded upon recognition of our nature as *Doctrina animalium*, the learning animals. Then we can enthusiastically embrace our genuine autonomy, self-determination, and the power this gives us to shape our future, near and far. Individually and collectively, our future is more or less what we choose, what we make it. Knowing this is the first essential step in making it so. We simply cannot continue to believe that big daddy in the sky has a blueprint already laid out for us. We *Doctrina animalium* must learn that our future and our fate are essentially in our own hands.

One evening, many years ago, my wife and I were enjoying the festivities at Carnival Village in St. Thomas, a small West Indian Island. We were eating some of the fantastic fried chicken so familiar to anyone who has ever been to Carnival Village when, all of a sudden, she found herself viscerally disgusted by the tendons and sinew of the chicken leg she was eating. That was well over 30 years ago, and she has been a vegetarian ever since. This despite having been raised as your average junk food loving, meat eating American kid. She just simply decided to not eat animals anymore.

A lion cannot do that. He cannot stop in the midst of eating his freshly killed gerenuk dinner and think, 'Hmmm. I wonder how this other animal feels when I chase it down and choke it out like that.' He cannot choose to embrace an alternative set of beliefs and behaviors. Something very much like free will is a vital part of being a member of the species *Doctrina animalium*. In spite of all the philosophy discussions in which 'free will' is called into doubt, something very much like free will is a real thing for us. We can choose our own future.

We are capable of doing what is right, or what is obligated, or what is best, even when it may be against our impulses and instincts to do so. We appear to be the only animal ever in Earth's history with a clear ability to step back, look at our impact upon the world in which we live, and choose to do things differently. We are capable of changing, and we do it all the time. Pinker's *Better Angels* documents how humanity has shifted away from violence in recent history, contrary to popular thought and the daily news-ertainment. In fact, we are doing just that when we choose to walk away from the lies, falsehoods, fictions, and problems inherent to religious faith. This may not be conscious, but it is very real change, nonetheless.

So, we are able to change and, slowly but surely, we are now doing so. This is great news. So, what's the worry?

What, Me Worry?

We are currently enjoying centuries of growing secular guidance and impact, an overall increase in the influence of atheist, humanist, scientific, and rational thought. There is a direct, causal connection between this and many of the improvements which humanity is enjoying, changes spanning every possible dimension of our lives, from cell phones and crop yields to human rights and social justice. This change is the gist of what *Rise of the Nones* is all about.

The future actually looks pretty good, so long as we keep being the problem solvers which evolution has shaped us to be. But we need freedom from religion in order to live up to our potential. Things have been getting better, in many respects. Unfortunately, there is no reason to assume that things will necessarily continue along in this progressive manner unimpeded. Religious resurgence and revival is always a very real threat. We need to be realistic about the fact that the rise of the nones is not itself a part of any plan, nor inevitable.

Quite to the contrary, there is a distinct possibility that all we have gained in the last few centuries of progress can be lost. One single major religious revival could set us back into the Dark Ages once again. The instinctive sources of religious faith are alive and well within us. They haven't gone anywhere. The progress we have made appears to be all nurture, no nature. Instinctive Mind, apotheosis, those cognitive biases, and the like? They are all still there, ready and willing to take control the moment we take our foot off the proverbial gas.

But it is not only the threat from without with which we should be concerned. The rise of the nones, the growing awareness and awakening, is threatened from within by at least two serious forces. Ignorance and apathy. You ever hear the one about ignorance and apathy? It goes like this:

Question: What's the difference between ignorance and apathy?
Answer: I don't know and I don't care.

Many of we nones believe that religion is 100% the result of indoctrination, for example. Embracing the 'tabula raza' school of thought, some of us contend that we are born as blank slates. As I argued in Chapter 2, *Born to Believe,* the evidence suggests otherwise, demoting this particular atheist belief to the level of mere faith.

Such ignorance is not merely erroneous, it is also dangerous. There is a distinct natural inclination, a suite of instincts, which predispose us toward religious faith and god belief when in a context of generalized ignorance. Failure to understand that we are actually hard wired for religious faith, that we have a 'belief instinct,' or a 'god instinct,'[194] may ultimately result in a failure to take proper preventative measures, with the result that religion, and its myriad attendant problems, might once again prevail, unquestioned and unchallenged.

The other threat to the growth of secularism is 'soft atheism'. Because we are afraid of being 'just like them,' we backpedal to the passive, soft atheist position. In so doing, we risk assenting to a sort of 'to each his own' subjectivity, which fails to out religion as the problematic and dangerous phenomenon it truly is. Fear of becoming what we are critical of keeps us from stepping into the fray and promoting godlessness, from being outspoken advocates for atheism, secularism, and humanism. It makes us afraid to be champions for reason and the truth.

If we are not on guard against religious belief, then our progress, our upward trajectory away from indoctrination and ignorance, can all be reversed. Our natural inclinations, our Instinctive Mind, could reassert itself. Imaginary supernatural beings or forces will start popping up everywhere the moment we take our feet off of the gas. And

---

[194] Jesse Bering's 2011 work was marketed in the atheist friendly environs of Europe as *The God Instinct: The Psychology of Souls, Destiny, & the Meaning of Life,* but the title was changed to *The Belief Instinct: The Psychology of Souls, Destiny, & the Meaning of Life* for the less tolerant, decidedly more religious market of the United States.

this is why we have a moral imperative to spread the message, as creepy as it feels to write that sentence.

Self-annihilation and extinction, or a utopian, sustainable human civilization: both are possible, both are in the cards. The difference between the two futures will *NOT* be determined by fate, karma, god, tarot, or a blueprint already written in the heavens, in the alignment of the planets and the stars, or in the words of scripture, be it the *Bible*, the Tibetan book of the dead, the Upanishads, or Joseph Smith's golden plates. Our future will be made by the combination of choices we all make today and going forward.

> I have a foreboding of an America in my children's or grandchildren's time—when the United States is a service and information economy; when nearly all the key manufacturing industries have slipped away to other countries; when awesome technological powers are in the hands of a very few, and no one representing the public interest can even grasp the issues; when the people have lost the ability to set their own agendas or knowledgeably question those in authority; when, clutching our crystals and nervously consulting our horoscopes, our critical faculties in decline, unable to distinguish between what feels good and what's true, we slide, almost without noticing, back into superstition and darkness.
>
> The dumbing down of America is most evident in the slow decay of substantive content in the enormously influential media, the 30-second sound bites (now down to 10 seconds or less), lowest common denominator programming, credulous presentations on pseudoscience and superstition, but especially a kind of celebration of ignorance.
>
> – Carl Sagan[195]

---

[195] Sagan, *The Demon Haunted World*, 1996.

Our future also depends on whether we go further in our opposition to rigid religious dogmas. In light of all the problems associated with religious faith, I believe we have a moral obligation to say that believing in god is wrong and bad. It is wrong in that it entails assenting to a range of lies and falsehoods, from the infinitesimal to the gargantuan. It is bad because religious faith causes very real problems in the world, including hindering individual human moral development, as well as social justice on the community level. I do not make it a personal mission to 'de-convert' individuals. If they ask what I think, I don't shy away. I speak truth, and I write about it. But there is no coercion nor falsehood here. I am hopeful that the truth will ultimately win out.

But I will not go back in the closet. The voices of we nones must be heard. The causal connection between secular thought and human progress must be recognized. I am indebted to those atheists and authors who helped convince me of the importance of being bold and outspoken in a world at times disapproving, even hostile, toward nonbelievers, nonconformists, freethinkers, blasphemers, and idolators. The bottom line is this: while I understand our reticence about being 'just like them,' the numerous zealots, missionaries, true believers, and proselytizers who have done so very much harm in our world, we need to speak out and speak up.

What we have is different, in form and content. Our position consists of no fictions nor falsehoods. We offer no violence, no coercion, and no disrespect for human autonomy. Ideally, while we may have a serious disrespect for the believer's religious views, we should always retain a fundamental sense of respect for the believer her or himself. In fact, our opposition to religious belief can be an expression of our respect for the impacted person or persons. As we oppose ignorance out of respect for the ignorant, we likewise oppose religion out of respect for the religious. Our message consists of nothing but the truth, the embrace of the human faculty for reason, and at all times a fundamental respect for our seemingly boundless potential for good.

Misanthropy

Misanthropy, meaning a sense of disdain for our own species of animal, is a considerable threat to the future of *Doctrina animalium*. These days especially, it is easy to get caught up in hating upon humankind. It is as if everywhere we look, another human or group of humans is engaged in something ludicrous and harmful, to people, to the non-human world, or to both. Many, myself included, can get swept up in a state of misanthropic ennui or despair. Once again, the backdrop of 2,000 years of Christian indoctrination can shed light upon the problem. Christian indoctrination inclines us toward misanthropy by virtue of Abrahamic dualism, which imbues us with an inherently negative take on the natural realm, not to mention its own overt emphasis upon human frailty in the doctrine of original sin, and our perpetual need for redemption or salvation.

Regardless of the cause of misanthropy, it is of the utmost importance that we get certain facts right here: *Doctrina animalium* is neither inherently good nor inherently bad, and yet inherently both. The overwhelming abundance of evidence we have accumulated and shared over the course of the last few hundred years makes it clear that we are less nature, more nurture, than any other species of organism which has ever evolved into being on this world. We have a choice. We are an animal characterized by something which looks very much like free will. The truth is that we are not bad by nature, but by nurture.

We can become whatever it is we wish to become. Human beings, well informed and rational, famously do amazingly good things. We can do right, live right, be harmonious, cooperative, and at peace in a sustainable manner with the rest of team human, and with the wider global environment, as well. Recall Chapter 10, *The Wolf in Sheep's Clothing*, and the example of education and progress on the Osa peninsula of Costa Rica. Ayaan Hirsi Ali's remarkable story of atheist enlightenment, as described in her 2007 work *Infidel*,[196] makes for an excellent read along those lines as well. Stories like these are abundant today. Properly nurtured, *Doctrina animalium* is a beautiful, good, just, responsible species of animal. The problem is not human nature. It is human nurture. To a large extent, the problem is merely that we are indoctrinated, rather than educated. Change this, and our future changes accordingly.

Out-Babied?

Religion has dominated, and spread its various messages, far, deep, and wide. When we look at our world, the ubiquity and import of religion to so very many peoples, its historical dominance, the power of its various myths and fabrications to ensnare and mesmerize us all, the rise of the nones can start to seem like a tiny, inevitably doomed little 'flash in the pan.' Consider these recent findings by Pew Research, which suggest that mere population dynamics alone are sufficient to promise an end to this little progressive ray of hope.

> For years, the percentage of Americans who do not identify with any religion has been rising, a trend similar to what has been happening in much of Europe (including the United Kingdom). Despite this, in coming decades, the global share of religiously unaffiliated people is actually expected to fall, according to Pew Research Center's new study on the future of world religions.
> To be clear, the total number of religiously unaffiliated people (*which includes atheists, agnostics and those who do not*

---

[196] Hirsi Ali, Ayaan. *Infidel*. Atria Books, 2008.

identify with any religion in particular) is expected to rise in absolute terms, from 1.17 billion in 2015 to 1.20 billion in 2060. But this growth is projected to occur at the same time that other religious groups—and the global population overall—are growing even faster.[197]

Essentially, we are in danger of being out-babied. Pew's article frightened me at first, until I realized that a dubious premise was at play. That premise? That, as in the past, people will generally tend to stick consistently with that which their parents and their wider culture believe. This is generally, and historically, a fair assumption. However, the growth in global literacy, in secular education, in communications technology and access to knowledge, and in our body of knowledge itself, all within the last several hundred years essentially, has changed the playing field entirely. It changes everything going forward, from here on out. To the extent that we promote and encourage literacy, secular education, and rational mind over religious indoctrination and instinctive mind, the threat of population dynamics can be, is being neutralized.

In fact, the very same disturbing demographics which Pew describes have been at work in the United States over the last decade, the very time and place in which we 'nones' have 'arisen.' More babies have been born to American Christians and Muslims than to we nones and nonbelievers over the last decade. Yet our numbers have famously increased, our percentage and proportion increased.

What explains this divergence? Education, knowledge, literacy, nurture over nature, and our being *Doctrina animalium* - the learning animal. Not only can the apparent threat to secularization and progress be halted, be neutralized, but we can even continue to turn the

---

[197] Lipka, Michael and David McClendon. "Why people with no religion are projected to decline as a share of the world's population." Pew Research Center, Washington, D.C., April 7, 2017. http://pewrsr.ch/2ogscCn

tide in the other direction. The rise of the nones could even 'go viral,' taking off at a rate heretofore unseen, sweeping the globe, regardless of where all of we global citizens are born or initially raised.

With this in mind, my sense of optimism actually increases. Achieving freedom from religion, and all that entails, generally seems nigh impossible. At best a slog, a long drawn out tedium of conflict and tension. But, what if, maybe, perhaps, we just turn around one day and it's gone. In the rear-view mirror. And our children's children are heard to exclaim 'Remember religion, back when that was still a thing?'

...all this talk of supernatural beings.
No one has believed that for countless generations.
Just as we no longer believe the stars control our fates,
or the spirits of the dead haunt the living.

– Star Trek: The Next Generation
Who Watches the Watchers, Oct 1989

Knowledge is Power. Nature is Not Destiny

One crucial take-home message emphasized throughout this book is the two-part message that *knowledge is power,* and *nature is not destiny.* Real knowledge gives us the power to choose and to change. It gives us the power to recognize and expose falsehood, to embrace radical new truths, and to choose more wisely than we did in the past. *Nature is not destiny* simply means that we are not strictly determined by our instincts and inclinations, that we are capable of change, of free choice, to a very pertinent degree.

As *Doctrina animalium,* we are largely the result of nurture, more so than nature. Again, this is both good news and bad news. It is bad news when we are so easily manipulated, coerced, indoctrinated, and raised to be mindless, blindly faithful sheep from childhood. But it is good news when we are awake, empowered, and well informed, and not under the coercive control of problematic ideologies such as the AIC. The better informed we are, the better we do.

Praemonitus, praemunitus. Forewarned is forearmed. The most obvious example would be this: fully informed of the AIC's problematic nature, the many respects in which religion is both wrong and bad for team human and more, we can choose to eschew indoctrination, to embrace atheism, and to emphasize empowering secular education and reason over faith and god belief, for ourselves, but often equally so for others, most importantly our children and our students.

Secularism means greater personal responsibility. Importantly, we must be armed with the fact that, as science and every single iota of evidence tells us, it is mistaken and ignorant to believe in an afterlife. We are shortchanging ourselves, our community, indeed the world, if we do not 'leave it all on the floor,' *carpe* the fucking shit out of each and every *diem*, giving life everything we've got, holding back nothing. Yet we are less inclined to such heightened awareness of personal responsibility, of the importance of the now and this one life we get, if we believe that there is another life after this one, or that some other being is in charge of it all. Belief in an eternal soul, an afterlife, and divine judgment do humanity far more harm than good, prevent us from maximizing, from even approaching, our potential. Yet they are central tenets of the Abrahamic religions. It is not really plausible to be a Christian without belief in these fundamental positions. This is why atheism must be the original awakening position.

Religion poisons everything. Hitchens got that right. Taking that a step further, religious indoctrination builds upon a foundation of natural predispositions which are highly problematic, inclining us toward theistic, magical, and superstitious beliefs. The problematic instincts at the root of religious faith are ubiquitous and universal. Religion is wired into our animal brains by evolution. Left unchecked, it will continue to hinder human civilization, prevent us from achieving the good so latent within our potential. Fortunately, we are *Doctrina animalium*. This problematic bit of nature can be overridden by a fairly simple dose of healthy nurture. That's why there are millions of atheists and nonbelievers in the world. That's why we are enjoying the rise of the nones.

Education

Rise of the Nones' focus is upon the key factors which are responsible for the growing influence of rational, scientific, and secular thought which we are currently enjoying. These include the period known as the Renaissance, beginning around 1500; at the same time as challenges to the dominant rule of Catholicism by Martin Luther and others; the long-term impact of Gutenberg's printing press, ultimately leading to the explosive and empowering growth in global literacy a few centuries later; the increasing influence of democracy and the rule of law; the growing emphasis upon human reason, and the revolutionary increase in scientific knowledge, particularly within the last two centuries; the radical growth in communications and transportation technologies, especially within the last century; the rising global population, hand in hand with steadily increasing globalism, multi-culturalism, and respect for human diversity; all building upon a foundation laid by *Doctrina animalium*'s uniquely developed evolutionary capacity for complex accretive and mutualistic intelligence.

Another pivotal factor has been the growth in increasingly secular public education, and the creation and growth in popularity of sophisticated secular universities around the globe. Higher education of this kind is no longer restricted to society's small, ruling elite and upper classes, but is increasingly accessible to the world's huge body of ordinary folk, those of us in the less privileged classes.

It is as a result of all of these collective forces that the works of such thinkers and authors as those whose names constitute the bulk of my 'Recommended Readings' section to come are reaching wider audiences since the turn of the 21st century. In an interactive dynamic, such works are both cause and effect of the literal rise of the nones, well documented during the last decade by Pew Research and others. Multiple millions of books by these authors, and others of their ilk, have sold in the U.S., and all around the world. Illegal downloads are surprisingly common in theocratic nations such as Saudi Arabia, in which such works are not merely illegal, but potentially life threatening.

Your average American parent is well aware of the importance of a decent 4-year university education today. But religiously inclined parents often end up wringing their hands over the fact that the standard university education tends to encourage atheist thought and belief. They are often anxious that their child will be brainwashed in the process of being educated, returning home with a basketful of dirty laundry, a heart filled with sin, and a head filled with radical ideas, including atheist blasphemy.

But this phenomenon of education encouraging the loss of religious faith is an unequivocal good for the individual recipient, the community, and the planet. It is actually more of a 'deprogramming' process than most people realize. Instead of stressing out over the fact that there is a direct, causal connection between the degree of education and freedom from religion, we should be celebrating. This should be considered as an excellent example of a university education's true value. We've found the cure! 'Defaithing' should be recognized as an important and obvious good.

Atheists should never go on the defensive anymore. In fact, this should be a selling point of a good university education, that it will free us from supernaturalist, superstitious, magical thinking and religious indoctrination. Readings in secular studies should become a more serious focus. The basic four-year university education should be considered an important touchstone, a model of something which we should seek to recreate, promote, encourage, and even celebrate. The rise of the nones should be celebrated as an unabashed, unqualified, undeniable good.

A good, science-inclusive, comprehensive liberal arts-type education lends itself toward so much that is good and important for humanity. Quality universities in modern times have served as a solid foundation for, and a source of, important social change. Modern secular universities have been the source of civil unrest and protest against elite and entrenched powers; have stimulated or supported important battles against misogyny, racism, and homophobia; have famously encouraged anti-war sentiments; and have also driven forward movements toward increased environmental awareness and responsibility.

Of course, the positive influences of a university education extend immeasurably beyond such undergraduate movements, well into post-university life. The well-educated human is a completely different animal from the one that entered into the university four years earlier. (Or in my own case, more like 7 years!) The fact that significant education and collegiate experience tend to make atheists out of former believers is just one example of the outstanding service which these secular schools provide to Americans, and to the world as a whole. It is not a flaw, but a feature.

Christianity teaches us that knowledge is evil. This is yet another lie, right there in the good book, in the story of Adam and Eve. But, entirely contrary to what the *Bible* and the church teach us, knowledge is not evil. It's just bad for religion. Knowledge and education are in fact very good things. Extremely important things.

I have said little about religion being used by those in power as a tool for maintaining order in a context which benefits their ruling status. Yet there is merit to the claim. The AIC systematically beat the anti-knowledge drum, and they do so for a reason. That reason, in many cases, has to do with the power of ruling elites, and the fact that an obedient, docile, and undereducated populace is far easier to control and exploit than is a well-educated, empowered mass of humans, who will ultimately become more intent upon such goods as autonomy and justice. It is undeniably the case that, historically, religious and political forces have allied and worked toward common goals, as we've seen in considering the joint exploits of conquistadors and missionaries, the disturbing commonalities between Christianity and capitalism, and the numerous historic alliances between religious and political authorities.

A good education alters us for the better. It changes us in important ways. It radically transforms people. And that change is the very solution we seek. A broad liberal arts type of education incorporates science and knowledge regarding the universe, earth and life; the study of ethics, morality, and philosophy; multi-cultural and anthropological studies; a true history of human beings; the arts in their various forms; learning about physical well-being, and about mental health issues, as well as such pertinent topics as gender and race studies, conflict resolution, and environmental studies. Ideally, universities provide incomparable worth in that they teach us both the truth about the real world, as well as how to reason and think critically.

Furthermore, the experience of living in a university context provides social engagements, athletic and team sport competitions, social or themed gatherings, be they parties, protests, classes, labs, or forums, and often international travel opportunities, all of which radically change people, making them wiser, larger, and more mature. University experience grows us up as citizens of the world. This phenomenon of mass enlightenment as the result of modern secular education is largely responsible not merely for our increasing secularism, but for changing our world for the better in every respect.

We are currently enjoying nothing less than a wholesale awakening based upon a foundation of knowledge as good, and of reason as essential. We must not take it for granted. It is not written in the stars, nor a part of any inevitable process of progression, nor inherent necessarily to history. Normalizing atheism and encouraging freethought, reason, respect for human autonomy, and the importance of freedom from religion are things for which we need to openly advocate. Promoting godlessness differs from religious proselytizing, and is a good thing which, above and beyond the normalization of atheism itself, we have a moral obligation to pursue.

Amen[198]

For some sad reason, apocalyptic hellscapes appear to be easier to conjure than is a peaceful, sustainable, beautiful civilization. We have a million movies about the dirty, chaotic, violent world which follows the apocalypse, but not a single serious one about what it would look like if things went *right*. If you sit down to watch a film, and it starts out utopian, just give it a sec' - it'll all go to hell in short order.

People tend to scoff at idealistic thinking, to have serious trouble imagining utopia as a realistic option. The ideal of a genuinely excellent, peaceful, beautiful, and sustainable civilization, right here on this little planet, upon which we all evolved, and for which we are accordingly most exquisitely adapted and attuned - all of this is seen as unrealistic and naive. Ironically, the people who deride such hopeful

---

[198] Amen: More wordplay. I was surprised to learn that 'amen' is, technically, not a specifically religious term. It simply means something like 'let it be so,' 'Hear! Hear!' or, in more contemporary American parlance: 'word!' – Amen: Old English - late Latin - Ecclesiastical Greek - Hebrew 'truth'; Used adverbially as an expression of agreement, to express solemn ratification or hearty approval.

thinking are often the same ones who believe in an immortal soul, virgin birth, life after death, a great god in heaven who judges us after we die, burning bushes, water into wine, parting seas, and a number of religion's other copious fictions.

The requirements for canonization today, in the year 2023, include credible witnesses who can attest to the fact that the candidate has performed two 'miracles,' literally defined in terms of the *suspension of the laws of nature* in one way or another. Amazingly, this goes on to this very day. Yet the folks who believe in all of this religious fiction, indoctrinated from birth in misanthropic notions of original sin and nature as inherently evil, will laugh off any suggestion that humans are capable of coming together in a significant way. This is irony at its very best. Or worst, perhaps.

A truly secular society may sound impossible, but no doubt the legal abolition of slavery seemed like a laughable ideal, far beyond reality, to anyone held captive in shackles 2000 years ago, or even a mere 400 years ago. Defeating Hitler seemed doubtful at one point. The belief that someday human beings would walk upon the moon was considered lunacy (see what I did there?). Amazingly, the little handheld phone/computer which is in your pocket right now is actually vastly more powerful than the massive computers which took us to the moon those 50 years ago. Any such handheld supercomputers globally interconnecting us all was the stuff of science fiction within my own lifetime, just as were mixed race persons in high office, such as Barack Obama and Kamala Harris.

The idea of a gay wedding between two men, sealed with an affectionate, public kiss, broadcast on network television, widely applauded, socially acceptable, and entirely legal, would similarly have been laughed off the table, all within the timescale of my own personal memory. Could we elect a married gay man, or even a black lesbian to the presidency today? I can remember a time when the answer would merely have consisted of more derisive laughter. Today, Americans would do it, and probably well before they'd elect an atheist, too.

Consider the *United Nations Universal Declaration of Human Rights*, crafted and proclaimed after the end of World War II. This is a fine articulation of human values, entirely god-free and secular. Imagine even conceiving of such a thing back in the time of Christ, Caesar, and Cleopatra. It would have seemed impossible, laughable, ludicrous. And yet here it is, an agreed upon statement of rational, entirely secular ideals, toward which all of us, globally, should, and could, realistically aspire. I highly recommend checking it out. It is well worth a read through.

When we *Doctrina animalium* can agree upon basic common goals and utilize our accumulated knowledge and reason, we are capable of accomplishing amazing things. The only prophecy which we need fear is the self-fulfilling kind. We must reject any and all mindsets which tell us that we cannot turn this ship around, precisely because, *if we believe them, then they are that much more likely to come to pass.*

There is no plan. The future is in our own hands. Progress is real, and it's happening. But it is not inevitable. Religious revival, atheist ignorance and apathy, or a combination of both, could easily derail the process any time. Especially when one realizes how unified the devout can be, as contrasted with the herd of cats which we nonbelievers tend to be. Plus, our skepticism so easily transforms into cynicism into misanthropy.

The good news is our adaptive, malleable nature as the learning animal. We can change and, in so doing, we can change the world. We can promote and encourage the conditions which lead to the holistic progress at the heart of the *Rise of the Nones*. And we should. We should counter falsehood and fiction with truth and reality. We should fight indoctrination, coercion, and disrespect for human autonomy with solid, secular education, rooted in respect for the incredible potential within each and every human being.

Can we reject, and move beyond, the Abrahamic religions of Islam and Christianity? Yes. We can. Absolutely. We are doing so as we speak. If we choose real needs over manufactured ones; Rational Mind over Instinctive Mind; Scientific epistemology over religious epistemology; education over indoctrination; autonomy over coercion; truth and reality over comforting fiction; reason over faith; and the natural over the supernatural.

If we do not, religion may indeed be the death of us all.

Let the *Rise of the Nones* be just the beginning...

Amen.

Acknowledgements

I would like to thank Hypatia Press and my excellent editor David McAfee, who helped turn *Rise of the Nones* into a significantly more clear and focused work, and who helped me *begin* to understand the importance of saying things just once. Rae McAfee perfected citations and images, and Rob Johnson offered everything from initial guidance to great design ideas.

I am forever indebted to the staff at *Free Inquiry* magazine for their support over the years. Heartfelt thanks to the late Tom Flynn, longtime editor of *Free Inquiry* magazine, who offered up the perfect blend of encouragement and critique. I am also grateful for the ongoing support of editors Nicole Scott and Paul Fidalgo.

I am genuinely thankful for the many great authors and thinkers who have impacted me over the years. Foremost among them are Christopher Hitchens, Richard Dawkins, Sam Harris, Michael Shermer, Greta Christina, Jesse Bering, Catherine Nixey, Neil Shubin, and Stephen Pinker. I would also like to thank my ethics professors and mentors, Professor Ellen Suckiel for her exemplary encouragement and her passion for lifelong learning, and the incomparable author and Professor John Doris. If I ever grow up, I want to be like him.

I am also very grateful to Michael Shermer, Matt Ridley, and John Doris for taking the time to peruse the manuscript and offer up support for the project that is *Rise of the Nones*. And big thanks go to Dan Barker, author and Co-President of the Freedom From Religion

Foundation, for generously taking time from his crazy busy schedule to write the foreword.

I am thankful to those friends and family who have been there for me, put up with my rants, offered shoulders to cry upon, and shared their thoughts on everything from book titles to writing style.

Finally, I truly cannot begin to convey my deepest heartfelt gratitude towards the two most important people in my life: my little twin sister Amy Beth, and my amazing wife of 35 years, Laura Joy. Rendering me speechless is a genuine accomplishment, indeed! Your support and love and wisdom mean everything to me.

Thank you all so very much. No man, nor woman, is an island. Least of all this one…

— Adam Neiblum

Recommended Readings

Barker, Dan. *God: The Most Unpleasant Character in All Fiction.* Union Square & Co. 2016.

Barker, Dan. *Godless: How an Evangelical Preacher Became One of America's Leading Atheists.* Ulysses Press, 2008.

Bering, Jesse. *The Belief Instinct: The Psychology of Souls, Destiny, and the Meaning of Life.* New York: W.W. Norton & Company, 2011.

Cristina, Greta. *Coming Out Atheist: How to Do It, How to Help Each Other, and Why.* Durham, NC: Pitchstone, 2014.

Coyne, Jerry A. *Why Evolution is True.* New York: Penguin, 2009.

Coyne, Jerry A. Faith Versus Fact: Why Science and Religion Are Incompatible. New York: Penguin, 2015.

Darwin, Charles. *The Origin of Species by Means of Natural Selection or, the Preservation of Favored Races in the Struggle for Life.* 1859.

Dawkins, Richard. *The Blind Watchmaker: Why the Evidence of Evolution Reveals a Universe Without Design.* New York: W.W. Norton & Company, 1986.

Dawkins, Richard. *The Ancestor's Tale: A Pilgrimage to the Dawn of Life.* New York: Houghton Mifflin, 2004.

Dawkins, Richard. *The God Delusion.* New York: Houghton Mifflin Harcourt, 2008.

De Waal, Frans. *Good Natured: The Origins of Right & Wrong in Humans and Other Animals.* Cambridge, MA: Harvard University Press, 1995.

Harris, Sam. *Letter to a Christian Nation.* New York: Vintage Books, 2006.

Harris, Sam. *The Moral Landscape: How Science Can Determine Human Values.* New York: Free Press, 2010.

Hirsi Ali, Ayaan. *Infidel.* Atria Books, 2008.

Hitchens, Christopher. *God is Not Great: How Religion Poisons Everything.* New York: Hachette Book Group, 2007.

Hitchens, Christopher. *The Portable Atheist: Essential Readings for the Nonbeliever.* Cambridge, MA: Da Capo Press, 2007.

McAfee, David G. *Disproving Christianity and Other Secular Writings.* Hypatia Press, 2022.

Nixey, Catherine. *The Darkening Age: The Christian Destruction of the Classical World.* HarperOne, 2018.

Nye, Bill. *Undeniable: Evolution and the Science of Creation.* New York: Saint Martin's Press, 2014.

Pinker, Steven. *Enlightenment Now: The Case for Reason, Science, Humanism, and Progress.* Penguin Books, 2019.

Pinker, Steven. *The Better Angels of Our Nature: Why Violence Has Declined.* New York: Penguin Books, 2011.

Sagan, Carl. *The Demon Haunted World: Science as a Candle in the Dark.* Random House Publishing, 1996.

Shermer, Michael. *The Moral Arc: How Science and Reason Lead Humanity Toward Truth, Justice, and Freedom.* New York: Henry Holt, 2015.

Shubin, Neil. *Your Inner Fish: A Journey into the 3.5-Billion-Year History of the Human Body.* New York: Vintage Books, 2008.

Singer, Peter. *The Expanding Circle: Ethics and Sociobiology.* New York: Farrar, Straus & Giroux, 1981.

United Nations. The United Nations Universal Declaration of Human Rights, https://www.un.org/en/about-us/universal-declaration-of-human-rights

Yong, Ed. *An Immense World: How Animal Senses Reveal the Hidden Realms Around Us.* New York: Random House, 2022.

Zuckerman, Phil. *What it Means to Be Moral: Why Religion Is Not Necessary for Living an Ethical Life.* Counterpoint, 2019.

www.ingramcontent.com/pod-product-compliance
Lightning Source LLC
Chambersburg PA
CBHW021132090426
42740CB00008B/751